ST GEORGE'S CHAPEL,
IN THE LATE MIDDLE AGES

HISTORICAL MONOGRAPHS RELATING TO ST GEORGE'S CHAPEL

General Editor: The Reverend Canon John A. White.

Historical Monographs relating to
St George's Chapel, Windsor Castle, Volume 17

ST GEORGE'S CHAPEL, WINDSOR, IN THE LATE MIDDLE AGES

Edited by

Colin Richmond and Eileen Scarff

WINDSOR 2001

Published by the Dean and Canons of Windsor

ISBN 0–9539676–0–3   (cloth bound)
ISBN 0–9539676–1–1   (paperback)

A catalogue record for this book is available
from the British Library

*Paperback cover illustration: John Norden's 1607 bird's-eye
view drawing of Windsor Castle from the north
(London, BL Harl. MS 3749, f. 3)
By permission of the British Library*

Produced by Maney Publishing
Hudson Road Leeds LS9 7DL UK

CONTENTS

GENERAL EDITOR'S FOREWORD

This volume, like the Conference (held under the auspices of St George's House) that gave it birth, signals an important advance in public access to the College of St George. For the present agglomeration of medieval buildings surrounding and including St George's Chapel, along with some more recent additions, serve merely as evidence of a continuous religious community life which has survived Reformation, revolution and review for over six hundred and fifty years. As members of the present day College strive to re-interpret the highest ideals inherited from their predecessors, encouragement in this up-hill task comes from clear evidence in these papers that throughout its history St George's has been served and sustained by human beings showing all the virtues and vices, strengths and frailties that 'flesh is heir to'. Ancient institutions and ancient heritage sites are the matrix of mythology but historians have a commission to be the sane correctives against our human tendency to roll down the green sward of romance straight into the nettles of nursery fantasy. This volume expresses the commitment of the monograph series to take seriously the record of the College's past and to subject it to historical scrutiny, thereby facilitating a reasonable assessment of the evidence in order to present a coherent and convincing picture of previous generations. In a time when the study of history is not everywhere thought to be of primary significance in the development of human self-understanding, the decision to preserve and develop the monograph series may be seen as a 'faith commitment' to the belief that the community that disregards or neglects its history is at serious risk of losing its soul.

My personal thanks must first be given to Dr Eileen Scarff who with characteristic application and remarkable good humour has steered this volume to the press, and to her co-editor Professor Colin Richmond who has helped to ensure the quality and significance of this collection of essays.

I must then thank Maney Publishing, and especially Mrs Wendy Sherlock, who have been helpful and encouraging from the outset of the project. Generous and essential financial support has come from the Richard III and Yorkist History Trust another cause for gratitude.

I also thank the following for permission to reproduce illustrations:-

Bibliothèque Nationale, Paris (Pls IIIA, VB)

J.A. Bowen (Figs 1, 8, 18, 19)

British Library, London (Pls IA and B, II, IIIB, VA, VIA and B, VIII, Figs 21, 23, 24)

College of Arms, London (Pl. VII)

Worshipful Company of Barber-Surgeons, London (Pl. IV)

Courtauld Institute of Art, London (Fig. 25a and b)

T. Tatton-Brown (Figs 2, 3, 9, 10, 11)

Wellcome Institute, London (Fig. 22)

C. Wilson (Figs 4, 5, 6, 7, 12, 13, 14, 20).

Last, but by no means least, I must thank all those who contributed of themselves to the Conference, and most especially those who went to the trouble not only of giving papers but preparing them later for publication. This volume must be seen as a good omen for a new phase in the development of a long established series as well as being of great value in its own right.

JOHN A. WHITE
Canon of Windsor

PREFACE

It takes a good historian, in any age, to judge what is important in the long term. We ourselves, who are involved in day-to-day administration of any organization, cannot see the wood for the trees. How can we be sure what to record for posterity? What will interest future generations? What will our successors need to know?

These are perennial problems for both the Chapter Clerk and the Archivist in any ecclesiastical foundation dating from the mediaeval period. It is exactly those details of everyday life, which we take for granted and therefore fail to record or to preserve, that are likely to interest researchers in the years ahead.

The lectures included in this volume were contributed to a memorable conference, 'St George's in the Fifteenth Century', organized by Dr Eileen Scarff the Archivist of the College of St George in Windsor Castle, and Professor Colin Richmond of Keele University. Their initiative has resulted in a publication which will stand alongside such earlier classics as *The English Secular Cathedrals in the Middle Ages* by Kathleen Edwards (1949) and *Life in a Medieval College, the Story of the Vicars-Choral of York Minster* by Frederick Harrison (1952).

In particular, the fourth essay by Dr A. K. B. Evans is the result of more than half a century of research into the affairs of the College of St George. The author has scrutinized the economic difficulties of the foundation throughout the period. Her motto seems to be that of Hugh of St Victor (*ob.* 1142): 'Learn everything: you will find in the end that nothing is superfluous'. Yet she has the ability to select from her material and present a balanced account.

Great imagination, allied to detailed knowledge of the period, was needed for the final chapter by Roger Bowers on the musical establishment of the College. We can almost hear the transition from plainsong to polyphony; we can understand the developing balance of choral forces and the emergence of the lay clerk; we can overhear the respective resonances of the old and new chapels; we can assess the provision for choristers; and, above all, we can believe that by the end of the fifteenth century the choir of St George's was the finest in England and became a model for other choirs.

On the architectural front, Tim Tatton-Brown has drawn on his experience as archaeological consultant to the Dean and Canons to correct and extend the seminal work of Sir William St John Hope in his *Architectural History of Windsor Castle* (1913) by proposing an historical sequence for the building of the Chapel and associated structures of the College. He also looks at the evolution of the topography of the lower ward in the later Middle Ages and how the Royal Palace there was absorbed into the College.

Each of the remaining seven essays is concerned with a specific topic within the period. We should welcome these vignettes of the Order of the Garter, what it meant to Margaret of Anjou, and how it fared in the crisis years of the mid-fifteenth century; of the English court physician who was as likely as not a canon of Windsor; of a typical mediaeval lawsuit involving a conscientious Knight of the Garter, Sir John Fastolf; of the meaning and value of chivalry to the Yorkist kings; of a St George cycle in English glass; of Canon James Denton who was a major benefactor of St George's (as well as of Lichfield Cathedral); and of the books and burial places of Edward IV, William, Lord Hastings, and Sir John Donne. They are fresh and authentic illustrations of the period.

As the life of the College continues, it is good to know that the problems of the present time are no greater than the problems of the past; and the opportunities of the future can be faced with deeper faith.

PATRICK MITCHELL
Dean of Windsor 1989–1998

The Constructional Sequence and Topography of the Chapel and College Buildings at St George's

TIM TATTON-BROWN

INTRODUCTION

St George's Chapel, in the lower ward of Windsor Castle, is one of the most remarkable buildings in the late Gothic style to be erected in England. It took almost exactly half a century to build (1475–1528), and its documented stages of building are fully discussed in Sir William St John Hope's great architectural history of Windsor Castle, written some ninety years ago.[1] Since that time there has been remarkably little new work on the architectural history, though a series of important articles have been published in the last half century, which throw new light on several aspects of the building history. These are, in chronological order of publication, Cave and Stanford London on the roof bosses,[2] Bond on the crucifix badges,[3] Harvey on the 'architects' (master-masons),[4] Kidson on the geometry,[5] Leedy on the vaults,[6] and Tracy on the choir stalls.[7] The documented history has also been carefully re-assessed by Colvin in the *History of the King's Works*.[8] In addition large-scale reconstruction work was carried out to the building (particularly the vaults) in the 1920s, under Sir Harold Brakspear,[9] and as a result some major alterations were made to the fabric, among them the addition of buttresses to the transepts. Brakspear also returned the 'king's beasts' to the tops of the pinnacles, nearly 250 years after they had been removed, on the advice of Sir Christopher Wren. Most recently, in 1969, a small chapel, the burial place of King George VI, was added to the west end of the north choir aisle.[10] Despite all of this new work, no new architectural history has yet been written. To undertake such a task a much more detailed study of the fabric is needed, using a series of

---

1. W.H. St. John Hope, *Windsor Castle: An Architectural History*, 3 vols, London 1913.

2. C.J.P. Cave and H. Stanford London, 'The roof bosses in St George's Chapel, Windsor', *Archaeologia*, 95 (1953), pp. 107–21.

3. M.F. Bond, 'The crucifix badges of St George's Chapel', *Report of the Society of the Friends of St George's and the Descendants of the Knights of the Garter* (1954), pp. 8–15.

4. J. Harvey, 'The architects of St George's Chapel, part II: the 15th and 16th centuries', *Friends Report* (1962), pp. 85–95.

5. P. Kidson, 'The architecture of St George's Chapel' in *The St George's Chapel Quincentenary Handbook*, ed. M. Bond, Windsor 1975, pp. 29–39.

6. W.C. Leedy, *Fan-vaulting: A study of form, technology and meaning*, London 1980, pp. 222–4.

7. C. Tracy, *English Gothic Choir Stalls 1400–1540*, Woodbridge 1990, pp. 48–51.

8. *History of the King's Works*, ed. H.M. Colvin, London 1963, ii, pp. 884–8 and, London 1975, iii pt.1, pp. 302–19. There is also a useful description in N. Pevsner, *Buildings of England: Berkshire*, Harmondsworth 1966, pp. 268–85.

9. For Brakspear's reports see Windsor, St George's Chapel Archives, IV.B.25. See also H. Brakspear, 'The work of repair to St George's Chapel in the castle of Windsor', *Journal of the RIBA*, 39 (6th Feb. 1932), pp. 253–67.

10. G.G. Pace, 'King George VI Memorial Chapel, St George's Chapel, Windsor Castle', *Friends Report* (1968–9), pp. 421–5.

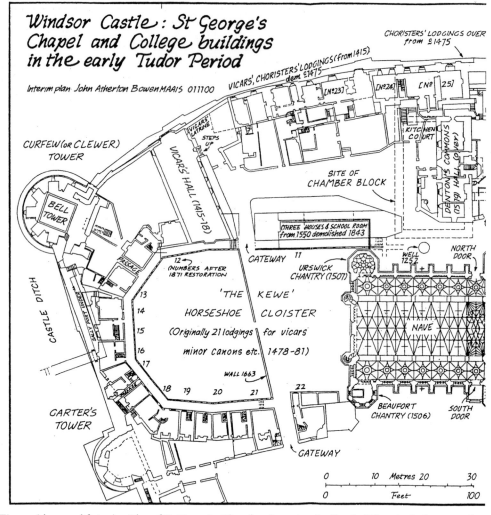

Fig. 1. *(above and facing)*   *Plan of St George's Chapel and associated college buildings in the lower ward at Windsor Castle (J.A. Bowen)*

measured drawings as the basis. The building materials and the masonry detailing also need to be studied archaeologically, as does the carpentry. The ironwork has recently been fully discussed by Jane Geddes.[11] This present essay is a provisional attempt at the basis for a new architectural history, using some of the more recent work mentioned above. It is also the result of my eight or so years as 'consultant archaeologist' to the Dean and Canons, which has allowed me the privilege of climbing all over the building.[12] This essay as well looks briefly at the topography of the area around the chapel, and at the

11. J. Geddes, *Medieval Decorative Ironwork in England*, London 1999, pp. 385–7.

12. I have also been able to study Bishop Beauchamp's work at Salisbury, as 'consultant archaeologist' to the Dean and Chapter of Salisbury Cathedral, and to study the Henry VII Chapel at Westminster Abbey.

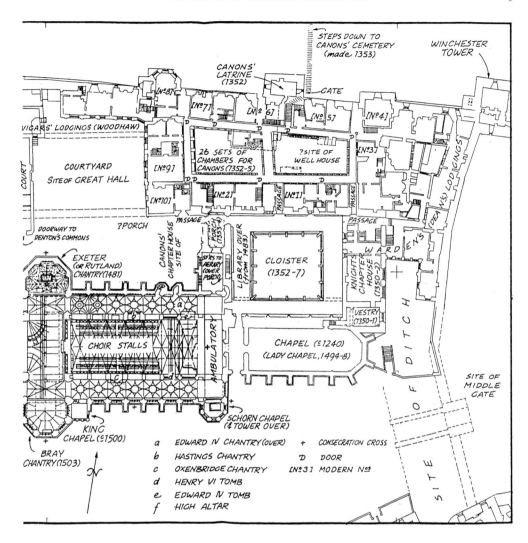

changes that were made to the buildings around the new chapel between the thirteenth and sixteenth centuries.

EDWARD IV'S NEW SCHEME

The first stage of the new work lasted for just about a decade and, as we shall see, was in many ways the most important phase. It was put in hand soon after Edward IV's total defeat (and murder) of Henry VI in 1471. The man chosen to carry out the new scheme was Richard Beauchamp, since 1450 bishop of Salisbury,[13] who had already reconstructed

13. Windsor is in the extreme north-east corner of Salisbury diocese, and Beauchamp had deputised for the Prelate to the Order of the Garter in 1453 and 1458. He did not become Chancellor of the Order, with an official lodging at Windsor, until 10 October 1475, see S.L. Ollard, *Fasti Wyndesorienses: The Deans and Canons of Windsor*, Windsor 1950, p. 34.

in 1456–7 the east end of his cathedral around a new shrine of St Osmund. Beauchamp also built himself a fine new external chantry chapel to the south of the shrine at Salisbury, and not far away from this he added a magnificent new chamber block and porch to the north side of the great hall of his palace.[14] On 19 February 1473 Beauchamp was appointed 'master and surveyor of the king's works' at St George's Chapel, and of 'divers other works' to be performed in the castle,[15] and over the next two years a very grand scheme was drawn up for the whole of the central part of the lower ward at Windsor Castle. On 12 June 1475 Richard Beauchamp was sent by Edward IV important letters patent, which instructed him 'to build and construct a new chapel in honour of the blessed Mary and St George the Martyr within our Castle of Windsor'. He was also given a free hand to demolish any old buildings in the lower ward that obstructed the building of the proposed new chapel,

both to and upon the walls on the north side and on the west in which the towers commonly called *Cluer ys Towre* and *Amener is Towre* and *Barner is Towre* are situated, and also on the south as far as the belfry.[16]

This implies that the whole of the new chapel, and almost certainly the Horseshoe Cloister (as it was later called) was being planned at this time, and to do this not only would major buildings need to be demolished, but also a great deal of earth moving and artificial terracing would have to take place, before the new foundations could be put in. This earth moving and the making of the new foundations probably happened in the two years of 1475 and 1476. It also seems likely from the evidence of the positions of the consecration crosses (see below), that as first planned the nave was to be one bay longer on the west,[17] and that the whole building was to be symmetrical about its north-south axis, as well as its east-west one. I would also speculate that four small semi-octagonal chapels were originally planned at each of the four corners, as well as two larger semi-octagonal chapels (transepts) in the centre of each side.[18] The two irregularities were the need to create an ambulatory at the east end in front of the west door of the existing early thirteenth-century chapel,[19] and the creation of a large new chantry chapel on the north-east side for King Edward IV above the east end of the north choir aisle.

A week after Edward IV sent the letters patent quoted above he wrote his will (dated 20 June 1475), and in this he refers to the chapel 'by us begoune of newe to bee buylded'. He goes on to say that his body is to be buried 'lowe in the grounde' of the new chapel with a stone laid over it. He also says:

14. R.C.H.M. *Salisbury, the Houses of the Close*, London 1993, pp. 53–72.

15. St. John Hope, ii, p. 375 and i, p. 242, n. 12.

16. Translated and fully transcribed in St. John Hope, ii, p. 376.

17. More recent writers like Colvin, *King's Works*, ii, p. 885, suggest it was originally a bay shorter than at present, basing this suggestion on the foundations discovered in 1927 in the penultimate bay of the nave. These foundations are, however, the top of the east side of the barrel-vault below the westernmost bay of the nave, and not an earlier 'west front'.

18. The north-eastern semi-octagonal chapel may have survived until the 1640s. It appears to be shown on the 1607 bird's-eye view of the chapel by Norden, with the canons' chapter house (demolished in *c.* 1650) to the west (Pl. VIII). The site of this chapel is now covered by the vestry, but the south wall of this vestry seems to be an infilling of an arch into the earlier chapel, and all of this area was rebuilt after the Restoration.

19. The main east wall of the new chapel was west of this ambulatory. At this time the chapel to the east was still the chapel made for Henry III, though inside it had been refurbished for the knights' and canons' stalls in the mid-fourteenth century.

Fig. 2.   *St George's Chapel from the south-west (T. Tatton-Brown)*

Fig. 3.   *External view of the south side of the choir at St George's Chapel (T. Tatton-Brown)*

Fig. 4.   *The north side of the east end of St George's Chapel, showing the Edward IV
Chantry Chapel (and royal pew) (C. Wilson)*

We wol that overe the same Sepulture ther bee made a vawte of convenient height as the place wil suffre it, and that upon the said vawte ther bee a Chapell or a Closet with an Autre convenient and a Tumbe to be made and sett there . . .[20]

The building of this new chantry chapel, in the north-east corner of St George's Chapel (Figs 4, 8), was clearly carried out rapidly at the beginning of the new works, and the low vault beneath, as well as perhaps the new ambulatory vault at the east end of the chapel, had probably been completed by 1481.[21] The idea of having a chantry chapel over an aisle, but also above the 'sepulture', must have come from the newly completed chantry chapel for Henry V above the eastern ambulatory of Westminster Abbey.

The plan of the new chapel, as laid out in 1475, was perhaps for a building that was about 250 feet long.[22] However, the west end of the structure, including its flanking chapels, was well down the hillside, and it must have been clear to Bishop Beauchamp, and to his master-mason, Henry Janyns, at an early stage, that an artificial basement would be required for the west end. When the work started on the walls themselves, in the spring of 1477, the lowest walling was probably built all the way around the whole chapel as far as the north and south ends of the sixth bay of the nave, where there is still a clear bonding break with the north-west and south-west chapels (later the Urswick and Beaufort Chantries). As part of this original masonry was set a series of square or lozenge-shaped panels, on each of which was carved a 'rose-en-soleil' with a crown above. These are clearly the badges of Edward IV. However, at the centre of each rose is a small crucifix and, as St John Hope pointed out,[23] these must have been intended to be consecration crosses as well, though no dedication or consecration ceremony is documented.[24] Maurice Bond made a careful study of all the 'crucifix badges' (as he called them) in 1954, when one of them was being renewed,[25] but he did not think that they were consecration crosses. Carved consecration crosses on the outsides of buildings are very rare in England, but at Salisbury Cathedral (where latten crosses were set into the carved masonry as well), and at two parish churches in Salisbury diocese, Edington and Uffington, they are still found on the external walls, and they must have been well-known to Richard Beauchamp, as bishop of Salisbury.[26] I would therefore suggest that they were intended to be consecration crosses, as well as the badges of Edward IV, even if the chapel was not actually consecrated in Edward IV's time. The ritual called for twelve external and twelve internal crosses with three on each cardinal face. At Salisbury Cathedral the three consecration crosses set into the north and south walls were all in the eastern arm on the transept walls, almost certainly because the eastern arm was to be built first (there are no crosses on the north and south walls of the nave). At Windsor, however, they were

20. St. John Hope, ii, p. 376.

21. Taynton stone 'called vowtynstone' for this is mentioned in the accounts for 1480–1, St. John Hope, ii, p. 379.

22. This figure is calculated by assuming the transepts and crossing were to be on the central axis, and that the nave was originally to have one more bay on the west.

23. St. John Hope, ii, p. 408.

24. For full details of such a ceremony, see E.S. Dewick, 'Consecration crosses and the ritual associated with them', *Archaeological Journal*, 65 (1908), pp. 1–34.

25. Bond, *Friends Report* (1954), *supra*.

26. See T. Tatton-Brown, 'The Salisbury Cathedral consecration crosses', *Transactions of the Monumental Brass Society*, 16, pt.2 (1998), pp. 113–16.

Fig. 5. *Vault in the Schorn Chapel, St George's Chapel, Windsor (C. Wilson)*

Fig. 6.   *South choir aisle vault with beyond the high pendant vault of the choir, St George's Chapel (C. Wilson)*

Fig. 7.　　*South choir aisle vault, St George's Chapel (C. Wilson)*

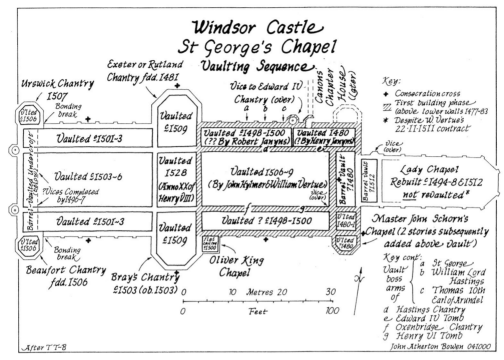

Fig. 8. *Plan of St George's Chapel, to show the constructional and vaulting sequence (J.A. Bowen)*

carefully spaced out with a cross in the centre of the north and south walls of the nave, transepts and choir.[27] Hence my suggestion that the chapel was originally intended to have a nave one bay longer. On the east wall of the chapel, three badges/crosses were also placed. That on the south-east (on the east face of the Schorn chapel) has been largely hacked off, but its lozenge form is still clearly visible with the moulded string-course carefully going around it. The north-east cross, perhaps set into the cloister wall of the former polygonal chapel, has gone, while the central cross is skilfully set into the panel work on the east face of the ambulatory (i.e. behind the high altar). This was clearly because the earlier chapel did not allow a cross to be put into the external east wall.

The use of the consecration crosses at St George's would suggest that the lowest outer walls of the chapel were very rapidly built in the first year, 1477. Unfortunately the building accounts for this first year are lost, but all the accounts from 11 January 1478 to 11 January 1484 do survive,[28] and these tell us much about the building work on the eastern arm (or choir), which was brought to completion during this time, though without

27. The badge and consecration cross on the north wall of the choir have gone. The internal consecration crosses at St George's were either never made, or perhaps painted, as was common elsewhere, the inside of the near contemporary Henry VII Chapel at Westminster Abbey, for example, where painted consecration crosses can still be seen on the west wall.

28. They are all transcribed in St. John Hope, i, pp. 243–5 and ii, pp. 398–406. Bishop Beauchamp also became dean of Windsor on 25 March 1477 (not 1478, as in Ollard, *Fasti*, p. 34), at exactly the time when the main building work was starting.

the vaults being made. These accounts tell us that Janyns was the master-mason, and he organised the purchase of Taynton stone and Caen stone for the project. All the external masonry was of Taynton stone except the window tracery which was Caen. Inside the softer Reigate stone, as well as Caen stone, was used. Among other chief workmen were John Squyer (the master carpenter), William Berkeley (the master carver) and John Tresilian (the master smith), and by 1480 timber and lead were being brought in for the roofs. As well as this, shrines were being created in the south-east corner of the chapel for both the 'Croes Naid' (a relic of the true cross, captured in Wales in 1283 by Edward I),[29] and for the Blessed John Schorn, a quasi-saint and former rector of North Marston, whose remains were brought to the south-east corner chapel at this time.[30] That this was very specifically the work of Bishop Beauchamp, who died on 18 October 1481, is shown by the unique vault-boss in the centre of the ambulatory vault in the south-east corner of the chapel, which depicts the kneeling figures of Beauchamp and Edward IV flanking the Croes Naid. Just beneath it, on the south side of the solid wall behind the high altar, is a niche for a book (probably originally a Sarum Breviary) with below it an inscription in English which starts:

Who leyde this booke here — The Reverend ffader in God Richard Beauchamp Bisschop of this Dioceyse of Sarysbury and wherfor to this entent that Preestis and minsters of Goddis chirche may here have the occupacion thereof seyying therin theyr divyne servyse . . .[31]

The making of 'crests' for the 'enterclose of Master John Schorn's chapel' is also mentioned in the accounts for 1481, and this corner of the new chapel was clearly of special importance to Bishop Beauchamp.

In 1481, once again just before Beauchamp's death, a new charter was given to the college by Edward IV which omitted Edward III's 'poor knights' but increased the number of clerks and choristers to 13 in each case. This was precisely the time when new choir stalls were first being put into the choir. These wonderful carved stalls have been fully described elsewhere,[32] and it is clear that, as first made, there were to be 50 back stalls (42 lateral and 8 return stalls) in which the knights of the Garter alternated with the canons. In front on each side were two blocks of substalls for the priest vicars, lay clerks and choristers, and each block contained ten stalls. To the east of the stalls doorways led out into the north and south aisles.[33] All this stallwork was being finished in 1482–3, and at the same time the roofs of 'lez side ilez' were being covered in lead, paving was being laid, and the windows were being made. At the west end of the choir and side aisles, there was a temporary partition with a door in it (and a window above), and at the time of Edward IV's death, on 9 April 1483 the eastern arm must have been nearly ready for use. In the year or so before the king's death, his tomb was being prepared and we hear in the accounts of 33 casks of 'touchstone' being acquired. This is black Tournai marble from

29. W.C. Tennant, 'Croes Naid' in *Friends Report* (1943), pp. 5–14.

30. A Papal Bull of Sixtus IV, in 1478, authorized the translation of the body of John Schorn to the chapel, transcribed in St. John Hope, ii, pp. 466–7. See also, R. Marks, 'A Late Medieval Pilgrimage cult: John Schorn of North Marston', *British Archaeological Association Transactions* (forthcoming).

31. Fully transcribed in St. John Hope, ii, p. 412.

32. St. John Hope, ii, pp. 429–46, and Tracy, *supra*.

33. The entrance on the south was finally blocked in the 1920s, but Henry VI's tomb, and the two additional stalls (made in 1786), already partly blocked the entrance. The door on the north was turned round, and moved eastwards.

Belgium, and some of this touchstone can be seen today on the north (choir aisle) side of Edward IV's tomb, as reorganized by Henry Emlyn in 1790. The black Tournai marble slab, that covers the burial place itself, has on it the fixing marks for the superb gilt wrought iron gates that were fixed here in 1483 by the master ironsmith, John Tresilian. These gates, which are by far the finest examples of medieval decorative ironwork in Britain, are now on the south side of the tomb, in the sanctuary, behind a 1790 screen.[34] Tresilian also made some superbly decorated lock plates for the doors into the choir, and for the door leading to the spiral stair to Edward IV's chantry.[35]

When Edward IV died on 9 April 1483 his chantry chapel was probably nearly ready, but his tomb was not by any means finished. After his burial, work seems to have stopped on the monument, but carried on at the chapel for the rest of the year, and the accounts mention ironwork for windows, the finishing of the stallwork and the putting in of a pulpit. The accounts end on 11 January 1484, and they also mention work on the vicars' lodgings. Later in 1484 the mortal remains of King Henry VI (murdered in 1471) were brought from Chertsey Abbey to be reburied in the south side of the sanctuary, and there is a payment of £5 10s 2d for the expenses of the removal.[36] Miracles were said to have happened at the tomb, and it was perhaps at this time that the magnificent iron offertory box was made for the tomb, probably by John Tresilian.[37] By the time of Richard III's death, at Bosworth Field on 22 August 1485, the choir was probably in use, though Richard himself had made no provision for his own burial at St George's or anywhere else.

HENRY VII'S WORK

For about eight years after Henry Tudor's victory at Bosworth, no work took place on St George's Chapel.[38] Then on 26 January 1492, Dr Christopher Urswick was appointed a canon of Windsor (he became dean four and a half years later),[39] and in the treasurer's account for 1492–3 there is a payment to Edrych the carpenter for three days' work in making a scaffold and putting up ladders and taking them down again upon 'le north cros yle' of the church. This same carpenter also repaired the pair of doors for the entry into the choir, and a glazier was also paid 'for glazing of the west window beside the end of the new quire'. The roof over the organs was also mended 'to keep out the rain'.[40] This may suggest that some new work was taking place on the north transept, as St John Hope and others suggest, but it could be nothing more than repair work to the temporary partition at the west end of the choir, where a pair of organs was already in use for the services. The organ must have been on a pulpitum screen, and it is possible that all four crossing piers, and the arches above them, had already been built by this time, and that the still existing roof over the crossing was in place by now. This was always meant to be a temporary roof, to be removed when the lantern tower was made, but the idea of having a lantern tower

34. See Geddes, *Ironwork*, pp. 261–4, and 386–7.
35. *Ibid.*, pp. 266–9, and 385.
36. St. John Hope, i, p. 241.
37. Geddes, *Ironwork*, pp. 264 and 386.
38. Though in 1490–1 some repairs were done, and a stall was made for the dean, St. John Hope, ii, p. 383.
39. Ollard, *Fasti*, pp. 118 and 37–8.
40. St. John Hope, ii, p. 383.

was only finally abandoned over thirty years after this in the later 1520s. It seems most likely to me that no real work took place on the main chapel for fifteen years, between about 1484 and 1498, and only after this did work continue rapidly on the transepts and the nave, thanks to Henry VII's two close friends, Dean Christopher Urswick and Sir Reginald Bray.

In 1493–4, however, Henry VII started to think about his own place of burial, and he quickly decided that it should be in a fine new Lady Chapel at the east end of St George's Chapel (Figs 9, 10). The existing thirteenth-century chapel was demolished, except for the lower parts of the west and north walls, and a completely new structure was rapidly built here between 1494 and 1498.[41] John Harvey has suggested that the surviving chapel (now the Albert Memorial Chapel) partly dates from Edward III's chapel of the mid-fourteenth century,[42] but all the masonry and window-tracery is uniform and must be of the late fifteenth century only. The plan of this new building, including the polygonal east end is probably the same as that for the original thirteenth-century chapel.[43]

By the spring of 1498, the new Lady Chapel was probably nearing completion, though no vault had been put in,[44] and a 'plat' had been made to show where Henry VII's tomb was to be, and nearby (perhaps at the centre of the new chapel) a new shrine-tomb was to be made for Henry VI. As is well-known, all of this came to nothing because, after a dispute between Westminster, Chertsey and Windsor, the abbot of Westminster managed to persuade the king that Henry VI had wanted to be buried in Westminster Abbey.[45] The whole scheme was, accordingly, moved to Westminster, and the result is the incomparable new Lady Chapel there, now known as the Henry VII Chapel.

The roofed, but empty, shell of the new Lady Chapel at Windsor was, therefore, abandoned in the spring of 1498,[46] and by this time work must have moved back to the main chapel. Probably the first new work at this time was the insertion of the aisle vaults on either side of the choir (Figs 6, 7). These fine fan vaults were, perhaps, designed by Robert Janyns, and Cave and Stanford London's study of the heraldry on the vaults suggests that this dates from the late 1490s, when the Hastings Chantry was finally being set up.[47] There is a payment in the treasurer's accounts, for 1498–9, to 'John Freman,

41. As is well-known, Henry VII got papal permission in October 1494 to suppress Luffield Priory and use its revenues to build a new Lady Chapel beside St George's, 'with a sufficient number of priests who are bound to celebrate in it for the safety of his soul'. In a second bull, the Pope granted an indulgence for the new Lady Chapel 'in which [Henry VII] intends to choose his place of burial', St. John Hope, ii, p. 498.

42. Harvey, 'Architects', p. 91.

43. I have discussed this more fully elsewhere, see T. Tatton-Brown, 'The building of the Henry VII Chapel at Westminister Abbey' (forthcoming).

44. The fine low four-centred barrel-vault at the western end of the Lady Chapel, which lies above the passage to the Dean's Cloister, was perhaps built at this time. The hollow cornice below it has Henry VII's and his queen's monogram on it.

45. A.P. Stanley, *Historical Memorials of Westminster Abbey*, 3rd rev. edn. London 1869, pp. 600–16. See also St. John Hope, ii, p. 479 and notes. The matter was officially determined by the Chancellor and the Privy Council.

46. The large sums given for the 'beleding of Seint George Chapell' in 1495–6 (St. John Hope, ii, p. 383) were perhaps for the Lady Chapel.

47. Cave and Stanford London, 'Roof bosses', *supra*.

Fig. 9.   *The new Lady Chapel of 1494–8 at St George's Chapel (T. Tatton-Brown)*

Fig. 10.   *The north side of the Lady Chapel, and the Dean's Cloister at St George's Chapel (T. Tatton-Brown)*

carpenter for making a scaffold for the painting of the arms of Lord Hastings' which seems to confirm this.[48]

One of the canons of Windsor during the first stage of the building work was Edmund Audley (canon in the 7th stall, 1474–80).[49] He became bishop of Rochester in 1480, then bishop of Hereford in 1492, and finally bishop of Salisbury in 1502 (he died there in 1524). At each place he brought the new Windsor style to his cathedral. At Rochester a new 'nave' was added to the south transept Lady Chapel,[50] almost certainly to accommodate stalls for the new choir for the singing of polyphonic Lady masses. A fine fan vault was intended for this chapel, but it was never built, perhaps because of Audley's move to Hereford. At his new cathedral Audley built for himself a new two-storeyed polygonal chantry chapel on the south side of the existing eastern Lady Chapel. This structure is very similar to one of the polygonal chapels at St George's, and the fan vault in it can be compared with the vault in the Schorn chapel.[51] In 1502 Audley moved on again to Salisbury where, as bishop, he also became Chancellor of the Order of the Garter. Here he built a free-standing, fan-vaulted miniature chantry chapel on the north side of the presbytery, and this too shows strong Windsor connections.[52] Many other examples (like Bishop Oliver King's work at Bath Abbey), could be cited of the influence Windsor and its canons had on the architecture of the last years of the fifteenth and the first years of the sixteenth century,[53] and it is at this time that the work on St George's Chapel was largely brought to completion. The key figures here were the dean, Christopher Urswick, and Sir Reginald Bray; the latter providing much of the funding, both before and after his death in August 1503. Bray, in his will, gave large sums for

the werke of the new werkes of the body [i.e. nave] of the church of the College . . . within the Castell of Wyndesore . . . accordyng and after the fourme and entent of the fundacion thereof as well in stone werke, tymbre, ledde, Iron, glasse, and alle other thinges necessary and requisite for the utter performance of the same.

He also asked for his 'sinfull' body to be buried

in the west ende and south syde of the same church within the chapell there newe made by me for the same entent.

This last passage must refer to Bray's intended place of burial in his own chantry chapel that was being made in the south transept, though earlier writers like Hope assumed it referred to the small south-west chapel (later the Beaufort Chantry). By 1503 the walls and arcades of the nave and transepts must have been complete, and it is worth noting that the large stone screens that separate off the Bray Chantry (and the Rutland Chantry in the north transept) are secondary and butted up against the adjoining outer walls of the chapel.

48. T. Willement, *An Account of the Restorations of the Collegiate Chapel of St George, Windsor*, London 1844, p. 15 n.

49. Ollard, *Fasti*, p. 108.

50. J.P. McAleer, *Rochester Cathedral 604–1504, An architectural history*, Toronto 1999, p. 161.

51. Leedy, *Fan-vaulting*, p. 171.

52. *Ibid.*, p. 198.

53. The rebuilder of Bath Abbey was Bishop Oliver King, a canon of St George's from 1480–1503, who was able to make for himself a very small chapel just outside the east side of Bray's chantry chapel in the south transept. See Ollard, p. 146 and St. John Hope, ii, pp. 413–14, and P.R. Mitchell, 'Bishop Oliver King and the Present Abbey (Priory) Church', *Bath Abbey 2000 Lecture*, 1996. Also see A.C. Deane, 'Sir Reginald Bray', *Friends Report* (1943), pp. 15–18.

Fig. 11.   *External view of the south side of the nave at St George's Chapel (T. Tatton-Brown)*

This suggests that the lower walls of this part of the nave and transepts were built well before this, possibly in the late 1470s as suggested above.

Unfortunately we have no detailed building accounts to help us, but the idea of shortening the original nave, and constructing the west front on its present site, must have been agreed in the later 1490s. The work of constructing the new vaulted basement and the new outer chapels must then have started soon afterwards. The two stair-turrets (vices) on either side of the great west window may be those mentioned in the accounts of 1496–7,[54] but all we can be certain of is that the whole structure, including the magnificent nave vault, was nearing completion in 1506. By this time the western chapels (Figs 12, 13) were being allocated as chantries to the Beauforts (south-west)[55] and to Dean Urswick (north-west). There seems to have been an earlier (1494) chantry at 'a certain altar on the

54. St. John Hope, ii, p. 383. Bolts for two doors in 'le vices' at the top of the church are mentioned.
55. M.F. Bond, 'The foundation of the Beaufort Chapel', *Friends Report* (1952), pp. 11–14. Also St. John Hope, ii, pp. 456–9.

Fig. 12.   *Vault in the Urswick Chantry and asymmetrical entry, St George's Chapel (C. Wilson)*

north side at the end of the new church', but its exact position is not known.[56] It was perhaps in the north transept, where a chantry for Anne, duchess of Exeter, had already been established in 1481. Work on the nave vault (Fig. 14) must have taken at least two years, and it is very likely that the nave vault was started soon after Bray's death in 1503, using Bray's money. The many punning rebuses (the hemp bray), and Bray's arms and garter (he became a knight of the Garter in 1501) on the vault all suggest this.

56. St. John Hope, ii, pp. 383–5 and 456. Hope assumed that this chantry was taken over by Urswick, but this is unlikely to be correct. Eileen Scarff points out that the earlier (1494) chantry was supplemented by grants of money in the will of Thomas Brotherton (dated 29 Dec. 1508) — SGC I.G.14. We also know that Canons John Arundell and John Seymour, as well as Thomas Brotherton (a yeoman of Windsor) wanted to be added to this chantry when they died, Denton, Black Book IV.B.3, ff. 241–4. Seymour became overseer of the works in 1481, after the death of Bishop Beauchamp, but in his will of 20 Sept. 1500 he asks for burial in the chapel of St Saviour, St Mary and St George, 'recently built by Bishop King in St George's Chapel'. This is the tiny chapel tacked onto the east side of Bray's chantry in the south transept.

Fig. 13. *Vault in the Beaufort Chantry and asymmetrical entry, St George's Chapel (C. Wilson)*

More importantly, however, the putting in of the nave vault started a new stage of work once all the major walls and roofs had been built. The completion of the nave vault then led quickly on to the building of the wonderful choir vault, and we are exceptionally lucky to still have the details of the contract drawn up with John Hylmer and William Vertue, freemasons, on 5 June 1506,[57] in which they agree to

vawlte or doo to be vawlted with free stone the roof of the qwere of the College Roiall of our Lady and Saint George within the Castell of Wyndesore, according to the roof of the body [i.e. nave] of the said College ther, which roof conteyneth vij severyes, as well the vawlte within furth as archebotens [i.e. flying buttresses], crestys, corses [i.e. shafts], and the King's bestes stondyng on theym to bere the fanes [i.e. weather vanes] on the outsides of the said quere, and the creasts, corses [and] beasts above on the outsides of Maister John Shornes Chapell, to bee done and wrought according to the other creastes, and comprised within the said bargayne: provided alway that the

---

57. St. John Hope, ii, pp. 460–1. Peter Begent kindly points out (in correspondence) that the nave was not finally completed until *c.* 1509, as it has 'K' and 'H' crowns on it, which commemorates the marriage of Henry and Catherine of Aragon in June 1509.

Fig. 14.   *Nave of St George's Chapel looking north-west (C. Wilson)*

principall keyes [i.e. bosses] of the said vawte from the high awter downe to the King's stall shall bee wrought more pendaunt and holower then the keyes or pendaunts of the body of the said colege, with the King's armes crowned with lyons, anteloppes, greyhounds and dragons, bering the said armes, and all the other lesser keyes to be wrought more pendaunt and holower than the keyes of the body of the said colege, also with roses, portecolys, floure-de-lyces, or any other devyce that shall please the King's grace to have in them.

This famous contract also very specifically says that the 'keyes' (bosses) are to be made 'more pendaunt and holower' than those in the nave, and that is exactly what we find today. The choir vault is still remarkable for its great width, and for its line of pendants down the middle. The contract also specified that the choir vault was to be finished by Christmas 1508, and it is at about this time that William Vertue was starting to make his virtuoso masterpiece, the high vault in the Henry VII Chapel at Westminster Abbey.[58]

THE COMPLETION OF THE CHAPEL

By the time of the death of Henry VII, in April 1509, nearly the whole of St George's Chapel, except the crossing where a lantern tower was still intended, had been vaulted. Over the next year or so, work on completing both chapels at Windsor and Westminster seems to have continued. At Westminster the burial of Henry VII in his new Lady Chapel took place, but the completion of the decoration work there, and the translation of the body of Henry VI from Windsor was never carried out. At Windsor much more work was needed, and another most interesting surviving contract was that drawn up by the dean, Nicholas West, and the canons with William Vertue on 20 December 1511:[59]

to vaute or doe to be vauted with freestone the roof of our Ladie Chapel . . . according to a platte devysed and drawend for the propos.

It goes on to say that Vertue was also to complete the outside of the Lady Chapel, including

embatteling the same as also in making up Crests, Corses and the Kings bests standing on them to beyre fanes or squychons with armes . . . and to make and perfectly fynish the Galarye betwixt the same Chapell and the Church after the maner and forme as it is begonnen and to vaute the same accordingly, and to make also a Botros butting on Maister John Shorne's Chapell.

All of this work was done, except sadly for the putting in of the main vault in the Lady Chapel. This was, no doubt, also going to be a virtuoso affair, and the contract specifies that the

principall keyes (bosses) of the said vaute of our Lady Chapell from the highe Altar down to the coming in of the same chapell shall be more hollowe than the keyes of the Body of the said College.

The work was to be complete by Michaelmas 1514, but before this time the dean and canons' funds may have run out, and the new young king, Henry VIII, had not yet decided whether to fund the project, let alone where he himself would be buried.

At exactly this time, however, a new canon of St George's, Thomas Wolsey, appeared on the scene. He left Magdalen College, Oxford in 1510, where he had been involved in building the great tower, and was from 1511–14 a canon of Windsor and Register of the

---

58. See Tatton-Brown, 'Henry VII Chapel at Westminster'. I would suggest that Robert Janyns (who died in 1506) designed the Westminster Lady Chapel, but that William Vertue designed the great vault, *pace* C. Wilson, 'The designer of Henry VII's Chapel, Westminster Abbey,' *The Reign of Henry VII: Proceedings of the 1993 Harlaxton Symposium,* ed. B. Thompson, Stamford 1995, pp. 133–56.

59. St. John Hope, ii, p. 481, though it is not very accurately transcribed here. See the original in the Chapel Archives, XVII.37.3.

Garter.[60] He left Windsor to become bishop of Lincoln in March 1514, and was by then already Henry VIII's right hand man. A decade later, in 1524, he acquired the whole Lady Chapel as his own place of burial and started to have a magnificent tomb built there. After Wolsey's fall, the incomplete tomb was acquired in turn by Henry VIII in 1530, but when Henry died in 1547 he was buried in the main choir of St George's Chapel, not in the Lady Chapel. Wolsey's sarcophagus, of course, now lies in the crypt of St Paul's Cathedral with the body of Nelson within it.

In the first few months of Henry VIII's reign, Nicholas West was appointed dean of Windsor.[61] As a brilliant diplomat, he served the king well as ambassador to Scotland and France, and as dean (1509–15) he drew up the Lady Chapel contract of 1511 mentioned above though, as we have seen, the money to complete the Lady Chapel vault was not found, and in 1513 plans for the completion of the chapel were still being discussed with the king. There is a most interesting letter in the archives from Dean West, in London, to the canons. It begins:

Masters and brethren, yesterday the king synyd that platt that he will have off hys chapell, which is the plate that was made acording to his first device. Howbeit ther schall no thing be done to it tell his cummyng agayne, which I pray Jesu may be schortly . . .[62]

The king seems not to have 'come again' to Windsor at this time, and West moved on to be bishop of Ely in 1515. At Ely he built himself an exquisite little chantry chapel in the south-east corner of the cathedral, which has a vault that has moved on from the late Gothic of Windsor to the early Renaissance style of the next generation.

With the departure of West in 1515 it was decided at a chapter of the Order of the Garter that:

The Knyghtes of late elected wiche never bare noo charge to the edefyeng of and vawtyng of the churche shuld bere summwhat towards the perfourmyng of hit, lyeke as they and oder Knyghtes in the tyme off King Henry Vij th had doon.[63]

Raising the money from the knights at this time was difficult (there was no Sir Reginald Bray), and virtually no work was done over the next decade or so. The 'parfourmance off the Roode lofte and lanterne' is mentioned, but the work never took place, and eventually it was given up. By 1528 a very large new fan vault was put over the crossing, almost certainly again to William Vertue's design (though he died in 1527). This impressive vault displays the arms of Henry VIII surrounded by the arms of all the knights of the Garter at that time, and the date, the twentieth year of his reign.[64]

By this time Henry was much more concerned with other ways of spending his money, and the age of Gothic ecclesiastical building had come to an end.

THE COLLEGE BUILDINGS

The lower ward at Windsor Castle probably first acquired buildings in the reign of Henry II. During the 1160s and 1170s a great hall and a series of associated buildings were perhaps

---

60. Ollard, *Fasti*, p. 119.
61. *Ibid.*, p. 39.
62. SGC XI.C.4, quoted in Colvin, *King's Works*, iii, p. 313.
63. St. John Hope, ii, pp. 462–3.
64. St. John Hope, ii, p. 463 and Cave and Stanford London, 'Roof bosses', p. 118.

erected on the north side of the lower ward, and as we shall see, the core of these buildings around the great hall was adapted for use by the college between the later fourteenth and early sixteenth centuries.[65] Remarkably one roofed fragment of the original buildings still survives as the present organist's house,[66] while much of the core of the northern defensive wall, on the clifftop, must date from the twelfth century. The masonry defences of the lower ward had not, however, been completed by the time of the siege in 1216, and many of the buildings were probably damaged at this time. Repairs were then carried out during the minority of Henry III, and most importantly three massive new semicircular towers (Clewer, Garter's and Salisbury towers) were built on the west side of the extended defences.[67] A new southern gatehouse was also probably completed at this time, though this was later replaced by the so-called Henry VIII gateway. When Henry III came of age, he was able to build a new private residence for himself and his queen in the north-eastern part of the lower ward, incorporating the reconstructed great hall and chamber block of Henry II's residence.[68] Henry III's principal new buildings were a king's and queen's lodging range (all under one roof and 100ft. long according to the documentary sources), and a chapel. Both of these buildings ran east-west and flanked the north and south sides of a 'grass plot' (later the Dean's Cloister) in the extreme north-east corner of the lower ward. To the north of these new buildings, whose dimensions are given in the accounts, was the twelfth-century north curtain wall (with a rectangular tower in it), while to the east was the ditch of the middle ward. These new buildings were put up in the 1240s, and we know that by 1249 the four chaplains, who served the new chapel of St Edward, had lodgings against the south curtain wall of the lower ward,[69] probably opposite the chapel. These chaplains were the forerunners of the canons of St George's.

In 1295–6 the private royal lodgings, by this time used by Edward I, were badly damaged in a fire and apparently abandoned.[70] The chapel to the south continued in use, as did the great hall complex immediately to the west, and this complex should be briefly discussed here, if we are to understand how the buildings were used by the college in the later Middle Ages.

In 1895, a series of excavations was made in the area immediately to the north of the nave of St George's Chapel,[71] and in them some massive north-south wall-foundations were discovered, which had been partly incorporated into Denton's Commons, the early sixteenth-century building which had been demolished in 1859 (see below). These walls were studied by St John Hope and he concluded that they must relate to the great hall of Henry II and Henry III's residence in the lower ward, which he thought ran north-south.[72] Hope also documents a series of repairs in the earlier thirteenth century to the

---

65. St. John Hope, i, pp.15–24 and Colvin, *King's Works*, ii, pp. 864–5. See Fig. 1 on pp. 4–5 above.

66. P.E. Curnow, 'Royal lodgings of the thirteenth century in the lower ward of Windsor Castle: some recent archaeological discoveries', *Friends Report* (1965), pp. 218–20.

67. Excavations carried out in November 1997, under the northern end of the later Vicars' Hall, found that the castle wall here dated from the thirteenth century, and contained a doorway leading to a garde-robe. It seems likely that the twelfth-century western limit to the lower ward was close to the later west front of St George's Chapel.

68. St. John Hope, i, pp. 52–5.

69. St. John Hope, i, pp. 58–9.

70. St. John Hope, i, pp. 86–7.

71. These are recorded on plan P. 75 in the Archives. Some drawn sections are also on this plan.

72. St. John Hope, i, p. 52.

great hall and 'great chamber of the same hall', as well as to the 'king's dais of the aforesaid hall'.[73] A new great kitchen was also made between 1227 and 1230, and a little later (in 1252–3) a timber alley was made from the kitchen to the hall, while at the same time (Nov. 1252) a well six ft. in diameter was ordered to be made 'so that a channel can come thence through a gutter to the kitchen'.[74] This well is almost certainly the well that still survives immediately to the north of the nave (now with a pump over it), and which in 1520 is called the Vicars' well.[75] By this time it had become the principal source of water for the vicars and all those living in that area. It was still being used, as the water supply with its pump, in the nineteenth century. The great kitchen was clearly covered by the site of the later St George's Chapel.

All writers after St John Hope have followed him in suggesting that the late twelfth-century and later great hall was the north–south building north of the nave, which runs up to the curtain wall on the north, and partly survives in the present organist's house. However, this cannot be correct as a royal great hall of this date must have been a large ground-floor aisled hall. It seemed to me more likely, therefore, that the north–south building was, in fact, the chamber block, and that the great hall ran east–west from this as far as the later Canons' Cloister. By reinterpreting the evidence from the 1895 excavation and from the still surviving organist's house, I would suggest that the north wall of the great hall ran eastwards from the main front wall of the organist's house,[76] and that the great hall was perhaps about 100ft. long (east–west) and 45ft. wide. This can be roughly compared with Henry III's great aisled hall in Winchester Castle, which is 111ft. long by 55 ft. wide.[77] Recently Dr Steven Brindle has drawn my attention to other documentary evidence, which confirms that the great hall ran east-to-west. In an inquisition concerning repairs at Windsor Castle made by Edward III, and dated 13 January 1331, the jurors mention:

the defects of the great hall with the pantry and buttery at the eastern head of the same

and

the defects of the chamber at the western head of the hall with a chimney in the same place which is ruinously weakened.[78]

This clearly tells us that the high end of the great hall with the dais was on the west, while the buttery and pantry with the screen's passage was at the east end, with a main porch no doubt to the south of this. The buttery and pantry must, therefore, have lain on the site now occupied by the front of St George's house (Nos. 9 and 10, The Cloisters). The 1331 Inquisition also tells us that there was a chamber with a chimney at the western end of the hall, and this must have been at first-floor level in the building that was partly used as Denton's Commons (in use from 1520) and was demolished in 1859. This building was, however, only the eastern part of the north chamber block, and the 1895 excavations

---

73. *Ibid.*

74. St. John Hope, i, p. 53.

75. St. John Hope, ii, p. 523.

76. Part of a thirteenth-century doorway in this north wall with an external plinth on the north side, still survives in the organist's house, which probably led into the north-west corner of the great hall.

77. See M. Biddle and B. Clayre, *Winchester Castle and the Great Hall*, Winchester 1983, p.25.

78. I am greatly indebted to Dr Brindle for this reference which is calendared in *Chancery Miscellaneous Inquisitions*, II (Edward II–III), no. 1220.

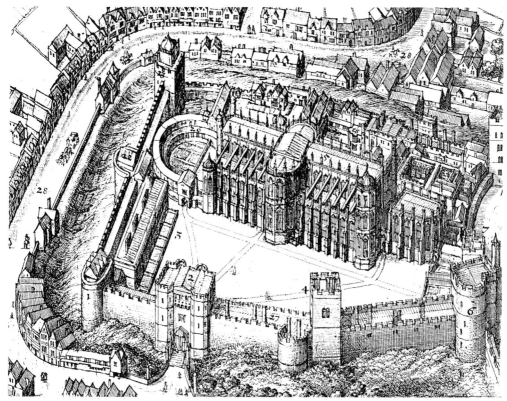

Fig. 15. *Detail of Wenceslaus Hollar's c. 1670 bird's-eye view drawing of the lower ward at Windsor Castle from the south-east (St. John Hope, Windsor Castle, i, pl. xxii)*

uncovered the main west wall of the western part which ran north to a still-existing pilaster buttress in the north curtain wall.[79] The house on this site (now No. 24) was built in the early eighteenth century, but Wenceslaus Hollar's bird's-eye view of the castle in the later seventeenth century shows two parallel north-south steep-pitched roofs here. These were probably the later twelfth- or early thirteenth-century scissor-braced roofs that covered the original chamber block.[80] Only one fragment of these roofs survive today in the flat over the organist's house (No. 25). The small first-floor chamber here still contains fragments of fine thirteenth-century wall-paintings, and it must originally have been part of Henry III's residence.[81] By the early sixteenth century, however, it was used as the choristers' lodgings at the north end of Denton's Commons.

As is well-known, a whole series of new buildings was erected on the north side of the chapel between 1350 and 1357 for the new foundation.[82] The earlier 'grass plot' to the

79. See note 71 above.

80. Hollar's view is to be found in St. John Hope, i, pp. 308–9 (see Fig. 15 above). Only the roof over the north-east corner still survives (see note 66), but more of this roof survived over Denton's Commons until 1859, as early photographs show.

81. See note 66 above and also D. Park, *B.A.A. Transactions* (forthcoming).

82. St. John Hope, i, pp. 134–59.

north of the chapel was turned into a new stone cloister (now the Dean's Cloister), and to the east of it a new vestry, chapter house and warden's lodgings[83] were erected along the edge of the middle ward ditch. To the north of the Dean's Cloister an old thirteenth-century masonry wall was partly retained, and in the area between this and the north curtain wall, a series of 23 or 26 timber-framed lodgings were contrived around a timber cloister for the lodgings of the canons.[84] The masonry back walls clearly contained fireplaces and flues, and the north curtain wall, and its three projecting rectangular towers, was rebuilt with the large central tower containing the canons' common latrine. A small postern gate was also built in the south-east corner of this tower which gave access to a series of steps (later called 'the hundred steps') that lead northwards down the hill to the canons' cemetery.

Remarkably the main timber-frame for most of the original canons' houses, built between 1352 and 1355,[85] still survives buried in the present buildings that occupy the site. Only on the west side was it apparently destroyed in the 1640s, and replaced with new buildings (Nos. 9 and 10, now St George's House) after the Restoration.[86] The canons' houses at Windsor are, therefore, some of the oldest (if not *the* oldest) timber-framed collegiate buildings surviving in Britain,[87] and the framing has surprisingly been little studied. Much careful survey work is needed, but it is possible, by looking inside, to see that the timber-framed houses were originally two-storied structures with shallow-pitched roofs, and that the cloister walks were tucked under the upper floor. Each bay was approximately 14–15 ft. wide, but at ground-level various through passages also had to be accommodated.[88] With the irregularity of the overall plan, it is not therefore possible to estimate the exact number of bays in the original timber-frame around all four sides of the cloister, but there must have been between about 22 and 26. This ties in well with the number of lodgings mentioned in the accounts i.e. 23 or 26,[89] and also with the number of priests (12 secular canons and 13 priest vicars) in the 1352 statutes.[90] St John Hope has suggested that the vicars occupied the smaller chambers on the ground floor, while the canons had the larger chambers, that oversailed the cloister walks, on the first floor. This is certainly a possible solution, but by no means the only one, and it would mean that each canon and priest vicar would have had a double bay in the timber-frame. On the ground floor there would have been a pair of small rooms for each lodging, each about 15ft. square, which the vicars perhaps used as a living and a sleeping chamber. There was also probably a fireplace in the masonry back wall of each lodging. In the larger upper floor

83. T. Tatton-Brown, 'The Deanery, Windsor Castle', *Antiquaries Journal*, 78 (1998), pp. 345–90.

84. St. John Hope, i, p. 147. Both 23 and 26 lodgings are mentioned in the accounts.

85. St. John Hope, ii, pp. 501–2.

86. There are also brick piers of the later seventeenth century in the west cloister walk, though parts of the top plate of the original west cloister arcade still survives in the north-west corner.

87. For a general survey, see W.A. Pantin, 'Chantry Priests' Houses and other medieval lodgings', *Medieval Archaeology*, III (1959), pp. 216–58.

88. To the Dean's Cloister on the south, and the passage to the Warden's lodgings on the south-east, and to the canons' latrine on the north.

89. See note 84 above.

90. Four clerks are also mentioned. See A.K.B. Roberts, *St George's Chapel, Windsor Castle, 1348–1416: A study in early collegiate administration*,Windsor 1947, p. 7.

chambers,[91] which were presumably reached by individual straight stairs going up through the corners of the lower chambers, the ceiling was higher (about 14ft. high, as opposed to about 8ft. in the lower chambers), and it is possible that only one of the bays in the upper chambers here was open all the way to the ceiling. In the second bay there could have been a half-floor from the beginning. This can, however, only be seen with ease in No. 2, and in this chamber the half-floor was put in at a later date.[92] In several of the first-floor chambers it is possible also to see simple braces from the central main posts to a central purlin that supports the rafters and this too must be an original feature.

With the provision of separate accommodation for the priest vicars in the early fifteenth century (see below), the canons could take over the ground-floor chambers as well,[93] and it is clear that by this time the buildings were already being modified, a process that is still continuing today. The first major visible changes, however, are those that had been carried out in the later fifteenth and early sixteenth century after the building of the new chapel. With the coming of many prominent new canons, new windows and oriels were put in,[94] lower ceilings were added,[95] and painted decoration was applied to the walls.[96] The chimney flues were also rebuilt in brick, and better staircases were put in. Parallel changes were also made at the Deanery.[97] The most elaborate house was that on the north side of the cloister in the middle (now No. 6), where a whole new timber-framed range, for an entrance, a staircase, an oriel and chimney stacks, was built in the cloister garth, and joined to the main lodging at first-floor level. The timber-framing, with a brick nogging infill, suggests an early sixteenth-century date for this work, but it is not known which canon built this or exactly when it was put up.

When these canons' lodgings were originally built in the mid-fourteenth century, they must have abutted onto the west end of the old great hall of the thirteenth-century royal palace, and the canons were able to make use of this, and its associated buttery and pantry. They were also able to use the great kitchen and other associated service-buildings to the south.[98] As a magnificent new main entrance to the whole complex, a very fine new vaulted porch was built on the north-west side of the Dean's Cloister, which had a fine outer doorway that faced south to the principal west front doorway to the chapel. Inside the porch, one doorway opened east into the Dean's Cloister, while another opened westwards, probably to connect with the earlier porch into the screen's passage of the

91. Each upper bay was about 21 ft. long by 15 ft. wide. This can best be measured today in the lodgings on the south side (Nos. 1 and 2). The principal partitions between lodgings often contained two long passing braces.

92. This area was opened up in the early 1970s to make offices for St George's House.

93. Though each canon no doubt already partly controlled his vicar's lodging beneath.

94. Some projecting out into the cloister garth, and including one [No. 2] that projects southwards over the north walk of the Dean's Cloister.

95. There is a fine sixteenth-century coved ceiling in the office of the warden of St George's House, for example.

96. The finest surviving painted decoration can now be seen in the so-called 'Catherine Room' at No. 2, see E.C. Rouse, 'The recently discovered wall paintings in the lower ward, Windsor Castle', *Friends Report* (1965–6), pp. 275–81.

97. See Tatton-Brown, 'Deanery', pp. 351–3.

98. The canons may originally have ate in common in the great hall, but they were soon eating in their own chambers, see Roberts, *Administration 1348–1416*, p. 78.

great hall. In the fifteenth century a second chapter house, for the canons, was built south-west of the porch.[99] This chapter house may first have been built early in the fifteenth century, when the chapter house in the east cloister walk was perhaps first used exclusively by the knights of the Garter. It was, however, almost certainly rebuilt in *c.* 1475–7, when the new St George's Chapel was being built, and a small doorway may have led directly from the south end of the canons' chapter house to the north choir aisle below the Edward IV chantry chapel.[100] Above the mid-fourteenth-century entrance porch, a small muniment room and counting house, now called the 'Aerary', was built in 1353–4,[101] and access was probably originally from a doorway on the west side, which perhaps led to a chamber above the old great hall porch. This remarkable room, which is covered by a stone vault, still has its original floor of Penn tiles.[102] In 1496 a new staircase to it was made in the east cloister walk,[103] and from 1483 a new library building had been made over the east cloister walk,[104] which had a connecting door to the 'Aerary'. By this time the 'Aerary' was also acting as a treasury for the chapel, but no longer as the counting house, which had moved to the Schorn Tower above the south-east corner of the chapel.[105]

In the later fourteenth and fifteenth century, many of the secular cathedrals in England were building separate new closes for their vicars, who now undertook most of the daily *opus dei* work in the cathedrals. Fine examples of these 'closes', with a separate vicars' hall and double ranges of lodgings around a court, still survive at Wells, Chichester, Lincoln, Hereford and Lichfield. At Windsor, as we have seen, a fine new range of vicars' lodgings (the Horseshoe Cloister) was laid out, and built, from 1475, in conjunction with the new chapel. However, there is documentary evidence to show that some new lodgings, as well as a vicars' hall, were built earlier in the fifteenth century. In 1409 the dean and canons were granted by Henry IV, 'a certain place within our Castle aforesaid called Woodhaw, beside the great hall, to build there houses for the vicars, clerks and choristers, because they were not fully endowed as to houses and lodgings for their vicars, clerks, choristers and servants . . .'.[106]

Running east from the twelfth–thirteenth-century chamber block, and near the east wing of No. 25 (the organist's house), is a fragment of a timber-framed range with a crown-post roof. This range, which lies adjacent to the north wall of the great hall (see above), and just inside the curtain wall, must have continued eastwards under the front part of No. 8, a new house that was built in the late seventeenth century after the destruction of the Commonwealth period.[107]

Some years after this, in 1415–16, there is a strange crossed-out entry in the treasurer's accounts 'for the new building of the houses of the vicars of the college' costing

99. It was in existence by 1477 at the latest, and was destroyed in the mid-seventeenth century, St. John Hope, ii, p. 506. It appears to be shown on Norden's 1607 bird's-eye view, with a lead roof (Pl. VIII).

100. The south end of this access route is perhaps the so-called 'sacristy'. See M. Bond, *St George's Chapel, Windsor: The quincentenary book of photographs*, London 1975, p. 47.

101. St. John Hope, ii, pp. 504–5.

102. See L. Keen, *B.A.A. Transactions* (forthcoming).

103. Heavily restored in 1862.

104. Now occupied by the mid-nineteenth-century 'Chapter Room'.

105. St. John Hope, ii, p. 505. Iron bars were added to the windows in 1496–7.

106. St. John Hope, ii, p. 517.

107. The south wall of this range, possibly incorporating part of the north wall of the great hall, can still be seen as a boundary wall in front of No. 8.

£67 14s 1¾d.[108] This probably relates to the range discussed above, but it could also relate to further works west of the thirteenth-century royal chamber block, where a new vicars' close was perhaps starting to be laid out. This had a new vicars' first-floor hall on the west (later the Chapter Library), with ranges of lodgings probably running east from the north and south side of this hall. Those on the south were no doubt replaced by the northern range of the Horseshoe Cloister, but the northern vicars' houses may in part survive in No. 23 (Marbeck), the present assistant organist's house and choir practice room. Unfortunately this range was very heavily restored in 1871,[109] but some original fifteenth-century timber work can still be seen in the building. To the west of it, and near the entrance of the vicars' hall, was probably the vicars' latrine, which must have discharged through the curtain wall to the north.[110]

The documentary evidence suggests that the building of the new vicars' close was still continuing in the later 1430s. In Archbishop Kemp's 'Injunctions' (issued in 1432, after a visit to the college on 22 May 1430), he says that:

since the chambers already constructed therein [i.e. in the 'mansion of the vicars'] are not sufficient for the full number of vicars. . .they shall construct or cause to be constructed and built one chamber fit and proper, like and corresponding to the other chambers in a place adjoining the said vicars' mansion.[111]

In a steward's roll of 1437–8 we hear of three vicars' chambers constructed *in mansione vicariorum*, and in another of 1439–40, we hear of nine vicars' lodgings being repaired.[112] The work was obviously very protracted, due to the college's poor financial health.

The vicars' hall itself is a fine first-floor hall (*c.* 70 ft. by 23 ft.) of at least six bays with a king-strut and crown-post roof. It too was heavily restored in 1870, but in its original form it was probably sub-divided into three sections. There is no doubt that it was built for the vicars in the early fifteenth century. In the years after 1475 its south end was rebuilt and incorporated into the Horseshoe Cloister. It, however, continued in use as the vicars' hall until 1550.[113] In summary, it seems that new lodgings for the vicars, clerks and choristers were built first to the north of the great hall (in the 'Woodhaw'), and then, from about 1415, a new close was created in the north-west part of the lower ward, centred on a new vicars' hall.[114] At about the same time, the royal great hall may at last have been demolished.[115]

With the building of the magnificent new chapel in the 1470s, a completely new seven-sided vicars' close was laid out immediately to the west of the chapel. Work on building the new timber-frames probably took place from about 1478 to 1480,[116] and in 1481 there

108. St. John Hope, ii, p. 517.

109. *Ibid.*

110. The site is now occupied by the underground boiler house.

111. John Kemp was at this time archbishop of York and chancellor of England. For the injunctions see J.N. Dalton, *Statutes*, typescript, 29, p. 28 and St. John Hope, ii, p. 522.

112. SGC XV.48.14 and 16.

113. St. John Hope, ii, p. 520.

114. The situation at this time is roughly on the mid-fifteenth-century 'Eton drawing', the earliest known depiction of the castle. See Fig. 16.

115. The great hall was used as a temporary chapel in about 1390 (during repairs to the chapel)- see St. John Hope, i, p. 222 , but after this references to the great hall disappear. Presumably it was not needed after the Vicars' Hall was built.

116. No documentary evidence for this survives.

Fig. 16. *Mid-fifteenth-century sketch drawing of Windsor Castle from the north (St. John Hope,* Windsor Castle, *i, pl. xix)*

are the accounts of Thomas Cancellar (Bishop Beauchamp had just died) which mention the making of 21 brick chimneys in 21 chambers for the vicars. 'Le brickefillyng' (i.e. the brick nogging in the timber-frames) is also mentioned, as are fireplaces and casting of lead for the roof.[117] All this suggests that these 21 new lodgings were complete by 1482, at a time when the new stalls in the new choir of the chapel were also nearing completion. By this time also the new choral establishment had been settled with a strength of 45 (16 vicars, one deacon gospeller, 13 lay clerks, two clerks epistoler and 13 choristers).[118] Some of the clerks probably still had lodgings along the south side of the lower ward, and others may have lodged north-east of the vicars' hall along the northern curtain wall in No. 23 (Marbeck). By this time the old great hall had certainly been demolished, but the northern part of the old chamber block had by now probably been adapted in part as the choristers' lodgings. The 21 new lodgings in the Horseshoe Cloister were probably built for all the vicars, as well as for some of the lay clerks.[119] These lodgings were very heavily restored in 1870–1, but they are still used, after more than 500 years, by lay clerks, the virger and others. As in the canons' houses, it is evident that the core of the original lodging still survives, despite many later alterations and additions at the rear. The original houses seemed to have contained just two rooms (a lower living chamber and an upper sleeping chamber) with a small staircase in each and a narrow through passage to a yard at the

117. St. John Hope, ii, p. 518.
118. See R. Bowers (*supra* p. 200).
119. Married clerks lived in the town, see Bowers, p. 201.

Fig. 17.   *View of Denton's Commons from the south-east in the 1850s, showing the main entrance and crenellated outer courtyard wall (St. John Hope, Windsor Castle, ii, pl. lxxxvii)*

back.[120] Each house also had a large brick chimney at the rear (now all rebuilt) with fireplaces in both the ground and first-floor chambers. A covered walk (cloister) ran all the way around the fronts of the houses, and this probably continued north of the nave, to the north door, to allow the vicars dry access to the chapel in all weather. Unfortunately the north-east part of the Horseshoe Cloister (about 5 original houses) was demolished in 1843,[121] but earlier views and plans show that the covered walk continued north of the Urswick Chantry and then up some steps near the well and pump on the north side of the nave. Immediately to the north of this one final new lodging was created in 1519 by Canon James Denton. This was a 'New Commons' for the 13 choristers and all the chantry priests, eight of them, who served various chantries in the chapel founded between 1481 and 1506.[122] This new lodging house, as we have already seen, was an adaption and rebuilding of the eastern range of the old thirteenth-century chamber block. It was surrounded on the east and west by a high brick wall, which enclosed yards, and had a common hall at the first-floor level with a pantry to the north. Beyond this again, in the only part of the building which still survives, was the choristers' *cubiculum*. On the

---

120. The lodgings on the west had no yard, but perhaps a way onto the battlements.
121. St. John Hope, ii, p. 523. By this time it was three houses and the schoolroom.
122. St. John Hope, ii, p. 512.

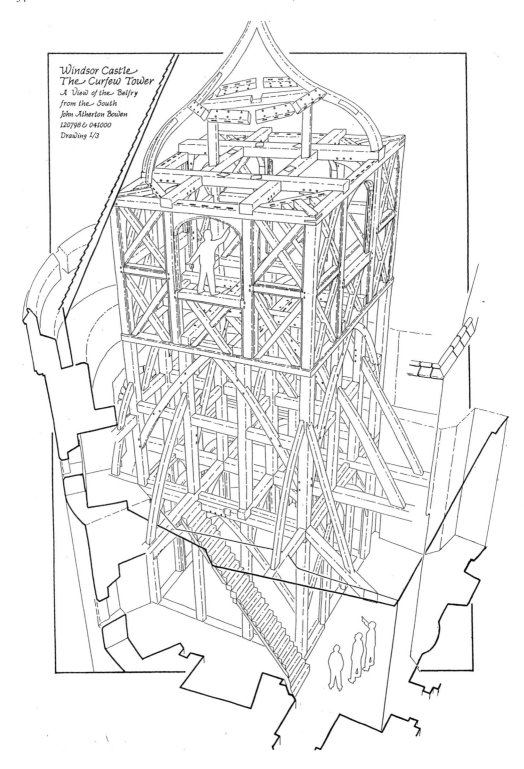

Windsor Castle
The Curfew Tower
A View of the Belfry
from the South
John Atherton Bowen
120798 & 041000
Drawing 1/3

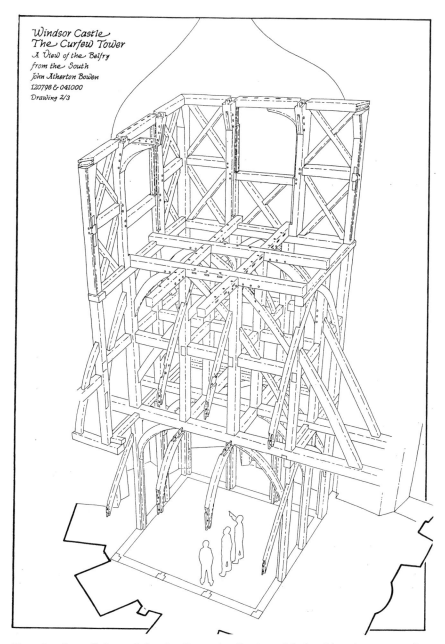

Windsor Castle
The Curfew Tower
A View of the Belfry
from the South
John Atherton Bowen
120798 & 041000
Drawing 2/3

Figs 18 and 19. *(facing and above) Perspective drawings of the late fifteenth-century timber-frame for the belfry in the Curfew Tower, Windsor Castle. All later timbers have been omitted (J.A. Bowen)*

ground floor was the kitchen with a buttery, larder and store. Sadly the building was ordered to be demolished by chapter in 1859, but its documented history and form were well described by St John Hope only half a century after its destruction.[123]

One final building should also be mentioned: the bell tower. With the creation of the new buildings for the Order of the Garter, a temporary belfry was erected on the roof of the chapel. However, soon afterwards a square tower on the south side of the lower ward, opposite the chapel, was rebuilt as the bell tower, and from at least 1361 it contained a clock.[124] From the 1370s various bells were added to the tower, so that by the early fifteenth century it had eight bells, including at least one for the clock. This bell tower is today the residence of the Governor of the Military Knights, but the tower still contains its original early fourteenth-century roof, and its original steep flights of steps up the four levels of the tower.[125] With the building of the new chapel from 1475, it was clearly intended eventually to have a new lantern tower over the crossing but, as we have seen, this was never built. However, a new bell tower was required for the chapel at an early stage, and the accounts tell us that a new timber-framed belfry was being made by 1478 in the Clewer Tower.[126] It was, though, only finally covered in lead in 1489–90. To this new tower were transferred the clock and all eight bells, and it has remained to this day the principal clock tower and belfry of the castle, though in 1863 the whole structure was covered with a prominent new conical roof.[127] The magnificent timber-frame (Figs 18, 19) inside the Clewer (now Curfew) Tower has also been little studied, even though it is one of the largest and finest timber belfries in Britain. The frame itself stands on the early thirteenth-century ribbed vault at the base of the tower, and is itself three stories high with an octagonal ogee roof on top.[128] It is massively braced, and the top stage, which still holds the bells, has extra cross-bracing in it, and four openings in each face with wide four-centred moulded timber arches above. Access to the tower was, and still is, via a through passage in the north-west side of the Horseshoe Cloister. A doorway in the masonry wall at the back of the tower leads immediately to a very steep blockwood stair to the first-floor level of the frame, which may well have been the original ringing chamber.

In sum, the surviving complex of stone and timber structures around St George's Chapel, in the lower ward of Windsor Castle, is one of the most interesting and least studied medieval and early Tudor complexes in Britain. A full modern archaeological survey is now needed.

ACKNOWLEDGEMENTS

I am exceptionally grateful to Dr Eileen Scarff for all her help (and patience!) with the writing of this chapter. Without this help, it could never have been finished. I am also most grateful to the

---

123. St. John Hope, ii, pp. 512–15. He also includes photos and drawings of the building before its destruction. See also Richmond (*supra* pp. 165–6).

124. A clock had been made for the round tower, as early as 1351–2. See St. John Hope, i, pp. 152–3. See also Roberts, *Administration 1348–1416*, pp. 96–8 and 100–1.

125. I am most grateful to Major General Sir Peter Downward for allowing us to inspect the inside of the tower, which today does not belong to the dean and canons.

126. St. John Hope, ii, p. 527.

127. The idea for this was probably suggested by Napoleon III, see Sir Owen Morshead, *Windsor Castle*, Windsor 1951, pp. 32–3 and T. Tatton-Brown, 'The Curfew Tower', *Friends Report* (1992–3), pp. 150–4.

128. The top of the roof was mutilated by the 1863 roof. From the base of the stone plinth to the top of the roof is over 100 ft.

Fig. 20. *High vault in the north transept (Rutland Chapel), St George's Chapel (C. Wilson)*

former dean of Windsor, the Very Revd. Patrick Mitchell, for introducing me to the delights of Windsor's architectural history, and to John Atherton Bowen for all his help with the provisional survey of the buildings. His notes and drawings have greatly aided my work. I would also like to thank Dr Christopher Wilson for allowing me to use photographs taken by him for his lecture to the conference on the rebuilding of St George's Chapel. Finally, as always, this chapter could never have been written without the word-processing skills of my wife, Veronica.

Margaret of Anjou, Chivalry and the Order of the Garter

DIANA DUNN

INTRODUCTION

In 1445 John Talbot, earl of Shrewsbury gave Margaret of Anjou a large richly illuminated book as a wedding present probably when she visited Rouen in late March on her way to England to meet her husband, King Henry VI. The manuscript, now preserved in the British Library (BL Royal MS 15 E. vi), has been described as a 'chivalric anthology', made up of a collection of chansons de geste, romances, chronicles and histories, treatises on government and warfare, and a copy of the Statutes of the Order of the Garter (see Pl. IA).[1] The choice of subject matter may be thought surprising for a woman, even a queen, and reflects the cultural interests and outlook of the earl of Shrewsbury whom contemporaries held in high esteem for his military prowess and leadership in the final humiliating years of the Hundred Years War.[2] It has been postulated that Talbot originally put the collection together for himself and then adapted it for the new queen once he learnt that the marriage had been formally agreed.[3] This may explain some obvious alterations made to the heraldry, though conveniently the marguerite, used throughout as a marginal decorative device, was equally appropriate to Talbot's own wife, Margaret Beauchamp.

Alternatively Talbot may have intended the book as a primer on chivalry for a future heir to the throne.[4] It is reasonable to assume that Talbot expected the queen to play an important part in directing the education of her children, at least in their early years, and it may have been that, given the lack of interest in things military and chivalric already evident in the king by 1445, Talbot regarded Margaret's role in shaping her children's future as crucial.[5] Whatever the queen's role, the contents of the Shrewsbury Book can

---

1. A. de Mandach, 'A Royal Wedding-Present in the Making', *Nottingham Medieval Studies*, 18 (1974), pp. 56–9. The contents of the manuscript are described in H.G. Ward, *Catalogue of Romances in the Department of Manuscripts in the British Museum*, London 1883, i, pp. 129–30, 469–70, 487–9, 598–600, 604–10, 615–19, 622–4, 627–9, 708–10.

2. A.J. Pollard, *John Talbot and the War in France 1427–1453*, London 1983, pp. 122–8.

3. *Ibid.*, p. 123; C. Reynolds, 'The Shrewsbury Book, British Library, Royal MS 15 E.VI' in *Medieval Art, Architecture and Archaeology at Rouen*, ed. J. Stratford, London 1993, p. 111.

4. Mandach, 'A Royal Wedding-Present', p. 59.

5. It is generally recognised that women had an important part to play in the education of their children in their early years, see N. Orme, *From Childhood to Chivalry: The education of kings and aristocracy 1066–1530*, London 1984; J. Hughes, 'Educating the Aristocracy in Late Medieval England', *History Today*, 49 (February 1999).

justifiably be considered appropriate reading matter for the education of a future king.[6] It contains accounts of deeds of valour in time of war, including those of Alexander the Great, Charlemagne and Guy de Warwick, French romances and chansons de geste, together with treatises on government and warfare, including Giles of Rome's *De Regimine principum*, Honoré Bouvet's *Arbre des batailles* and Christine de Pisan's *Livre des fais d'armes et de chevalerie*.

I

Did Margaret, then, have any understanding of, or interest in, the chivalric culture of later medieval England and France, which is reflected so strongly in the Shrewsbury Book? The two key people likely to have been important influences on her early life, playing a major part in her education and shaping her literary tastes, were her father, René, duke of Anjou and her grandmother, Yolande of Aragon with whom Margaret spent a considerable amount of time as a young girl. Yolande of Aragon, who acted as regent during her son's absences overseas, was a highly educated woman and patron of the University of Angers where she founded faculties of theology, medicine and arts.[7] René of Anjou was also a significant patron of the arts and possessed wide-ranging artistic talents as a musician, writer and illuminator of manuscripts. His court at the castles of Angers and Saumur on the Loire was renowned across Europe for its artistic brilliance and its tournaments, such as the one held at Nancy in 1445 in celebration of the marriage of his daughter to the king of England.[8] In 1448 he founded the Order of the Croissant and instructed his King of Arms to keep a record of the high deeds of prowess of the companions of the Order.[9] He wrote a pastoral love poem *Regnault et Jeanneton*, and an allegorical work *Le Mortifiement de Vaine Plaisance* in the early 1450s followed in 1457 by his most famous book, *Le Livre du Cuers d'Amours Espris*, an allegorical romance.[10]

---

6. In March 1460 Alesia, Lady Lovell was discharged from service to Edward, prince of Wales who was 'now so grown as to be committed to the rules and teachings of men wise and strenuous, to understand the acts and manners of a man befitting such a Prince, rather than to stay further under the keeping and governance of women', *Calendar of Patent Rolls 1452–61*, p. 567. During his time in France, Prince Edward's education was supervised by Sir John Fortescue, Chief Justice of the King's Bench and chancellor of the Lancastrian court in exile. In the preface to his *De Laudibus Legum Anglie*, Fortescue remarks on the prince's love of jousting and fierce horses, at the same time as expressing concern about his ignorance of the law, see Fortescue, *De Laudibus Legum Anglie*, ed. S.B. Chrimes, Cambridge 1942, pp. 2–3, 16–19. A number of books of instruction were written specifically for Prince Edward. These include a collection of 'sayings and opinions of various philosophers' by George Ashby; Peter Idley's *Instructions to his Son*, based in part on two Latin works of the thirteenth-century Italian author Albertano da Brescia; as well as Fortescue's *De Laudibus*. See Orme, *The education of English kings*, pp. 102, 105–6, 130, 154, 184, 189.

7. A. Lecoy de la Marche, *Le Roi René: sa vie, son administration, ses travaux artistiques et littéraires*, 2 vols, Paris 1875, i, pp. 549–52; J. Harthan, *Books of Hours and their Owners*, London 1977, pp. 84–5.

8. Lecoy de la Marche, *Le Roi René*, i, p. 237, but see the discussion of Lecoy's account in B.M. Cron, 'The duke of Suffolk, the Angevin marriage, and the ceding of Maine, 1445', *Journal of Medieval History*, 20 (1994), pp. 77–99. One of the most detailed surviving accounts of the organisation of a tournament in the later fifteenth century is René of Anjou's treatise of *c.* 1455–60, *Livre des tournois*, see R. Barber and J. Barber, *Tournaments: Jousts, Chivalry and Pageants*, Woodbridge 1989, pp. 180–6.

9. M. Keen, *Chivalry*, London 1984, p. 192.

10. F. Unterkircher, *King René's Book of Love*, New York 1980, p. 14.

In René of Anjou's great art collection books figure prominently amongst the paintings, sculpture, tapestries, medals, armour and devotional objects. The catalogue of his library 'housed in a new gallery overlooking his oratory and the little garden', at the castle of Angers, describes the collection of over 200 volumes in Latin, Greek, Hebrew, Arabic, French, Italian and German on subjects as diverse as theology, philosophy, geography, history, law, literature, and physical and natural science.[11] As a child therefore, Margaret had access to one of the largest private book collections in Europe and her literary tastes and ideas were open to the influence of that chivalric culture so beloved of her father. The Shrewsbury Book was a fitting wedding present for Margaret and there is every likelihood that she would have read it with pleasure and appreciated its contents.

The inclusion of Christine de Pisan's *Livre des fais d'armes et de chevalerie* in the Shrewsbury Book is particularly interesting as the only known medieval treatise on warfare written by a woman. It was also fortuitous given Margaret's own position in a country experiencing civil war in the1450s and 1460s. Whilst Christine's qualifications for writing on warfare have been debated from her own lifetime to the present day, there is no doubt that her treatise was well-received and widely circulated amongst the aristocracy of Europe during the fifteenth and early sixteenth centuries.[12] It was amongst the earliest printed books in both France and England, three versions appearing in each country before 1527 (the earliest English printed edition translated by Caxton for Henry VII in 1489).[13] The treatise had a clear educational purpose, being commissioned around 1410 by John the Fearless, duke of Burgundy for his thirteen-year-old son-in-law the dauphin, Louis de Guyenne. The collapse into insanity of King Charles VI resulted in responsibility for the upbringing and education of the dauphin being placed in the hands of the duke of Burgundy.[14] This was a time of acute political tension with periodic outbreaks of civil war in France, and all hopes of future stability were vested in the dauphin, hence the concern for his education. These circumstances find an obvious parallel for the situation in which Margaret of Anjou found herself in 1453 when Henry VI also succumbed to a serious physical and mental disorder shortly before the birth of their son.

Christine de Pisan was already experienced in writing educational texts having produced two for the sons of John the Fearless, as well as her *L'Epître d'Othéa* of 1399 which has as its central concern the instruction of a young man, perhaps her fifteen-year-old son, Jean de Castel. Here she states that the knight should seek good repute in virtuous ways rather than through egotism and vainglory. In addition to her emphasis upon moral education, she also stresses the need for a knight to receive a proper military training to equip him for a successful career.[15] This epistolary allegory from the goddess of Wisdom

---

11. The catalogue is dated 1471, see Lecoy de la Marche, *Le Roi René*, ii, pp. 184–90.

12. C.C. Willard, 'Pilfering Vegetius? Christine de Pizan's Faits d'Armes et de Chevalerie' in *Women, the Book and the Worldly*, ed. L. Smith and J. Taylor, Woodbridge 1993; *The Reception of Christine de Pizan from the Fifteenth through the Nineteenth Centuries: Visitors to the City*, ed. G.K. McLeod, Lewiston, Queenston, Lampeter 1991, pp. 25–43.

13. *The Book of Fayttes of Armes and of Chyvalrye: Translated and Printed by William Caxton from the French Original by Christine de Pisan*, ed. A.T.P. Byles, EETS, os 189 (1932) and the new edition *The Book of Deeds of Arms and of Chivalry: Christine de Pizan*, ed. C.C. Willard and trans. S. Willard, Pennsylvania 1999.

14. C.C. Willard, *Christine de Pizan: Her Life and Works*, New York 1984, pp. 91–9, 173–93.

15. S.L. Hindman, *Christine de Pizan's 'Epistre Othéa': Painting and Politics at the Court of Charles VI*, Toronto 1986.

and Prudence to the Trojan hero Hector was very popular and copies were made for three members of the French royal family between 1400 and 1415: for Louis, duke of Orleans (Paris, BN MS. fr. 848); for John, duke of Berry (Paris, BN MS. fr. 606); and for Queen Isabeau of Bavaria (BL Harley MS. 4431).

Throughout her life, Christine de Pisan was concerned about the unstable political situation in France and, in many of her writings, she took the opportunity to put across her view that every effort should be made to restore peace. She regarded the reign of Charles V as a golden age for France, and in her biography of the king, *Le Livre des fais et bonnes meurs du sage roy Charles V*, commissioned by Philip, duke of Burgundy before his death in 1404, she expresses her admiration for his wisdom and intelligence. The book draws heavily on French history, especially the *Grandes Chroniques de France*, and contemporary political ideas, a strong influence being Giles of Rome's *De Regimine principum*. In the second part of the biography entitled 'Chivalry', Christine discusses Charles V's chivalric virtues evident not so much in physical prowess but strength of character, common sense, good fortune and diligence.[16] His example of wise kingship, worthy of emulation, contrasts with the disastrous reigns of Charles VI and Henry VI which led to civil war.

Christine believed that women in positions of authority had a particular role to play in time of war as mediators and peacemakers. In her book of advice for women, *Le Livre des Trois Vertus*, written in 1405, she cites examples of queens who had successfully played this role in the past.[17] In 1402 Queen Isabeau of Bavaria was given full powers of mediation in the dispute between the dukes of Burgundy and Orleans, with authority to deal with finance and any other major matters of government business when the king was incapable of acting, powers further clarified in 1403 when it became clear that the king's illness was worsening.[18] There is a remarkable similarity in the personal experiences of Isabeau of Bavaria and Margaret of Anjou although the nature of their husbands' illnesses was different. Both queens became embroiled in politics and both were to be blamed for the outbreak of civil war in their respective countries. In a letter dated 5 October 1405, written by Christine de Pisan to Isabeau of Bavaria, she makes it clear that it is the queen's role to try to find a remedy for the evils afflicting France. She cites examples of noble ladies from the past who succeeded in obtaining peace against all the odds. The perfect woman, Mary, Queen of Heaven and Mother of God, is held up as the model for all women to imitate, one of her essential roles being that of comforter of her people in times of strife. Here, as elsewhere, Christine writes of the horrors and suffering that are brought about by civil war and, in particular the effects of war on the helpless children and widows, the poor and infirm.[19] These ideas are reiterated in other works such as her *Lamentacion sur les maux de la France*, written in 1410, addressed to all French princes especially the venerable and wise Jean, duke of Berry, brother of Charles V, to whom she appeals to use

16. Willard, *Christine de Pizan*, pp. 115–33.

17. In particular she cites the example of Queen Blanche of Castile, mother of St Louis, see Christine de Pisan, *Le livre des trois vertus*, translated S. Lawson, Harmondsworth 1985, pp. 49–51. This book was written for Margeurite de Nevers, eldest daughter of the duke of Burgundy on her marriage to the dauphin Louis de Guyenne in 1405.

18. R. Gibbons, 'Isabeau of Bavaria, Queen of France (1385–1422): The Creation of an Historical Villainess', *Transactions of the Royal Historical Society*, 6th ser. 6 (1996), p. 54.

19. *Anglo-Norman Letters & Petitions*, ed. M.D. Legge, Oxford 1941, pp. 144–50.

his wisdom and experience to work for peace. She exhorts the French nobility to remember the chivalric ideals of the past and urges the queen and all women to open the eyes and hearts of men to the horrors of civil war and to appease the anger flowing from their selfish ambitions. She advocates prayer as a means of bringing about peace.[20] Although a peace treaty was signed between the Burgundians and the Armagnacs on 2 November 1410, the peace did not last. In 1412–13 Christine wrote her *Le Livre de la Paix* dedicated to the dauphin Louis and presented in the style of a 'mirror for princes', urging the French to unite against the English. She describes the blessings of God-given peace in contrast to the cruelties and destruction of civil war. Here she expresses her fervent belief that the main objective of a good ruler should be to govern in such a way as to prevent civil war.[21]

Christine was not the only French writer to express views on the evils that result from civil war. A strong anti-war movement developed in later fourteenth-century France, growing out of the devastation and social dislocation caused by the Hundred Years War, and the internal conflict that followed.[22] The remedy proffered by such writers was strong leadership, both political and military, a well-trained and highly-disciplined army, and the encouragement of a sense of the 'common weal' amongst the ruling and fighting classes in society. Concern was particularly expressed by Honoré Bouvet for the neglect of the rules of 'worthy chivalry'. Likewise Christine de Pisan's *Livre des fais d'armes* placed chivalry firmly in the context of service to the common weal. These theories were put into practice by Charles VII during an interlude in the Anglo-French War provided by the truce of Tours in 1444. In the following years he devoted considerable attention to the establishment of what became in effect a permanent standing army controlled by the crown. This army was to play a crucial part in the final defeat of the English in Normandy and Gascony after the renewal of war in 1449.[23]

The situation in England during the 1440s was very different. The country was ruled by a weak king who failed to provide the necessary leadership to unite the nobility in the prosecution of a successful overseas war. Instead, Henry VI's main concern was to bring the war with France to an end by the negotiation of a satisfactory peace settlement, cemented by his marriage to a French princess. The marriage of Margaret to Henry VI seems to have been popular at first bringing high expectations of a permanent peace.[24] Talbot's own expectations of the new queen are clearly stated in the dedicatory verse written on the second folio of his wedding present. Here he expresses his hope that the marriage will not only unite the two royal families and bring peace but also lead to the

20. 'La Lamentacion sur les maux de la France de Christine de Pisan' in *Mélanges offerts à Charles Foulon*, ed. A. Kennedy, Rennes 1980, pp. 177–85. The translation by R. Blumenfeld-Kosinski is printed in *The Selected Writings of Christine de Pizan*, ed. R. Blumenfeld-Kosinski, London and New York 1997, pp. 224–9.

21. *Selected Writings of Christine de Pizan*, ed. Blumenfeld-Kosinski, pp. 229–48.

22. Other examples are Philippe de Mézières and Honoré Bouvet, see Keen, 'War, Peace and Chivalry', reprinted in *Nobles, Knights and Men-at-Arms in the Middle Ages*, London 1996, pp. 8–16, and C.T. Allmand, *The Hundred Years War*, Cambridge 1988, pp. 153–7.

23. Keen, 'War, Peace and Chivalry', pp. 17–18; *The Book of Deeds*, ed. Willard, p. 8.

24. See F. Carleton Brown, 'Lydgate's Verses on Queen Margaret's Entry into London', *Modern Language Review*, 7 (1912), pp. 225–34; V.J. Scattergood, *Politics and Poetry in the Fifteenth Century*, London 1971, pp. 155–6. The marriage negotiations are discussed in detail in Cron, 'The duke of Suffolk, the Angevin marriage, and the ceding of Maine, 1445', pp. 77–99. See also R.A. Griffiths, *The Reign of King Henry VI*, London 1981, pp. 482–90 and B.P. Wolffe, *Henry VI*, London 1981, pp. 169–83.

production of an heir to continue the illustrious line.[25] The inclusion of the ornately decorated genealogical table showing French and English royal descents from St Louis, uniting in the figure of Henry VI, is a clear statement of Talbot's belief in the rightness of Henry's claim to the French crown (see Pl. IB).[26] But the marriage placed Margaret in an impossible position, and it is difficult to know exactly what the young queen's expectations were in 1445. She was very much under the influence of her uncle Charles VII who sent two embassies to England in July and October 1445 to conclude the peace negotiations. On 22 December 1445 Henry VI wrote a personal letter to Charles VII agreeing to the surrender of Maine to the French by 30 April 1446.[27] This was done without the knowledge of the royal council and, it was believed, under pressure from his wife. As the Lancastrian government lost credibility in the late 1440s, public opinion began to turn against the queen. She was blamed for the loss of England's French possessions and became the scapegoat for the breakdown of government and the decline into civil war.[28]

The real problem, however, lay with the weak personality of the king. By 1450 he had amply demonstrated his unsuitability to rule when strong leadership at the centre of government was essential, especially in time of war. Henry VI, however, was inclined towards religion and peace rather than war, and preferred the company of churchmen to soldiers.[29] Unlike René of Anjou or Henry V, Henry VI appears to have had no interest in the art or practice of war, and on no occasion led an army onto the field of battle. There is little evidence to indicate whether he had any real understanding of the concept or practice of chivalry. A way in which this might be assessed is by an examination of his attitude towards one of the great outward manifestations of late medieval chivalry in England, the Order of the Garter. The most detailed study of this subject has been carried out by Hugh Collins who argues that Henry VI upheld the ceremonies associated with the Order of the Garter at least until the collapse of effective government in the later 1450s.[30] An analysis of the king's attendance at the annual chapters of the Order of the Garter, recorded in the Order's Register, shows that it was only in exceptional

25. BL Royal MS 15 E.vi, f. 2. Pollard is not impressed with the quality of the verse which he describes as 'so execrable that one cannot help feeling that he [Talbot] composed it himself', see Pollard, *John Talbot*, p. 128.
26. Reynolds, 'The Shrewsbury Book', p. 113.
27. *Letters and Papers Illustrative of the Wars of the English in France during the Reign of Henry VI of England*, ed. J. Stevenson, Rolls Series, 2 vols. in 3, London 1864, i, pp. 164–7, ii, pt. ii, pp. 639–42.
28. *The Brut*, ed. W.F.D. Brie, EETS, os 131, 136 (1906–8), pp. 511–12. Margaret was blamed for the lack of good government as early as 1447 in an indictment for seditious speech brought before the court of King's Bench, London, Public Record Office, KB9/256/13.
29. Ralph Griffiths has put forward the idea that as a child, 'being surrounded by ageing, distinguished soldiers too early in life', Henry VI was constantly reminded of his dead father's martial exploits and may have reacted against this in later years, see Griffiths, *Henry VI*, pp. 250–1.
30. This was the subject of Hugh Collins' doctoral thesis, 'The Order of the Garter, 1348–1461: Chivalry and Politics in Later Medieval England' (unpublished D. Phil. thesis, University of Oxford, 1996), published as H. Collins, *The Order of the Garter, 1348–1461*, Oxford 2000. See also H. Collins, 'The Order of the Garter, 1348–1461: Chivalry and Politics in Later Medieval England' in *Courts, Counties and the Capital in the Later Middle Ages*, ed. D.E.S. Dunn, Stroud 1996, pp.155–80.

circumstances that deputies were appointed in his stead.[31] Henry did not apparently take much interest in the college or chapel of St George at Windsor, directing his attention instead to his new foundations at Eton and King's College, Cambridge; in 1458, however, a statue of St George mounted was commissioned by the Garter chapter, each member contributing to its cost, the king paying one hundred shillings (see Pl. II). This may be an indication of Henry's interest in the Order's religious significance at least, if not its martial dimension.[32]

Margaret of Anjou herself did not receive the Garter until 1447.[33] As a woman she shared this distinction with the wives and widows of other Garter knights, who were

31. Even during the minority, the young king attended regularly from 1427. The first record of attendance is in 1425 when he was only aged three and a half years, see J. Anstis, *The Register of the Most Noble Order of the Garter*, 2 vols, London 1724, i, p. 88 *sic* p. 90; the following year his presence was excused on the grounds of his 'infancy' and 'being at Leicester', *ibid.*, p. 94. Absences are recorded in 1430–1 when he was in France for his coronation. After he assumed his majority in 1437, Henry was absent on five occasions: in 1444 'The King was absent, intent on his matrimonial affairs', *ibid.*, p. 124; 1450 'The King was absent, being at Leicester where he had called a Council or Parliament', *ibid.*, p. 139; 1451 'The King was absent being at Westminster where he held a Parliament', *ibid.*, p. 144; 1454 'the King being sick kept himself within the Castle', *ibid.*, p. 151; 1457 'the King was at that Time with his Household at Kenylworth', *ibid.*, p. 160; the exact part played by the king at the chapter meeting held at the bishop of London's palace on 8 February 1461 is unclear: he was in effect a prisoner of the earl of Warwick at the time, *ibid.*, pp. 166–8.

32. 'Their Minds being disposed to advance the Honour of their tutelar St. George', the Sovereign contributed a hundred shillings, each Duke forty shillings and Earl 26s 8d, Baron 20s, Knight 13s 4d 'for making out of Hand an Image of that Saint sitting on Horseback', Anstis, *Register*, i, p. 163. See also the illumination in BL Royal MS 15 E.vi, f. 439, discussed by Collins, 'Order of the Garter' (thesis), pp. 209–10. Reynolds points out that the image of St George, beloved of Talbot as the distinguishing emblem of the English armies in France, is prominent as a decorative device in the Shrewsbury Book, see Reynolds, 'The Shrewsbury Book', p. 111. Talbot's other associations with St George are referred to in Pollard, *John Talbot*, p. 124: 'in 1452 he willed that a chapel dedicated to Our Lady and St George be founded in his home church of St Alkmund's, Whitchurch, where masses for his soul might be celebrated'. 'He donated to the church of the Sepulchre in Rouen ornaments for the altar decorated with the emblem of the Garter specifically for use in services celebrating the feast of St George.' Rouen, ADSM, série G, 9336. Margaret's Household Accounts of 1452–3 record payments to John Prudde, the king's glazier, for glazing a window of two lights in the chapel of Our Lady of the Pew, Westminster to be worked with images of the King and Queen kneeling in salutation to the Virgin Mary emblazoned with the queen's flowers (margeurites?) and her motto, with an escutcheon of the arms of St Edward to be placed in the old glass, at a cost of 2s, and another escutcheon of the arms of St George at a cost of 12d, see A.R. Myers, 'The Household of Queen Margaret of Anjou 1452–3', *Bulletin of John Rylands Library*, 40 (1957–8), pp. 423–44.

33. The king's order to the keeper of the Great Wardrobe for the issue of Garter robes to the queen is dated 12 April 1447, PRO, E101/409/19. Margaret's name does not appear on the list of recipients of Garter robes in the Great Wardrobe accounts until 1449. There has been some speculation over the reason for the delay in Margaret's receipt of Garter robes after her marriage in 1445, see Collins, 'Order of the Garter' (thesis), pp. 66–7. The lapse of time between Margaret's marriage and her receipt of Garter robes does not seem to be unusual for a queen: Richard II's first queen Anne of Bohemia (married 1382) received her robes in 1384 and his second queen Isabella of Valois (married in 1396) in 1397; Henry V's queen Catherine of Valois (married in 1420) in 1421; Henry VII's queen Elizabeth of York (married in 1486) in 1488.

chosen personally by the king, rather than elected by members of the Garter fraternity.[34] The role of female members is unclear since they were not required to fulfil the martial obligations of the knights of the Order. They were excluded from the formal chapter assemblies held annually on the eve of the feast of St George but attended the St George's Day festivities including high mass.[35] As ladies were not routinely honoured by the receipt of Garter robes for the St George's Day festivities, it could be argued that the occasions on which they were included were intended to be particularly magnificent. The records do not always provide a complete picture of the number of Garter Ladies but it seems that Richard II and Henry IV were both generous distributors of Garter robes to women, including their queens, other members of the royal family and wives of high-ranking noblemen as well as some foreigners. There is some uncertainty over the identities of Garter Ladies during the majority rule of Henry VI, apart from Margaret herself and Eleanor, duchess of Somerset, daughter of the earl of Warwick and wife of Edmund Beaufort.[36] What considerations determined the choice of ladies as recipients of Garter robes apart from convention? Collins speculates that, although a significant percentage of Garter Ladies were related to knights and could be regarded as complimenting their brothers, the disbursement of livery to a lady had a more overtly political function.[37]

In Henry VI's reign a significant number of women so honoured belonged to families with close connections at court which had always been an important factor. During the minority, when Humphrey, duke of Gloucester and John, duke of Bedford were in charge of government, the opportunity was taken to give robes to their wives. One of the most obvious examples of a beneficiary of the honour, through the influence of her husband at court, was that of Alice Chaucer, wife of William de la Pole, earl of Suffolk, who received her Garter robes shortly after their marriage in 1432, along with Isabel,

---

34. Part of the section on 'The Habit and Ensigns of the Order' in E. Ashmole, *The Institution, Laws and Ceremonies of the Most Noble Order of the Garter*, London 1672, is devoted to 'The Robes anciently assigned to the Queen and great Ladies'. See also Anstis, *Register*, ii, pp. 122–9, dealing with 'The Robes of this Order given to Ladies'. The Ladies of the Garter have been listed by G. Holmes, *The Order of the Garter: Its Knights and Stall Plates 1348 to 1984*, Windsor 1984, pp. 168–78. The most detailed study of the subject is J.L. Gillespie, 'Ladies of the Fraternity of Saint George and the Garter', *Albion*, 17 (1985), pp. 259–78. See also chapter 6 of P.J. Begent and H. Chesshyre, *The Most Noble Order of the Garter: 650 Years*, London 1999, which contains a useful discussion of the problems of evidence for the association of ladies with the Order.

35. According to an account of the festivities of 1476 written by Francis Thynne, Lancaster Herald, the queen and her Ladies sat in a closet in the rood loft to hear mass because they had no stalls allocated to them in the choir, see Anstis, *Register*, i, p. 197; Gillespie, 'Ladies of the Fraternity', p. 274; Begent and Chesshyre, *The Most Noble Order*, p. 101 and n. 24, p. 379. Anstis states that 'the Queens at Windsor made offerings at the High Mass celebrated on St George's Day in the same manner as the King did,' see Anstis, *Register*, ii, p. 123.

36. Holmes includes Lady Anne Moleyns, Lady Saye and Sele, Margaret, Lady Beauchamp and Alice Norreys, wife of Sir John Norreys as recipients of Garter robes in 1448, *Order of the Garter*, pp. 175–6, but Gillespie, 'Ladies of the Fraternity', p. 273, says that this is based on a misreading of the Great Wardrobe Account for 1448 which, after reciting the recipients of robes, lists these ladies as recipients of 'divers res . . . de dons domini Regis', PRO, E101/409/18. The Wardrobe Account for 1452–3 (Longleat MS. Misc.1) records the gifts of Garter robes to Eleanor Beauchamp, duchess of Somerset and Margaret Beauchamp, countess of Shrewsbury for the St George's Day festivities in 1453, neither of whom are included in Holmes' list. Although the earl of Shrewsbury attended the Garter ceremony in 1452, in 1453 his absence was excused 'being at Bordeaux', where he died at the battle of Castillon on 17 July 1453. Somerset was killed at the first battle of St Albans on 22 May 1455.

37. Collins, 'Order of the Garter' (thesis), pp. 66–7.

countess of Warwick.[38] Suffolk's rise to power in Henry VI's government in the 1430s and 1440s was swift and dramatic. An indication of his closeness to the king is provided by the fact that in 1444 he was sent to France to negotiate a marriage partner for the king, stood proxy for Henry VI at the betrothal ceremony with Margaret held at Tours in May 1444, and again at their marriage celebrated at Nancy in March 1445. His wife was one of the young queen's principal companions on the long journey to England to meet her husband in 1445, and the two women appear to have remained close at least until 1451.[39]

II

Hugh Collins has made a detailed study of the elections to the Garter fraternity in the late medieval period in order to assess whether there is any accuracy in the charge that there was a diminution in the status of membership. Selection for outstanding military service to the crown, especially in France, based on diligence in arms, courage, honour and loyalty, was allegedly giving way to outright political considerations.[40] The fellowship was fixed at 26 knights including the superior, the king of England. The election of a new companion could only take place on the death, resignation or degradation of a member and the statutes closely regulated the election procedure. Seven voting scrutinies dealing with nominations of companions between 1445 and 1460 survive; they reveal that political considerations did indeed play a significant part in determining the final choice, courtiers being particularly favoured.[41] Collins argues, however, that military service remained an important route to election at least until 1453 and martial considerations were never wholly overlooked.[42] For the purpose of this paper the most pertinent question to ask is whether a change is discernible in the later 1450s when the king's position was weak and,

38. Richard Beauchamp, earl of Warwick had been appointed the young king's tutor in 1428. According to Anstis, the duchess of Suffolk's Garter robes were issued by order of the Privy Council dated 21 May 1432, *Register*, ii, p. 124. The tomb effigy of Alice, duchess of Suffolk, in the parish church of Ewelme, Oxfordshire, provides us with a rare surviving example of a lady wearing the Garter insignia on her left forearm. See also the tomb effigy of Margaret Byron, wife of Sir Robert Harcourt in the church of Stanton Harcourt, Oxfordshire, illustrated in Anstis, *Register*, ii, between pp. 128 and 129. These are the only two known examples of medieval tomb effigies of women wearing the Garter device, see F.H. Crossley, *English Church Monuments*, London 1933, p. 154.

39. After the final collapse of the Lancastrian government and the death of Henry VI in 1471, Margaret was placed in Alice's custody until, having been pensioned off by Edward IV in 1475, she returned to her homeland. See the biography of Alice Chaucer by Rowena E. Archer in the *New DNB*, Oxford, forthcoming.

40. Collins, 'Order of the Garter' (thesis), *passim*, and Collins, 'The Order of the Garter,' in *Courts, Counties and the Capital*, pp. 155–80. A much more pessimistic view is presented by J. Milner, 'The Order of the Garter in the Reign of Henry VI, 1422–1461' (unpublished MA thesis, University of Manchester, 1972), who argues that the Order went into serious decline in Henry VI's reign, reflected in both the nature of the chapter meetings and the quality of the new members. By 1450 the Order had become 'virtually useless' and none of the intentions of the statutes could be fulfilled', see Milner, 'Order of the Garter' (thesis), p. 189.

41. The king had a considerable amount of freedom over the election of new members. Regardless of the number of nominations a particular candidate received, he was not obliged to elect the preferred choice. Henry VI rarely adhered to the advice of his companions, often making quite arbitrary choices and excluding some obvious candidates, Collins, 'Order of the Garter' (thesis), pp. 30–1; Milner, 'Order of the Garter' (thesis), pp. 61–8.

42. This was particularly true of the election of Edward Hull in May 1453, see below p. 48; Collins, 'The Order of the Garter' in *Courts, Counties and the Capital*, pp. 161–3, 179. After the disastrous end to the war with France in 1453 there was necessarily a decrease in opportunities for distinguished military service overseas.

it is generally agreed, his wife was in control of government. Can it be argued that Margaret of Anjou manipulated Garter elections for her overriding political purpose of buttressing support for the Lancastrian regime on behalf of her husband and her son? Alternatively, it might be argued that the queen possessed a lively appreciation of the chivalric background to the Order and the honour attached to election. As a daughter of King René, and the recipient of the Shrewsbury Book with its pointed dedicatory verse, this would seem to be a perfectly tenable conclusion.

In the early years of Henry VI's majority rule the composition of the Garter reflected both the rise of court factionalism and the decline of English military fortunes in France. Under the control of a pacific king, who was easily influenced by those closest to him at the centre of government, admissions closely followed the political composition of the royal council. Power was in the hands of a small group of court favourites led by Suffolk and Somerset (Suffolk being elected to the Garter in 1421 and Somerset in c. 1440).[43] Connections with the royal household were an important factor in this period, as with the elections of Ralph Botiller, Lord Sudeley; John Viscount Beaumont and Sir John Beauchamp of Powick; Thomas Hoo, Lord Hastings, chancellor of Normandy and Richard Woodville, Lord Rivers. They all had close connections with Margaret of Anjou.[44] Edward Hull, elected at a chapter held on 7 May 1453 in the King's bedchamber in the palace of Westminster, was an established member of the court party, an esquire of the king's body who had close links with Margaret, having been a queen's carver from 1448, and a feoffee of the duchy of Lancaster. Yet, as Collins points out, Hull's military credentials were strong: he served as constable of Bordeaux from 1442–51 and was active in the defence of Jersey and Gascony, indenting to serve with the earl of Shrewsbury in 1453 in the final campaign of the Hundred Years War.[45]

The collapse of Henry VI into an acute depressive stupor for a period of about eighteen months in August 1453 created a serious problem of authority at the centre of government resulting in a state of inertia. This was only resolved by the need to take action following

43. Collins, 'Order of the Garter' (thesis), pp. 112–19. For a discussion of Henry VI's personal rule in the period 1437–53, see Griffiths, *Henry VI*, esp. Part 2; Wolffe, *Henry VI*, Part 3; J. Watts, *Henry VI and the Politics of Kingship*, Cambridge 1996, chs. 4–7.

44. Thomas Hoo had been a member of the embassy appointed to assist Suffolk in the negotiations at Tours in 1444. Beaumont was appointed chief steward of the queen's duchy of Lancaster estates in 1452. They all received gifts of jewels from the queen between 1445 and 1453, see Margaret of Anjou's Jewel Accounts, PRO, E101/409/14 and 17; E101/410/2, 8, and 11, the latter account is published in A.R. Myers, 'The Jewels of Queen Margaret of Anjou', *BJRL*, 42 (1959), pp. 113–31. The Wardrobe accounts for 1452–3 (Longleat MS. Misc. 1) record the distribution of Garter robes for the 1453 St George's Day festivities to Queen Margaret, William Waynflete, bishop of Winchester, the dukes of York, Buckingham, Somerset and Norfolk, the earls of Salisbury and Shrewsbury, Viscounts Beaumont and Bourchier, Lords Willoughby, Scales, Sudeley, Fauconberg, Beauchamp, Hastings and Rivers, Sir John Fastolf, the duchess of Somerset and the countess of Shrewsbury.

45. The election scrutiny for 1453 survives, see Anstis, *Register*, i, pp. 150–1. Collins points out that, according to the election scrutiny, the names of other prominent courtier knights close to the queen were put forward, including those of Thomas Stanley and Edmund Hungerford but, although both were high in royal favour, Hull was selected over his rivals, see Collins, 'The Order of the Garter' in *Courts, Counties and the Capital*, p. 179, n. 64. Hull was a prominent member of the queen's household, appointed queen's carver in 1448. He was a feoffee of the duchy of Lancaster and a regular recipient of gifts of jewels from the queen (he features in four out of her five surviving Jewel Accounts, along with his wife Lady Margaret). He lost his life with Shrewsbury at the battle of Castillon on 17 July 1453.

the death, on 22 March 1454, of John Kemp, archbishop of Canterbury and chancellor of England. This was a time of extreme political uncertainty, evident in a letter written from London by John Stodeley to the duke of Norfolk on 19 January 1454.[46] The tense atmosphere in the capital can also be discerned in the description of the poorly attended meeting of the Garter chapter at Windsor on 11 May 1454. The duke of Buckingham presided, for 'the King being sick kept himself within the Castle'. Somerset was imprisoned in the Tower and the only knights present were Lord Sudeley and Viscount Bourchier. Despite the fact that Richard, duke of York had been appointed protector and defender of the realm and chief councillor on 3 April 1454, he chose not to attend. The excuses given by members for non-attendance are illuminating: the duke of York said 'That the Sovereign had for some time been angry with him, and therefore he durst not come nearer, for fear if he did so, of giving unnecessarily an Occasion of greater Offence, whereby the King being out of Order, (which God avert he said) his Resentment and perhaps his Distemper might gain ground.' The earl of Salisbury was excused by the Deputy 'because his Foot was so hurt, that he could neither come on Foot or Horseback without Danger' and Lord Beauchamp was excused by Lord Sudeley 'because he was so much out of order in his Feet, that he could neither walk nor ride'. William Neville, Lord Fauconberg was excused 'because having been lately kept in Prison [in France], he had now got Leave to see his House and Lands.' Sir John Fastolf 'was so very old and weak (as Lord Sudeley said in his Behalf) that he could neither go nor ride without very great Danger of his Health'. The absences of the duke of Norfolk, Thomas Hoo, Lord Hastings and Thomas Bourchier, Lord Scales were not excused and penalties of the Statutes were imposed.[47] This is the longest and fullest list of excuses for non-attendance given for any chapter meeting during this period and, because of the low attendance, there could be no election to fill the vacancy caused by Shrewsbury's death the previous summer.

The appointment of Richard, duke of York as protector proved a short-lived arrangement. Henry resumed control of government soon after New Year 1455. His fitness to govern remained questionable, though he attended the meeting of the Garter chapter on 22 April 1455 along with Buckingham, Beaumont, Lord Sudeley and Lord Beauchamp.[48] The Register records that the 'Duke of York was sick' and that the absences of the earl of Salisbury and Lord Bourchier were excused. Others were not so fortunate: the duke of Norfolk, Lord Scales and Sir John Fastolf 'because they had not sent the causes of their being absent, were left to the sentence of the statutes'. Lord Fauconberg is recorded as being 'out of the Kingdom' and Lord Rivers as 'at Calais'. There is no mention of the duke of Somerset, despite the fact that he had been released from the Tower on 26 January and restored to his former position as Henry's principal councillor soon afterwards. Again, because of low attendance, there could be no elections of new members. The stalls of Emperor Sigismund and the earl of Shrewsbury remained vacant, as well as that of Lord Hastings who had died since the last chapter meeting.

---

46. *The Paston Letters*, ed. J. Gairdner, Gloucester 1983, ii, pp. 295–9.
47. Anstis, *Register*, i, pp. 151–2.
48. *Ibid.*, i, p. 154. The date recorded in the Black Book for this meeting is 22 May 33 Hen. VI, but this must be an error. The Registrum Ordinis Chartaceum (Oxford, Bodleian Library, MS Ashmole 1128, f. 72v) has 22 April ('Marsdy le xxii jour Daurill lan du Regne . . . xxxiiie'.)

The political situation was no less tense when the king presided over the chapter meeting held on 22 April 1456 attended by Buckingham, Salisbury, Bourchier and Sudeley. The dukes of York and Norfolk, Lord Scales and Lord Beauchamp, Viscount Beaumont and Sir John Fastolf were all excused by the sovereign 'for Reason that he saw fit'. Once again no elections could be held because of low attendance.[49] Despite Somerset's death at the first battle of St Albans the previous year, and another short period when York acted as protector, divisions at the centre of government remained. The king was growing progressively weaker and more ineffective, while the queen became increasingly powerful. She sought to build up a court party with strong connections in the duchy of Lancaster, using her son, Edward, prince of Wales (born 13 October 1453) as the focus of patronage, and to counterbalance the power of Richard, duke of York whom she increasingly regarded as a dynastic threat.[50] In the summer of 1456 Margaret moved the court out of the capital to Kenilworth castle and the nearby city of Coventry in the heart of her duchy estates in the midlands with good communications north-westwards towards Chester and north Wales.[51] They were joined there by the king in late August.

The chapter meeting held on 14 May 1457 was presided over by the newly installed earl of Shrewsbury, deputed by the king who 'was at that time with his household at Kenilworth'. The exact date on which John Talbot, earl of Shrewsbury (son of the great soldier who had lost his life at Castillon), together with Thomas, Lord Stanley and Lionel, Lord Welles were elected is unknown; perhaps it occurred quietly at Kenilworth under the queen's influence.[52] Stanley, whose estates lay in Cheshire, Lancashire and north Wales, emerged as a key figure in the Lancastrian government of the late 1450s, and was particularly closely associated with the queen. He was created justiciar and chamberlain of north Wales and justiciar of Chester at a time when Margaret was actively recruiting

49. *Ibid.*, i, pp. 155–7. There was now a fourth vacant stall created by Somerset's death at the first battle of St Albans on 22 May 1455. His trophies were offered at the mass for the dead held on St George's Day 1456.

50. See the frequently quoted letter written by John Bocking to Sir John Fastolf on 9 February 1456: 'The Quene is a grete and strong labourid woman, for she spareth noo peyne to sue hire thinges to an intent and conclusion to hir power', *Paston Letters*, ed. Gairdner, iii, pp. 74–6. A Council for the prince of Wales was set up on 28 January 1457 and this became a powerful instrument in the hands of the queen, see Griffiths, *Henry VI*, pp. 781–3; Watts, *Henry VI*, pp. 326–37. A Garter stall was reserved for Edward, prince of Wales in 1458, but he was never formally installed, see Collins, 'Order of the Garter' (thesis), p. 65.

51. Coventry was described as 'the queen's secret harbour' because of her frequent use of the city for her political schemes, see the section on Coventry in *The Atlas of Historic Towns*, 2 vols, ed. M.D. Lobel, ii, London 1975, p. 1.

52. The reason for the appointment of a deputy is given in the commission dated 18 April, 35 Henry VI (1457) at Hereford: 'Forasmuch as various Affairs press upon us, so that we are not able to be in Person at the next Feast of St George', Anstis, *Register*, i, p. 159. Anstis has added a note to the bottom of the page about the omission of a record of the election of new members i.e. the earl of Shrewsbury, Thomas, Lord Stanley and Lionel, Lord Welles in 1457. He refers to the Wardrobe accounts kept by Henry Fylong, Keeper of the Great Wardrobe for 35–36 Henry VI (1457–8) which contain an entry for the delivery of Garter robes to the earl of Shrewsbury and Lord Stanley, PRO, E101/410/14, f. 6v; E101/410/19, m. 4. There is also a complete list of recipients of Garter robes E101/410/14, f. 21v.–22r; E101/410/19, m. 5: Queen Margaret received 200 gold garters; the bishop of Winchester, the dukes of York, Buckingham and Norfolk each received 120 garters; the earls of Salisbury and Shrewsbury each received 100 garters; Viscount Beaumont and Viscount Bourchier each received 90 garters; Lords Scales, Sudeley, Fauconberg, Beauchamp, Rivers, Stanley, and Welles each received 80 garters; and Sir John Fastolf received 70 garters. Anstis also states that the earl of Shrewsbury was installed by Lord Sudeley, while Mass was being celebrated, at the chapter meeting held on 14 May 1457, 'and immediately after presided in virtue of his commission'.

supporters in Cheshire and north Wales.[53] There was again a large number of absentees at the chapter meeting of 1457, the duke of Buckingham, Viscount Beaumont, Lord Beauchamp and Lord Rivers being with the king at Kenilworth, and the dukes of York, Norfolk, the earl of Salisbury and Sir John Fastolf sending excuses for non-attendance. Lord Scales 'pleaded no excuse' and therefore suffered the penalty of a fine.

The court returned to Westminster in October 1457, marking the start of a brief period when the king appeared to be asserting his authority over that of his wife. In the vain hope of patching up the feuds between his magnates, Henry organised a public Loveday procession through the streets of London on 17 March 1458, when Somerset walked hand-in-hand with Salisbury, before the king, who was followed by the queen with the duke of York. Nothing was achieved by this 'grand, formal, empty state occasion'.[54] A chapter meeting attended by the king was held on 22 April 1458 when the duke of Buckingham, Lords Stanley, Sudeley, Beauchamp, Welles and Rivers were present. The duke of York, the earl of Salisbury and Viscount Bourchier were excused, 'the king speaking for them'. Viscount Beaumont also had a 'Letter of Excuse' from the king, but the absences of the duke of Norfolk and Lord Scales were 'not approved' and they were 'put under the penalty of the Statutes, and the latter was, by way of memorial of his default, obliged to pay 20 marks to the College'. William Neville, Lord Fauconberg was 'put in prison'.[55]

Henry also attended the chapter meeting on 21 April 1459, the earl of Wiltshire, Lords Sudeley, Welles, Beauchamp, Berners, Dudley and Fauconberg, and Viscount Beaumont being present. The dukes of Buckingham, York and Norfolk, the earls of Shrewsbury, Salisbury and Pembroke, Viscount Bourchier, Lord Rivers and Sir John Fastolf 'were represented by messengers with the causes of their absences which the sovereign approved'. Lord Scales 'was left to the Fine put upon him'.[56] There is some uncertainty over the dates of the elections of the new members who were either present or excused attendance in 1459, namely Jasper Tudor, earl of Pembroke, James Butler, earl of Wiltshire and Ormond, John Sutton, Lord Dudley and John Bourchier, Lord Berners. They were all closely connected with the queen, either as the king's blood relations or through membership of the prince of Wales' council. It is likely that their election as Garter knights was closely linked to the queen's desire to buttress support for the Lancastrian regime by any means available to her. The position of Lord Berners is less clear-cut: the Bourchier family is usually regarded as mainstream and conciliatory in this period, yet by 1459

---

53. For Margaret's links with Lord Stanley see Griffiths, *Henry VI*, pp. 778–9, 781–3. In the late 1450s the queen was openly preparing for a military confrontation: in 1459 she toured her Cheshire estates with her son, distributing liveries of the swan and ostrich feathers to the gentlemen of the county, *An English Chronicle of the Reigns of Richard II, Henry IV, Henry V and Henry VI*, ed. J.S. Davies, Camden Society, os 64 (1856), pp. 79–80.
54. Wolffe, *Henry VI*, p. 312.
55. Anstis, *Register*, i, pp. 162–3. According to Bodl. MS Ashmole 789, f. 526, Lord Scales was ordered to present a jewel worth 20 marks to the College for his unexcused absence, see Collins, 'Order of the Garter' (thesis), p. 164. Milner points out that Thomas, Lord Scales, a fervent Lancastrian supporter, was the worst offender in terms of consistent non-attendance without an official excuse (he missed seven chapters between 1445 and his death in 1460), thus incurring fines. The duke of Norfolk was also absent without proffering a formal excuse in 1457 and 1458, see Milner, 'Order of the Garter' (thesis), pp. 56–7. Does this imply a casual attitude towards the Order during the later years of Henry VI's reign, or simply political expediency?
56. *Ibid.*, i, pp. 163–4.

Berners had become one of the queen's knights.[57] Lord Berners alone of the entire Garter companionship was present at Windsor to celebrate St George's Day in 1460 with the deputy of the Order, Jean de Foix, earl of Kendal.[58]

The final chapter meeting of Henry VI's reign at which elections of new members took place was held at the bishop of London's palace on 8 February 1461. The scrutiny survives giving an insight into the changed political situation at a time when King Henry was being held captive in London by Warwick and other Yorkist lords. The election of four new members in February 1461 reflects the Yorkist ascendancy: Warwick took Buckingham's stall; William, Lord Bonville took Lord Scales's stall after he had been murdered by Londoners following the battle of Northampton; Sir Thomas Kyriell took Shrewsbury's stall; and Sir John Wenlock took Beaumont's stall. Kyriell and Wenlock had both been staunch Lancastrian supporters until late 1459, but were quick to change sides as the political climate shifted.[59]

The first chapter meeting of Edward IV's reign was held at Windsor on 17 May 1461, in the wake of his decisive victory at Towton. The new king was not present 'being continually taken up with the many great and various affairs of the Kingdom'; he appointed Viscount Bourchier as his deputy, who was attended by the duke of Norfolk, Lord Berners and Lord Fauconberg.[60] The elections of Warwick, Bonville, Wenlock and

57. This is a particularly significant group of new knights in terms of their connections with the queen and her son: Jasper Tudor, earl of Pembroke, the king's half-brother, had been steadily promoted from the time of his ennoblement in 1452, and he played a crucial part in securing control of south Wales for the crown in the later 1450s; James Butler, earl of Wiltshire (and, from 1452, earl of Ormond) was a member of the royal council in the 1450s and was appointed to the prince of Wales' council in 1457, becoming chief steward of the duchy of Lancaster estates south of the Trent in succession to Lord Stanley after his death in February 1459, and treasurer of England after Shrewsbury's death also in 1459. He became bitterly unpopular for his efforts to raise money to prop up the Lancastrian regime in its final years, see Griffiths, *Henry VI*, pp. 860–2, who refers to the virulent Yorkist propaganda against the earl in 1460. Along with Shrewsbury and Viscount Beaumont, he was blamed for misguiding the king and poisoning his mind against the Yorkists, see J. Gairdner ed., *The Historical Collections of a Citizen of London in the Fifteenth Century*, Camden Society, ns 17 (1876), p. 206; 'John Benet's chronicle for the years 1400 to 1462' ed. G.L. and M.A. Harriss, Camden Society, 4th ser. 9 (1972), p. 225; *An English Chronicle*, pp. 91–4. John Sutton, Lord Dudley was another member of the prince of Wales's council appointed in 1457. He succeeded Lord Stanley as chamberlain of north Wales in 1459, and jointly commanded the queen's army at the battle of Blore Heath where he was captured by Salisbury's men. He stood to be a beneficiary after the attainder of York in October 1459, but he threw in his lot with the Yorkists in 1460, see Griffiths, *Henry VI*, pp. 826 and 865. The political stance of the Bourchier family is discussed in Griffiths, *Henry VI*, p. 798, and that of John Bourchier, Lord Berners, in Collins, 'Order of the Garter' (thesis), p. 123 and Milner, 'Order of the Garter' (thesis), p. 100.

58. Bodl. MS Ashmole 789, ff. 338–9; Collins, 'Order of the Garter' (thesis), p. 123.

59. The election scrutiny for 1460 survives, see Anstis, *Register*, i, pp. 166–8. The nominations were as follows: Warwick (9), the earl of March (9), William, Lord Bonville (9), the earl of Oxford (8), Sir John Wenlock (6), Sir Thomas Kyriell (6), Lord Stourton (4), Sir John Neville (4), Lord Grey of Ruthyn (3), Lord Fitzwarin (3), Sir Thomas Harrington (3), Sir Thomas Neville (2), and one each for the earl of Arundel, Lord Hungerford, Lord Montagu, Lord Duras, Lord Richmond (Richemont-Grey?), Sir John Shotesbroke and Sir William Oldhall. Jean de Foix, earl of Kendal chose not to participate, 'not knowing the Lords and Knights of this Kingdom, who were without Reproach, committed what was in the Power of his Vote to the other subjects of the Kingdom'. Collins points out that 'the irony of the nominations of 1460 was that whilst ostensibly representing a return to the Order's traditional values, the underlying criteria dictating eligibility was involvement in, or acceptance of, the overthrow of the ruling monarchy', Collins, 'Order of the Garter' (thesis), p. 127.

60. Anstis, *Register*, i, pp. 172–3.

Kyriell, held earlier that year were confirmed, although Bonville and Kyriell had since died, both being executed by the Lancastrians after the second battle of St Albans (17 February 1461), traditionally said to have been carried out on the orders of the prince of Wales, urged on by his mother.[61] The Register provides us with a dramatic picture of the treatment of Garter knights who were either dead or no longer in favour, including the deposed king Henry VI:

There were heard Letters which the Sovereign had sent to his Deputy and the rest of the Knights, in which they were required to take the Ensigns of the late king out of the Choir, and hang up those of the King now reigning which they who were present readily took care to have done. For the King's herald by order of the Nobles taking away those of the former sovereign, carried them into the Vestry, and hung up the new ones of our now most dread King in their stead. By authority of the same Letters, also the Ensigns of the Earl of Wiltshire and Lord Wells were taken down and carried out of the Choir.

In the Mass the next Day for the Dead, the swords and Helmets with the Appurtenances of the Knights who were now dead viz. the Dukes of York and Buckingham, Earls of Salisbury and Shrewsbury, Viscount Beaumont and Lord Scales were offered, according to ancient usage, and because there were no more present, the Deputy himself with his Colleagues performed the whole Office.

Moreover it was there also by Authority of the Sovereign enacted by the Knights, that the swords and Helmets with their Appurtenances that were taken down for any cause whatsoever, and carried out of the Choir, should be converted to the use and profit of the Hospital or College of St George in the same manner, as the Ensigns of the deceased Companions, which were offered by the survivors on the Day after the Feasts, though some of them opposed this Determination, and desired the contrary.[62]

What conclusions can be drawn from this brief survey of the chapter meetings of the Order of the Garter between 1445 and 1461? Did Henry VI and his queen contribute to a devaluation of its membership by attempting to turn it into an instrument of political control? It cannot be denied that the raison d'être of membership of the Order, as a means of honouring individuals who had given outstanding military service, largely disappeared after the end of the war with France in 1453. Henry VI's lack of interest in military affairs must have had an impact upon his relations with his nobility and, as these relations deteriorated in the late 1440s, it could be argued that the cohesion of the body of the Order also suffered, evidenced by the poor levels of attendance at meetings of the chapter between 1445 and 1460.[63] There were considerable delays in carrying out elections to fill vacancies most notably between 1453 and 1457. Apart from a handful of foreigners such as Alfonso V, King of Portugal, the Arragonese knight François de Surienne, the Emperor Sigismund and Emperor Frederick III, new members elected in this period were either of the royal family or were Lancastrian partisans, members of the higher ranks of the nobility

---

61. *An English Chronicle*, p. 108.

62. A note added by Anstis states that: 'The later practice hath been in cases of Attainders and Degradations, to fling down the Hatchments into the Choir and thence to kick or spurn them through the Church, and through the Quadrangle into the Ditch of the Castle', Anstis, *Register*, i, pp. 174–5; Ashmole says that Henry VI's achievements were taken down and carried out of the Choir into the Vestry by order of Edward IV on the Feast Day of St George 1461, *Institution, Laws and Ceremonies*, p. 629.

63. There were particularly low levels of attendance between 1450 and 1460 when the number of knights present at each assembly only exceeded four on three occasions (1452 (6), 1458 (6) and 1459 (8)), see Collins, 'Order of the Garter' (thesis), p. 180. Milner argues that chapter meetings lost their appeal to members as the king's interest in the Order waned, Milner, 'Order of the Garter' (thesis), pp. 52–7.

being preferred to those of lesser rank. Loyalty to the dynasty was of prime necessity.[64] Most of the new knights during this period had no special public service to commend them, being either very young courtiers with no military experience or other forms of service, or elderly mediocrities like Welles and Dudley. Only Thomas, Lord Stanley had had a moderately distinguished career at court.[65] But it is surely going too far to say that the Order 'declined into an acute state of disorder' reflecting personal and political animosities at the centre of power.[66] Collins holds a more favourable view, asserting that: 'Even towards the end of Henry VI's reign, a considerable percentage of banneret-knights elected, regardless of their court connections, had enjoyed careers in France or were still militarily active'. In the ranks of baron and banneret by the late 1450s 'election had become even more synonymous with royal favour' yet 'martial considerations were never wholly overlooked.' He has, however, to admit that among the higher nobility, 'the majority of earls was selected on account of their curial or partisan associations' and that 'in periods of courtier domination, many of the higher magnates owed their Garter elections to royal favouritism.' Nevertheless, he concludes that 'Henry's selection of household men for Garter nomination should not be seen as a departure from established precedent.'[67]

How significant, if at all, was Margaret of Anjou's influence on elections and did political considerations interfere with the process of election of new Garter knights? From 1453 the queen played an important part in politics as she sought to establish a secure power base for her son, using the duchy of Lancaster estates and offices as a source of patronage. New members elected in this period all had close links with the royal household and many were connected with the council of the prince of Wales set up in January 1457. Margaret did not, however, succeed in getting some of her closest advisers elected, for instance Sir James Fiennes (proposed in 1445) and Sir Roger Fiennes (proposed in 1445, 1446 and 1447), Sir Andrew Ogard (proposed in 1445, 1446, 1447, 1453), Sir Thomas Stanley (proposed in 1445, 1447, 1450, 1453) and Sir Richard Harrington (proposed in 1450 and 1453). There were difficulties in getting new members elected between 1453 and 1461 when the level of absenteeism from meetings of the Garter chapter was especially high. This was at the exact time when the queen's political influence was strongest and the future direction of government was so uncertain. Fear of the queen's intentions may have kept members away, thereby placing a curb on any attempts she may have made to control elections.

Margaret's main enemy and political rival Richard, duke of York continued to be issued with Garter robes in the 1450s, although he consistently failed to attend the St George's Day festivities after 1447, usually sending an excuse. It could be argued that one of the reasons for York's persistent absence was his fear of the queen, whose actions he increasingly came to regard with suspicion. But, there is no evidence to indicate that there

---

64. *Ibid.*, p. 146.
65. *Ibid.*, p. 148.
66. See especially Milner's conclusions, *ibid.*, pp. 187–93.
67. Collins, 'Order of the Garter' (thesis), pp. 39–43, 54–7, 62, 116.

was any personal antagonism between them before 1453.[68] The collapse of the king and the birth of a Lancastrian heir in 1453 completely changed Margaret's relationship with York whom she saw as a political threat. York attended a meeting of the Great Council held at Coventry in October 1456 when he swore an oath of loyalty to Henry VI but, after the charade of the Loveday in London in March 1458, he left the capital and withdrew to his estates. His wariness proved to be well-founded: at a meeting of the Great Council held at Coventry in June 1459, York, Salisbury, Warwick and other prominent Yorkists were indicted at the queen's instigation on unspecified charges.[69] In response the Yorkist lords prepared for armed confrontation and clashed with the queen's army of Lancastrian supporters under the command of James Tuchet, Lord Audley at Blore Heath on 23 September 1459.[70]

CONCLUSION

Exactly what the Order of the Garter meant to Margaret of Anjou, or whether she ever actually read the Statutes included at the end of the Shrewsbury Book cannot be known for certain. The first folio of the section of the book containing the Statutes is headed by an exquisite illumination of Henry VI presenting a sword to the earl of Shrewsbury, witnessed by a group of courtiers and clerks to one side, and knights in armour to the other. Was this a source of inspiration to Margaret's son as he grew up in his mother's care? There is some evidence to indicate that Prince Edward, perhaps inheriting some of his mother's more belligerent characteristics, might have matured into a warlike king, resembling his grandfather Henry V more than his pacific father.[71] Unlike his father, who died in captivity, Prince Edward died on the battlefield at Tewkesbury on 4 May 1471, aged 17, thus ending the queen's hopes for the restoration of the Lancastrian monarchy.[72] Queen Margaret was held captive in England in the care of Alice, dowager duchess of Suffolk, until Edward IV negotiated with Louis XI for her return to France in 1475. By the time she died in 1482 Margaret seems to have been reduced to a state of poverty and

---

68. This is clear from a letter written by York's wife, Cecily Neville, in 1453 asking the queen to use her influence with the king to mediate on York's behalf. The letter, in the Huntington Library, San Marino, California, Battle Abbey MS 937, has been published, see C. Rawcliffe, 'Richard, Duke of York, the King's 'obeisant liegeman': A New Source for the Protectorates of 1454 and 1455', *BIHR*, 60 (1987), pp. 232–9.

69. 'John Benet's chronicle', p. 223.

70. See my chapter, 'The Queen at War: the Role of Margaret of Anjou in the Wars of the Roses' in *War and Society in Medieval and Early Modern Britain*, ed. D. Dunn, Liverpool 2000.

71. Fortescue describes the prince's delight 'in attacking and assaulting the young companions attending him, sometimes with a lance, sometimes with a sword, and sometimes with other weapons, in a warlike way and according to the rules of military discipline', *De Laudibus Legum Anglie*, ed. Chrimes, pp. 2–3. In 1467 the Milanese ambassador wrote: 'This boy, though only thirteen years of age, already talks of nothing but of cutting off heads or making war, as if he had everything in his hands or was the god of battle or the peaceful occupant of that throne', *Calendar of State Papers, Milan*, i, p. 117.

72. There is some uncertainty about the circumstances of Prince Edward's death. Contemporary accounts are unanimous in stating that Edward was killed on the battlefield of Tewkesbury but other versions of events quickly grew up, some saying that he was killed fleeing from the field of battle, and others claiming that he was executed after the battle as an act of vengence by Edward IV. This latter story was elaborated by the Tudor chroniclers culminating in the scene in Shakespeare's *Henry VI, part III*, act 5, scene 5, where the prince is brutally murdered by Clarence, Hastings and Gloucester. For a discussion of the sources, see P.W. Hammond, *The Battles of Barnet and Tewkesbury*, Gloucester 1990, appendix 2, pp. 123–6.

her short will makes no reference to any personal possessions such as books.[73] The survival of the Shrewsbury Book in the collection of the King's Library (now the British Library), would seem to indicate that she was forced to leave her precious wedding-present in England when she departed for France in 1475, and that it passed into the hands of her enemy, and builder of the new St George's Chapel, Edward IV.[74]

73. Margaret's will is published in Lecoy de la Marche, *Le Roi René*, ii, pp. 395–7.
74. Ross speculates that the manuscript may have been amongst 'the chattels of Henry VI' acquired by Edward IV in 1471, see C.D. Ross, *Edward IV*, London 1974, p. 266. See also M. Kekewich, 'Edward IV, William Caxton, and Literary Patronage in Yorkist England', *Modern Language Review*, 66 (1971), pp. 481–7.

PLATE I

A. *John Talbot, earl of Shrewsbury, dressed in his Garter robes, presents his book to Margaret of Anjou: taken from a French manuscript book presented by John Talbot to Margaret of Anjou on her marriage to King Henry VI in 1445 (London, BL Royal MS 15 E. vi, f. 2v)*

B. *Genealogical table showing French and English royal descents from St Louis uniting in the figure of Henry VI, King of England. The decorative border contains the arms of Anjou and an initial M crowned within a garter (London, BL Royal MS 15 E. vi, f. 3)*

PLATE II

Figure of St George with an assembly of Garter Knights (London, BL Royal MS 15 E. vi, f. 439)

PLATE III

A. *This illumination from a fifteenth-century French text of the* Danse Macabre *shows a society physician in fur-trimmed taffeta robes, holding a jordan for the examination of urine samples in one hand to denote his profession. For all his skill, however, he cannot escape Death, who seizes his elegant sleeve (Paris, Bibliothèque Nationale, MS Francais 995, f. 11v)*

B. *The text of this lavishly illuminated presentation copy of the* Secreta Secretorum, *made for Edward III in 1326, warns the successful prince against the pleasures of the flesh and the snares of women (London, BL Add. MS 47680, f. 15v)*

PLATE IV

Hans Holbein the Younger's heavily restored painting of Henry VIII and the Barber Surgeons of London depicts the merger of the two companies in 1540. To Henry's right kneel his influential physician, Sir William Buttes, his colleague, John Chamber, and the royal apothecary (London, Worshipful Company of Barber-Surgeons)

PLATE V

A.   *Aristotle's advice to Alexander the Great about the importance of consulting the heavens before medical treatment is illustrated in Edward III's 1326 copy of the* Secreta Secretorum *(London, BL Add. MS 47680, f. 53v)*

B.   *A fifteenth-century illumination from a French text of Bartholomaeus Anglicus's* De Proprietatibus Rerum *depicts expensively dressed practitioners treating patients. On the left the physican examines a urine sample brought by a servant, while his colleague, a surgeon, comes in closer contact with a wounded patient (Paris, Bibliothèque Nationale, MS Francais 22531, f. 115r)*

PLATE VI

A.   *St George is beheaded by a heathen soldier*
     (London, BL Add. MS 71474, f. 153)

B.   *St George is scourged (London, BL Add.*
     MS 71474, f. 156v)

PLATE VII

Performance of three-part secular song by soloists and minimal chorus, boys and men, early sixteenth-century England (London, College of Arms MS Vincent 152, f. 178)

PLATE VIII

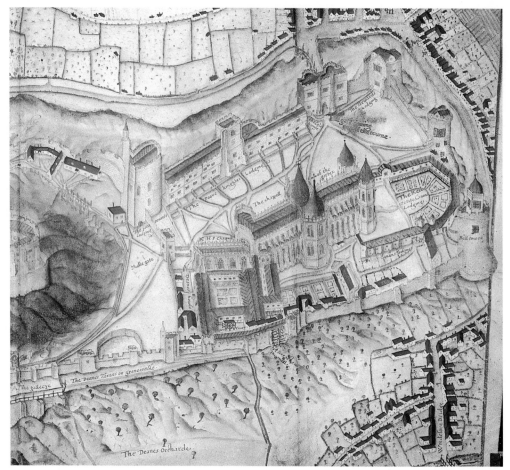

Detail of the chapel area from John Norden's 1607 bird's-eye view drawing of Windsor Castle from the north (London, BL Harl. MS 3749, f. 3)

'My Confessors have exorted me gretely ther too . . .': Sir John Fastolf's Dispute with Hickling Priory

ANTHONY SMITH

Medieval legal disputes have perhaps two main interests to historians. One is what they can tell us about the technicalities of the law and legal institutions. The other is the insight which they can afford into wider issues of political and social history. It is on the second of these emphases that this study of aspects of a dispute between Sir John Fastolf (1380–1459) and the Norfolk Augustinian house of Hickling Priory is more particularly focused. The disagreement over an annual rent of 25 marks charged on the manor of Hickling Netherhall was a major preoccupation of the last fifteen years of Fastolf's life. Here I shall look very briefly at the background and progress of the dispute, the research by Fastolf's servants which it prompted, the broader social and political context in which it took place, and the ways in which it seems to have affected Fastolf's own outlook.[1]

The complex history of ownership of the manor of Hickling Netherhall had a direct bearing on the dispute between Fastolf and Hickling Priory. In the fourteenth century the manor was owned by Sir Brian Hickling and subsequently by his daughter and heir Joan. Her marriage to Sir Edward Berkeley brought Berkeley the manor, together with another Hickling family manor at Rishangles (Suffolk). Joan died without surviving issue in c. 1362 and her co-heirs were Sir Thomas Bardolf of Spixworth (Norfolk), Sir Bartholomew Antingham and Sir Thomas St Omer, though Berkeley retained Joan's property for life 'by the courtesy of England'.[2] As a result of the existence of these three reversionary interests Hickling Netherhall was divided into three equal portions and each portion was eventually acquired by Hickling Priory.

The three owners of the reversionary interests each disposed of his Hickling Netherhall property before Berkeley's death in 1380. Sir Thomas Bardolf sold his interest to Adam Stokynland and his heirs in February 1375. Stokynland's feoffees subsequently (apparently in July 1380) conveyed Bardolf's portion of the manor to Hickling Priory, on condition that religious services, including burning a lamp at Hickling high altar, were celebrated for

---

1. Discussion of Fastolf's lawsuits, including that with Hickling Priory, is in A.R. Smith, 'Aspects of the Career of Sir John Fastolf (1380–1459)' (unpublished D.Phil. thesis, University of Oxford, 1982), pp. 169–218, and A. Smith, 'Litigation and Politics: Sir John Fastolf's Defence of his English Property', *Property and Politics: Essays in Later Medieval English History*, ed. A.J. Pollard, Gloucester 1984, pp. 59–73. The President and Fellows of Magdalen College, Oxford, have generously granted me permission to cite documents owned by the college; I am grateful to the college's Archivist, Dr. R. Darwall-Smith, for his friendly assistance in making them available. An authoritative examination of another of Fastolf's more important lawsuits is P.S. Lewis, 'Sir John Fastolf's Lawsuit over Titchwell, 1448–1455', *Historical Journal*, I (1958), pp. 1–20.

2. M[agdalen] C[ollege, Oxford], Hickling 126, 146 (1) and 149. Berkeley died about 4 July 1380 (*Calendar of Inquisitions Post Mortem*, xv, p. 128). Robert Brandeston and John Jakys, rector of Rishangles, were appointed administrators of his goods on 16 December 1380 (MC, Hickling 63).

Stokynland's soul.[3] Sir Bartholomew Antingham alienated his interest in 1362 to Sir William Kerdiston, who, in February 1381, granted his estates in Hickling Netherhall and Rishangles to the Benedictine nuns of Redlingfield (Suffolk). The nuns conveyed the Hickling portion of this benefaction to Hickling Priory in January 1386, though they retained the Rishangles property.[4] Sir Thomas St Omer died in 1367 and his executors sold his interest to Sir Thomas Ufford, from whom it later passed to Sir Edward Berkeley himself.[5] In his will of 1380 Berkeley enjoined that his property in fee (as opposed to that held as a life interest) at Hickling and Rishangles should be sold for the purpose of clearing his debts, with first refusal being offered to his feoffee and executor Sir Lewis Clifford.[6] Clifford bought this property but soon afterwards, in May 1383, he conveyed his Hickling Netherhall estate to several men living near Hickling, in return for an annual rent charge of 25 marks. These feoffees (John Stiward, vicar of Stalham, William Blackson, parson of Catford, Robert Hert, parson of Palling, John Eccles, Geoffrey Somerton and John George) were evidently acting for Hickling Priory, for on the same day the priory made a conditional grant to Clifford of an annual sum of £20, to be paid if ever the rent charge of 25 marks fell into arrears.[7] In this way, by 1386, Hickling Priory had consolidated its possessions at Hickling Netherhall.

The rent charge secured by Sir Lewis Clifford on the third part of Hickling Netherhall formerly owned by Sir Thomas St Omer is the one which was eventually acquired by Sir John Fastolf. On Clifford's death in 1404 it passed to his nephew William Clifford, who conveyed it to the London citizen Henry Barton in 1410 and subsequently sold it outright to Barton in 1421.[8] Fastolf purchased the rent charge from Barton in 1428.[9] The evidence we have gives no indication that Hickling Priory ever denied its obligation to pay the rent charge in the six decades which passed between its inception in 1383 and the outbreak of the dispute with Fastolf. The priory confirmed without much delay its obligation to pay the rent both to Barton (in early 1411 and again in 1422) and to Fastolf (in 1429). Surviving receipts and accounts, moreover, show that the rent was paid to Barton and to Fastolf between 1421 and early 1444.[10] It seems, however, that it was the priory's failure to pay what was owing to Fastolf which prompted him, on 30 October 1444, to enter the priory's manor at Palling and, by way of distraint, to seize three horses, valued by the

---

3. MC, Hickling 146 (5) and (6); *Calendar of Patent Rolls* (hereafter *CPR*) *1377–81*, p. 525.

4. MC, Hickling 149 (2), 127, 85, 146 (7) and 134. W.A. Copinger, *The Manors of Suffolk*, 7 vols, London 1905–11, iii, p. 294, notes that the nuns of Redlingfield were endowed with Rishangles manor.

5. MC, Hickling 52 (2), 146, 126, 146 (4), 54, 55 and 146 (3).

6. MC, Hickling 62 (fifteenth-century copy of Berkeley's will of 21 September 1380), 60. Berkeley's executors were Sir Lewis Clifford, Sir John Clanvow and John Fordham (later bishop of Ely). Clifford and Clanvow were Lollard knights, whose careers have been discussed by K.B. McFarlane, *Lancastrian Kings and Lollard Knights*, Oxford 1972, Part Two, *passim*.

7. MC Hickling 80, 87, 106.

8. MC Hickling 64 (award by the executors and feoffees of Sir Lewis Clifford to William Clifford of 1406) and 49 (conveyance by William Clifford for a term of sixteen years dated 1410); MC, Hickling 51 (13 February), 47 and 82 (15 May), and 46 and 48 (21 May) record Clifford's sale to Barton in 1421. Clifford informed Hickling Priory of this sale by letter in 1422 (MC, Hickling 66).

9. MC, Hickling 58.

10. MC, Hickling 50 (1411) and 93 (1422); receipts of rent 1422–8 are MC, Hickling 76, 78, 79 and 84. Richard Norwich, the prior of Hickling, delayed acknowledging Fastolf's title in 1428–9 (see MC, Hickling 157 (4)) but must eventually have done so; record of payments having been made survives in MC, Fastolf Paper 9 and 14 and Hickling 157 (7) and (8), the last dated May 1444.

priory at twelve marks.[11] This inaugurated a dispute which was still unresolved at Fastolf's death fifteen years later.

The object of Fastolf's action at Palling was to recover arrears and to compel the priory to honour its obligations. Plainly it was not sufficient as Fastolf soon found it necessary to confirm his right to the rent by means of further legal action, in the Court of Common Pleas. In November 1445 Fastolf obtained a writ of praecipe requiring the priory to show what right it had to withhold payment of the rent charge. The priory countered with a writ of trespass in connection with the distraint taken at Palling. This was in process during Michaelmas 1446. In the same term Fastolf sued out a writ of disseisin directed against the priory.[12] The proceedings continued inconclusively in the Trinity and Michaelmas terms of 1447 but thereafter were discontinued as Fastolf, now subject to other, more serious, legal challenges, began to look for alternative means of settling the dispute.[13]

Some details of the arguments deployed in this phase of litigation can be known from the collection of Fastolf's legal case papers now at Magdalen College, Oxford.[14] The basis of Fastolf's case was that the rent charge had descended to him in the manner already described. In having distrained upon the priory at Palling, it was claimed, Fastolf was seeking to recover arrears of the conditional annual rent of £20, which the priory had undertaken to pay Sir Lewis Clifford if ever the 25 marks rent fell into arrears. This was a weakness of his case, as his lawyers came to appreciate, for it was doubtful whether he was entitled to do so as merely an assign rather than an heir of Clifford.[15] In reply, to justify withholding the 25 marks rent charge, the priory seems first to have argued that Sir Lewis Clifford had enjoyed only a life interest at Hickling Netherhall and that the priory, having recovered the rent charge at Clifford's death, was consequently under no obligation to pay Fastolf. This recovery, it was claimed, was of record in Chancery, though no evidence of the recovery was ever in fact adduced. The priory further denied that Hickling Netherhall had been divided into third portions as a result of the reversionary interests of Joan Bardolf's heirs, suggesting instead that she had been succeeded by a son and heir to whom it had passed whole. This heir, it was said, was none other than Sir Thomas Bardolf. It was subsequently argued by the priory that, if it were the case that a rent charge was payable, then it was owed not from Clifford's but from Bardolf's portion of the manor. From case papers contemporary with the litigation we know that Fastolf's agents had already accumulated documentary evidence to controvert these claims and that his counsellors were able to demonstrate their mutual inconsistency.[16] His lawyers had, for example, record of the priory having attorned the rent to Clifford's feoffees, heirs and assigns, information about its arrangements with Clifford in 1383 and knowledge of deeds of grant of the reversionary interests in Hickling Netherhall after c. 1362. They were able to cite

11. MC, Hickling 137.

12. MC, Hickling 108, 137, 139 and 142.

13. The most notable challenge was that of the duke of Suffolk, who seized Fastolf's properties at Dedham (Essex) in 1447: Smith, 'Property and Politics', p. 66.

14. The formal proceedings in the Court of Common Pleas and the reasoning of Fastolf's lawyers on them are recorded, particularly in MC, Hickling 59, 130, 137 and 147 and Fastolf Paper 29.

15. MC, Hickling 71 (letter from William Wangford and William Jenney, 6 February 1445 or 1446).

16. A summary of the principal points raised is given here: for further details see Smith, 'Aspects of the Career of Sir John Fastolf', pp. 195–9.

Sir Thomas Bardolf's sale of his reversion to Adam Stokynland in 1375 and the grant by Stokynland's feoffees to the priory in 1380. They could thereby show that Clifford had never owned Bardolf's portion and that the rent could never have been charged on that portion. Once the strength of Fastolf's case became evident in court the priory could only have recourse, as it did with some success, to a series of delaying tactics.[17]

One tactic adopted by the priory was to convey the rent charge on 17 November 1447 to Sir John Cheyne of Drayton Beauchamp (Buckinghamshire), 'kinsman and heir' of the Lollard knight Sir John Cheyne. The Lollard Cheyne had been one of the feoffees of Sir Lewis Clifford, another Lollard knight, for the rent charge, by a conveyance of 10 June 1395, and was the last of Clifford's feoffees to die. The priory thus, with at least some semblance of legality, tried to remove the rent far from Fastolf's reach by claiming Cheyne as the legal heir to it. However, it is clear enough from the surviving evidence that the Lollard Cheyne had, as Sir Lewis Clifford's trustee, acquiesced in the inheritance of the rent by Clifford's heir William Clifford.[18] Moreover, it was to protect himself from the possibility of such a challenge that Fastolf had on 1 July 1440 obtained a release of right in the rent charge from Sir John Cheyne of Drayton Beauchamp.[19] Fastolf's attorney in the court of Common Pleas nevertheless employed the appropriate procedure of summoning to court the young Clifford heir Alexander Clifford in order that he might vouch for Fastolf's case, apparently in the full knowledge that he was legally a minor and ineligible to appear for some years.

Another such tactic, adopted by the priory during Michaelmas term 1447, at the instance of the common lawyer John Heydon, a member of the duke of Suffolk's East Anglian affinity, was to summon to warranty a boy named Robert Eccles, who (it was claimed) was the grandson and heir of John Eccles, one of the men to whom Sir Lewis Clifford had in May 1383 granted his third part of Hickling Netherhall manor in exchange for the 25 marks rent charge. Fastolf's attorney immediately challenged the sufficiency of this warranty, arguing that Eccles had not been seised of the rent at the time Fastolf was put out of it and that neither had his ancestors ever been seised of it. Shortly afterwards, when the youth of Robert Eccles was discovered, Fastolf's attorney asked the court that examination of the boy be postponed until he reached adulthood.[20]

While this common law litigation was underway, Fastolf, his lawyers and estate officials were busy undertaking research with a view to extending the range of their knowledge of the issues under consideration in the Court of Common Pleas. This aspect of the dispute is well illustrated by the investigation conducted into the background to the summoning of Robert Eccles. In a letter of 21 October 1447 written from London to Thomas Howes

17. It is notable that in 1452 Prior Okkham's successor told Chancery that Fastolf, without being entitled to the rent, was paid as long as the priory could afford to do so; but he did not explain how the allegedly rightless Fastolf first came to be paid. Fastolf responded that, through malice towards him and in anticipation of gain, certain men had advised the priory to withhold payment (MC, Hickling 139 and 142 (the prior), 132 and 141 (Fastolf)). The priory's estates were valued in 1535 at £100 18s. 7¼d., of which the property at Hickling itself contributed about £45, so Fastolf's rent, though a not insignificant charge, would presumably not have been an overwhelming burden (*Victoria History of the County of Norfolk*, ed. W. Page, 2 vols, London 1906, ii, pp. 383–4).
18. MC, Hickling 98, 154 and 109 (a fifteenth-century copy of the 1395 deed). For the Lollard Cheyne: McFarlane, *op. cit.*, Part Two, *passim*.
19. MC, Hickling 105.
20. MC, Hickling 130, 137, 59.

at Caister Fastolf ordered Howes to gather information about Eccles, 'yth ony such heyr be' and to 'ghete suffisaunt record & wytnesse that he toke no proffitz of the seid rent charge ne the lond sith that the pryour decesed me of my rent . . . I suppose,' Fastolf remarked, 'there ys none such Robt Eccles heyr to John Eccles as the pryour councell have allegged. And therefor I desyr to have such a notable record of thys mater that it may be a suffisaunt wytness to me for my aunsuer'.[21]

Howes's long letter of 26 October 1447 in reply to Fastolf is particularly revealing about the work that Fastolf had wanted done.[22] Howes began by telling Fastolf that he was sending him notes about the last testaments of Thomas Bardolf of Spixworth, Edmund Ufford, Edmund St Omer, Adam Stokynland and others once involved with the Hickling property. He reported that he had not been able to locate the testaments of Sir Bartholomew Antingham and Sir Thomas St Omer: 'we can not fynde them as yet and we suppose it is not lyke we shull fynde them here ffor yf a man have lyvelod in ii dyocese or in more than one then his testament and wyll shall be proved and registred at Caunterbury as lerned men enforme me.' It is certain, though, that access was gained to the archbishop of Canterbury's records, for Fastolf's own muniments include a copy of the 1380 will of Sir Edward Berkeley extracted from Archbishop Sudbury's register.[23] From the evidence of legal memoranda, dateable to the summer of 1447, the interest of Fastolf's servants in the earlier history of the rent is evident.[24] They were seeking to discover whether Joan Berkeley had been married before her marriage to Sir Edward Berkeley and whether (as had been alleged by the prior's counsel) Thomas Bardolf of Spixworth was her son by such a marriage. They wanted to know where Joan was buried and what arms were on her tomb, how her co-heirs were related to her and what their arms and descents were. Howes's letter of October 1447 was bringing Fastolf up to date with the fruits of some of the research carried out on these points.

Most of Howes's letter, however, is about the work that had been done in trying to identify the young Robert Eccles, whom the prior of Hickling had vouched to warranty in the Court of Common Pleas. Howes began by speaking of Reginald and John Eccles, who were interred, as Fastolf's servant Walter Shipdam had discovered, in the chancel of Billockby parish church in Norfolk. Howes wrote:

ther was Regnald Eccles a sergeaunt of lawe or a prentys of court and com up in poverte as Heydon dooth which Regnald was hefded in the ryflyng tyme [that is, beheaded during the Peasants' Revolt of 1381] and hie hed set at Norwich as Lynford told Spirlyng whiche had sone John Eccles and that John Eccles dwelled in Byllokby and ther is beried by his fader Regnald as her . . . testaments and wyllys specyfye and that John Eccles sold and gaf dyvers of his maneres londes and tenements to dyvers men and specyfieth non yssue. Natwythstandyng the specifications of hys wyll and testament we have do inquired and many men can telle her of and sey pleynly yat John Eccles had none yssue.

Howes enclosed for Fastolf's information extracts of the wills of Reginald Eccles and his wife Agnes taken from the bishop of Norwich's registers, together with a copy of John Eccles's testament 'word for word as it is regestred.' He reported that he had consulted

21. MC, Hickling 130.
22. MC, Hickling 140.
23. MC, Hickling 62 (from Lambeth Palace Library, Register of Archbishop Sudbury, ff. 106–106v).
24. MC, Fastolf Paper 29; MC, Hickling 96 is a similar paper of about the same date containing an abstract of Fastolf's title to the rent charge and memoranda of inquiries to be made about Joan Berkeley and her co-heirs.

Fastolf's neighbour and associate John Lynford of Stalham, who lived near Hickling Priory, and that Lynford believed that John Eccles had had no children, but died in debt little more than three years after his father.[25]

Howes then referred to an Eccles family of Martham (Norfolk). 'In as muche,' he wrote, 'as we were informed that ther wer other Eccles in Martham we sent ther Jefray Spirlyng and Robert Botiller to inquire sadly yf any yong man or chyld wer ther clepid Robert Eccles . . .' Howes said that the Eccles families of Billockby and Martham 'were non of kynred ner of stok ffor Regynald Eccles com up of poverte as Heydon dooth and was a sergeaunt in law and these other Eccles com of berthe of gentilmen of an old stok . . . as it sheweth right pleynley in a bille annexed to this letter.' Yet, as Howes revealed in the remainder of his letter, the history of the Eccles family of Martham was not as simple as it might have been, for, he wrote,

ther was one Wyllyam Eccles whom dyvers men in Martham knew yt lyven yet at this day whiche Wyllyam dwelled in yarmuth and was a draper and is beried at yarmuth whiche had yssue Robert Eccles dwellyng in Belton in a place yat sumtyme was John Spitelyng and yat Robert had yssue Robert and yat second Robert had yssue the thrid Robert whiche is nowe lyvyng in Martham of viii yeer of age and was ward to the lord Cobham whiche wardship one Thomas Chirche of Martham hath bought of the lord Cobham and fyndeth the chylde at this day to scole for that same Thomas Chirche hath wedded the modre of that heyr . . . Where it is . . . rehersed [Howes explained] that Lynford seyd that the Eccles of Martham were gentylmen of old aunscestry the cause that they be reported as gentylmen is this as we suppose yt the seid Wyllyam purchased xx marc worth of lyvelod in Martham of a man sum tyme clepid Martham . . .

Howes's concluding words are worth quoting at length. He wrote:

Please you to gef credence to this writyng for it hath be labored by Watkyn Shipdam at Byllockby and by me and my clerk in the Register and by Spirlyng at Martham and other places of the iiide part and alle folowen upon one conclusion by cleer informacion of dyvers men yat John Eccles had never yssue and yat yong heyr yat now lyveth clepid Robert Eccles was sone of Robert Eccles and yat secund Robert was sone of the thrid Robert and yat thridde Robert was sone to Wyllyam Eccles sumtyme of yarmuth draper whiche accordeth to Heydons plea yf Wyllyam Eccles had be clepid John Eccles. But as to yat name John Eccles ther was non suche but John Eccles of Byllokby whiche had never yssue and by this mean it may weell be conceyved and opynly how he is set in untruth of the mater.

In this letter we see Howes struggling with notions of gentility: he suggests that a successful lawyer from a humble background (like Heydon) cannot be a gentleman and thinks that the son or at least the grandson of a Yarmouth draper (who had bought a country property worth 20 marks a year) could probably qualify as a gentleman, possibly even one of 'an old stok'. But Howes appears a little uneasy with this idea and it is evident that he does not wish to perceive Fastolf's antagonist the common lawyer John Heydon as a gentleman. There is a tangible distaste for Heydon. Howes seems pleased that his enquiries suggest that Heydon's tactic of vouching young Robert Eccles to warranty would founder at law because of facts of genealogy either overlooked or ignored by Heydon. The means of enquiry are instructive too. They were: locating and consulting

25. Roger Virgoe regarded Reginald Eccles as an active JP ('East Anglia under Richard II', in F.R.H. Du Boulay and C.M. Barron ed., *The Reign of Richard II*, London 1971, p. 233; for appointments to commissions of the peace and oyer et terminer see *CPR 1377–81*, pp. 47, 96, 303, 418, 513, 515, 571, 574, 579, 581. Eccles's house at Billockby was attacked by the rebels: B. Cornford, W.F. Edwards, G.F. Leake and A.W. Reid, *The Rising of 1381 in Norfolk*, Norwich 1984, p. 42.

relevant legal documents such as deeds, wills and testaments; viewing informative monuments, as when Walter Shipdam examined those of the Eccles family in Billockby church; recording the recollections and opinions of local gentlemen such as John Lynford of Stalham; and interviewing inhabitants of the countryside whose knowledge and memories could provide information to enable a case to be made against Hickling Priory and its supporters. These activities are reminiscent of those of the antiquary William Worcester. As a colleague of Thomas Howes and Fastolf's other servants Worcester presumably found his interests stimulated and his opportunities for research enhanced by his involvement with this kind of work.[26]

Fastolf's surviving papers provide plenty of other evidence of this search for knowledge in connection with the Hickling dispute. The archives of Magdalen College now contain not only the deeds he acquired on purchasing the rent charge but also numbers of mid-fifteenth-century copy deeds relating to the estates in the other two thirds of Hickling Netherhall manor as well as many contemporary abstracts of title to these estates.[27] From these it seems that Fastolf never gained access to the muniments of Hickling Priory, presumably (as we shall see) because of the opposition of its patron Thomas, Lord Scales. Efforts were made before 1450 to see the archives of Redlingfield Priory, and these were eventually seen during 1450 after the death of William de la Pole, duke of Suffolk, a patron of the nuns, whose convent was situated near to Suffolk's estate at Eye (Suffolk).[28] The Redlingfield archive was important for the evidence it was supposed to contain of the descent of Sir Bartholomew Antingham's third of Hickling Netherhall, which, it will be recalled, had been sold by Antingham to Sir William Kerdiston, and granted by Kerdiston to the nuns, who had conveyed it to Hickling Priory. A working paper of c. 1447 shows

26. The work done by Fastolf's servants is similar to that done in connection with the lawsuit over Titchwell (see Lewis, *op. cit.*). Their assertions about John Heydon's origins were correct, as I hope to demonstrate on another occasion.

Howes's letter and other Hickling papers much interested K.B. McFarlane. He wrote to Norman Scarfe on 16 May 1950 (at 4.20 p.m.): 'I'm nearly blinded by reading fifteenth century handwriting: I've been transcribing Fastolf letters in the college muniment room. William Worcester's hand is frightful enough but today I came upon some runs of memoranda about Redlingfield (you remember the hens and the nettles in the ruins of the garden of the rectory). They've taken me since noon, and aren't all deciphered yet . . . I liked the statement that one Reginald Eccles was "hefded" [beheaded] in the Ryfling time [the Peasants' Revolt]; an admirable name for it; no other instance of it appears to be known . . .'. *K.B. McFarlane. Letters to Friends 1940–66*, ed. G.L. Harriss, Magdalen College, Oxford 1997, pp. 75–6. Besides Howes's letter McFarlane was particularly thinking of the memoranda in MC, Hickling 145 (see notes 28 and 29).

27. An inventory survives of original Hickling deeds removed at Fastolf's request on 27 November 1446 from Caister Castle tower to London. This mentions five releases for Sir Lewis Clifford of 5 Richard II, a grant from the Priory to Clifford of 6 Richard II and a further indenture of 6 Richard II (sealed with six seals) between Clifford and John Stiward, as well as the deed of 7 Henry VI by which Fastolf acquired the rent from Henry Barton. These were not all the Hickling muniments then in Fastolf's possession; rather they were sent to assist Fastolf's lawyers in coming to conclusions about particular disputed points (MC, Hickling 67).

28. MC, Hickling 145 (see note 29); London, British Library, Add. MS 39848, no. 223 (7 May 1450). In this letter Fastolf claimed that the prioress of Redlingfield had placed all her original deeds in the duke of Suffolk's custody but had retained a book of copies, which might now be seen. Copies of Redlingfield muniments were obtained by August 1450 (BL Add. MS 39848, no. 224); study of them by Fastolf's servants is mentioned in letters of 7 and 15 September 1450 (*loc. cit.*, nos. 245, 253). In the May letter Fastolf complained that copies would have been available sooner but for the dilatoriness of the bishop of Norwich's chancellor. The case papers at Magdalen College include abstracts of deeds whose provenance must have been the Redlingfield Priory archive.

that efforts were made to employ the bishop of Norwich's influence to obtain information from the Redlingfield archive.[29] One memorandum reads: 'Item. That my lord see the evidence of Ridelyngfeld and ye fundacion and how thei came by here rent of xxv marc . . .'. This manuscript also shows that the nuns were sheltered by the duke of Suffolk. The bishop of Norwich's servant Richard Doket, the paper notes, had been sent to the duke to ask about the 'dischargyng hem of her evidence'. More knowledge was also sought of William Clifford (d. 1438), the man who had inherited the rent charge and sold it to Henry Barton. By about 1447 Fastolf's servants had a note of his Kent property and place of burial. They knew that his grandson and heir Alexander Clifford (son of his son Lewis Clifford, esquire) was a nine-year-old boy residing at Windsor as a ward of Lord Saye and Sele, who had custody of the Clifford family muniments, which included documents relating to Hickling Priory.[30] Having glanced then at the research undertaken by Fastolf's servants, it is to the bishop of Norwich (Walter Lyhert) that we must now turn, as the bishop was considered by Fastolf to have an important part to play in resolving the dispute with Hickling Priory.

Action at common law was not Fastolf's preferred method in this dispute. He sought to bring ecclesiastical pressure to bear on the priory, apparently on the advice of his legal counsellors but perhaps also on that of his confessors. His aim was to depose the offending prior of Hickling and reform the priory through a visitation of it by the bishop. This policy had some effect but it was not a complete success, as we know from a letter of the bishop to Fastolf, apparently written in August 1451.[31] Bishop Lyhert wrote:

29. MC, Hickling 145 (this undated document was written before 1450 and seems from its contents to be of *c.* 1447). Amongst other details, it notes the location of Redlingfield Priory and its Rishangles property ('fast by Debenham Market') and includes a memorandum to inquire about the overlordship of Rishangles, together with a statement that 'Antingham by hise attorney called Kerdiston gaf to the hous of Riddlyngfeld the iii part . . . of Rysangle in which thei have and nowe ben pesibly sesid of . . .'. This remark reveals a sound grasp of that descent.

30. MC, Fastolf Paper 29. The property was recorded as Ditton (rightly described as three miles from Maidstone), Milton (identified as Milton by Gravesend) and Bobbing (correctly noted as situated a mile from Sittingbourne); the burial place was rightly reported as St Margaret's, Canterbury. William Clifford had married Elizabeth, daughter and heir of Arnald Savage of Bobbing (son of the famous Speaker). He and his son Lewis had lived at Bobbing. E. Hasted, *The History and Topographical Survey of the County of Kent*, 12 vols, 1972 reprint of the 2nd Canterbury edition of 1797–1801, iv, p. 457, v, p. 364, vi, pp. 148, 195, vii, pp. 338, 446; J.S. Roskell, 'Sir Arnald Savage of Bobbing', *Archaeologia Cantiana*, lxx (1956), pp. 68–83; *Calendar of Fine Rolls 1437–45*, p. 2; *CPR 1436–41*, p. 43). Fastolf's servants noted the names of Kent *jurisperiti* to whom inquiries might be directed. The list included the infamous Stephen Slegge and William Isley (see B. Wolffe, *Henry VI*, London 1981, pp. 124, 125, 234) and the less controversial John Bamborough (*CPR 1446–52*, v, pp. 41,189, 590; *Cal. Close 1447–54*, p. 100), John Rowe (*CPR 1446–52*, pp. 339, 346, 579), William Moyle (*Cal. Close 1447–54*, pp. 97, 270, 355, 358, 364) and John May (*CPR 1446–52*, pp. 216, 365; *Cal. Fine R. 1430–7*, p. 79).

31. MC, Hickling 89; 18 August, year not stated. The content of the letter and Lyhert's presence at St Benet's on the Sunday before St Laurence's Day (10 August) makes either 1450 or 1451 certain. Allusions in the letter to Lyhert's interview the previous Michaelmas with the new prior, to recent attempts at private arbitration and possibly to the affairs of Sir Henry Inglose (died 1 July 1451) tend to suggest 1451. It seems probable that in the autumn of 1450 Lyhert had attempted to make the new prior settle the dispute or at least permit Fastolf access to the priory's archives. Fastolf's later statement in Chancery (Hickling 132, 141) that common law proceedings were discontinued about the time of the former prior's deposition makes clear what his strategy was.

And as touchyng your matier hangeng in contraversie betwyn yow and the house of hykelyng I have put my sylf gretly in my devour that goode ende shuld have be had in the same wherof sufficient evidence may be undrestoode by my importune besinesse whiche I made to the precessour of the pryore that now is the whiche was cheef cause of his resignacion and also to hym that now is pryore whiche moved hym sytthe michelmesse to come to me to London as I suppose ye can remembre where I were instaunced by the lord Scales not to medel in the matier for by cause of importune laboures therin I was take as a suspecte personne . . . Wherefore I advyse yow to take sum othre weye wherby ye may obteyne yowr entent as far as reson and law wole.

The alternative which Lyhert had in mind was the duke of Norfolk's good lordship. 'I hertily desir,' Lyhert continued, 'that ye take myghtily unto yow your knyghtly hart and dispose yow to come hidir to the eyre of yowr natural byrthye where I know right wel ye shal fynde my lord of Norfolk yowr good lord and suche attendaunce as I and other gentiles of the cuntrey may doo redy unto yow at all tymes after your desir . . .' Lyhert, however, plainly was alarmed by Lord Scales, for within a few weeks, in September 1451, Fastolf is found complaining that the bishop was dragging his heels in his attempts to resolve the Hickling dispute.[32]

The bishop of Norwich's letter, though, does make clear that the offending prior of Hickling (Roger Okkham) had been removed in 1450 or a little earlier and that his successor as prior had been brought under episcopal pressure. The resignation had apparently come in the wake of an episcopal visitation of the priory.[33] The letter, moreover, appears to refer to Fastolf's attempts to capitalise on the changes there, for in the few months before mid 1451 he sought to use private arbitration to settle the dispute. In May 1451 he offered to abide by the ruling of Bishop Bourgchier of Ely and whoever the priory should nominate and about this time he also proposed to employ the bishop of Norwich himself as an arbitrator.[34] A draft of this proposal to Lyhert survives and in it Fastolf says that he 'is so disposed that he wille not occupye ner take onye thyng of person or persones othyr wyse then right lawe and conscience will' and is therefore prepared to abide by the ruling of the bishop, who is to consult two lawyers, one each named by the priory and by Fastolf. Fastolf also proposed to pay the priory's costs and to discontinue all litigation if the award was made against him. Neither of these proffered arbitrations nor a petition from Fastolf to the Lord Chancellor Cardinal Kemp for an impartial commission of enquiry into the Hickling dispute, also attributable to late 1450 or early 1451, produced any discernible outcome at all.[35]

Local East Anglian and national politics help to explain these failures. During 1449 Bishop Lyhert, having previously lacked influence, was becoming prominent in the royal council of Henry VI but he was still a man of less political weight than Thomas, Lord Scales, who warned him against intervening in the Hickling dispute. Scales, hereditary lord of the manor of Hickling Overhall and overlord of Hickling Netherhall, was the most powerful landowner in the vicinity of Hickling Priory and, by the late 1440s, he was closely associated with the East Anglian affinity of William, duke of Suffolk, the dominant

---

32. BL Add. MS 34888, f. 75 (23 September 1451).
33. This was evidently before September 1451 (see Smith, 'Aspects of the Career of Sir John Fastolf', p. 200, note 114).
34. MC, Hickling 107 (Bourgchier, 21 May 1451: Smith, *op. cit.*, p. 200, note 117); MC, Hickling 95 (Lyhert).
35. MC, Hickling 99 (Smith, *op. cit.*, p. 200, note 118).

figure in royal government. Scales's power was temporarily eclipsed by the fall of Suffolk's regime from power in the spring of 1450, which was, of course, also directly advantageous to Fastolf. With Suffolk dead, Fastolf expected that he would be able to obtain copies of the valuable documents owned by the nuns of Redlingfield: 'seth it ys soo the world ys changed gretely over it was y pray you and charge you . . .', he wrote in May 1450 to Thomas Howes, 'labour ye . . . so as I may come by a copy of theyr evidens'.[36] The copies were available early in August and undoubtedly they helped Fastolf's cause for, by the end of that month, he had reached an agreement with Scales over the future of the disputed rent payable by Hickling Priory.[37] Scales did not abide by this agreement, the details of which are not known, as can be seen from Fastolf's revealing letter of 23 November 1450, in which he told Howes that 'there ys a baylly of hykelyng that meynteynyth the pryour yn hys wrong ayenst me and hath proud langage and unfyttyng of me', whom Fastolf wished to be indicted for maintenance before the commissioners of oyer and terminer then in Norfolk.[38] This bailiff, presumably one of Scales's officials, could only have been acting with his lord's protection and support. Scales went further and defended members of Suffolk's affinity when the oyer and terminer commissioners met to try them at King's Lynn in January 1451 and at Walsingham the following May. Scales had allied himself with a new court party, led by Edmund Beaufort, duke of Somerset, which had replaced that of the duke of Suffolk, and emerged when the duke of York failed to find a place in the ruling regime after the political disturbances of 1450. By protecting and thereby gaining the support of Suffolk's former East Anglian associates, Scales had consolidated his own local power. In 1451, for instance, he gained joint custody, with Sir Miles Stapilton, of the late duke's estates, and he was in a position to thwart Fastolf's attempts to defeat Hickling Priory.[39]

    In these circumstances it is difficult to conceive how another of Fastolf's tactics in 1451 could have been expected to succeed. Negotiations were opened with Alexander Clifford, now of age and entered upon his inheritance, who was sent copies of deeds concerning his ancestor Sir Lewis Clifford's endowment of Hickling Priory with land in exchange for the 25 mark rent charge. An agreement was reached with him by September 1451 whereby Hickling Netherhall manor was to be sued out of the priory's possession (presumably through an action in the court of Chancery) and granted to Clifford. The grounds for this seem to have been that the priory's failure to pay the rent to Fastolf constituted a breach of its agreement with Sir Lewis Clifford. Once in possession, Alexander Clifford would resume payment of the rent to Fastolf. Fastolf's letter to Thomas Howes of 23 September 1451 about this says that Clifford

---

36. BL Add. MS 39848, no. 223 (7 May 1450); see also note 28.
37. BL Add. MS 39848, no. 224 (8 August 1450).
38. MC, Fastolf Add. 2. The bailiff alleged that Fastolf possessed forged evidences of the rent, 'off whych he lyeth falsly'.
39. Smith, 'Litigation and Politics', pp. 68–9; *Cal. Fine R. 1437–45*, p. 220. Evidence of Scales acting as a 'good lord' to Tuddenham and Heydon includes his taking Tuddenham's part in a dispute over Tuddenham's sheep in June 1451 (J. Gairdner, *The Paston Letters*, 6 vols, London 1904, ii, p. 249). This may be connected with Scales's alleged protection of Tuddenham and Heydon's property through the pretence that their cattle and sheep were his own (BL Add. MS 34888, f. 53). For another example of Scales's help to Tuddenham and Heydon see Gairdner, *op. cit.*, ii, p. 206.

shall entree in the hole maner that ys chargeable wyth my xxv marc rent, which the Pryour and Convent have forfeted the seid hole maner to the heyers undre her Convent seele of record, because of myne nonne payment of xxv marc; and so then the Pryour shall lese for ever IIIIxx [four score] marc of rent, and that wythout onye concience, for they have be fals both to the Clyffordys and to me thys vii yeere day. And y trust to God to correct hem so by spirituell law and temporell lawe, that all othyr Relygyoux shall take an example to breke the covenant or will of any benefactor that avauncyth hem wyth londs, rents, or gode; and my confessours have exorted me gretely ther too.

Nothing seems to have come of this ambitious scheme and in September the priory refused to attorn the rent to Fastolf's feoffees, on the occasion of a new settlement of the property to the use of Fastolf's will.[40]

This refusal possibly prompted Fastolf to try another tactic, for in the summer of 1452 he summoned Hickling Priory to the court of Chancery to answer for non payment of the disputed rent charge. The prior was compelled to attend and, in addition to denying Fastolf's title, made a new allegation that Fastolf had seized from the priory a property called Hickling Hall in Caister, as retaliation for losing the rent charge. The prior then requested that the dispute be returned to the court of Common Pleas. Fastolf had no difficulty in showing that Hickling Hall was in fact held on a twenty year lease from Hickling Priory, agreed with Prior Okkham in 1442. The mass of surviving legal papers at Magdalen College indicate that this chancery suit was taken as seriously as the earlier common law litigation.[41] However, Fastolf's careful preparations were plainly unavailing, as no decision on the case seems ever to have been reached by the court.

Arbitration was tried again in 1455 when, on 15 March, Fastolf and the priory agreed to refer their dispute to the decision of the common lawyers John Paston (acting for Fastolf) and John Fyncham (acting for the priory). If they were unable to agree on any points, these issues were to be submitted to Archbishop Bourgchier of Canterbury and Walter Lyhert, bishop of Norwich, who were to seek advice from any two secular judges.[42] Fastolf, in a letter of 2 May 1455, requested Paston to remind Lyhert of the agreement and to ask the bishop 'to comaunde the seid priour to be bound by obligacion to stand to the seid appoyntment in lyke forme as I at all tymes lefull am redy for to do to th'entent yat my lord may verily knowe that the complysshyng of ye seid appoyntement is nat deferred ner delayed by me'. The same letter reports a related harassing manoeuvre by Lord Scales, who now claimed that Fastolf owed him homage for an estate called Essex situated in Hickling.[43] A day was evidently appointed for Paston and Fyncham to meet in London but it does not seem that they had made any progress before negotiations were

---

40. *Cal. Close 1447–54*, p. 309 (Sir James Fiennes, afterwards Lord Saye and Sele, received Clifford's wardship on 5 October 1440 — repeated on 21 October 1440: *CPR 1436–41*, pp. 488, 508); BL Add. MS 34888, f. 75 (partly printed in Gairdner, *Paston Letters*, ii, pp. 253–4); MC, Hickling 144 mentions the prior's refusal to attorn in connection with Fastolf's settlement of 28 September 1451.

41. Records of the case are not amongst the Early Chancery Proceedings in the Public Record Office. Copies are MC, Hickling 103, 132, 139, 141, 142, and 144, with other working copies in Hickling 102 (1), 136, 145 and 151. The 1442 lease is MC, Hickling 101. The pleadings in court refer to Fastolf's attempt to remove the land bearing the rent charge from the priory into the king's hand on the grounds that it (St Omer's third) had been acquired without royal licence. This is possibly a reference to the scheme involving Alexander Clifford.

42. MC, Hickling 152.

43. BL Add. MS 35251, f. 24; Gairdner, *Paston Letters*, iii, pp. 82–3; N. Davis, *Paston Letters and Papers of the Fifteenth Century*, 2 vols, Oxford 1971, 1976, ii, no. 547. Though dated 1456 by Gairdner and Davis the letter, which mentions the arbitration just noted, is clearly of 1455.

overtaken by the Battle of St Albans later in May, which propelled Fastolf's patron the duke of York to political power. Indeed it is possible that Paston and Fyncham had not even met by then.

Soon after St Albans, presumably in the light of the priory's slowness in coming to an agreement and with a realistic appreciation of the likely beneficial impact of York's supremacy on the course of his own litigation, Fastolf chose to return the case to the court of Common Pleas. On 24 June he told John Paston to 'remembre sadlye myne atturney Raulyns . . . to take more tendernesse yn thys mater . . . that hath so manye yeeres and days be dryve off yn the lawe to my grete dammage'.[44] Fastolf was quickly rewarded with news in July that the justices had ordered the issuing of a writ of distress per omnia bona et catalla against Hickling Priory. Less welcome was information, recorded in Fastolf's letter to Paston of 31 July, about the actions of Lord Scales.[45] Fastolf wrote that he had been informed that the monks of Hickling had 'sente the Lord Scales all there evidences and he wil come and dwelle yere hym-silf. And I am also enformed for certeyn that the Bishop of Norwiche, for all ye truste I hadde to hym yat by his meane I shulde haue knowen yere fundacion, he hathe warned his officeres nought to haue a doo yerjnne by-cause of the Lord Scales . . .' In other words, Scales had frightened the bishop sufficiently to prevent him from doing anything further to help Fastolf. At this point stalemate seems to have ensued — the court issued the writ Fastolf needed but nothing could be done to enforce it locally in the face of Scales's hostility, for making Scales comply would have been very low on the list of objectives of the duke of York's embattled regime.[46] The rent remained unrecovered at Fastolf's death four years later in 1459. The dispute preyed upon his mind even as he made his will in November of that year; he then stipulated that his feoffees and executors should 'porsewe lawfully my right and title that I have in xxv marke of yeerly rente, with all the areragis that of right and concience is dewe to my feffees feffyd there in to myn use to dispose for my soule helthe chargyd and payable out of a maner in Hiklyng, callid Nethyrhalle, which the priour and convent of Hiklyng for the tyme beyng, be bounden and astrict be wrytyng undyr here convent sealys to paye yeerly'.[47]

This lawsuit illustrates well the ineffectiveness of the Lancastrian common law courts in resolving property disputes deriving from the complex contemporary land law. It gives evidence of the use of alternative means of resolving them, such as private arbitration, recourse to the equitable jurisdiction of the court of Chancery, and the employment of ecclesiastical discipline to bring pressure to bear on a litigant. Clear too is the connection between such disputes and the deployment of social and political power, or lordship, which is particularly evident in the activities of Lord Scales. Scales's support for Hickling Priory was decisive in preventing Fastolf from securing justice. His actions were effective because he was both a local landowner and magnate and a politician who cultivated (and could rely upon) the assistance of the factions which dominated the court of Henry VI for many years between 1447 and 1459 — first that of the duke of Suffolk and afterwards that

---

44. Davis, *op. cit.*, no. 554; dated 1456 by Davis but evidently of 1455 (see note 43 above).

45. Davis, *op. cit.*, no. 560; dating as in note 44.

46. This is a summary account of the last years of the dispute (for which see also Smith, 'Litigation and Politics', pp. 69–70, and 'Aspects of the Career of Sir John Fastolf', pp. 201–4). I intend to discuss the difficulties of Fastolf's last few years more fully elsewhere.

47. Gairdner, *Paston Letters*, iii, p. 154; another passage in the will reveals Fastolf's obsession with forged muniments and authentic seals (*ibid.*, pp. 155–6).

of the duke of Somerset. The intractableness of the dispute owed much to the fact that Scales, in order to sustain his reputation and power as a good lord in local society, could not permit Fastolf to win the dispute.[48]

This dispute reveals Lancastrian England as a society preoccupied with information of a particular kind — archival, genealogical and topographical. Such a preoccupation derives from the importance in the common law (and to common lawyers) of matters of fact and from the social pressure upon lords and others to act with the semblance of right and justice rather than with naked force. Research of the kind undertaken by Fastolf's servants was therefore unavoidable for litigants and lords of men. And there was too a politics of information. Scales, the duke of Suffolk, and Suffolk's associate Lord Saye and Sele (the guardian of young Alexander Clifford) all exerted themselves at times to prevent Fastolf obtaining access to archives and documents of relevance to his dispute with Hickling Priory.

It is tempting to regard disputes of this nature as a form of social ritual or games playing, another form of chivalric tournament. But, of course, they were not. No one reading Fastolf's letters can doubt his conviction of the justice of his case in his dispute with Hickling Priory. This being so, it would have seriously damaged his reputation and status if he had not fought this battle, particularly as he had the means to do so.[49] His consulting his confessors about this dispute, moreover, seems to reveal a spiritual anxiety or scrupulosity which goes beyond religious conservatism or worry about the forms of the law. The confessors were asked to advise about a manoeuvre which would result in the partial disendowment of Hickling Priory. Fastolf was concerned that this should not be to the disadvantage of his soul. For, as we know, he was a committed benefactor of churches and monasteries, particularly St Benet's Holme (Norfolk), and believed sincerely that such benefactions were spiritually advantageous to him.[50] Further evidence of the anxiety which the dispute with Hickling Priory caused Fastolf is contained in a letter of 23 November 1450 in which he reported to Thomas Howes that he had been urged by Hugh Acton, master of the Hospital of St Giles in Norwich, to sell his manor of Mundham

48. Scales's attitude is illustrated in his letter of 22 April 1450 to John Paston (Davis, *Paston Letters and Papers*, ii, p. 34 (no. 449)) about claims by Thomas Daniel against Osberd Mundford. Scales observed that as the 'said Osberd is my tenaunt and homager it is my part to holde with hym rather than with Danyell in hise right, which I will do to my pouer', in the event of Daniel seizing Mundford's property. Scales's published letters (Davis, *op. cit.*, nos. 449, 495, 561, 563, 592–8 and 879) reveal a man of commanding temperament. His brevity borders on peremptoriness; he seems keen to intervene directly in his associates' affairs; and he has a preference for the private settlement of his own disputes. (In 1386 his ancestor Roger Scales granted licence to the priory to acquire Clifford's and Redlingfield Priory's third parts of Hickling Netherhall, said to be held by knight service of his manor of Hickling Overhall: MC, Hickling 134.)

49. See Smith, 'Litigation and Politics', pp. 60 and 73, on the relative cost of Fastolf's lawsuits.

50. Early testimony to Fastolf's benefactions to St Benet's is in Bishop Lyhert's letter already cited (MC, Hickling 89). Lyhert wrote that he had visited St Benet's the 'soneday byfor seint Laurence day last passed gretly reiocyng in suche work and notable cost whiche ye have do ther whiche must nedes remeane in to a perpetuel memory of yow all dayes to come be hit unto the worship of god who ever preserve yow'.

cheaply to the Hospital.[51] Acton, Fastolf wrote, 'wold I shuld hafe do almesse on hem and relessed hem som money but ye may sey hym the untrouth of the pryour of hykelyng drawyth awey my devocion in such causes'. In other words, Fastolf was becoming unwilling to assist existing religious houses. However, as is well known, one of the preoccupations of his last years was to endow, in the absence of an heir, a college of priests at his own seat of Caister Castle for purposes specifically stipulated by himself and supported by his own landed estates. His fundamental faith was unchanged; but it does not seem unreasonable to suggest that his desire to use his wealth in this particular way owed much to the disillusioning lessons of his dispute with Hickling Priory.

51. MC, Fastolf Add. 2. Fastolf's attitude is particularly striking because of his esteem and goodwill for Hugh Acton. In this letter he told Howes to speak 'wyth maister piere seint ffeyth to sende me . . . aunsuer whethyr he wolle resseyve the benefice of Taverham or no and that I hafe . . . suffisaunt witnesse as maister hue acton wolle remembre yow for I hafe graunted hym the presentacion to such an honest preest as he wolle name'. If Fastolf typically had this disinterested and responsible attitude towards ecclesiastical patronage it is not surprising that his dispute with Hickling Priory caused him anxiety and dismay.

More than a Bedside Manner: The Political Status of the Late Medieval Court Physician

CAROLE RAWCLIFFE

Honour a physician with the honour due unto him for the uses that ye may have of him: for the Lord hath created him. For of the most High cometh healing, and he shall receive honour of the king. The skill of the physician shall lift up his head: and in the sight of great men he shall be in admiration.

Ecclesiasticus, XXXVIII, vv. 1–3

In a society preoccupied with the external trappings of wealth and status, the fifteenth-century English court physician cut a fine figure. A long tradition of advice literature, stretching back to Hippocratic times, which urged the practitioner to adopt a sober style of dress in keeping with his professional gravitas and discretion, sat uneasily with an understandable desire to advertise. Attacks made in France on the type of 'pernicious and diabolical' imposter who posed as a society physician by dressing in 'superb and magnificent clothes, wearing at his neck chains of gold which he, perhaps, *borrowed* from a goldsmith' underscored the fact that a genuinely successful practitioner would have *earned* his handsome apparel, rather than acquiring it by fraud.[1] John Somerset, who treated Henry VI almost continuously from 1427 to 1451, at a basic fee of £140 a year, received an annual allocation from the royal wardrobe of ten yards of blood-red and of yellow or green cloth, as well as nine bundles and ten back furs of 'scachegrey' and 18 bundles and 17 back furs of 'cristegrey' [types of squirrel] for his livery. From time to time he sold on to the wardrober items (such as a hood of 32 miniver skins, and ten yards of violet grosgrain, in 1443–4 alone) for which he no longer had much use.[2] He ranked in these accounts immediately after the lawyer, John Throckmorton, a prominent Worcestershire land-owner, who had frequently represented the county in parliament, while also serving as chamberlain of the Exchequer and under treasurer of England.[3] Since Somerset was himself then chancellor of the Exchequer, warden of the royal mint in the Tower of London, almoner of the king's household, and a former shire knight for Middlesex, where he had accumulated substantial estates centred upon his 'great messuage' at Isleworth, the

---

1. A.K. Lingo, 'Empirics and Charlatans in Early Modern France: The Genesis of the Classification of the "Other" in Medical Practice', *Journal of Social History*, 19 (1986), p. 586. For the Hippocratic tradition, see H. King, *Hippocrates' Woman: Reading the Female Body in Ancient Greece*, London 1998, pp. 42–4.

2. London, British Library, Add. MS 17721, f. 38r; London, Public Record Office, E101/409/12, ff. 9v, 12r, 77v. Henry's other physicians, John Faceby and John Raundes, also wore squirrel and miniver: E101/409/2, f. 42v; E101/409/12, f. 80v. Somerset's annual pension from the crown comprised £40 from the fee farm of London awarded retrospectively from 1427 (*Calendar of Patent Rolls* (hereafter *CPR*) *1422–9*, p. 460); £60 from the issues of Warwickshire and Leicestershire awarded in 1432 (*CPR 1429–36*, p. 241); and 50 marks a year (1437) rising to £40 in 1438 from the abbey of Bury St Edmunds (*CPR 1436–41*, pp. 70, 130). In 1439 he received the manor of Ruislip, Middlesex, for life, and subsequently surrendered the first and last of these fees (*CPR 1436–41*, pp. 286, 359).

3. J.C. Wedgwood, *History of Parliament: Biographies of the Members of the Commons House 1439–1509*, London 1936, pp. 851–2.

pair seemed evenly matched.[4] Here, then, was a man of consequence: as he strode through the corridors of power for his daily consultations with the king, whose own sartorial standards were notoriously shabby, a mere glance revealed his authority, not least because of the furs and jewels lavished upon him by other grateful clients and patients. How had he become so influential?

In 1993 a book by two American psychologists, Jerrold Post and Robert S. Robins, attracted considerable attention in medical circles. Dramatically entitled *When Illness Strikes the Leader: The Dilemma of the Captive King*, and bearing on its cover the photograph of a ravaged Franklin D. Roosevelt at Yalta, it dealt with assorted questions of medical ethics arising from the treatment of the sick or terminally ill head of state in the twentieth century. At the crux of the issues addressed by the two authors lay the relationship between the ruler and his medical advisors. This, they observed, with a striking reference to the fundamental principles of Galenic medicine:

is likely to be one of extraordinary intimacy. *Good medicine is preventative medicine.* A principal obligation of the royal physician is to maintain the health of the royal patient in optimum condition so that he will be able to withstand the stress of high office and address the tasks of leadership with full effectiveness and vitality . . . The leader, ill or well, is apt to see his physician often.[5]

They then proceeded to illustrate how rarely this objective has been achieved over the last century, and how fraught the conflict between politics, medicine and patronage can become once a head of state or other powerful patient has succumbed to illness.

The symbiotic nature of the physician–patient relationship, the intimacy of the bonds between the two and the influence thus accruing to the practitioner appear even more striking as we move back into an age when the personal authority of the monarch was infinitely greater, and the viable alternatives to preventative medicine virtually non-existent. A chronically sick or mentally unstable monarch was especially dependent upon his medical advisors, who might well (as in the case of John Somerset) represent the interests of a particular group or faction bent on seizing the political initiative. Yet comparatively little attention has been paid by English medievalists to the role, influence and standing of the baronial or royal physician. Talbot and Hammond's *Dictionary of the Medical Practitioners in Medieval England* (1965) serves as a useful starting point for such a survey, although it presents little in the way of analysis or historical background.[6] Hammond's subsequent reassessment of the career of Cardinal Wolsey's Venetian physician, Augustine de Augustinis, whose involvement in the murky world of Tudor *realpolitik* has tended to overshadow his professional and intellectual achievements, provides

4. Somerset became chancellor and warden in December 1439 (*CPR 1436–41*, p. 418), was royal almoner by January 1441 (PRO, E28/66/18–19), and MP for Middlesex in 1442. On one estimate the wardenship alone was worth £160 a year (PRO, C1/19/65). His inquisition *post mortem* records an annual landed income in Middlesex of £19, excluding properties in which he had a life interest (PRO, C145/319/20). Wedgwood, *History of Parliament*, pp. 780–1, notes his parliamentary service, offices and various commissions, but is otherwise unreliable. Another outline — but also incomplete — biography of the physician appears in C.H. Talbot and E.A. Hammond, *The Medical Practitioners in Medieval England*, London 1965, pp. 184–5.

5. J. Post and R.S. Robins, *When Illness Strikes the Leader: The Dilemma of the Captive King*, New York 1993, p. 96.

6. This volume was up-dated by F. Getz, 'Medical Practitioners in Medieval England', *Social History of Medicine*, 3 (1990), pp. 245–83. See C. Rawcliffe, 'The Profits of Practice: The Wealth and Status of Medical Men in later Medieval England', *ibid.*, 1 (1988), pp. 61–78, for some preliminary reflections on the standing of the court physician.

a welcome reminder of the many attributes and accomplishments such men were expected to possess.[7] Generally speaking, however, no sustained attempt has been made to rectify the impression that fifteenth and early sixteenth-century royal physicians were little more than 'corrupt and ineffective placemen, wheeler-dealers on the fringes of power, fully part neither of the court nor of the universities'.[8]

The question as to *why* men of the stamp of William Buttes, Lewis Caerleon and Gilbert Kymer wielded so much authority and grew so affluent remains largely unexplored, partly because political historians have yet fully to appreciate the enormous differences between medieval and modern medical practice and set the former in a meaningful context. For these differences go far beyond the obvious disparities in medical technology and the understanding of human physiology which separate the fifteenth century from the twentieth. As we shall see, the medieval physician plumbed the recesses of the soul as well as those of the body, often being more familiar with his patients' spiritual health and psychological anxieties than he was with their bodily infirmities. Those medical historians who, in turn, *are* interested in questions of professional power and status seem consistently to underestimate the essentially intangible role of the counsellor in an age of clientage and 'good lordship'. It is easy to forget that the late medieval royal or baronial physician ranked on a par with the household knight — the most trusted and important figure in any elite establishment, whose function was to advise and guide his patron.[9] At some point shortly before June 1442, Thomas Beckington, secretary to Henry VI, who had been sent to Bordeaux to negotiate a marriage between the king and the count of Armagnac's daughter, wrote in desperation to his 'right welbeloved and entirely trusted Maister', John Somerset. Complaining that the mission seemed likely to founder 'withoute hasty *remedy* be hadde in this behaf', he urged his friend to 'sture and call upon my lords of the king's counsaill to pourvey such *remedye* in this partie, in all goodely hast, as yt may be to the king's pleasure, and the wele of us all', a punning request which underscores Somerset's diplomatic as well as medical qualifications.[10] As John Watts reminds us, this was a time when King Henry's shortcomings as a ruler gave such 'mandarins' an unusual degree of political freedom.[11]

This essay will examine in general terms some of the more significant factors contributing to the influence and image of the English court physician during the late medieval period. Even without a detailed prosopographical analysis of careers, fees and patronage, it is evident that we are dealing with an academic and social elite comprising a very small group of men, whose ubiquity was entirely disproportionate to their numbers. For a variety of reasons, neither Oxford nor Cambridge produced more than a handful of fully qualified physicians at any one time. In all, only 94 individuals are known to have graduated in medicine from Oxford University between 1300 and 1500, and a mere 59 from Cambridge, although many other students succumbed to the lure of mammon and left to practise before taking their degrees. Attempts in the early fifteenth century to

7. E.A. Hammond, 'Doctor Augustine, Physician to Cardinal Wolsey and King Henry VIII', *Medical History*, 19 (1975), pp. 215–49.

8. V. Nutton, ed., *Medicine at the Courts of Europe 1500–1837*, London 1990, p. 9, where he calls for a more positive evaluation of the role of the sixteenth-century royal physician.

9. Rawcliffe, 'Profits of Practice', pp. 63–4.

10. C. Munro, ed., *Letters of Queen Margaret of Anjou*, Camden Society, os 86 (1863), pp. 85–6.

11. J. Watts, *Henry VI and the Politics of Kingship*, Cambridge 1996, p. 167.

establish a professional collegiate structure, of the kind to be found in other parts of Europe, were doomed to failure because the two English Faculties of Medicine were so weak, conservative and relatively undistinguished.[12] As might be expected under the circumstances, the bulk of talented graduates opted for lucrative employment at court or in the retinues of lords and prelates rather than an academic career. Among their ranks we find Nicholas Colnet (one of the most energetic and successful pluralists in Lancastrian England); John Arundel (a canon of Windsor who was promoted to the bishopric of Chichester in 1458); and William Hattecliffe (now chiefly remembered as secretary of the privy seal under Edward IV).[13] In noble households, too, physicians occupied a prominent position. Thomas Moscroff, a graduate in medicine, was supported by that archetypical renaissance prince, Edward, duke of Buckingham, the highest ranking and richest peer in early sixteenth-century England, while he was still at Oxford. As his 'counsellour in fysyke' he occupied a seat on the duke's inner council, which managed the largest lay estate in Tudor England; he acted briefly as Buckingham's cofferer, or financial agent, and as receiver general of his revenues; and he eventually assumed the post of secretary — while still attending to his employer's health.[14] A fit and active man, who died on the block and not in his sickbed, Buckingham may have been less inclined to follow the advice of medical practitioners than his nemesis, Henry VIII, whose last years were dogged by illness.

The name of Sir William Buttes appears frequently in studies of humanism and evangelism at the Tudor court, where he served as King Henry's favourite physician. The first of such men to receive a knighthood, he was one of several influential members of the royal household to be painted by Hans Holbein the Younger (d.1543), a telling mark of social status. His wife, Margaret, who also sat to Holbein, shared his religious beliefs, and became a lady-in-waiting to Katherine Parr.[15] Buttes was a learned man, as indeed were all the other practitioners to be mentioned in the course of this essay. He showed considerable skill in dealing with a difficult and demanding patient, and successfully exploited the king's dependence upon him in the wider interest of religious reform. A staunch and tireless advocate of the evangelical cause, he played a notable part in the advancement of Hugh Latimer, whose promotion to a bishopric was said to have been as much due to him as to his friend, Thomas Cromwell.[16] Foxe's *Book of Martyrs* provides a memorable (and essentially convincing) vignette of Buttes at work, defending the

12. F.M. Getz, 'Medical Education in Late Medieval England', in *The History of Medical Education in Britain*, ed. V. Nutton and R. Porter, Amsterdam 1995, pp. 76–93; C. Rawcliffe, *Medicine and Society in Later Medieval England*, Stroud 1995, chapter five, *passim*.

13. Talbot and Hammond, *Medical Practitioners*, pp. 115–16, 220–2, 398–9; Rawcliffe, 'Profits of Practice', p. 72.

14. In June 1519, while Moscroff was evidently acting as his receiver general, Buckingham paid the generous sum of £10 a year towards his exhibition at Oxford (PRO, SC6 Henry VIII 5841, m. 5r, Henry VIII 5807, m. 1r). See also PRO, E36/220, f. 11v, and SP1/22, f. 58r.

15. P. Ganz, *The Paintings of Hans Holbein*, London 1950, nos 124–5, plates 165–6.

16. M. Dowling, 'Anne Boleyn and Reform', *Journal of Ecclesiastical History*, 35 (1984), pp. 36–8 (where she notes that Buttes's 'unobtrusive services to the gospel were to play a key part in the course of the Henrician Reformation'); *eadem*, 'The Gospel and the Court: Reformation under Henry VIII', in *Protestantism and the National Church in Sixteenth Century England*, ed. *eadem* and P. Lake, London 1987, pp. 48–53, 69–70; *eadem*, *Humanism in the Age of Henry VIII*, London 1986, p. 65 and note 84 on p. 73. As these sources reveal, Robert Huycke, another royal physician with evangelical tendencies, was also a noted humanist.

protestant preacher, Richard Turner, who ran into trouble in 1543 for his outspoken attacks on traditional religion. Turner's patron had written to Buttes, asking him to use his influence with the king, which he did with telling effect. Years of practice had perfected an extraordinarily accomplished bedside manner:

When the king was in trimming and washing (as his custom was at certain times to call for his barber) Dr Buts (whose manner was at such times ever to be present, and *with some pleasant conceits to refresh and solace the king's mind*) brought with him in his hand this letter. The king asking what news, Dr Buts pleasantly and merrily beginneth to insinuate unto the king the effect of the matter, and so, at the king's commandment read out the letter.[17]

Turner was spared. Only after Buttes's death, in 1545, did the persecution of protestants begin in earnest, leading to the set piece burnings at Smithfield in the following year as the ultra-conservative Howard faction regained the initiative. In Germany, too, physicians such as Johann Krafft von Crafftheim became embroiled in the doctrinal struggles of the age.[18]

The Cambridge-trained physician, mathematician, priest and astrologer, Lewis Caerleon, deployed his diplomatic skills for political rather than religious ends. He was *medicus* and counsellor to the Lady Margaret Beaufort, mother of the future Henry VII, whom he helped in 1483 to plan the abortive rebellion against Richard III. The chronicler and Tudor propagandist, Polydore Vergil, noted that, 'because he was a grave man and of no smaule experience', Margaret often confided in him, seeking his advice about the possibility of a dynastic alliance with the house of York to overthrow the usurper. In his capacity as 'a very learnyd physytion', Lewis was able to communicate with the widowed Queen Elizabeth at Westminster Abbey, where she had taken sanctuary, representing the scheme 'as devysyd of his owne heade' to render it more acceptable.[19] Eustace Chapuys, Imperial ambassador at the court of Henry VIII, was later to observe that he 'like[d] to make acquaintance with men of that profession [physicians] because they can come and go to all places without suspicion'; and Caerleon's 'scyence' clearly provided ideal cover for clandestine operations.[20] As we shall see later, his accomplishments as an astrologer added further to his value as a confidant.

There can, therefore, be little doubt that English court physicians exercised considerable influence at a national level. Why else would the hard-headed realists of late medieval England have bestowed such extravagant gifts of robes, money, plate and jewels upon them? It was in return for his 'notable industry and for his labour expended with the king for expediting [the award of] the new charter, and other arduous business assiduously facilitated and undertaken by him on behalf of the city' that the Corporation of London

17. S.R. Cattley, ed., *The Acts and Monuments of John Foxe*, 8 vols, London 1837, viii, pp. 31–4, at p. 34. See also *ibid.*, v, p. 605, and vii, pp. 454, 461.

18. Nutton, *Medicine at the Courts of Europe*, pp. 9–10.

19. H. Ellis, ed., *Polydore Vergil's English History*, Camden Society, os 29 (1844), pp. 195–6; Rawcliffe, *Medicine and Society*, pp. 118–20.

20. *Calendar of Letters and Papers, Foreign and Domestic, Henry VIII*, viii, no 48, p. 15. Chapuys was writing, in January 1535, of Augustine de Augustinis, who was then conveying messages to him from Lord Sandys, his patient, in Hampshire 'at his house pretending to be ill' (*ibid.*, no 1034; Hammond, 'Doctor Augustine', p. 235). Augustinis and Caerleon were certainly not the first physicians to act as diplomats, secret agents and possibly spies. The fascinating history of Peter of Milan, a Lombard *medicus* who served Richard Courtenay, bishop of Norwich, and various members of the household of Henry V, is described in Talbot and Hammond, *Medical Practitioners*, pp. 249–51.

made a remarkably generous settlement upon John Somerset. Notwithstanding his subsequent claim never to have taken 'brybes for forderaunce of men . . . ne for spedyng of causys, bot evere [to have] kepte myn handys inpollute fro accepcions of gyftys and lyved on esy lyvelod *that never man of myn occupacions in any kynges tyme of so lytel lyved*', the facts speak otherwise.[21] In 1445–6 alone Somerset was awarded a robe, a fur-trimmed cloak and 20 marks every year for life, along with a one-off cash payment of 100 marks, by the grateful rulers of London, who also agreed to admit one of his clients to the freedom.[22] Indeed, for the rest of the decade the mayor and aldermen regularly consulted him about civic business. How could a physician promise — and deliver — so much? This is an important question, not least because medieval medicine is often perceived as being ineffectual as well as overpriced, and its practitioners powerless in the face of disability and disease (Pl. IIIA). The short answer is that Somerset exploited his hold over the King, whom he attended almost daily, to advance the interests of the city and other clients. For many years a member of the *familia regis*, he was one of the unpopular favourites who, in the words of Cade's rebels, clustered 'dayly and nyghtely abowte his hyghnesse'.[23] That his calling as a physician legitimised his constant attendance upon a weak and malleable young monarch carried little weight with the Commons of 1451, who unsuccessfully demanded his removal from the royal presence as an undesirable influence.[24] The long answer appears rather more complex.

Medieval satirists, such as John Gower and William Langland, ridiculed the medical profession's fatal combination of ignorance, rapacity and hubris with a venom rarely encountered in today's media.[25] But theirs was only one of many responses to the physician's exercise of the healing arts. To many he was neither a cynical opportunist nor a charlatan, but a *mediator* between life and death, sin and redemption: especially if, as so often proved the case in England, he was also a priest. In order to understand the relationship which bound the royal or aristocratic patient to his or her *medicus* we must go back to one of the most significant events in the history of medieval medicine. The Fourth Lateran Council of 1215 passed two rulings of crucial importance to the development of the medical profession in the later Middle Ages. The first concerned confession, and underlines the intimate relationship which, in a pre-Cartesian world, was perceived to

21. PRO, C1/19/65; D.A.L. Morgan, 'The House of Policy: The Political Role of the Late Plantagenet Household', in *The English Court from the Wars of the Roses to the Civil War*, ed. D. Starkey, London 1987, pp. 39–40. Somerset's defence of his probity was made in 1450, three years after he reluctantly leased out the wardenship of the mint at £40 a year, and accepted 1,000 marks for the reversion of the chancellorship at the behest of the duke of Suffolk (*CPR 1446–52*, p. 54). He claimed to have spent the money on 'dedys of devocion, mercy and pitee', such as his almshouse and guild at Brentford, established under royal letters patent in 1446 (*ibid.*, p. 29). For the background to this foundation, see A.F. Sutton and L. Visser-Fuchs, 'The Cult of Angels in Late Fifteenth-Century England', in *Women and the Book: Assessing the Visual Evidence*, ed. L. Smith and J.H.M. Taylor, London 1996, pp. 242–3.

22. Corporation of London Record Office, Journal IV, ff. 84r, 90v, 144r.

23. Watts, *Henry VI*, pp. 170, 207.

24. *Rotuli Parliamentorum*, v, p. 216. King Henry refused to accede to this request, on the ground that Somerset was one of those 'persones which shall be right fewe in nombre, the which have been accustumed contynuelly to waite upon his persone . . .', and he remained in the household (PRO, E101/410, 7, 9).

25. See, for example, William Langland, *The Vision of Piers Plowman*, ed. A.V.C. Schmidt, London 1978, B text, passus VI, vv. 268–74, passus XX, vv. 168–9; G.C. Macaulay, ed., *The Complete Works of John Gower*, 4 vols, Oxford 1899–1902, i, pp. 283–4.

exist between the body and the soul. This ruling was actually headed 'that the sick should provide for the soul before the body' and stipulated that the priest, or *physician of the soul*, should confess and absolve the patient before treatment began.[26] The injunction was taken very seriously, although in practice it proved hard to enforce and was deemed by some practitioners to have harmful psychological effects. The fourteenth-century French surgeon, Henri de Mondeville, who rose to prominence in the service of Philip the Fair, deplored the prospect of unedifying squabbles between surgeons and priests as patients in urgent need of medical attention expired for want of attention. Mondeville, whose command of anecdotal material must greatly have enhanced his own bedside manner, clearly recognised a conflict of professional interest, but it was by no means uncommon for surgeons to join with their patients in seeking confession and absolution before they wielded the lancet.[27]

By this date surgeons were invariably laymen or clergy in lower orders, whereas the overwhelming majority of physicians trained in English universities continued to be ordained as priests, and were thus able to administer the sacraments as well. In other words, the confessor and the physician were often one and the same person. John Arundel, future bishop of Chichester, was, for example, employed as both medical consultant and chaplain by the deeply pious Henry VI, Gilbert Kymer similarly by Humphrey, duke of Gloucester, and the busy Thomas Moscroff by Edward, duke of Buckingham. Diagnosis and treatment of the diseases of the soul consequently went hand in hand with the care of the body. Deploying their prognosticatory skills through the examination of urine and scrutiny of the heavens to determine how long the patient might survive, such *medici* were able to safeguard against the terrors of *mors improvisa* by offering all the consolations of the Christian Church. Recognising with grim inevitability that 'there is no medicine for death', medieval men and women had very different expectations of their medical practitioners, who routinely managed the transition from one world to the next.[28] A confessor (as critics of the friars constantly complained) might acquire great authority in secular affairs, too. The confidences of a sick monarch or nobleman would almost certainly touch upon matters of national importance, which, in turn, could be seen to exercise a direct influence upon both spiritual and physical wellbeing.

It is instructive to examine the vocabulary used in the Middle Ages to describe the process of confession. As in so many other areas of religious activity the terminology is often medical.[29] Henry, duke of Lancaster's *Livre de Seyntz Medicines*, a title which speaks for itself, is a long, sustained meditation composed in 1354, during the aftermath of the

---

26. N. Tanner, ed., *Decrees of the Ecumenical Councils*, 2 vols, Georgetown 1990, i, pp. 245–6.

27. M.R. McVaugh, 'Bedside Manners in the Middle Ages', *Bulletin of the History of Medicine*, 71 (1997), p. 217; J. Ziegler, *Medicine and Religion c.1300: The Case of Arnau de Vilanova*, Oxford 1998, pp. 250–4; M.C. Pouchelle, *The Body and Surgery in the Middle Ages*, Oxford 1990, pp. 46–8; Rawcliffe, *Medicine and Society*, pp. 71, 95.

28. Talbot and Hammond, *Medical Practitioners*, pp. 60–3, 115–16; PRO, SC6 Hen VIII 5841, m. 4v; F. Getz, *Medicine in the English Middle Ages*, Princeton 1998, pp. 3–4, 15–16. The deathbed of Bishop Grosseteste (d.1253) provides a classic example of the learned physician, in this case the Dominican theologian, John de St Giles, 'as a constant companion . . . offering consolation of both body and soul': Talbot and Hammond, *Medical Practitioners*, pp. 179–80.

29. See, for example, Zeigler, *Medicine and Religion*, chapter four, *passim*, and the collected writings of D.W. Amundsen, *Medicine, Society and Faith in the Ancient and Medieval Worlds*, Baltimore 1996, notably chapter seven.

first outbreak of plague in England. It compares the slow process of spiritual healing and the conquest of sin with a physician's struggle against disease. We should remember that many English noblemen were, like the duke, highly sophisticated, well-educated men, who clearly relished the society of a learned and eloquent physician, noted for his *urbanitas verborum*. The remedies suggested by duke Henry offer direct analogies: the theriac of a good sermon, the ointment of Christ's blood, the salve of the Virgin's kiss, the amputation of penance, and the *gratia Dei* applied to a festering mouth after cleansing by confession.[30] This metaphor is itself revealing, since the name *gratia Dei* was given to one of the most common ointments for wounds and sores to be produced in the later Middle Ages.[31]

The second important ruling of the 1215 Lateran Council concerned the prohibition henceforth placed on the shedding of blood or deployment of cauteries by clergy of the order of sub-deacon or above.[32] Hitherto, medicine and surgery had often been practised together by distinguished ecclesiastics, such as Baldwin, abbot of Bury St Edmunds, who attended both Edward the Confessor and William the Conqueror, itself a remarkable testimony to his skill.[33] A number of reasons lay behind the conciliar ruling about bloodshed. Blood was seen to be polluting: men of God, especially in the newly reformed church of Innocent III, should not have hands stained with the bodily fluids of their patients while celebrating the sacrament. And what if surgery, so often a brutal and terrifying experience, resulted in accusations of manslaughter? The risk of accidental homicide was especially great given the dangers inherent in surgery without antisepsis, reliable anaesthesia or blood transfusion.[34] Questions of snobbery also obtained. Senior clergy understandably wished to distance themselves from the practice of what was essentially a craft rather than an art, and to emphasise their higher, more cerebral calling. Since most of the health care available in medieval England was to be had at the hands of apothecaries, empirics, unlettered women and other assorted 'irregulars', the erection of clear-cut boundaries seemed all the more important. The rise of the universities, with their burgeoning faculties of medicine, proved another powerful incentive towards the specialist and essentially theoretical study of medicine by senior clergy. In England, unlike France and Italy, no significant attempt was made during the Middle Ages to integrate the surgeon into an academic programme of training by offering anatomy classes, or even occasional dissections. Nor, despite efforts in the 1420s by a group of court practitioners (including John Somerset and Gilbert Kymer) to set up a joint college or confraternity of

30. Henry of Lancaster, *Le Livre de Seyntz Medicines*, ed. E.J. Arnould, Oxford 1940, part two, *passim*. 'And since a man's tongue may help to heal a wound in his mouth and keep it clean, grant, O Lord, that my tongue may help me clean my festering mouth by confessing my sins. Then let it be covered with the bandage of your mercy and the precious ointment of *gratia Dei*': ibid., p. 181.

31. See, for example, W.R. Dawson, ed., *A Leechbook or Collection of Medical Recipes of the Fifteenth Century*, London 1934, pp. 117–19; BL Royal MS 18 A. vi, f. 15v.

32. D.W. Amundsen, 'Medieval Canon Law on Medical and Surgical Practice by the Clergy', *Bulletin of the History of Medicine*, 52 (1978), pp. 40–2.

33. Talbot and Hammond, *Medical Practitioners*, pp. 19–21.

34. D. Jacquart, *La médecine médiévale dans le cadre Parisien*, Paris 1998, pp. 26–40; Amundsen, 'Medieval Canon Law', pp. 39–40; M.J. Haren, 'Social Ideas in the Pastoral Literature of Fourteenth-Century England', in *Religious Belief and Ecclesiastical Careers in Late Medieval England*, ed. C. Harper-Bill, Woodbridge 1991, p. 54; V.I. Kennedy, 'Robert Courson on Penance', *Medieval Studies*, 7 (1945), pp. 322–3.

physicians, surgeons and apothecaries on the continental model in London, was any progress made in this direction before 1518.[35]

For all these reasons the ruling of Lateran IV had profound consequences for English medical and surgical practice. Surgery passed exclusively into the hands of laymen trained in artisan guilds or members of the lower clergy; it was an *ars mechanica*, a practical, hands-on activity, like stone masonry or carpentry, to which it was so often compared. To the surgeon fell the unpleasant, bloody or dangerous tasks, which not only involved what we today understand as surgery but also the intimate aspects of prophylactic humoral therapy, such as the administration of the 'laxatives, medicines . . . clysters, suppositories, medicines for clearing the head, gargles, baths, complete or partial, poultices, fomentations, embrocations, shaving of the head, ointments, plasters, waxes, cupping, with or without cutting the skin, and inducements to bleeding' prescribed in 1454 for the ailing Henry VI.[36] The surgeon was also often responsible for embalming, and sometimes dismembering, the royal dead, which may have given him a better grasp of human anatomy but set him even further apart from his more academic colleagues.[37] We have already noted the presence of Sir William Buttes when the royal barber went about his business, probably phlebotomising Henry VIII as well as cutting his hair.[38] As might be expected, this dichotomy is reflected in the respective garb and rank of the two types of practitioner. Royal surgeons were often extremely learned men, well versed in medical theory, yet they rarely enjoyed the social or intellectual prestige of their senior associates and did not, as so often happened on the Continent, attend university. At the court of Edward IV, for instance, surgeons, however erudite, ranked somewhere between yeomen and esquires, and dressed as such in more functional robes, while the physicians were, as we have seen, senior members of the royal household with long gowns and fur-trimmed liveries (Fig. 21).[39]

Physic had, indeed, increasingly become an academic subject, studied at English universities from a syllabus which — from the European humanist perspective — appeared increasingly outdated and obfuscated by scholastic accretions. Yet, to the advocates of this system, Hippocrates' first aphorism, '*ars longa, vita brevis*' unquestionably justified a training which built on the foundations of the liberal arts. For them the *trivium* (grammar, rhetoric and logic) and *quadrivium* (mathematics, music, geometry and astronomy) constituted useful preparation for a medical career, especially one to be pursued in high places, where learning, wit and an easy social manner carried a high premium. The study of rhetoric, for example, was believed to make it easier for the physician to manage difficult or fearful patients, while at the same time establishing a reputation for eloquence which was part of his professional *persona*. The development in the early fourteenth century of increasingly complex *formulae* for calculating the degrees of moisture, heat, dryness and cold in medical

35. T. Beck, *The Cutting Edge: Early History of the Surgeons of London*, London 1974, pp. 63–7.

36. T. Rymer, ed., *Foedera, Conventiones, Litterae et cuiuscunque Acta Publica*, 20 vols, The Hague 1704–35, v, part 2, p. 55. Two surgeons, Robert Wareyn and John Marshall, were recruited at this time to implement the *regimen*: CPR 1452–61, p. 147.

37. Pouchelle, *Body and Surgery*, p. 72; C. Gittings, *Death, Burial and the Individual in Early Modern England*, London 1984, p. 216.

38. See note 17 above.

39. A.R. Myers, *The Household of Edward IV: The Black Book and the Ordinance of 1478*, Manchester 1959, pp. 124–5.

Ｎ ᴄᴇ meſime an emuron my
nung vint vne tılgrant ma
ladie a moſſ jeban duc de noʒ

Fig. 21.   *A consultation at the bedside of Louis IX's eldest son, as seen through late medieval eyes. Having carefully scrutinised the royal urine sample, the two physicians, wearing their furred robes, discuss the next stage of treatment with a colleague, who is perhaps an apothecary (London, BL Royal MS 20 C. vii, f. 78v)*

preparations and foodstuffs meant that physicians required advanced mathematical skills.[40] A training in syllogistic argument likewise offered valuable preparation for professional debate, and undoubtedly helped its exponents to hold their own in the council chamber. It is worth noting that John Somerset's first posting after he graduated from Cambridge University in 1418, *artium grammatices professor et bachilarius in medicinis*, was as master of grammar at Bury St Edmund's school, a post acquired through the patronage of Thomas Beaufort, duke of Exeter.[41] A man of such diverse talents soon found employment in the ducal household, where he served as a physician rather than a grammarian, tending Exeter during his last illness and attesting his will. His friend, the royal surgeon, Thomas Morstede, who also assisted at the deathbed, almost certainly helped to arrange his move to Henry VI's court.[42] The award of a doctorate in medicine at this time did not, however, lead Somerset to abandon his interest in education, for he was retained both to teach and 'preserve the health' of the young king.[43] The two activities were, indeed, deemed synonymous. 'It is greet honuere and greet good', ran one late medieval advice manual, 'when Princes have knowlege and undirstandinge of clergie and science . . . and in especiall that they undirstande and convenabely speke latyn . . . for than shall they more wysely and sagely governe both thayme self and theire lordshippes.'[44]

It was in the dual capacity of pedagogue and physician that Somerset accompanied Henry to France, in 1430, his presence beside the nine-year-old monarch in Rouen being recorded on the fly-leaf of the presentation copy of the Bedford Book of Hours.[45] Not surprisingly, given his impressive academic background, Somerset was later to play a major role in implementing, and perhaps even formulating, Henry's two most cherished projects: the foundation of the school at Eton and of King's College, Cambridge.[46] The best documented account of a physician's role in the education of a young prince occurs somewhat later, in the reign of Louis XIII of France, most aspects of whose upbringing were supervised and carefully recorded by the humanist physician, Jean de Héroard. Like Somerset before him, the Frenchman moved easily from medicine (he began his career at court as a veterinary surgeon in charge of the royal horses) to training a future head of

40. Ziegler, *Medicine and Religion*, p. 19; McVaugh, 'Bedside Manners', pp. 215–17; Jacquart, *Médecine médiévale*, pp. 467–70.

41. BL Cotton MSS Tiberius B ix, f. 180r.

42. E.F. Jacob, ed., *The Register of Henry Chichele II*, Oxford 1937, p. 362. Morstede was another of the reformers involved in the projected college of surgery and physic: Beck, *Cutting Edge*, pp. 63–7, 79–86, 92–7; Rawcliffe, *Medicine and Society*, pp. 140–1.

43. *CPR 1429–36*, p. 241.

44. J.P. Genet, ed., *Four English Political Tracts of the Later Middle Ages*, Camden Society, 4th ser. 18 (1977), p. 205. The leading English physician, John of Gaddesden, began his *Rosa Medicine* of *c*. 1230 with the advice, taken from Galen, that 'one ought not to enter into the halls of princes without a knowledge of books': Getz, *Medicine in the English Middle Ages*, p. 42.

45. PRO, E404/46/299; BL Add. MS 18850, f. 256r; J. Stratford, ed., *The Bedford Inventories*, London 1993, p. 120.

46. Somerset was a trustee in 1440 of alien priory lands to be settled on Eton College (*CPR 1436–41*, pp. 454, 471; *Rotuli Parliamentorum*, v, p. 48) and a surveyor of works there (*CPR 1441–46*, p. 82); he helped draw up the statutes of King's College in 1441 and 1446 (*CPR 1436–41*, pp. 521–2; *Calendar of Charter Rolls, 1427–1516*, p. 74), and of Queens' College in 1448 (*CPR 1446–52*, p. 143), while also holding land in trust for the former (*CPR 1436–41*, pp. 557, 565; *1446–52*, p. 172). See J. Watts, *Henry VI*, pp. 169–71, for the suggestion that he and the other members of the king's *familia* involved in these endowments were actually engaged in a 'corporate enterprise' responsible for formulating as well as executing royal policy.

state, composing authoritative texts on both topics.[47] John Somerset has been suggested, along with various other learned members of his circle, as a putative author of the *Tractatus de Regimine Principum ad Regem Henrici Sexti*, which survives in one fine presentation copy, probably intended for the monarch himself. Since he was not, as the writer describes himself, a *religiosus* (and, in fact, abandoned the celibate life espoused by many English court physicians in favour of matrimony), his authorship may be ruled out, although he would clearly have been more than capable of writing a manual of this kind.[48]

Such activities bring to mind Christine de Pisan's remarks in *Le Livre du Corps de Policie*, which was widely read in fifteenth-century England, about the health of princes, and the close connection between learning, virtue and physical wellbeing:

. . . in order to govern the body of the public polity well, it is necessary for the head to be healthy, that is virtuous. Because if he is sick the whole of the body will feel it. Therefore we begin by speaking of medicine for the head, that is for the king or princes . . . [she proceeds to discuss the therapeutic powers of education].[49]

The reader may feel that such training qualified medieval physicians for everything but the hands-on treatment of living, suffering patients. Yet the English *medicus* did not lack practical expertise. His role was simply different from that of a modern physician, and might, in today's parlance, be more appropriately described as a cross between a dietician, confidant and advisor on matters of life-style and health.[50] It is easy to see why medicine developed along these lines. Given the enormous risks of surgery, and the likelihood of death or debilitating illness as a result of even quite minor complaints, preventative medicine assumed overwhelming importance. This was in keeping with the all-pervasive classical Greek tradition, as mediated through the schools, which in the later Middle Ages found popular expression in the widespread circulation of manuals about healthy living. One such, *Li Livres dou Sante*, was commissioned in 1256 by Beatrice of Savoy from the physician, Aldobrandino of Siena, an exquisite presentation copy being made for her daughter, Eleanor, then queen of England. Since this was the first medical text ever to be composed in French rather than Latin, it was clearly intended to serve a more than decorative purpose, although the volume itself shows few signs of regular usage.[51]

Many *regimina* derived from the medical parts of the *Secreta Secretorum*, a text of Arab origin, comprising exhortatory, albeit entirely fictitious, letters supposedly sent by Aristotle to his pupil, Alexander the Great, on the conduct and lifestyle befitting a successful

47. M. Foisil, ed., *Journal de Jean Héroard*, 2 vols, Paris 1989, i, pp. 1–249, *passim*, notably pp. 43–51. I am grateful to Dr Gillian Lewis for drawing my attention to this source.

48. Genet, *Four English Political Tracts*, pp. 40–168. Conflating Talbot and Hammond's biography of Gilbert Kymer with that of John Somerset, Ralph Griffiths asserts that the latter was a chaplain who served in Humphrey, duke of Gloucester's household, and thus seems a prime candidate for authorship of the treatise (*The Reign of Henry VI*, London 1981, pp. 245–7, 265 note 47, 332). But Somerset was twice married, and never benefited from ecclesiastical preferment. In 1441 he and his first wife, Agnes, were awarded a royal corrody at Merton priory in return for his 'praiseworthy service' to King Henry (*CCR 1435–41*, p. 479). Five years later Henry set up a chantry at St Stephen's church, Colman Street, London, where, in 1448, prayers were to be said, *inter alios*, for her soul and the salvation of Somerset and her successor, Alice (*CPR 1446–52*, pp. 176–8).

49. Christine de Pisan, *Le Livre du Corps de Policie*, ed. A.J. Kennedy, Paris 1998, p. 3.

50. John Somerset described himself in 1430 as '*domini regis ad personam servitor et sanitatem vitaque conservationem consulens*': J.H. Wylie and W.T. Waugh, *The Reign of Henry V*, 3 vols, Cambridge 1914–29, iii, p. 433.

51. BL Sloane MS 2435; described in P. Murray Jones, *Medieval Medical Miniatures*, London 1984, pp. 132–6.

prince.[52] A lavishly illuminated text of the *Secreta* was produced in 1326 for the young Edward III, just before he became king. The implicit comparison between Edward and Alexander, underscored by the exuberant use of martial and heraldic iconography, probably appealed rather more to him than the philosopher's somewhat tedious advice about sexual abstinence and moderation (Pl. IIIB).[53] Successive outbreaks of plague served, however, to concentrate the minds of monarchs as well as their subjects. After the Black Death, mass-produced *regimina sanitatis* circulated widely in the vernacular, while the wealthy had their own custom made after protracted consultations with a resident physician.[54] A Latin *regimen* of 1424 drawn up by the distinguished Oxford physician, Gilbert Kymer, for his patron, Humphrey, duke of Gloucester, offered a salutary caution against the dangers of sexual indulgence, which, he warned with remarkable candour, given the duke's tortuous marital history, would undermine his already enervated constitution.[55] This highly personal list of recommendations certainly suggests that a remarkable degree of intimacy had been established between physician and patient. Duke Humphrey, part of whose library Kymer secured for Oxford University, was an avid collector of books on natural science, which they may well have studied together. John Somerset, who subsequently played a less than creditable part in the administration of Gloucester's estate, apparently making free with certain volumes to bolster his personal reputation as a patron of learning, was also a bibliophile.[56] One of his own books, bequeathed to Peterhouse, Cambridge, but first loaned to the physician, Roger Marshall, *pro totam vitam suam*, contains a *Tractatus utilis de Regimine Sanitatis*, as well as a copy of part of the pseudo *Medicine Aristotelis ad Regem Alexandrum*.[57] As a young man, before mounting the throne, Edward IV had likewise owned (and inscribed his name in) a working volume of astrological and medical texts, including a *Liber de Secretis Secretorum Aristotelis* prefaced by extracts from the astronomical writings of Roger Bacon.[58] As

52. Getz, *Medicine in the English Middle Ages*, pp. 53–64. Examples of vernacular versions of the *Secreta* may be found in R. Steele, ed., *Three Versions of the Secreta Secretorum*, Early English Text Society, extra ser. 74 (1898).

53. BL Add. MS 47680. See M.R. James, ed., *The Treatise of Walter de Milemete*, Roxburghe Club 1913, pp. xxxviii–lxiii, and for facsimiles pp. 159–86. It is worth noting that Milemete sent Edward another tract, *De Nobilitatibus, Sapientiis et Prudentiis Regnum*, just after his coronation (*ibid.*, pp. ix–xxxvii).

54. See, for instance, L.C. Arano, *The Medieval Health Handbook*, New York 1992, and L. Garcia-Ballester, 'Changes in the *Regimina Sanitatis*', in *Health, Disease and Healing in Medieval Culture*, ed. S. Campbell, B. Hall and D. Klausner, New York 1992, pp. 119–31. H.C.E. Midelfort, *Mad Princes in Renaissance Germany*, Charlottesville 1994, pp. 49–51, 67–8, 85–9, 103, 105–7, describes a number of *regimina* devised on the Galenic model for sick or unstable rulers.

55. BL Sloane MS 4, ff. 63–104, discussed by Getz, *Medicine in the English Middle Ages*, pp. 63, 86, 127.

56. *CPR 1446–52*, p. 45; *Rotuli Parliamentorum*, v, p. 339. Gloucester reputedly died intestate, but Somerset and his fellow administrators, who had little affection for the deceased, may have suppressed his will and were later investigated on (unproven) charges of embezzlement. For Somerset's increasingly acrimonious exchange with the University about Gloucester's legacy and his own gift of at least one of these books to Gonville Hall, Cambridge, see D. Rundle, 'Two Unnoticed Manuscripts from the Collection of Humfrey, Duke of Gloucester: Part II', *Bodleian Library Record*, 16 (1998), pp. 306–9.

57. BL Sloane MS 59. See also L.E. Voigts, 'A Doctor and his Books: The Manuscripts of Roger Marshall (d.1477)', in *New Science Out of Old Books*, ed. R. Beadle and A.J. Piper, Scolar Press 1995, pp. 250, 281.

58. BL Royal MS 12 E. xv, notably ff. 19r–116r. John, duke of Bedford, was also an enthusiastic collector of medical and scientific works. One of his commissions, a 'moderately luxurious' copy of Guy de Chauliac's *Inventarium*, contains a depiction of him (or another distinguished patron) receiving the finished text: K.L. Scott, *Later Gothic Manuscripts*, 2 vols, London 1996, i, plates 267–9; ii, pp. 203–4.

unrepentant hedonists, neither he nor Gloucester showed any more practical enthusiasm for the austere lifestyle urged by their physicians than Edward III had done before them, but each clearly recognised the wider implications of such ideas.

The essence of medieval therapeutics was to keep one's four bodily humours (blood, phlegm, black bile and choler) in a state of balance, treading the tightrope between deficiency and excess through the regulation of six external factors known as non-naturals. The physician was thus an advocate of that 'mesure and attemperaunce' so beloved by writers of political and moral advice literature for princes, while the good ruler presented himself as a Christ-like model of perfect equilibrium.[59] Since it was believed that the humours were generated from food and drink through a cooking process in the stomach, diet remained the most important and most easily managed of the non-naturals, being universally recognised as 'the first instrument of medicine'. The royal practitioners licensed in 1454 to treat King Henry were thus to begin by 'moderating' his diet, before moving on to more aggressive measures, such as phlebotomy.[60] According to the terms of their employment, the principal responsibility of Edward IV's physicians was the continuous regulation of his eating habits, an unenviable task, given the king's notorious sybaritism. In the words of one household ordinance, each holder of this office

stondith muche in the presence of the kinges meles, by the councelyng or awnswering to the kinges grace wich dyet is best according, and to the nature and operacion of all the metes. And comynly he shuld talke with the steward, chambrelayn, assewer, and the master cooke to deuyse by counsayle what metes or drinkes is best according with the kinges dyet; and whan he woll at mete and souper in the kinges chambre or hall or in his own chambre, deuysyng the kinges medecens . . .[61]

But it was not enough to watch what one ate. The whole of life, including sexual activity — another of Edward's weaknesses — had to be carefully ordered, and this, as we have seen, was also the physician's task, achieved through protracted and intimate consultations with the patient. It took weeks, if not months, to devise a *regimen*, and even longer to implement one. Rather than spend long periods in attendance on one specific patient, many physicians liked to work on short term contracts, keeping their options open and using drugs in preference to diet.[62] But once at court or in a baronial household, they had to be available, or at least on call, as and when required. The factors of continuous presence and close proximity to the patient are crucial, in a political as well as a medical context.[63] To establish his credentials as an agent at the Imperial court, in 1531, Augustine de Augustinis emphasised the fact that his duties in England involved daily attendance upon Henry VIII at dinner.[64] The historian can only speculate as to the degree of personal influence such a relationship bestowed. The citizens of London who enlisted the support of royal physicians had, presumably, made a shrewd assessment of what went on behind

59. Genet, *Four English Political Tracts*, p. 193.

60. Rymer, *Foedera*, v, part 2, p. 55.

61. Myers, *Household of Edward IV*, pp. 123–4. Pope Clement VII always kept two physicians beside him at table to discuss his diet: R. Palmer, 'Medicine at the Papal Court in the Sixteenth Century', in *Medicine at the Courts of Europe*, ed. Nutton, pp. 62–3.

62. L. Demaitre, *Doctor Bernard de Gordon: Professor and Practitioner*, Toronto 1980, pp. 35, 148. Gordon was critical of colleagues who cut corners in order to take more patients.

63. A theme explored by D. Starkey, 'Intimacy and Innovation: The Rise of the Privy Chamber 1485–1547', in *idem*, *English Court*, pp. 71–118, notably with regard to the groom of the stool, pp. 78–9.

64. *Calendar of Letters and Papers, Foreign and Domestic, Henry VIII*, v, no 283.

closed doors. Trust and confidence were not commodities to be compartmentalised or confined within a narrow domestic sphere.

In this context the extent to which concepts and practices based upon the *regimen sanitatis* entered the vocabulary of the late medieval preacher is highly significant. Far from denigrating the skill of earthly practitioners, which to modern eyes seems all too fragile and limited, these ideas reinforced the image of the 'good physician', following in the steps of *Christus Medicus*. The letters patent of 1454 authorising Henry VI's physicians and surgeons to implement their regimen of diet and purgation observed that his 'bodily illness' came by divine visitation and might only, in the last resort, be cured 'if it should please Him who is the health of all things'. Following 'the advice of ecclesiastical counsel', however, more immediate remedies were to be sought at the hands of men expert in the use of medicines 'which the Almighty created for the relief of human weaknesses'.[65] From time to time preachers attacked the greed and lack of compassion shown by successful *medici*, but this did not prevent them from harnessing the specialist terminology of the university-trained physician when they wished to exhort their flocks to moral improvement. Christ, 'the most sovereign leech' had, after all, devised a *regimen* for each of his patients, who by following it might achieve spiritual health and eternal life.[66] Not surprisingly, the bibliophile Gilbert Kymer, who had served for many years as chancellor of Oxford University, made much of this *topos*. He was buried next to the relics' altar at Salisbury Cathedral (where he was dean), itself an appropriate reflection of his position as earthly and spiritual physician to Humphrey, duke of Gloucester, his brother, Henry V, and eventually to the latter's son, Henry VI.[67] The profits of practice paid for the glazing of a nearby window, which bore his image and an invocation begging the *Summus Medicus*, through the healing saints, to administer medicine to his soul so that he might enjoy the everlasting health of heaven.[68] The association in the public mind between medicine and Christ was everywhere: in sermons, statues, iconography and funerary monuments (Fig. 22). It saturated the discourse of the social and intellectual elite.

The good prince was, moreover, enjoined to take the medical practitioner as his model. Such a ruler, or so John of Salisbury had urged, should follow moderate counsels, playing the part of a physician 'who cures diseases sometimes by starvation of the overfed, sometimes by refreshment of the malnourished, and who sedates pain sometimes by cauterising tissue, sometimes by poultice'.[69] Richard, duke of York's attack, in the Parliament of 1460, upon the 'long festered canker' of Lancastrian rule drew eloquently

65. Rymer, *Foedera*, v, part 2, p. 55. It is interesting to note that the theologians called upon to propose treatment for the melancholic Johann Wilhelm, duke of Jülich-Cleves, in 1590, agreed with the diagnosis and recommendations of his physicians, suggesting in addition that a priest should deal with his *animi infirmitate*: Midelfort, *Mad Princes*, pp. 108–10.

66. P. Heath-Barnum, ed., *Dives and Pauper I*, EETS, 275 (1976), p. 68. See also, S. Wenzel, ed., *Fasciculus Morum: A Fourteenth-Century Preachers' Handbook*, Pennsylvania 1989, pp. 255–7; *idem*, ed., *Summa Virtutum de Remediis Anime*, Athens, Georgia 1984, pp. 21, 266, 268, 274 (where the preacher refers to Galen's recommendations regarding abstinence); Ziegler, *Medicine and Religion*, chapter four, *passim*.

67. Talbot and Hammond, *Medical Practitioners*, pp. 60–3; PRO, E404/33/19; SC1/43/182.

68. C. Wordsworth, ed., *Ceremonies and Processions of the Cathedral Church of Salisbury*, Cambridge 1901, p. 301.

69. John of Salisbury, *Policraticus*, ed. C.J. Nederman, Cambridge 1990, p. 50. John is here quoting Lucius, but on pp. 49–50 he expands the metaphor to embrace surgery, the third and last instrument of medicine, violence towards the subject being similarly the last resort of the monarch.

Fig. 22.   Christus Medicus *does the rounds of a sixteenth-century hospital ward, holding a physicians's jordan in one hand and surgeon's instruments in the other. To his right, works by Galen and a wicker basket for transporting urine samples represent the physician's command of both theory and practice (London, Wellcome Institute Iconographic Collection, line engraving after H. Glotzius)*

upon this tradition of social pathology. In describing himself as the 'principall physician' of the realm, and in enlisting the support of the Commons as 'trew and trusty appotecaries', the duke invited his audience to reflect upon the inadequacies of a royal *medicus* who had so conspicuously failed to heal either himself or the ills of his kingdom.[70] For as Giles of Rome had explained in his aptly titled and influential *Regimine Principum*, the ruler's primary task was to keep the body politic in a state of balance:

We must understand that just as the essence of medicine, by the diet and by potions and by syrups and other things which concern it, relates principally to the management of the humours and to make the human body healthy, so the science of governing cities and realms relates principally to ruling human affairs by law.[71]

70. E. Hall, *Hall's Chronicle Containing the History of England*, London 1809, p. 245.
71. J.L.G. Pichert, *La métaphore pathologique et therapeutique à la fin du moyen age*, Tübingen 1994, p. 20. See also *ibid*., pp. 19, 31; and Watts, *Henry VI*, pp. 20–1.

Holbein's 'great picture' of Henry VIII and the barber surgeons of London (1540) is surmounted by a tablet recording how, after a serious outbreak of plague, God bade the king 'undertake the office of good physician . . . that will be a remedy for a mind diseased', most notably by encouraging the study of Galen's works in their most recent translation (Pl. IV).[72] This is a strong, persuasive image, associating monarch and practitioner in a common goal and purpose; and one which had appeared in various guises for centuries. It enhanced the status of those whose vocation had about it something of the regal and much of the divine. The thaumaturgic aspects of kingship were most dramatically manifest in the ceremony of touching for the king's evil, or scrofula, a ritual with which physicians and surgeons alike were understandably keen to identify themselves. Louis XIII's assiduity in this regard was enthusiastically encouraged — and carefully documented — from boyhood by his physician, Jean Héroard, who records statistics comparable with the medieval period while the king was still a child. But not all monarchs possessed this sacred power. Counter-propaganda mounted by Sir John Fortescue against the victorious Yorkists in the 1460s had denied Edward IV the capacity to cure his subjects. Only the legitimate sovereign, Henry VI, as God's anointed, could offer 'his own pure hands' as a conduit of healing grace.[73]

A whiff of sulphur, or something of the night, also hung about many of the physicians who achieved influence at court in the fifteenth century: at least in the eyes of those who denounced the practice of judicial astrology and its sister art, alchemy. Emphasis upon the importance of environmental factors in the preservation of health, and a widespread belief that man was a microcosm of the wider universe, meant that from Hippocratic times a knowledge of the heavens was deemed essential for the effective practice of medicine (Pl. VA). William the Conqueror's suave and accomplished Norman physician, Gilbert Maminot (d.1101), somewhat grudgingly described by Orderic Vitalis as 'a man of great learning and eloquence', was, for example, famous for his 'inspiring teaching . . . in arithmetic and astronomy, the main branches of natural science and other profound subjects'. Although many churchmen opposed the dissemination throughout the Christian West of arab texts on astronomy and astrology, by the fourteenth century astrology was recognised as a fundamental part of the medical syllabus. Since it was believed that each of the planets influenced the humoral composition of individuals born under its sway, and that each sign of the zodiac exercised a powerful control over specific parts of the body, neither diagnosis nor treatment could safely proceed without consulting the heavens.[74] Physicians were, however, tempted to go further, and venture down the forbidden but

72. J. Sawday, *The Body Emblazoned: Dissection and the Human Body in Renaissance Culture*, London 1995, p. 190. Henry was, indeed, something of a practitioner, collaborating closely with his physicians in devising salves and ointments for his own ulcerated legs: BL Sloane MS 1047. For a development of the idea of the physician-king, see J.G. Harris, *Foreign Bodies and the Body Politic: Discourses of Social Pathology in Early Modern England*, Cambridge 1998, pp. 56–63.

73. M. Bloch, *Les Rois Thaumaturges*, Paris 1924, pp. 111–14, 362–3. The surgeon, Henri de Mondeville, compared both the monarch who 'touched' and Jesus Christ with a surgeon rather than a physician, since the former had more contact with the human body: Pouchelle, *Body and Surgery*, p. 50.

74. M. Chibnall, ed., *The Ecclesiastical History of Orderic Vitalis*, 6 vols, Oxford 1972–80, iii, pp. 20–3; R. French, 'Astrology in Medical Practice', in *Practical Medicine from Salerno to the Black Death*, ed. L. Garcia-Bellester and others, Cambridge 1994, pp. 30–59.

primrose path of divination, often at the behest of royal or baronial patrons. Notwithstanding his impeccable background as a canon first of Windsor and then of St Stephen's Westminster, Thomas Southwell took the lure. One of the leading practitioners of his day and a sometime associate of John Somerset, he was condemned to death in 1441 for assisting his patron, Eleanor, duchess of Gloucester, to forecast the demise of her nephew, Henry VI. As the king's chief medical advisor, Somerset either himself undertook the task of compiling a more optimistic horoscope or else commissioned his young friend, the Cambridge physician, Roger Marshall, to do so. Both men were expert astrologers, as, indeed, was Lewis Caerleon, the owner of the only surviving copy of this work.[75] Because of his part in Margaret Beaufort's conspiracy against King Richard, Caerleon spent some time as a prisoner in the Tower of London, being permitted to continue his work on the compilation of astronomical tables while in custody.[76] Divination was a risky business, which promised to consolidate the hold already exercised by a practitioner over his patient. It could, on the other hand, end in disgrace, banishment or the stake.

Each of these four physicians, and many of their colleagues, shared with leading members of the royal court an academic, if not overtly practical, interest in alchemy. Even more enticing than the prospect of converting base metal into gold was the hope that they would master 'the restoral of all fallen and infirm bodies and how to bring them back to a true balance (*temperamentum*) and the best of health'.[77] Roger Bacon's belief that health and longevity might be assured 'bi power of astronomye, alkamye and prospectif and of sciences experimental' assumed a particular urgency during the last years of Henry VI's reign.[78] To his contemporaries, the young king must already have displayed signs of a potentially dangerous humoral imbalance long before the dramatic mental collapse of 1453, which many historians have come to regard as the first real manifestation of his medical problems.[79] Notwithstanding Thomas Southwell's prediction that the king would die of melancholia, Henry presented a classic example of the phlegmatic temperament, which was unstable, effeminate, withdrawn and forgetful. An excess of this watery humour made such men fearful, pallid and child-like, their moonish faces reflecting an affinity with *luna*, the planet of madness. This was a heavy cross for any individual to bear, but for a king — and for the distempered body politic — the burden must have seemed

75. R.A. Griffiths, 'The Trial of Eleanor Cobham: An Episode in the Fall of Duke Humphrey of Gloucester', *Bulletin of the John Rylands Library*, 51 (1968–9), pp. 381–99; Voigts, 'A Doctor and his Books', pp. 252–3. Somerset's skills as an astrologer are noted by the author (the pseudo-Elmham) of a *vita* of Henry V, who presented him with the text and paid extravagant compliments about his learning: T. Hearne, ed., *Thomae de Elmham Vita et Gesta Henrici Quinti*, Oxford 1727, p. 339; Wylie and Waugh, *Reign of Henry V*, iii, pp. 432–3.
76. BL Royal MS 12 G. i, a book of astronomical calculations made by Caerleon in 1482. Notes in a contemporary hand on ff. 1r and 6r record that he later produced other tables and canons while incarcerated in the Tower by Richard III.
77. G. Roberts, *The Mirror of Alchemy: Alchemical Ideas and Images in Manuscripts and Books*, London 1994, p. 37. See Jacquart, *Médecine médiévale*, pp. 488–500, for a discussion of 'la tentation alchimique'. The involvement of late medieval medical practitioners in alchemy is currently being explored by Dr Jonathan Hughes, to whom I am grateful for the opportunity to discuss many of the ideas advanced in this essay.
78. Trinity College, Cambridge, MS R.14.52, f. 53r. See Getz, *Medicine in the English Middle Ages*, pp. 53–64, for a discussion of Bacon's ideas concerning the regimen of health.
79. See, for example, Griffiths, *Reign of King Henry VI*, p. 715. An attempt at post-mortem diagnosis, notable for its anachronistic view of late medieval medical practice, has been made by B. Clarke, *Mental Disorder in Earlier Britain*, Cardiff 1975, chapter seven, *passim*.

intolerable. Although intended to provide evidence of Henry's sanctity, and thus counteract far less flattering interpretations of his increasingly erratic behaviour, the short memoir compiled by Henry's confessor, John Blacman, describes a pattern of behaviour to be found in any late medieval encyclopaedia or medical text under the general heading of 'superflyte of flueme'.[80] If, as seems likely, Henry seemed to teeter on the edge of a precipice long before the 1450s, his physicians and surgeons must have grown increasingly desperate with the passage of time. By 1456, as he became slower, duller and sleepier, the prospect of another long period of royal collapse and attendant civil unrest necessitated emergency measures.[81] The grant of licences to practise alchemy, which had been pronounced illegal at the beginning of the century, to three of Henry's medical advisors was made in the express hope that they would discover the 'empress of medicines' through which 'all curable infirmities would be easily healed . . . human life would be prolonged to its natural term, and man would be marvellously sustained unto the same term in health and natural virility of body and mind, in strength of limb, clearness of memory and keenness of intellect'. One of the recipients was Gilbert Kymer, who had been urgently summoned to Windsor, in June 1455, to tend a king 'occupied and laboured with sikenes', and who subsequently appears to have composed a treatise on alchemy.[82]

Far from finding the philosopher's stone, John Somerset had, meanwhile, experienced a considerable loss of status well before his sudden death in 1454.[83] All favourites, however skilled or learned, were subject to the turn of fortune's wheel, and none more so than those royal physicians who took the gamble of engaging in high politics during one of the more turbulent periods of English history. Disillusionment first set in during the late 1440s, when the hitherto inviolable *medicus* had been obliged to concede some of the spoils of office to younger courtiers hungry for patronage. A simmering grievance over the earlier award of his manor of Ruislip to the very Cambridge college he had helped to found was exacerbated by this unwelcome reminder of declining influence.[84] Putting his skills as a grammarian to good use, Somerset composed a *Queremonia*, bewailing in Latin hexameters the instances of princely and academic ingratitude which had blighted his later

---

80. M.R. James, ed., *Henry the Sixth: A Reprint of John Blacman's Memoir*, Cambridge 1919, pp. 25–44. 'For a verray fleumatik man is in the body lustles, heuy and slowgh; dul of wit and of thought, forgheteful . . . whitliche in face, ferdeful of herte . . . ful of slothe and slepinge': M.C. Seymour and others, ed., *On the Properties of Things: John Trevisa's Translation of Bartholomaeus Anglicus De Proprietatibus Rerum*, 3 vols, Oxford 1975–88, i, pp. 156–7.

81. R.L. Storey, *The End of the House of Lancaster*, London 1966, p. 184, citing PRO, KB9/287, no 53.

82. D. Geoghegan, 'A Licence of Henry VI to Practise Alchemy', *Ambix*, 6 (1957–8), pp. 15–16; PRO, SC1/ 43/182; *Thomas Norton's Ordinal of Alchemy*, ed. J. Reidy, Oxford 1975, p. 50. In an admirable article which examines the connections between medicine and alchemy in this period, Michela Pereira ignores the question of Henry VI's collapse and suggests that the purpose of the 1456 commission was to produce a pharmaceutical cure for the plague. It seems impossible, however, to divorce this burst of activity from the political circumstances, especially as a sick realm was often held to reflect the health of the monarch: '*Mater Medicinarum*: English Physicians and the Alchemical Elixir in the Fifteenth Century', in *Medicine from the Black Death to the French Disease*, ed. R. French and others, Aldershot 1998, pp. 26–52.

83. Somerset died intestate after succumbing to an unexpected 'seknesse', but not apparently before setting aside 100 marks for his aged mother and £20 for a servant (PRO, C1/26/329; E13/146, rot. 51r).

84. *Rotuli Parliamentorum*, v, p. 87; PRO, C1/19/60–65; Watts, *Henry VI*, p. 218; Morgan, 'House of Policy', pp. 38–45.

career.[85] He was one of many casualties in a general scramble for preferment which characterised the last years of William, duke of Suffolk's ascendancy over King Henry. Yet it was not until the duke's downfall and death, in 1450, that he sought to distance himself from a once generous patron, and only then that steps were taken to investigate his alleged embezzlement of the duke of Gloucester's estate.[86] Given the fate of certain members of his circle, he was fortunate to escape unscathed.

It is fitting to conclude with another poignant reminder that court physicians who elected to play for high stakes were as vulnerable as any other ambitious careerists to conspiracy, intrigue and retribution. Little has been made of the presence of one Thomas Nandyke, chaplain, 'nigromansier' and physician, in the retinue of Henry, duke of Buckingham, just before the latter's execution for treason in the above-mentioned 1483 rebellion.[87] Nandyke, whose divinatory skills were clearly flawed, escaped with his life, but was henceforward obliged to live in considerably reduced circumstances. He apparently never found another aristocratic patron, returning instead to Cambridge, where he had first studied medicine in the 1470s. An inventory of his goods taken after his death in 1491 shows that he had indeed seen better days in the service of one who expected more from his medical advisors than simple recommendations about diet and exercise. The great quantities of plate and jewels, so characteristic of the wills of successful practitioners in this period, had almost all been confiscated or sold, but Nandyke managed to retain 'ij estrolabes of latton price vjs viijd' and other instruments, as well as unspecified books on physic and astronomy.[88] That he had once put them all to profitable use is evident from what remained of a now moth-eaten and threadbare wardrobe. His collection of fur-trimmed and silk-lined gowns must once have marked him out, like John Somerset, as a leading member of his profession (Pl. VB). Two gowns trimmed with black lamb, two furred with fox, a red robe lined with squirrel, a murrey gown lined with 'brode menyver', a green robe with a taffeta lining, another lined with chaumlet, and — once the prize of his now rather mangy collection — a great cloak of 'calabour wombys',

---

85. Hearne, *Thomae de Elmham Vita et Gesta Henrici Quinti*, pp. 347–50. Somerset, who clearly enjoyed turning his hand to verse, is said to have written a tract *De Facultate Metrica*, now lost: A.B. Emden, *Biographical Dictionary of the University of Oxford to 1500*, 3 vols, Oxford 1957–9, iii, p. 1728.

86. Somerset was eventually exonerated by the royal commission of inquiry set up in 1450 by Archbishop Stafford into the administration of Duke Humphrey's effects, but he had a suspenseful wait of three years: Rundle, 'Two Unnoticed Manuscripts', p. 310. Although he claimed in retrospect never to have enjoyed Suffolk's 'luf and affeccion' (PRO, C1/19/65), the physician was mocked in one version of the satirical '*dirige*' composed in 1450 after de la Pole's death as a creature of the unlamented duke (F.J. Furnivall, ed., *Political, Religious and Love Poems*, EETS, os 15 (1866), p. 9). The designation 'Master Somerset' here eliminates any confusion with Edmund Beaufort, duke of Somerset (Watts, *Henry VI*, p. 209).

87. Notably by the present author, who mentions Nandyke only briefly in *The Staffords, Earls of Stafford and Dukes of Buckingham, 1394–1521*, Cambridge 1978, pp. 34, 227. His inventory is cited by C. Richmond, 'Religion and the Fifteenth-Century English Gentleman', in *The Church, Politics and Patronage in the Fifteenth Century*, ed. R.B. Dobson, Gloucester 1984, p. 200 and note 49. Edward, duke of Buckingham's precise date of birth to the hour was recorded in the family cartulary, which suggests that his father displayed an interest in astrology: Staffordshire Record Office, Bagot Collection, D.1721/1/1, f. 222r.

88. His estate was valued at just over £19, although he owed his creditors £7 in unpaid debts: PRO, PROB 2/48. A comparison with the will of the successful society physician, William Goldwyn MB, who died in 1482, is instructive. The latter bequeathed over £240 in cash, as well as large quantities of jewellery, plate, fur-lined robes and a library destined for All Souls (PRO, PCC, 5 Logge). His executors recovered at least £114 in debts due to him (*CPR 1485–94*, p. 362).

or skins of Calabrian fur. The rich and unscrupulous *medicus* in Langland's *Piers Plowman* wears just such a garment, with solid gold buttons further advertising his success.[89] Christ may have been a physician, but apostolic poverty was not one of the many features of a profession whose weaknesses as well as strengths made it all the more important to create a powerful impression of omniscience.

89. Langland, *Piers Plowman*, B Text, passus VI, vv. 268–70.

The Years of Arrears: Financial Problems of the College of St George in the 15th Century

A.K.B. EVANS (A.K.B. ROBERTS)

For the first three-quarters of the fifteenth century the College of St George in Windsor Castle was faced with an insoluble administrative problem: how to run the institution with insufficient funding. When Edward III founded it in 1348 he intended its income to be princely: £1000 a year, and the Exchequer was to make up the difference while its endowment fell short of that sum. But Edward III's intentions outran his resources; and by 1360 he had decided that property bringing in £655 a year would be adequate. Even that was not quite achieved: the last £50 a year never materialized. The college's income was just over £600.[1] This meant that there had to be economies, of which the most apparent was the restraint tacitly undertaken by the monarch in appointing poor knights to be supported by the foundation. The college statutes allowed for twenty-six, but in practice there were never more than three at a time, and usually fewer, and from time to time none at all.[2]

During the fourteenth century income kept pace with expenditure, though the margin was small. But in the first decade of the fifteenth century the problem of underfunding became acute. Of the properties which made up the original endowment of St George's, the church of Simonburn in Northumberland was the most valuable.[3] In 1370 it brought in £142. But thereafter border warfare steadily eroded its value. From 1402 to 1432 it brought in nothing at all.[4] This meant that at the beginning of the fifteenth century the college's potential income of £600 was reduced to £500, which was a reduction to a half of the £1000 Edward III originally intended. This situation was aggravated by the failure of the tenants of the college's other properties to pay their due rents: a general problem at this time, owing to a far-reaching economic depression.[5] Depopulation, attributed to

1. A.K.B. Roberts, *St George's Chapel, Windsor Castle, 1348–1416: A study in early collegiate administration*, Windsor 1947 (hereafter cited as Roberts, *Administration 1348–1416*), pp. 43–4.

2. E.H. Fellowes, *The Military Knights of Windsor 1352–1944*, Windsor 1944, pp. xvii–xxi. From 1385 to 1402 and from 1415 to 1428 there was only one or none (see n. 26).

3. Simonburn was described by A. Hamilton Thompson, *The English Clergy in the Late Middle Ages*, Oxford 1947, p. 102 n. 2, as 'probably the richest parochial benefice in England' at the time. See Roberts, *Administration 1348–1416*, p. 23, and below, n. 48.

4. Roberts, *Administration 1348–1416*, appendix 1.

5. J. Hatcher, *Plague, Population and the English Economy 1348–1530*, London 1977, pp. 35–54; J.L. Bolton, *The Medieval English Economy 1150–1500*, London 1980, ch. 7; J. Hatcher, 'The great slump of the mid-fifteenth century', in *Progress and Problems in medieval England*, ed. R.H. Britnell and J. Hatcher, Cambridge 1996, pp. 237–72.

recurrences of plague and other diseases,[6] caused the market for agricultural produce to contract. Land went out of cultivation, and tenants could not meet their liabilites. They fell behind with their rents, with disastrous results for those who depended on rent income.

In the first years of the fifteenth century the accounts of St George's barely balanced; and from 1406 there was a deficit, which in 1421–2 amounted to nearly £300.[7] In that year salvation seemed to be in sight, for John, duke of Bedford, Henry V's brother, gave the college a handsome gift of the spiritualities of the alien priory of Ogbourne, which he had acquired, with the temporalities, by grant of his father Henry IV.[8]

The Ogbourne grant should have solved the college's financial problems. But it did not. Partly this was because of the difficulty of identifying the smaller spiritualities, and, when they were identified, of securing payment of the forty-three pensions and portions of tithes which were due. But even without the pensions and portions there were nine rectories which between them were worth £150 a year. It might have been enough to keep the college solvent; but it was not enough because of the problem of arrears. This affected nearly all the properties of the college: most of its tenants were in arrears with their rents. Even in 1406 there were some arrears which had been accumulating over three decades.

But in 1422, with the grant of the Ogbourne spiritualities, the future looked bright. The dean and canons had already tried to put their affairs in order by hiring a consultant to reform their accounting system.[9] John Burton, who spent eight weeks at Windsor in 1416, had reviewed the college's financial records from 1406 when the deficits began. He made changes in the form of the accounts, designed to eliminate unnecessary duplication, and also carried out a strict examination of payments made out of the common funds. Particularly stringent was his disallowing certain benefits which had been shared during the previous ten years by the resident canons. They were required to make restitution of £162 7s 11¼d. This did not represent a great sum received in each of the ten years and when shared between nine or more canons (there were thirteen canons, including the dean, of whom nine or ten kept residence); but it was uncomfortably large when required to be repaid. The £162 7s 11¼d appeared as a debt still owing in the treasurer's accounts of the next two years, and then, with a change of accounting practice, was specifically mentioned no more. But in 1423, the year after the Ogbourne revenue was acquired, a decision was made to pay off this debt, by deducting each canon's share from the stipend due to him in the coming year. Unfortunately, the college's income did not improve enough that year to allow the canons to be paid at all. So the debt remained outstanding. But it was not forgotten. In 1442–3, a quarter of a century after the debt was incurred,

6. Hatcher, *Plague, Population* (as n. 5), 17–18, 57–8; J. Hatcher, 'Mortality in the fifteenth century: some new evidence', *Economic History Review*, 2nd ser, 39 (1986); J. Bolton, 'The World Upside Down: Plague as an agent of economic and social change', in *The Black Death in England*, ed. W.M. Ormrod and P. Lindley, Stamford 1996, pp. 17–78; M. Bailey, 'Demographic decline in late medieval England: some thoughts on recent research', *Econ. Hist. Rev.* 2nd ser, 49 (1996), pp. 1–19.

7. St George's Chapel Archives (hereafter cited as SGC) Treasurer's Account, XV.34.33 (1421–2) m. 3d. St George's Chapel has an unrivalled collection of its surviving medieval accounts, notably those of the treasurer and steward (see J.N. Dalton, *The Manuscripts of St George's Chapel, Windsor Castle*, Windsor 1957, sections xxxiii and xxxiv). These accounts are the main source for this paper. For reference, see the accounts of the years in question. Specific references are given here for selected details only.

8. *Calendar of Patent Rolls* (hereafter CPR) *1401–5*, p. 466; *1416–22*, p. 441.

9. Roberts, *Administration 1348–1416*, pp. 226–9.

Edmund Lacy, by then bishop of Exeter, who had been a canon of Windsor until 1417 when he became bishop of Hereford, was struck by conscience and repaid his share of it, which amounted to £14 1s 4d.[10] By this date, Lacy seems to have been the only survivor of the canons who were in post in 1416; but his was not the last instalment to be repaid. There were three others still outstanding, of canons by then deceased whose executors had still not been paid their stipends for 1423–4 from which their share of the debt would be deducted.

This means that, twenty-five years after Burton's reforms, the college was still in financial difficulties. The immediate results of Burton's efforts were equally ineffective. In 1418, the payment of the canons' prebends (40 shillings each) had to be postponed, and in 1422 half their prebends and all their quotidians: the daily shilling credited to canons present in chapel, which made up the bulk of their emoluments since it could amount to £18 5s 0d a year, when the prebend was only £2.[11] At Michaelmas 1422 the college's accumulated deficit had risen to nearly £300. It is true that £73 of the deficit was caused by expenditure incurred in easing the transfer of the Ogbourne properties (travel expenses, hospitality and gifts to officials, fees and gifts to lawyers); but this was considered money well spent, for the Ogbourne grant was the first addition to the college's revenues since the original endowment under Edward III.

At first, the high hopes for future solvency seemed to be justified. In 1422–3 the Ogbourne properties brought in £162 12s 2d, even though only fifteen of the forty-three pensions and portions of tithes had been secured. It took forty years to identify and claim the remaining pensions and portions, and with little benefit. Of the eight pensions, only one was paid with anything approaching regularity, one other was paid intermittently, and the rest rarely if ever. Of the thirty-five portions, fewer than half produced revenue and that intermittently. But the nine Ogbourne rectories were productive. The problem was that the revenues due from them, like those from the college's original endowment, soon fell into arrears. The decision to pay off the residentiaries' debt to the college out of their stipends for 1423–4 was made in good faith when the Chapter thought the lean years were over. The Chapter was mistaken. By 1426 arrears owed to the college from all its properties amounted to over £477, and of this nearly £100 was due from the Ogbourne rectories.

It was not that the college's tenants were wilful defaulters. They too were victims of the recession, and found themselves unable rather than unwilling to pay their rents. The Chapter apparently appreciated this, especially with regard to long-standing tenants. For instance, Weedon Bec, one of the Ogbourne rectories, was at farm for £12 a year to John Brother when St George's acquired it in 1422. Brother retained the lease each time it came up for renewal, which was every five years, since the college statutes forbade leases of longer duration. From time to time Brother fell into arrears, but paid them off in instalments when he could. Throughout the 1430s he was more than a whole year's rent in arrears. Nevertheless, in 1441 the Chapter granted him and William Brother (presumably his son) an unprecedented lease for the duration of both lives at the same

---

10. Treasurer's Account, SGC XV.34.41 (1442–3), dorse.
11. Roberts, *Administration 1348–1416*, p. 8.

rent.[12] Because of the statutory embargo on long leases, the rectory had to be restored to the college every five years; but the lease was to be renewed each time, as indeed it was until William Brother's death, despite his mounting arrears which stood at £32 (nearly three years' rent) when he died in 1476.

Some recent historians have suggested that competent estate management could surmount the problems of the fifteenth-century recession, and that it was incompetent officials who steered landlords into insolvency.[13] This view was held in the 1430s by the dean of Windsor, John Arundel, who complained repeatedly to the Lord Chancellor, the college's official Visitor, about the steward and the treasurer. The dean's problem was that these offices were not held by hired administrators who could be dismissed, but by canons of the college, who were elected annually by the Chapter and received an additional remuneration of £5 a year. Since prebends at Windsor were in the king's gift, many of the canons were king's clerks, with administrative experience in royal service. More than half of the canons took a turn in office, as precentor, treasurer or steward,[14] but some proved more capable or more public-spirited than others, and accepted re-election. There seems to have been a tacit understanding, until the last quarter of the fifteenth century, that no canon should be returned for the same office for more than four consecutive years.[15]

From 1422, when the Ogbourne properties increased the responsibilities of the steward and the treasurer, until 1434, when the dean complained for the second time, the two offices were held by at least ten different canons. But for seven of those thirteen years the office of steward was held by John Coryngham, an able man who became canon of Windsor in 1416. At Michaelmas that year he was elected treasurer of the college, and next year he also became Register of the Order of the Garter. Apparently he was considered to be the wisest of the canons, for the Garter Statutes required that the canon chosen as Register of the Order should be *le plus savant dudit college*.[16] He was treasurer again in 1420–1, and then began a four-year tenure of the office of steward. This meant that he was steward during the complex negotiations for the handover of the Ogbourne properties. He managed these so skilfully that the Chapter voted him a bonus payment of ten marks.[17]

The dean, John Arundel, had been in France with Henry V when he was appointed in January 1419. Since he remained with the king in Normandy, he was an absentee for two

---

12. SGC XV.7.8. This is probably the earliest lease granted by the college specifically for more than five years (Roberts, *Administration 1348–1416*, pp. 143–5): it ran for 35 years.

13. J.R. Lander, *Conflict and Stability in fifteenth-century England*, 3rd edn, London 1977, pp. 30–3; Bolton, *Medieval English Economy*, pp. 227–8. For arguments against this view, see Hatcher, *Plague, Population*, pp. 39–44; Hatcher, 'Great Slump', pp. 240–8, 257–61.

14. Roberts, *Administration 1348–1416*, pp. 50–1, 114–139.

15. The first canon to hold the same office for more than four years in succession was Thomas Passhe (canon 1449–89), who was elected treasurer for each year from 1476 to 1481. He had served as precentor, treasurer and steward many times between 1454 and 1476, and was steward in 1483–4 before being returned as treasurer again in 1485. He was still in office as treasurer at Michaelmas 1489 shortly before he died in November (Bill, SGC XV.57.28 (1488–9); Treasurer's Account, SGC XV.34.62 (1489–90), sheet 1).

16. L. Jefferson, 'MS Arundel and the Earliest Statutes of the Order of the Garter', *English Historical Review*, 109 (1994), p. 384. The office of Register of the Order, like that of Garter King of Arms, was established by the earliest Statutes of the Garter, issued in 1415. Coryngham seems to have been the first to hold the office, probably from 1417.

17. Treasurer's Account, SGC XV.34.32 (1422–3), m. 3.

years; but when he returned his close connexions with the king and the duke of Bedford proved invaluable in promoting the gift and the transfer of the Ogbourne spiritualities. He made five visits to the duke of Bedford in 1421, and also went back to France in April 1422 to ask Henry V for confirmation of the duke's grant and permission for the college to hold extra property in mortmain. His success in these negotiations earned him, too, a bonus from the Chapter: 100 marks, to be paid in ten annual instalments of ten marks each.[18]

Both the steward, Coryngham, and the dean were in high favour with the Chapter in 1422. Despite the fact that there was no money in hand to pay any quotidians nor the dean's stipend; and only half the canons' prebends and the college officers' fees could be paid, and many other dues could not be met, there was optimism about the financial future. The college's outstanding debts were to be paid off in instalments.[19] This policy meant that although long-standing debts slowly diminished, new ones were incurred, as current dues had to be left unpaid.

Coryngham and the dean had made many journeys on college business, severally and together; and it was Coryngham who was sent to meet the dean when he returned from Normandy in 1422. It would seem that Arundel was on good terms with the college officers at the time. This did not last. The policy of paying off old debts at the expense of current commitments began to irk the dean. In 1426, not only was his current stipend as dean unpaid, but £100 was owing to him for the two previous years. When he collected the rent from the tenant of a group of Ogbourne portions he felt justified in keeping it, in part payment of what was due to him.

Coryngham had given up the stewardship in 1425, but in 1427 he was elected treasurer, and next year he was returned as steward again for what became a three-year tenure of the office. It was during these years that the dean lost patience and began to complain to the Chancellor. It was not only that his pay was in arrears. As dean, he was entitled to an annual fee of 100 marks in addition to his prebend of 40s and the quotidians of one shilling a day when present in chapel or absent on college business. The college statutes allowed the dean sixty days' non-residence each year, but if he exceeded this concession he was fined (mulcted) half a mark a day, which was deducted from his fee as dean and paid to the resident canons. During his initial absence in Normandy in 1419–21, the residentiaries had claimed the whole of his 100 marks, forfeited as dean's mulcts. After his return, they continued to claim mulcts each time he exceeded the permitted sixty days' absence a year. There was disagreement about when his absence was on college business and when not. Arundel also complained about the elected officers of the college, whom he blamed for the college's problems: they did not keep him informed about the financial position, and exceeded the statutory limits of their office. Here he was on strong ground, since the college statutes could be invoked. By statute, the steward's duty was confined to receiving the income of the college: the money collected was to be delivered to the treasurer, who was responsible for expenditure.

The Chapter sent the steward, Coryngham, to talk the matter over with the Chancellor, Archbishop John Kemp, and with Humphrey, duke of Gloucester, then regent for the young Henry VI, before the Chancellor made his Visitation on 22 May 1430. Kemp ruled

18. *Ibid.*, m. 4.
19. Treasurer's Account, SGC XV.34.33 (1421–2), m. 3d.

that the financial matters in dispute were to be settled by auditors and arbitrators, and he postponed issuing his judgments on disciplinary matters until he had their report. In the meantime, it seems that he made clear that the statutes must be observed, for a Chapter Act enforcing and defining the statutory duties of the treasurer and the steward was issued in 1430:[20] it added that in future the steward was to retain no money in his own hands for more than three days after receiving it or returning from his collecting journeys, and to make no payments without express command or consent of the Chapter.

It is not surprising that the steward had been doing more than merely collecting revenue. Before the Ogbourne grant, he was dealing with only about twenty properties.[21] Suddenly, with the Ogbourne spiritualities, he was responsible for twice that number, and for discovering and laying claim to as many again. He had to find tenants, negotiate leases, arrange for the management of properties between leases, supervise repairs, travel widely to collect rents, hire escorts where travel was dangerous, procure writs against defaulters, consult lawyers and take action on their advice, and do any business of the college that could conveniently be done on his many journeys. It was impossible to do all this without spending money. Before 1422, his normal expenditure had been limited to necessary local outgoings on properties (wages, stock, labour, repairs), but he did on occasion while in London pay the fees of the college's legal advisers and the costs of litigation, and for the cloth and furs bought for the liveries of the college servants.[22] From 1422, his responsibilities expanded widely, but in quantity rather than quality. He had more properties to deal with, so had to spend more. And, since he had so many building repairs to pay for on the estates, it was convenient for him also to deal with repairs within the college's domain in Windsor Castle,[23] hitherto the sphere of the treasurer. Since he had so much legal business to deal with, it was convenient for him to pay the legal fees of the college attorneys and all legal costs.[24] And since he and his assistants did so much travelling, it was practical for him to pay all the travel expenses of those engaged on college business. Since he was so often in London, it was sensible for him to make any necessary purchases there on behalf of the college. Whole categories of expenditure previously in the treasurer's province gradually were transferred to the steward.

It was Coryngham, as steward, who arranged and paid for the accommodation of the Chancellor's commissaries when they came to arbitrate in 1431. He also paid for the feast given for Humphrey, duke of Gloucester visiting Windsor that year: and he paid the travel expenses of the dean when he went to see the executors of the duke of Exeter about a legacy to the college. It is clear that the Chapter was continuing to be liberal in giving consent to the steward's activities.

While the auditors and arbitrators were at work, the Chapter, well aware that the underlying problem was the inadequacy of the college revenues, drafted a petition to the king drawing attention to the impossibility of meeting commitments with current income. The draft adapted the text of an earlier petition, made in the lean years before the Ogbourne grant, which quoted income and expenditure in 1410–11. The amended text

---

20. S. Bond, *The Chapter Acts of the Dean and Canons of Windsor 1430–1672*, Windsor 1966, pp. 1–4. This is the earliest Act of the Windsor Chapter of which there is surviving record.

21. Roberts, *Administration 1348–1416*, pp. 14–46.

22. *Ibid.*, pp. 74–7.

23. E.g. in 1425–6: Steward's Account, SGC XV.48.8 dorse.

24. By 1429–30 the steward was accounting for all costs of litigation: SGC XV.48.9.

quoted revenues and commitments in 1429–30. By then, the original endowment of the college, worth nearly £562 in 1411, had fallen in value to £423 9s 0d. To this the Ogbourne properties were now added, worth nearly £207, making a total of £630 7s 8d. But the college's commitments that year amounted to £801 10s 5d: there was a shortfall of just over £171.[25] The Chapter also appealed to Humphrey, duke of Gloucester (regent while Henry VI was in France) not to appoint any more poor knights.[26]

The arbitrators suspended all payments to the dean while they were examining the accounts. They worked out how much was due to the residentiaries for dean's mulcts over the years. Then the Chancellor drew up his Injunctions, which were very far-reaching and were issued with the reinforcement of royal command on 22 February 1432.[27] The Chancellor deplored the discord which he had found in the college, and made some token rulings in the dean's favour: he should not have been mulcted when initially absent with Henry V in France, since his absence was not wilful and he was useful to the college while with the king; all members of the college owed obedience to the dean; and the officers were to keep him informed about the state of the college. But he went on to admonish the dean to refrain from injurious revilings, insults and reproaches; he ordered him to listen to the advice of his canons, and to take it, unless it went against his conscience. If he could not agree with the Chapter, or with the canons who audited the accounts, he was to refer the matter to the Chancellor. He was not to hinder the officers of the college, nor usurp their functions, nor take action without the consent of the Chapter. Moreover, if he planned to be absent from the college for more than eight days, he was to appoint a deputy with full power to act in his absence.

On the other hand, the Chancellor was also severe with the canons. The common seal was not to be affixed to documents without their being read in Chapter and agreed. No loans of more than 100 marks were to be contracted, and those only for the permanent benefit of the college, not for paying the quotidians of the canons when revenues were insufficient. When there was a shortfall of income, the canons must bear with not being paid.

The college officers received only mild rebukes. They were not to spend the common funds on matters which benefited only the residentiaries; and only minor repairs, costing up to twenty shillings, might be authorized by the steward alone. The steward's position was indeed strengthened by the Chancellor's ruling that if the dean or any canon collected payments due to the college, they were on no account to retain them (as Arundel had done in 1426) but to pay the money over to the steward within three days of their return.

General opprobrium was reserved for a lesser official, John Colkyrke, who combined writing documents, as clerk to the Chapter, with travel on college business. Most of his time was spent on journeys to the properties of the college, so that he was in effect an assistant to the steward.[28] He had been employed since 1422, when his predecessor

---

25. Draft Petition, SGC XV.34.27.
26. Steward's Account, SGC XV.48.11 (1431–2), m. 6. There had been no poor knights to be supported at Windsor from 16 July 1420, when William Lisle died, until the appointment of John Kiderowe in June 1428. In May 1430 a second poor knight, John Trebell, was appointed. There had not been more than one since at least 1415: hence the Chapter's alarm.
27. Archbishop Kemp's Injunctions, SGC XI.D.7; also in Arundel White Book, SGC IV.B.1, ff. 84–8.
28. The Chapter paid Colkyrke £4 a year, plus travel expenses at one shilling a day. He is variously described in the accounts as *deputatus collegii* or *deputatus senescalli* and in the Injunctions as *clericus capitularis*.

resigned, perhaps because of the massive increase in travel required after the Ogbourne grant: Colkyrke's first recorded assignment was to ride from Windsor to the college's rectory at Saltash in Cornwall, calling on the way at Cleeve Abbey in Somerset to ask for the Ogbourne pension the abbey owed.[29] Colkyrke seems to have been the whipping-boy whom all could agree to blame. The Chancellor's Injunctions describe him as incompetent, unpleasant, and more of a hindrance than a help to the college.[30] He was to be dismissed forthwith. He was replaced by Thomas Lerbek, as deputy steward. Lerbeck was apparently a success in his post. Two years later he was appointed to a position which fell vacant as one of the chantry chaplains of the college, with a stipend of £8 a year, twice his salary as deputy steward. He continued for another five years to travel on college business, for which he submitted bills of expenses like other members of the college who assisted the steward in this way.

Although concord between the dean and canons was agreed in 1432,[31] their dispute did not end here. In 1434, another Visitation by the Chancellor (now John Stafford, bishop of Bath and Wells) was necessary, since the dean was still complaining about the steward and the treasurer: they were spending far too much on repairs, and paying their own emoluments while keeping those of the rest of the college in arrears.[32]

Coryngham had given up the stewardship in 1431, and in 1434 was holding the less controversial office of precentor. But in 1435 he was voted into the office of treasurer, and next year was elected steward, being voted back again for a four-year stretch. It is clear that the Chapter had confidence in him. Something needed to be done, for the college's financial situation was steadily worsening. At Michaelmas 1436, when the Chancellor sent his own clerk to audit the accounts, the arrears of pay of members of the college alone amounted to £637 1s 10d; for instance the choristers' arrears of pay went back seven years.[33] The dean continued to complain to the Chancellor. In 1437 he accused the steward and treasurer of squandering the college revenues, of leasing its properties to insolvent persons, of indulging in litigation without consulting the dean and Chapter, and of making payments by favour instead of impartially.[34] Again payments to the dean were suspended while the complaints were investigated. At the end of that year (Michaelmas 1438) the dean's arrears of pay amounted to £238 1s 8d: the college's total deficit was over £803. Debts owed to the college by its tenants amounted to £1137 3s 5½d, of which £300 were deemed irrecoverable. The remaining £837, if it could have been collected, would have cleared the college's own debts.

On two occasions in the following year, the Chancellor sent for Coryngham for discussions. The previous Chancellor, Archbishop John Kemp, had in his Injunctions of

---

29. The rectory of Saltash was part of the original endowment of the college. The pension from Cleeve Abbey was one of the Ogbourne spiritualities: it was the yearly rent for the lease of the prebend of Cleeve in Wells Cathedral.

30. '. . . Johannes Colkirke clericus capitularis dicti Collegii secundum detecta omnium Canonicorum eiusdem ipsi Collegio reputetur valde inutilis onerosus et nocius.'

31. Bonds to ensure concord between the dean and canons were drawn up with advice from lawyers: Steward's Account, SGC XV.48.11 (1431–2), m. 6.

32. CPR 1429–36, p. 349.

33. Treasurer's Account 1435–6, in Winchester Cathedral Library, MS L38/4/12 (Box 62), m. 4d. The choristers were paid in full this year, but more than £30 was owed to them for the years 1429–33.

34. CPR 1436–41, p. 129.

1432 given some guidance regarding the practical problem of running the college with inadequate funds, ruling that when income was insufficient the canons should not expect to be paid. This did not go far enough: for, even without paying the dean and canons, the college's commitments could not be met; so that in 1438 all its members, vicars, chantry priests, poor knights, clerks, choristers, virger, bellringers, and the college officers, could only be paid in part, with the balance to be paid in the unforeseeable future.[35] Kemp's successor as Chancellor, Bishop John Stafford, tried in 1440 to deal with the underlying problem: how to bring in the theoretical but so far unrealizable assets of the college: the arrears of revenue owed by the tenants and farmers of its properties. If that money could be collected, the college's troubles would be over.

Bishop Stafford's solution was to command the college to create a new officer whose sole duty was to collect old arrears, which were defined as arrears incurred before Michaelmas 1439. Moreover, he decreed that the new Receiver of Old Arrears should be Master John Coryngham. The task facing the Receiver of Old Arrears was an unenviable one: presumably Bishop Stafford had talked Coryngham into accepting it when he had sent for him to discuss the college's problems. Coryngham knew only too well, from his long experience as steward, how time-consuming and unprofitable it was to pursue debtors at law. As steward in the 1420s and 1430s he had sued out writs against defaulters, which involved paying fees to attorneys, clerks, and custodians of government archives, and sending messengers to deliver the writs to sheriffs; and he knew that debtors who had been pursued through courts of law nevertheless did not pay up. A case in point was the pension of £5 a year payable by the vicar of Wantage in Berkshire:[36] one of the Ogbourne spiritualities. The Wantage pension first appears in the college accounts in 1425–6. The vicar, William Lee, new in the previous year, paid the part pension due from him for that year from the date of his admission to the living. For the next year he made a part payment but thereafter paid nothing at all. When in 1432 his arrears were over £29 legal proceedings were begun in the king's court at Westminster. The problem was to secure Lee's appearance in court. He ignored citations; and the sheriff of Berkshire was unable to compel him since he had no lay property in the county by which he could be distrained. Consequently, the college secured a writ of *venire facias* to the bishop of Salisbury, requiring him to cause Lee to appear at Westminster. When the bishop's command was ignored, the Wantage benefice was sequestrated. This prompted Lee to embark on a counter-suit. He appealed to the archbishop, claiming that, since Wantage was in the peculiar jurisdiction of the dean of Salisbury, and the bishop had no primary jurisdiction there, the sequestration was not legal. The college's response to this move was adroit. By securing a royal prohibition to the archbishop it was able to cause proceedings in the

35. Treasurer's Account, SGC XV.34.39 (1437–8), m. 3d. Members of the college below the rank of canon were always given priority in the matter of pay. Whenever possible they were paid in full, and always were paid in part, whereas the dean and canons were often not paid at all. In August 1435, in response to a petition from the dean and canons, the pope granted them licence to hold other benefices, with and without cure, while resident at Windsor. The petition had not, however, cited non-payment of stipends in support of the request, but that the canons of St George's were entitled to only £2 a year unless they resided at Windsor and qualified for quotidians (*Calendar of Papal Letters 1427–47*, p. 576).
36. Such pensions, payable by the incumbent to the patron of the living, were said to date from time immemorial. Probably they formed part of the original arrangements made when the advowsons were granted to a religious institution in the eleventh and twelfth centuries.

archbishop's court to be suspended until the suit concerning non-payment of the pension had been decided in the king's court.[37] The case dragged on, involving the college in expenses for writs and legal counsel, copies of documents, rewards to members of the duke of Bedford's household for producing proofs of title to the pension, travel to London and to Wantage, and hospitality and gifts to the sheriff and others who were involved. Meanwhile, although the pension remained unpaid, Lee's debt was frozen, presumably while his benefice was sequestrated. After judgment was given in the college's favour in 1436, his liability was still £29 18s 3d plus £5 for the current year, 1436–7. Of this he paid £12, and the college forgave him £12, leaving arrears of £10 18s 3d. Next year, since he paid nothing, the debt rose to £15 18s 3d. This seems to have been his parting shot, for he vacated the vicarage, leaving the debt outstanding.

This was the situation with regard to the Wantage pension when Coryngham became Receiver of Old Arrears in 1441; and this pension was only one of the fifty-eight different properties from which the college should have been drawing revenue. Moreover, Coryngham, although wise and experienced, was getting on in years. Even if he was only in his teens when he became a fellow of Merton College, Oxford, in 1374,[38] he must have been over eighty when he took on this new and daunting task. Both he and the steward had a valuable deputy in John Gardener, who had succeeded Lerbek in assisting the steward in 1439.[39] Such was Gardener's diligence in serving the college that he had received a bonus of 13s 4d in 1440, and also the cost of a replacement saddle and girths, and medical attention for his horse which was almost dead when he arrived in Ipswich on one of his journeys.[40]

Coryngham seems to have organized a methodical onslaught on Old Arrears. Writs were sued out, some for debts as small as 4 marks, and warrants for the arrest of defaulters; and not only were debtors pursued, and their heirs and executors if deceased, but also their guarantors. In this way, the Old Arrears owed by William Lee for the Wantage pension were eventually secured in 1444, paid off by his surety, John Stokes, gentleman, of Brimpton in Berkshire.[41] Some tenants were forgiven arrears because they had been overburdened by too-high rents.[42] Just over £100 of Old Arrears were recovered in 1441; but no amount of energy and determination could wring money out of the insolvent. A writ against Agnes, widow of Robert Andrew, who had farmed the rectories of Ogbourne St George and Ogbourne St Andrew from 1421 to 1436, and died in 1437 leaving arrears of £83 13s 9¼d, had no effect: the debt was till owing in 1453 and probably was never paid. The separate treatment of Old Arrears (from before Michaelmas 1439) was marked by a change in accounting methods: in local accounts,[43] submitted by tenants and bailiffs,

---

37. Record of proceedings, SGC XV.58.3.

38. A.B. Emden, *A Biographical Register of the University of Oxford to A.D. 1500*, i, Oxford 1957, p. 494.

39. Lerbek was given one of the benefices in the college's gift, the vicarage of Wantage, Berkshire, in 1439. John Gardener appears in the accounts in this year (1439–40) as *clericus collegii* and riding on college business. In 1442 he was officially appointed for life as assistant to the steward (Arundel White Book, SGC IV.B.1, ff. 96v–97).

40. Steward's Account, SGC XV.48.16, mm. 4, 7d.

41. Local Accounts, SGC XV.53.39, m. 8.

42. For example, Richard Sampson, former bailiff at Deddington rectory, Oxon, was forgiven part of his old arrears *quod . . . fuit superoneratus de dicta firma . . . tempore quo fuit ballivus Rectorie predicte* (Local Accounts, SGC XV.53.39 (1443–4), m. 8d).

43. A collection of local accounts, for individual properties, survives for 1443–4: SGC XV.53.39.

they were now given a separate entry, presumably so that progress in securing their payment could be monitored.

Coryngham died in November1444, and the office of Receiver of Old Arrears died with him. Instead, the canon who held office each year as steward resumed the responsibility. For another ten years Old Arrears continued to be noted separately from more recent arrears in both the steward's accounts and the accounts of each individual property. In 1450 outstanding *Arreragia Vetera* amounted to £398 6s 10½d,[44] which was an improvement on the £837 3s 5½d of Michaelmas 1438. But this was at the expense of *Arreragia Nova*, which had accumulated to £675 5s 3½d,[45] making a total of over £1073. The steward's actual receipts that year were £412 10s 9d, and the college's annual commitments (as given in the petition of 1431) were nearly twice that sum.

In 1449 and 1450 Convocation of Canterbury had voted to the king, for the war with France, grants from the clergy which included those normally exempt from clerical taxation. As might be expected, given their circumstances, the canons of Windsor petitioned the king to allow the college's long-standing privilege of exemption to stand, claiming that otherwise it would be *to theym greet Hurt, Hyndryng and Utter Undoing.* Probably they quoted the accounts of 1449–50, for the steward was responsible for the petition. Henry VI was convinced by it. He confirmed the college's exemption in 1451, on account of their *greet poverte.*[46]

By 1453 the steward was aware that the onslaught on Old Arrears had outlived its usefulness, and recommended that most of those still outstanding should be written off as irrecoverable.[47] The Chapter agreed. But, surprisingly, the auditors (who were the dean and two of the canons, elected each year by the Chapter) looked again at each case, and wrote off fewer than half of them. One which was not written off, despite the Chapter's having forgiven the debt, was £83 7s 5d owed by two former farmers of the rectory of Simonburn, one of whom had died without assets, and the other deemed too poor to be distrained.[48] Another debt not written off was the £83 13s 9¼d of the unfortunate Agnes for the arrears of the two Ogbournes owed by her late husband who had died sixteen years before.

Nevertheless, changes gradually appeared in the way Old Arrears were regarded. Instead of the operative date being Michaelmas 1439, Old Arrears came to be defined as those incurred longer ago, before Michaelmas 1435.[49] By the 1460s the steward was rarely mentioning Old Arrears specifically in his accounts. Although Old and New Arrears were still being pursued through legal process, increasingly debts were being compounded. For instance, in 1462 William Neele, the rector of Streatham, Surrey, was sued for four years' arrears of the pension he owed for his rectory, and seven years' arrears of the portion of tithes of Tooting Bec, for which he was also liable. After four years without progress, the matter was settled by negotiation. In 1466 the Chapter agreed to forgo what was owing

44. Steward's Account, SGC XV.48.22 (1449–50), m. 3d.
45. *Ibid.*, mm. 1d–2d.
46. Arundel White Book, SGC IV.B.1, f. 73–73v.
47. Steward's Account, SGC XV.48.23 (1452–3).
48. After a long period of producing no revenue at all, the rectory of Simonburn was leased to the vicar from 1432 to 1452 at £10 a year. From 1452 the rent was reduced to £6 13s 4d.
49. The new cut-off date for Old Arrears was adopted after 1453 and before 1459, when it first appears in Steward's Account, SGC XV.48.25.

for Tooting in return for payment of the arrears for Streatham. Neele paid the £8 he owed for Streatham (now for eight years at 20s a year), and in return the Chapter forgave him the £10 debt for Tooting (also at 20s a year).[50] Moreover, the college officers pursued the sensible policy of reducing the rents for most of the college properties:[51] otherwise tenants could not be found.

Arrears both old and new continued to encumber the steward's accounts. For each property there was a long and confusing paragraph, giving instalments paid of arrears both long-standing and recent, together with current payments, so that the name and liability of the current tenant are almost totally obscured. For one year, 1471–2, a new format was adopted. The steward relegated all £1292 19s 9¼d of arrears to an entry of one sentence, leaving the entries for the individual properties clear and straightforward. The steward was Thomas Passhe,[52] the John Coryngham of his day. He had already held office as precentor, steward, or treasurer on many occasions, and in 1471 he was not only steward but also president of the Chapter during a vacancy of the deanery. His account as steward for 1470–1 was drawn up in the established, confusing way: in sharp contrast was the clarity of the account for 1471–2. The improvement was not maintained by his successors as steward. By 1473–4 the receipts section of the account was almost as long and confused as before.

Fortunately, the days of deficits were nearly over, for Edward IV provided the only solution to the financial problems caused by the recession: a further endowment so massive that it could surmount the difficulties of reduced rents and long-standing arrears. In 1471 the first of Edward IV's grants, a pension of £20,[53] was mentioned in the steward's accounts though not yet received. In 1475 another five grants (three manors and two rectories) appeared in the accounts though not yet fully paid.[54] And thereafter, the grants and the steward's receipts increased by leaps and bounds. In 1476 the steward was able to hand over to the treasurer, after all necessary expenses had been paid, £525 10s 1d; in 1479 it was £704 6s 3¼d, and the treasurer also received £98 from St Anthony's Hospital in London, which had been granted to St George's by Edward IV, with effect from October 1476, to pay the stipends of the seven clerks and seven choristers he added to the foundation.[55] In 1483 the college's total income was £1091 2s 8½d, and since total commitments amounted to £841 12s 10¼d, there was nearly £250 in hand.[56] The salaries of members of the college, some of whom were owed in 1472 arrears dating back as far as ten years, were all paid up. A new, more splendid St George's Chapel was being built.

50. Steward's Accounts, SGC XV.48.27 (1461–2) mm. 8, 10d; XV.48.35 (1466–7), sheets 14, 13d. Neele had in fact paid nothing at all for Tooting in the 12 years he had been rector of Streatham, and no payment was ever again received for the Tooting portion: it had last been paid in the 1440s.
51. Steward's Account, SGC XV.48.35 (1466–7) mentions both the present and previous rents for many properties.
52. Passhe was sub-almoner to the king when appointed in December 1449 to a canonry of Windsor (CPR 1446–52, p. 302), which he held until his death in November 1489. He was elected to office as precentor, treasurer or steward at least eighteen times (see note 15).
53. The pension was payable by the Cistercian abbey of Rufford, Notts. In 1471 it was already three years in arrears. From 1473 payment was received for the current year.
54. The manors were Membury, Devon; Preston Bowyer and Monksilver, Somerset; and the rectories, Puriton and Woolavington, Somerset: Steward's Account, SGC XV.48.43, sheet 7d.
55. Treasurer's Account, SGC XV.34.55, sheet 1.
56. Treasurer's Account, SGC XV.34.59 (1482–3), sheet 8d.

Past arrears owed by tenants were not forgotten, but could be sustained. In the 1490s a memorandum of arrears had a total of just over £2690 outstanding, of which £1076 9s 5d was described as desperate and irrecoverable.[57] This was no longer a major problem, for by then St George's had ninety-three individual properties on its books, and even if twenty or so of them were in hopeless arrears, clear income was still over £1000 a year.[58] The establishment to be supported had been increased by the additional clerks and choristers, and existing vicars, clerks, and choristers had been granted an increase in pay, but the cost was minimal compared with the extra income, which left a balance in hand each year. The first three-quarters of the fifteenth century had been, for St George's, years of continual arrears. The last quarter of the century began for the college, as for the Chapel itself, the years of regeneration.

57. SGC XV.48.66 (Michaelmas 1497), sheet 5.
58. Treasurer's Account, in Oxford, Bodleian Library, MS Berkshire Roll 4 (1495–6). The treasurer received from the steward that year £868 3s 10¼d; with £200 from St Anthony's Hospital and other small receipts the total income was £1069 10s 6¼d. Expenditure that year was £929 11s 2d.

'Chevalerie . . . in som partie is worthi forto be comendid, and in some part to ben amendid': Chivalry and the Yorkist Kings

ANNE F. SUTTON AND LIVIA VISSER-FUCHS

We take our text from Gower, the *Confessio Amantis*, written about 1400, printed by Caxton early in the reign of Richard III, 2 September 1483.[1] It has often been said that chivalry is a difficult word. Not only did it have a wide variety of meanings in the later middle ages, all very alien to us, but it was also revived and 'remade' in the late eighteenth century when scholars began to study seriously the chivalric romances of the middle ages.[2] In the late fifteenth century the word meant — to follow the *Medieval English Dictionary* — a body of mounted warriors; the nobility, that is knights and their superiors, as a social class; knighthood as a ceremonially conferred social rank; any feat of arms or act of war; the moral code of chivalry or knighthood including the qualities of honour, valour, generosity and courtesy. The *OED*'s list of modern usage of the revived word is much the same because it survives essentially to describe medieval practices. But there is a tincture of unreal 'medievalism', notably when the moral or ideal dimension is meant. For example when a knight or man-at-arms is referred to, there is the 'extended and complimentary sense', says the *OED*, of 'gallant gentleman' (*OED* 1:f) with all its nineteenth-century accretions and associated social misconceptions. We have to beware that the word 'chivalry' does not blind us to the fact that one of its meanings is the waging of war, one man killing another, more often than not in order to seize something belonging to the other. It is as well to remember that Bouvet's 'Tree of Battles' was the 'Tree of Suffering' (*arbre de deuil*) drenched in blood and bristling with weapons while kings and knights fought among its branches.[3] It is occasionally advisable to use the dirtier, harsher words of 'war' and 'soldier' instead of 'chivalry' and 'knights'. We need to remember that killing and greed, vanity and showing-off, army camps and drilling, even administration and committees, were also part of 'chivalry'.

There were similar complexities and ambiguities of meaning and interpretation for medieval people. The juxtaposition of brutal reality and Christian and humane ideals inside and outside the literature consumed by the reading public of the fifteenth century

---

1. J. Gower, *The Complete Works*, ed. G.C. Macauley, 4 vols, Oxford 1899–1902, *Confessio Amantis*, bk 8, lines 3007–10.

2. *OED*: chivalry. For definitions of chivalry and the difficulties: M. Keen, 'Huizinga, Kilgour and the decline of chivalry', *Medievalia et Humanistica*, ns 8 (1977), pp. 1–20; S. Anglo, 'Introduction', *Chivalry in the Renaissance*, ed. S. Anglo, Woodbridge 1990, esp. pp. xi–xii; H. Chickering, 'Introduction', and J.D. Adams, 'Modern views of medieval chivalry, 1884–1984', in *The Study of Chivalry: Resources and Approaches*, ed. H. Chickering and T.H. Seiler, Kalamazoo, MI, 1988, pp. 1–89, *passim*.

3. *Oxford English Dictionary*, 'chivalry' in the sense of gallant gentleman, 1.f. G.W. Coopland, ed., *The Tree of Battles of Honoré Bonet . . .*, Liverpool 1949, p. 81; ill. e.g. M. Keen, *Chivalry*, New Haven and London 1984, fig. 48.

can be disconcerting. The gorgeous display of knights in armour, fine war-horses, and all the magnificent works of art produced by craftsmen, made an entertainment out of war, glorified it, and drew young men into the game of killing for profit and glory, which someone somehow always managed to call a 'just' war. Authors might admire a recently dead or living figure using terms borrowed from a classical text, hagiography or romance with no feeling of anachronism or inappropriateness. In the midst of that most lavish and carefully chivalric of displays, the Smithfield tournament between Anthony, the Great Bastard of Burgundy, and Anthony Woodville, Earl Rivers, Rivers himself — a man frequently hailed by historians since Horace Walpole as a paragon of chivalry — was suspected of dishonesty in his stratagems to win. Literate people in the middle ages were as aware of the contradictions between ideals and reality as their twentieth-century equivalents, and sometimes the political circumstances encouraged the expression of arguments in favour of non-aggression, for example in the summer of 1475 when the English-Burgundian invasion of France petered out, or in September 1484, when the Scots ambassador Archbishop Whitelaw addressed Richard III.

The twentieth-century arguments of historians over the supposed decline of chivalry, its golden age, its 'waning' and its Indian summer, are all well known, and we shall assume that there is now a general acceptance that there never was a golden age when men behaved according to universally recognised ideals.[4] We will take Gower's words as summing up the truth of the matter: chivalry always had some good points, but it was always in need of improvement. Taking the arguments of modern commentators as settled, does not clear the field, however: historians are still up against the gloss of chivalry with which medieval chroniclers and theorists usually clothed the realities of politics and war in their own time. They wanted to render the realities more palatable and they wanted to find heroes. It was natural for a London poet celebrating the Barnet campaign to compare Richard of Gloucester to Hector of Troy and for a classical scholar like Abbot John Whethamstede to call Edward IV 'a second Achilles'. A dozen years later William Whitelaw, the Scots diplomat, compared King Richard to Tydeus, the Greek hero. We must look behind these words, if we can, in order to see 'chivalry' as it really was in the reigns of Edward IV and Richard III.

Of the five meanings given to the word 'chevalerie' by the *MED* which might be studied in relation to the Yorkist kings we will not consider the 'body of mounted warriors', nor these kings' opinions of 'knights and nobility as a social class'. There is plenty of evidence that 'chivalry' was equated with 'nobility', and as we have argued elsewhere, the Yorkist kings and their contemporaries no doubt accepted the fact and importance of nobility by blood without argument, although they would also not have denied the need for the nobly born to be 'virtuous'.[5]

We would like to know whether either of these kings had a deep belief in 'chivalry' at its most idealistic, or were they both plain, practical men? How were they taught the ideals, what manuals and treatises were they expected to know and which did they own?

---

4. J. Huizinga, *Herfsttij der Middeleeuwen*, Haarlem 1919, esp. chs 6 and 7; L.R. Kilgour, *The Decline of Chivalry*, Cambridge, Mass., 1937, *passim*; Keen, *Chivalry, passim*; M. Vale, *War and Chivalry*, London 1981, *passim*; and see n. 1.

5. A.F. Sutton and L. Visser-Fuchs, *Richard III's Books. Ideals and Reality in the Life and Library of a Medieval Prince*, Stroud 1997, ch. 6.

What did they do about the crusading ideal? What did their contemporaries think about their 'chivalry'? We need to look at their attitude to knighthood as a 'ceremonially conferred rank', as embodied, for example, in the Order of the Garter, and try to perceive the ideals and the policy behind their use of this Order. Did they, and their subjects, find any contemporary heroes to admire, and how were such men rewarded by these kings? Lastly, and most of all, we want to find out what value was placed on the plain sister of chivalry, *peace*, and who valued her. In short, we must look at what Edward and Richard did, what they said and what they (could have) read. Inevitably the various areas of our inquiry, like the complex meanings of the word 'chivalry', run into each other and overlap, and many of these questions cannot be given more than partial answers.

'Chivalric' behaviour, it was believed, could be taught, and the educated were under an obligation to behave according to what they had been taught. In the Burgundian *Débat d'honneur entre trois chevalereux princes*, a fictional debate between Alexander the Great, Hannibal and Scipio Africanus about which of them was the most virtuous and the best soldier and commander, Hannibal blamed Alexander for his lascivious life and said that such behaviour might have been excused in himself or someone else who had little education, but Alexander who had read Homer and who had been taught 'day and night' by Aristotle himself should have known better.[6]

Vegetius, Giles of Rome, Ramon Lull, Christine de Pisan, the de Lannoy brothers, Sir John Fortescue, all wrote down their advice and knew that 'virtue' and proper conduct, and chivalric virtue and conduct in particular, could be taught. The queen in the romance of *Parthonope of Blois* and the lady in *Petit Jehan de Saintré* spend much time coaching their young lover or protégé in the rules of love and chivalry. If you did not have such a magical or mysterious lady to teach you, you turned to the many books available. The evidence suggests that the two Yorkist kings had completely different attitudes to books, chivalric, didactic, or otherwise. While in Richard's case we have been able to conclude that he had a genuine interest in learning and that his choice of books was personal and deliberate, Edward gives the impression of rarely having acquired a book for pleasure. It is dangerous to assume that ownership of a book indicates that it was read, but Richard is at least known to have signed most of his books himself, and it is significant that almost all his surviving books were second-hand acquisitions. Of Edward's manuscripts only two have personal *ex libris*,[7] all the others are either large illuminated books showing little sign of individual selection, or they are dedications.[8]

Among Edward's 'chivalric' manuscripts there were books of ancient and near contemporary history that often were part of the library of any nobleman able to read French at the time: Josephus' *Jewish Wars*, Caesar's life and work in one version or another, the *Romuleon*, William of Tyre's *History of the Crusades*, and the chronicles of

---

6. Scipio was the victor because he fought to defend his country and did not shed blood for his own honour. The 'Debate' was adapted from an edited Latin version of Lucian's dialogue (2nd century AD) by Jean Miélot for Philip the Good in 1449. A. Vanderjagt, *Qui sa vertu anoblist*, Groningen 1981, pp. 151–80, esp. 169.

7. London, British Library, Royal MS 12 E. xv, a composite MS containing a version of the *Secreta secretorum* and medical treatises, all in Latin, owned by Edward when earl of March, and BL Harl. MS 3352, a collection of legal formulas in Latin, owned by Edward when duke of York.

8. See the present authors, 'Choosing a book in late fifteenth-century England and Burgundy', *England and the Low Countries in the Late Middle Ages*, ed. C. Barron and N. Saul, Stroud 1995, pp. 84–6.

Froissart, as well as a few works of contemporary history, some of them dedicated anew to Edward. Richard also had chronicles covering the histories of Troy, England and France almost up to his own time, as well as a few chivalric romances, *Ipomedon*, *Tristan*, Chaucer's *Knight's Tale* and Lydgate's *Siege of Thebes*. The history books and the chivalric romances they owned taught the examples of the real and fictional past, and between them the Yorkist kings also owned a number of the standard didactic texts on the subject of 'chivalry' and 'nobility', including so-called 'mirrors for princes'. Such 'mirrors' included Vegetius' *De re militari* and Giles of Rome's *De regimine principum* which relied heavily on Vegetius, and Christine de Pisan's *Fayttes of Armes* which also relied on Vegetius and was very much in favour of educating knights. Richard owned a Vegetius in English and a *De regimine* in Latin; Edward had an unidentified text called the 'Gouvernement of Kinges and Princes', probably a *De regimine* in French.[9] He also had a collection which included the *Chemin de vaillance* or *Songe Doré* (the *Road to Courage* or the *Golden Dream*, a manual for knights written in the 1420s by an aged Norman nobleman, Jean de Courcy[10]), the *Epistre d'Othea*, by Christine de Pisan (which is no longer automatically regarded as a chivalric courtesy book by modern commentators, but probably was just that to readers in Edward IV's time[11]), and the *Bréviaire des nobles*, by Alain Chartier. Such literary works tended to be nostalgic about the former glory of the order of knighthood and to elaborate on the present failings of knights, reminding them of their duties. Of particular interest are Ramon Lull's *Order of Chivalry*, of which Edward had a French text, and of which the English translation was dedicated to Richard by William Caxton, and William Worcester's *Boke of Noblesse*, dedicated to Henry VI, Edward and Richard in turn.

Lull's work was by far the greater work of the two, it is one of the key texts which set out the ideals of chivalry. Ramon Lull was the son of a wealthy Majorcan knight and served in his youth at the court of James II of Aragon until, in 1266, he had a vision of Christ and began his life's task of converting the Saracens of North Africa. He was killed there at the age of eighty in 1313. Although he led some missions himself his main activity was writing and teaching missionaries. The *Order of Chivalry* was inspired, therefore, by a strong missionary zeal which sought to engage all classes in a crusade against paganism. He begged the princes of his day to open schools for potential knights and he set out an uncompromising list of the duties of the knight: to defend the Christian faith and protect the church; to defend his lord; and to maintain justice. A knight must exercise his soul in justice, wisdom, charity, loyalty, truthfulness, humility, strength, hope, swiftness, and 'al

---

9. 'Choosing', p. 85.

10. Jean de Courcy, Lord of Bourg-Achard, see e.g. A. Piaget, '*Le Chemin de Vaillance* de Jean de Courcy', *Romania*, 27 (1898), pp. 582–91, for a summary of the story, and B.D. Dubuc, '"Le Chemin de Vaillance": mise en point sur la date de composition et la vie de l'auteur', in *Medieval Codicology, Iconography, Literature and Translation. Studies for Keith Val Sinclair*, ed. P.R. Monks and D.D.R. Owen, Leiden, New York and Cologne 1994, pp. 276–83. The text only survives in BL Royal MS 14 E. ii, where it is followed by the *Epistre Othea*, the *Bréviaire des Nobles* of Alain Chartier, the *Des ix malheureux et ix malheureuses*, and Ramon Lull's *Ordre de Chevalerie*.

11. For the latest interpretation see S.L.Hindman, *Christine de Pizan's 'Epistre Othéa'. Painting and Politics at the Court of Charles VI*, Toronto 1986.

other vertues'.[12] Few readers could be unaffected by Lull's text. In 1484, having just translated this advocation of the professional training of young men for knighthood by the kings of Europe, William Caxton, the merchant, ardently took up the theme. He wanted Richard III to hold public tournaments and jousts as encouragement to the youth of England to improve their fighting skills, exactly as Lull had advised. In imitation of Lull, Caxton also asserted that the text of the book had been given him by a squire to be published, and he hoped that King Richard would see to it that every potential knight in the country obtained a copy; Lull's scenario had an aged knight entrust the text to a young and untutored squire, who was on his way to court to be knighted and who was to make the book known to his king and his court.

William Worcester's book takes up a similar tutorial role towards Henry VI, Edward IV and Richard III — or indeed any king of England who would undertake the reconquest of France. In the text of the *Boke of Noblesse*, presented to Edward before he embarked on his French expedition, he begs that the youth of the nobility and gentry while 'they are of green age, be exercised in . . . usage of a school of arms' so that they may be ready to support the king in defending the realm — the truly legitimate aim of war. This he contends was the practice in the time of Edward III,

whereby their honour spread and increased in renown in all lands . . . But now of late, more the pity, many who are descended from noble blood and are born to arms . . . set themselves . . . to learn the practice of law or customs of land, or of civil matter, and so waste greatly their time in such needless business as to hold courts, to keep and bear out a proud countenance at the holding of sessions and shires, also there to embrace and rule among your poor and simple commons of bestial countenance that wish to live at rest. And he who can be a ruler and put himself forward in such matter is, as the world goes now, more esteemed . . . than he who has spent 30 or 40 years of his days in great jeopardy in your ancestors' conquests and wars . . . And such singular practice ought not to be accustomed and occupied unduly with such men that come of noble birth, unless he be the younger brother, having not the livelihood wherein to live honestly.[13]

Worcester's message is suited to an English audience but it was common to all tutors of chivalry. Christine de Pisan put it more generally in 1408: in old times men 'made not theyr children to be norisshed in the kyngis & pryncees courtes for to lerne pryde, lechery nor to were wanton clothing'.[14]

The humble scribe and secretary, William Worcester, adopted the views of his aristocratic betters without question when he enthusiastically advocated the conquest of France. His knowledge of the horrors of the French war did not apparently encourage him to think twice about promoting its renewal — it was Edward IV's laziness, Charles the Bold's different priorities and Louis XI's cleverness which prevented that. As soon as Caxton the merchant, who had traded through the troubled years of the 1450s, 1460–1, 1470–1, let alone the wars of Charles the Bold, emerged from the euphoria induced by reading Lull's *Order of Chivalry*, no doubt he would have expressed himself very differently

12. Present authors, 'Richard III's books: XI. Ramon Lull's *Order of Chivalry*, translated by William Caxton', *The Ricardian*, 9 (1991–3), pp. 110–29, esp. 119–22; Ramon Lull, *The Book of the Ordre of Chyvalrye. Translated and printed by William Caxton*, ed. A.T.P. Byles, EETS, os 168 (1926, repr. 1971), esp. chs 2 and 3; quotation p. 31.

13. William Worcester, *The Boke of Noblesse*, ed. J.G. Nichols, Roxburghe Club 1860, pp. 77–8; spelling modernised.

14. C. de Pisan, *The Book of the Fayttes of Armes and of Chyvalrye*, trans. W. Caxton, ed. A.T.P. Byles, EETS, os 189 (1932), p. 29.

on the subject of soldiers and war. Lull himself knew very well that there were bad knights and recommended that they be killed by their knightly peers. Above all and in spite of their occasional reservations about war all these fifteenth-century commentators, French, English and Burgundian suffered from the illusion, apparently a complete illusion, that there was once a golden age when things were different, were better done, and that with effort things could be improved. Presumably the Yorkist kings would have agreed.

Though this rule was not always followed, the statutes of the Order of the Golden Fleece laid down that the life and deeds of all members, including the duke himself, the sovereign of the Order, should be the subject of enquiry by their brother knights at each chapter. Edward IV was elected at the chapter of 1468; in May 1473 — two years after his successful return from exile in the Low Countries — at Charles the Bold's second chapter of the Order, the king of England's actions, too, were reviewed. During his exile Edward must have met many of the knights of the Golden Fleece personally and they probably knew him better than would have been possible under ordinary circumstances. In their formal criticism they said that if only he had better gauged the situation which led to his exile, he would never have found himself in such danger; but, it was added, after his return he made everything right, *vertueusement* by great *vaillance*. His foreign brother knights then struck a very personal note, saying that he seemed to have so little confidence in himself that if those who were near to him and whom he trusted did not praise his plans and his undertakings, he did not have the courage to execute them, and he did nothing if not supported by his people. This was not caused, however, by anything bad in his character or by any evil in him, and one did not know whether it was caused by his character or his upbringing (*nature* or *nourriture*) and therefore he could not be blamed for it. Finally he was highly praised for his very great *vaillance et prouesse*, his *bon sens* and many other unspecified virtues, and it was emphasised that he meant well (*veult bien*) and was a good friend.[15]

If the first point of criticism was not in fact a veiled compliment to Duke Charles, who — it has been claimed — had warned Edward about the dangers of his situation in 1470,[16] the king of England was being blamed for a lack of foresight — a serious failure in any soldier or commander — and perhaps for being too casual in his approach to his duties as a prince. The second point, that he always needed the encouragement of his entourage, which may be in its turn a complimentary reference to Charles's encouragement and support of Edward, appears to confirm that his contemporaries had the same impression of

---

15. Vienna, Österreichisches Staatsarchiv. Haus-, Hof- und Staatsarchiv, Archiv des Ordens vom Goldenen Vlies, Register Nr. 3 (1473), f. 24v: *Apres sest faicte lenqueste sur la personne de treshault et tresexcellent prince **le roy Eduart, Roy dAngleterre etc**. En laquelle enqueste a este touchie et dit que se le roy Edouart pieca devant son departement dAngleterre eust bien volu entendre son cas, comme besoing estoit, il neust pas souffert le danger ou quel il sestoit trouve depuis, mais apres son retour il lavoit tout repare, vertueusement et par grant vaillance. Combien que de soy il semble avoir telle diffidence que se ceulx qui sont dalez lui et dont quil se fie ne lui louent et prisent son concept ou emprise il ne la ouseroit faire ne excuter, et ne fais comme riens sil nest advoue de ses gens. Ce que ne lui vient pas de maise condicion ou par malice, ne scet lon se cest ou de nature ou de sa nourriture, parquoy on ne le lui impute a blamer. Mais en conclusion a este ledit roy Edouart moult grandement loue et recommande par mesdisseigneurs de lordre de tresgrant vaillance et prouesse, de bon sens et dautres vertus pluseurs et mesmement a este dit quil veult bien et est bon amy.* (Capitals and punctuation modernised). We are grateful to Dr René Stuip for checking the exact meaning of the comments.

16. Contemporary historians have said and modern commentators have repeated that Edward was blind to the dangers and Charles frequently warned him. See C.D. Ross, *Edward IV*, London 1974, p. 148, and references given there.

his laziness and unwillingness to bestir himself which modern commentators have also noticed. Whether they correctly interpreted the cause of it is another matter.

The last comments of his brother knights concerned martial and 'chivalric' matters; Edward's knightly *vertue* (courage), *vaillance* and *prouesse* could in any case hardly be denied after the two major victories that put him back on the throne and made him again a useful and powerful ally to the duke of Burgundy. The two characteristics noted by these contemporaries, a passive attitude and military competence, or at least good fortune in war, seem to sum up Edward's personality and achievements.[17] Only a few years after he had come to the throne, by personally winning the battles of Mortimer's Cross and Towton, the opinion of Richard Neville, earl of Warwick, concerning Edward appears to echo this mixed reputation in its lack of enthusiasm for the king playing an active, military role. Writing from Newcastle in October 1463 Warwick, perhaps making play with Edward's motto, admitted that it gave him and all the king's subjects 'confort and reioysing' to hear that Edward was planning to come north to subdue Scotland and that he was sure the king would be successful, but he implied that Edward's coming would only be of use if he came well provided with victuals, 'grete guns' and other artillery, powder, stones, 'grete quantitie of bowes, arows, stringes, speres and all othre habilimentes of werre' and above all, troops; if he did not bring all those it was politely suggested that he stay away.[18] Earlier in the same year William, Lord Hastings had written to the Burgundian Jean de Lannoy that Warwick had the situation in the north well in hand, while the king was 'at his sport and entertainment of the hunt without any fear for his very honourable person or any of his subjects'.[19] Was Hastings expressing criticism of Edward, or admiration for his *sang froid*, or was he merely telling de Lannoy that the king knew there was *no* danger, or he would be doing something himself?[20] A poem celebrating Edward's life after his death in April 1483 was to write admiringly that the king made Scotland yield and gained Berwick, while he was 'rydyng a-hunting himself to sport and play'.[21]

Edward knew very well that his most basic, primal duties as king involved fighting personally to protect his realm and his subjects. They were the same as his duties as a knight: protect the weak and those dependent on him and preserve peace. He referred to these duties frequently: on 21 December 1461 he prorogued parliament and thanked the members for their service to him '. . . and yf Y had eny better good to reward you with all then my body ye shuld have it, the which shall alwey be redy for youre defence, never sparyng nor lettyng for noo jeopardie . . .'. In June 1468, when he declared to parliament that he intended to live of his own and only to ask for financial assistance in time of danger, and '. . . Y shall be to you as good and gracious kyng, and reigne as rightwissely uppon you

---

17. On Edward IV's reputation as a soldier and general: J.R. Lander, 'The Hundred Years War and Edward IV's 1475 campaign in France', in *Tudor Men and Institutions*, ed. A.J. Slavin, Baton Rouge, Louisiana, 1972, pp. 70–100; Ross, *Edward IV*, pp. 176–7; C.A.J. Armstrong, 'Politics and the battle of St Albans', repr. in the same, *England, France and Burgundy in the Fifteenth Century*, London 1983, pp. 1–72, esp. 25; A. Goodman, *The Wars of the Roses*, London 1981, pp. 84–5; M.K. Jones, 'Richard III as a soldier', in *Richard III. A Medieval Kingship*, ed. J. Gillingham, London 1993, pp. 93–112, esp. 94–5.

18. M. Kekewich *et al.*, eds, *The Politics of Fifteenth-Century England. John Vale's Book*, Stroud 1995, pp. 171–2.

19. Printed C. Scofield, *The Life and Reign of King Edward the Fourth*, 2 vols, London 1924, ii, pp. 461–2.

20. Compare the opinion of Michael Jones on this remark in his 'Richard III as a soldier', p. 95.

21. Manchester, John Rylands University Library, MS Eng. 113, f. 3.

as ever did eny of my progenitours upon commons of this my reame in dayes past, and shall also in tyme of nede applie my persone for the wele and defence of you and of this my reame, not sparing my body nor lyfe for eny jeoparde that mought happen to the same'.[22] In the speech thought to have been given to the parliament of 1474 by the chancellor, Robert Stillington,[23] he defended the planned campaign in France, and referred to these earlier remarks. He also claimed again that the king was prepared for 'dangerous fetes of werre' and with 'his knightly courage' would 'not spare to employe his owne person', and asked his audience to 'considre the knyghtly courage, grete proesse, and disposicion of our Soverain Lord the Kyng, whoos good Grace will eschewe payne, perell, ne jeopardie'.[24] When asking for benevolences Edward used the same language: 'we shulde put forthe our owne personne to perill and iupardie'.[25] He may have repeated himself — or his counsellors and clerks did — but he was saying the right things, which were expected of him and understood. The same poem which expressed so much admiration of Edward after his death, reminded his subjects that the king had always been 'in every field full ready for our right; it was no need to pray him for to fight'.[26]

The ultimate aim of all this waging of wars and the king putting himself at risk was peace, peace in England itself: 'comforte and wele of alle . . . trewe subgiettes . . . and perfite tranquilite';[27] 'thonour and weele of thayme and all the remanent of our sugettes . . . and the peax and tranquilite of the same'.[28] It was the king's duty to preserve this peace: 'he knoweth hym silf to be moost bounde of all the creatures of the world to bethynk, studie, and fynde the most convenable moyens and weyes that myght sette his people in ease, welth, and prosperite', tranquillity and assured peace being the only means by which a country could prosper.[29] Of all the ways by which peace and prosperity might be found, when everything else had been tried, there was none 'so honourable, so necessarie, nor so expedient' as external war. Just as the Roman Scipio defeated Hannibal by crossing the sea and striking at Carthage so Edward would take the war abroad and defend his country by victories in France.[30]

From the same period as the Warwick and Hastings letters quoted earlier a letter from Edward himself survives which repeats some of his official attitude to peace and mentions chivalry. To James III of Scotland, who was harbouring the deposed Henry VI and his wife and son in late 1462, he wrote of the 'tendirnesse or good highe zele to that perfeccion of peax that stablissith the salvacion, encrease and conservacion of the numbre of Cristen feithe to the blessid entent that recheth to the confusion and repression of thennemyes therof' and 'the good and tendir zele that God knowith we have to the said peax'. This

---

22. S.B. Chrimes and A.L. Brown, eds, *Select Documents of English Constitutional History, 1307–1485*, London 1961, pp. 325–6, 329.

23. Lander, 'Hundred Years War', pp. 70–100, esp. 82, n. 38.

24. *Literae Cantuarienses*, ed. J.B. Sheppard, Rolls Series, 3 vols, London 1887–89, iii, pp. 278, 284–5.

25. *John Vale's Book*, p. 145.

26. John Rylands University Library, MS Eng. 113, f. 3v.

27. Warwick in his letter to Edward, describing the purpose of an invasion of Scotland, *John Vale's Book*, pp. 171–2.

28. *John Vale's Book*, p. 145.

29. *Lit. Cant.*, pp. 274–5.

30. *Lit. Cant.*, pp. 278–9. In the contemporary French redaction of one of Lucian's dialogues, the popular *Débat d'honneur*, Scipio was judged the best knight, above Hannibal and Alexander, both expansionist conquerors; Scipio fought to defend his own country. Vanderjagt, *Qui sa vertu anoblist*, ch. 2.

peace, Edward said, was endangered by James's actions which were 'ageinste the natur of verray nobley' — that is chivalry — but if he handed over Henry VI 'peax shulde growe and continue . . . as acordith with Goddis pleasur and causith every reaulme joye in parfite peax and to floure in honoure, nobley and prosperite'. Edward's enemies were also acting 'agenste the ordir and custume of reason and knighthod in auncion daies shewed and grounded in Cristen princes professid and assured in the vertueux and honorable order of verray nobley'.[31]

In the chivalric manuals and mirrors for princes that Edward and Richard owned this basic idea that a king or a knight should defend the weak and the humble, protect their land and their people and establish peace can be found again and again. In the *Breviary of Noblemen* the first virtue of the nobility is 'loyalty', which ensures that a knight 'serves his king and protects his dependents'.[32] According to the *Order of Chivalry* (Caxton's translation)[33] it is the duty of a knight to uphold justice, by force if necessary, and peace will follow: 'in the tyme in whiche chyvalry beganne was thyoffyce of chyvalrye to pacyfye and accorde the peple by force of armes'.[34] In Giles of Rome's *De regimine principum* there is no doubt about the need for military competence. In the introduction to his third book, which deals with a king's role in time of war and leans heavily on Vegetius' *De re militari* in its practical advice, Giles states that military science is a separate section of what he calls 'prudence' and very necessary to a king, for the main purpose of waging war is 'fighting for justice and removing whatever endangers the common good'.[35] At the very end of his work, when he has stopped quoting Vegetius, he writes:

It remains to explain why war is waged. You must know that according to the philosopher [Aristotle] we make war not for its own sake but to have peace. It does happen that wars are fought because people are evil, and for profit, or to satisfy some other form of anger or greed, but just wars are meant to make peace and quiet for the people, and are waged for the sake of the common good. Wars should have the same effect on society as potions and bloodletting have on the human body: . . . the superfluity of bad humours which disturbs its health should be removed. . . . When kings and princes are intent on the common good and the peace of their people they themselves will earn that eternal peace in which there is perfect rest.[36]

Other books in Edward's library, such as the *Chemin de Vaillance* and the *Epistre d'Othea*, were less specific on the duties of a knight or prince, but they taught by means of stories, examples and allegory. Detailed classical examples of every possible virtue, including those necessary to princes and commanders, were to be found in Valerius Maximus' *Memorable Deeds and Sayings*, of which two copies in French translation survive among the royal manuscripts, one containing the arms of Edward and his sons.[37] It had many stories, for

31. *John Vale's Book*, pp. 144–5.

32. J.C. Laidlaw, ed., *The Poetical Works of Alain Chartier*, Cambridge 1974, pp. 396–7. For the meaning of 'loyalty' see also below.

33. Lull, *Ordre*, ed. Byles, pp. 39, 87–8.

34. *Ordre*, pp. 45–6.

35. Giles of Rome (Aegidius Romanus, Aegidius de Colonna), *De Regimine Principum Libri III*, Rome 1556 (repr. in facsimile Frankfurt 1968), bk 3, pt 3, ch. 1.

36. *De regimine*, pt 3, bk 3, ch. 23.

37. BL Royal MS 18 E. iii, iv; also Royal 17 F. iv.

example, about Scipio Africanus, to whom Edward was compared for his planning of outward war to save England.[38]

Among the king's counsellors, who wrote or inspired his speeches, there were many well-read men who knew how to use texts like Valerius Maximus' *Memorable Deeds and Sayings* and Giles of Rome's *De regimine principum*. Much is known about the learning and libraries of men such as Thomas Rotherham, John Alcock, James Goldwell, Robert Stillington, John Russell and George Neville.[39] We know that Richard Neville, earl of Warwick, of whose library nothing else survives, owned one of the contemporary Burgundian didactic works on the duties of knights, the *Enseignement de la vraie noblesse*.[40]

Straightforward and unequivocal contemporary comments on Edward's character, knightly virtues or his talents as a soldier are rare. The criticism from his brother knights of the Golden Fleece is unique. John Whethamstede, abbot of St Albans, whose writing was steeped in classical imagery, called the young Edward: 'a new Hector and a second Achilles' and hoped that he would reign 'more happily than Augustus and better than Octavianus',[41] but these were merely standard superlatives for a Latin scholar. Jean de Wavrin, the Burgundian chronicler, in his history of England covered the first ten years of Edward's reign in detail,[42] but nowhere does he voice an opinion of the king's character and achievements — he does comment on Warwick's and Henry VI's. Wavrin's report of Edward's accession and first battles reads like a chivalric romance and the young king behaves exactly as he should: mourning his father and his friends, haranguing his troops before battle, dismounting to fight on foot with his men,[43] expressing his gratitude to Warwick and other supporters before his splendid coronation, *and* looking the part, 'twenty-two years old, fair and a pleasure to behold, his whole body well proportioned, as good as anyone you could find in the whole of England'.[44] The general impression of Edward created by Wavrin is on the one hand that he was young and trusting and often asked and followed advice, on the other that he could at times be very energetic and successful. This apparent dichotomy, however, does not have any significance in Wavrin, as it is caused by this author's slavish use of a wide range of very different sources including rumours as well as factual reports and propagandist newsletters.

Better known is the image of Edward created by Philippe de Comines, the French historian, an expert at subtle calumny, whose apparent 'modernity' has made his work very influential until the present day. He painted a picture of a man generally successful, but always by means of others or circumstance, and all the virtues that Comines admits Edward had are counteracted by his vices: laziness, carelessness, credulity — Warwick

---

38. The same Scipio is mentioned briefly in William Worcester's *Boke of Noblesse*, in his *Tulle: Of Olde Age*, and in his *Declamacion of Noblesse* (printed in R.J. Mitchell, *John Tiptoft*, London 1938, p. 222), when the aristocratic Publius Cornelius Scipio reminds his audience of the great deeds of his ancestors from whom he derives his noble status.

39. E.g. *Richard III's Books*, pp. 258–62.

40. See *Richard III's Books*, p. 30, and references given there.

41. T. Wright, ed., *Political Poems and Songs relating to English History*, Rolls Series, 2 vols, London 1859–61, ii, pp. 264–5.

42. Jean de Wavrin, *Recueil des Croniques et Anchiennes Istories de la Grant Bretaigne, a present nomme Engleterre*, ed. W. Hardy, Rolls Series, 5 vols, London 1864–91, v, pp. 335 to end.

43. A very important action, see Vale, *War and Chivalry*, p. 101, and compare Wavrin's and other chroniclers' comments on Warwick's habit of keeping his horse ready.

44. Wavrin, ed. Hardy, vol. 5, p. 349.

thought his master *un peu simple* — and, towards the end of his life, lasciviousness. As a knight Edward also failed: though he had a far greater army than Louis he did not fight and gave up his advantage, leaving the initiative completely in Louis' hands; he had no mercy for defeated enemies, witness Henry VI and the adversaries he executed on the field of battle; he did not keep his promises; he only married Elizabeth Woodville because he could not have her any other way and he had already tricked another lady.[45] The list is endless and the picture very persuasive; with its partial truths it has insinuated itself into the mind of every historian since Comines.

It is likely that Edward IV — once he was king — never particularly desired to fight battles or to start a war. Even the campaign into France, which at first sight is difficult to interpret as a war that was merely forced on Edward by circumstance — as his recovery of his crown was — has been said, by one historian, to be 'not . . . a revival of the genuinely aggressive policies of Henry V, but . . . a reaction to this background of deep, intense suspicions and fears, a somewhat defensive reaction . . .'.[46] The treaty of Picquigny — commemorated in the misericord of the king's own stall in St George's Chapel — remains the best evidence that Edward IV knew the value of peace. Louis XI and Edward IV could both refute their critics by using a less commonly expressed recognition that a wise prince might conquer and achieve military and diplomatic success by spending money rather than waging war. Christine de Pisan gives great praise to conquerors who stay in their palaces[47] and refers to her special hero, Charles V:

And me semyth that to the propos of thes thynges may wel serve that that the wyse Charles the fyfeth kinge of Fraunce sayde whan men said unto him that grete shame it was that with money he recovered his fortresses that som of his enemyes held . . . wrongfully, seeyng that he was of might grete ynoughe for to have recovered theym by strengthe. It semith me sayd he that that whiche may be bought ought not to be bought with mannys blode.[48]

This point of view counters the comments of Edward's fellow knights of the Golden Fleece and emphasises the value of peace, encourages a sense of humour, and even a contempt for the warrior, those 'very fierce' men who needed controlling, as Bishop Russell said in 1470 (see below). Both Louis XI and Edward IV valued money, and peace was cheaper. Two of the surviving poems on Edward's death regarded the French campaign as a great victory, emphasising that France had to pay 'tribute',[49] and that it was such a clean victory, 'without a stroke, and afterward came home'.[50] Some subjects agreed with Edward and Louis over the value of peace.

It is difficult to achieve a full understanding of the meaning of medieval mottoes, but a man who, like Edward IV, had the courage to chose for his motto *comfort et liesse* (comfort and joy), when his peers had courtly, martial and virtuous 'words' such as *Aultre n'auray* (I will never have another),[51] *Je l'ay emprins* (I have undertaken it, i.e. a martial venture)[52] or

45. For all this see J. Dufournet, *La destruction des Mythes dans les Mémoires de Ph. de Commynes*, Geneva 1966, pp. 506–10, where Edward is ranged under Comines' *princes bestiaux*.
46. Lander, 'The Hundred Years War', p. 81.
47. Pisan, *Book of Fayttes*, trans. Caxton, p. 20. Written 1408, trans. and printed 1490.
48. Pisan, *Book of Fayttes*, pp. 128–9; use of *u/v* modernised by present authors.
49. John Rylands University Library, MS 113, f. 3.
50. *Ibid.*, f. 3.
51. Philip the Good.
52. Charles the Bold.

Malo mori quam foedari (I would rather die than be dishonoured),[53] cannot have considered himself above all a soldier, or even a courtly knight. He is more likely to have had in mind both his own comfort and the peace and prosperity of his people, and their joy at his accession.

Few people during his lifetime or later have denied Richard some merit as a soldier and commander, and every aspect of his reputation has often been discussed. We will not go into detail here, but we have been able to conclude elsewhere that he may perhaps be called a knight *sans peur*, though not *sans reproche*, and that he probably thought himself — and was so considered by others — reasonably successful in his chivalric role. He fought efficiently, both in his brother's battles and most of his own, he owned and read the right books and had had the right training in his youth. The main blot on his chivalric blazon is the fate of his nephews, but he may have seen the deposing of Edward V as part of his unpleasant duty as a prince and ruler, acting for the good of the kingdom.[54]

At present we will only ask how Richard's reputation fares when the subject considered is peace. His short and troubled reign gives us little to go on. There is no doubt he knew from his chivalric manuals, including Giles of Rome's *De regimine*, which we have already quoted, the concept of a just war and its severe limitations. A knight's soul was in great danger 'over the grete evyeles that necessaryly behoveth hem for to doo' if he fought in any but a just war, that is for the Christian faith or for justice.[55] All unjust wars were caused by pride and greed.[56] The most obviously just war was 'the true deffense of the lande, or for the commonwele, or for to kepe the fraunches [freedom] and good customes of the place or countrey'.[57] In Richard III's copy of Guido delle Colonne's *Historia Troiae*, which he acquired and signed when king, there is a passage concerning the great advantages of fighting to protect one's own home along with relatives and friends. A fifteenth-century hand has written in the margin: 'note well the fair words'. The dictum is illustrated by the story of the crow courageously defending its nest against the stronger falcon.[58] It is impossible to say with certainty whether Richard wrote the marginalia, but even if not they were there to draw his attention to the message of the text.

Both Scotland and England were convinced of this truth concerning the defence of one's own, when the ambassadors of Scotland arrived in Nottingham on 12 September 1484 for the major peace negotiations of Richard's reign. James III would have preferred to achieve a *peace* rather than a *truce* — with the return of Dunbar and Berwick — and the problems that beset Richard III since the death of Edward IV had given him some hope that he might win back his towns. But no king of England, and certainly not the victor of Berwick — a castle which materially improved England's defences against Scotland — was going to give up these towns unless forced to do so; as Edward IV had said to the pope

---

53. Ferdinand I of Aragon, King of Naples (1431–94).
54. See e.g. *Richard III's Books*, ch. 4.
55. Pizan, *Book of Fayttes*, pp. 282–3 (Christine in conversation with Bouvet).
56. *Ibid.*, p. 148. And see Giles, *De regimine*, cited above, before n. 36.
57. *Ibid.*, p. 282.
58. St Petersburg, Saltykov-Shchedrin State Public Library MS Lat. F IV 74, f. 43: *nota bene pulchra verba*, and *nota de cornice et eius strenuitate* ('note the crow and its vigour').

in 1482: 'we are bound to recover what was ours'.[59] The two sides had manoeuvred throughout 1483 and the first half of 1484, playing off their ancient weapons of a Scottish-French alliance and support for the 'Scottish fifth-column', that is James III's rebellious brother, the duke of Albany. The chronology of events is confused: a Scottish attempt to besiege Dunbar was unsuccessful; English plans for a large-scale attack did not materialise; Richard III won a sea-battle against the Scots and French off Scarborough in early July; Albany was routed at Lochmaben on 22 July — but from at least early July, negotiations, often secret, were underway for full-scale talks.[60]

An eminent Scots embassy arrived in Nottingham on 12 September and was met by Richard III, surrounded by an impressive array of advisors.[61] James's erudite and expert secretary, intimately concerned with the king's foreign policies, delivered a model address to Richard which was calculated to appeal to a man who — we maintain — read books. A truce of three years and a marriage contract were concluded, but Dunbar and Berwick did not change hands and no long term peace could be accepted by the Scots without the return of 'their' towns. Richard made the small but telling concession that if Dunbar should be the subject of local fighting it should not affect the truce — it was Berwick which was really important to the English and their king. It is probable that Richard himself conducted the negotiations, for after ten years of experience of the north he was uniquely qualified to do so. His hand has been seen particularly in clause 16, which set up judicial machinery for the border area linked to the English council of the North on one side and to the king of Scotland's council on the other. Early in 1485 Richard authorised commissions to implement the Nottingham truce and investigate any breaches, and a second conference was arranged with the Scots in May for later in the year. The suggestion by Alexander Grant that Richard saw the Nottingham truce as part of his programme for the peaceful and beneficent government of the North is a persuasive one — and James's policies dovetailed with Richard's at all crucial points, though the exigencies of diplomacy between the ancient enemies ensured it took a long time for them to admit this publicly. Both kings, and many, if not all, of their subjects wanted peace and the king of England's personal experience of the area made him uniquely able to understand and foster that.[62] It is worth emphasising that the two kings themselves showed every sign of being in

---

59. *Calendar of State Papers . . . Venice*, i, *1202–1509*, ed. R. Brown, Rolls Series, London 1864, p. 146, cited A. Grant, 'Richard III and Scotland', in *The North of England in the Age of Richard III*, ed. A.J. Pollard, Stroud 1996, p. 122.

60. The most detailed examination is Grant, 'Richard III and Scotland', in *The North of England in the Age of Richard III* (see last note), pp. 115–48, 194–202, esp. pp. 134–7. See also N. Macdougall, *James III*, Edinburgh 1982, pp. 208–15, and A.J. Pollard, *North-Eastern England during the Wars of the Roses. Lay Society, War and Politics 1450–1500*, Oxford 1990, pp. 240–4.

61. BL Cotton MSS Vesp. C xvi, ff. 75–9 and Cotton Caligula B v, ff. 151–2; printed in *The Bannatyne Miscellany*, ed. H.D. Laing, Bannatyne Club, Edinburgh 1836, pp. 41–8. The surviving account of this meeting, unfortunately not complete, appears to be an almost contemporary transcript of minutes made at the time, by someone who had too little Latin to record Whitelaw's speech accurately.

62. For the truce and this positive view-point, Grant, 'Richard III and Scotland', pp. 140–5. His earlier arguments that at the beginning of his reign Richard wanted war with Scotland are less convincing (pp. 128–9): no solid evidence is cited of this but only the off-handedness of diplomatic exchanges; Richard's private authorisation of Lord Dacre and Sir Thomas Percy to make local truces on the borders at the end of 1483 seems rather to be evidence that a deep-seated desire for peace for the subjects he had governed closely for over 10 years existed behind all the slow, double-talk manoeuvres of civil servants.

agreement, and that their wishes were paramount in a discussion conducted by Richard himself and the king of Scotland's highly trusted personal secretary, Whitelaw.

It is instructive to look again at the Scots speech which opened the proceedings, because it shows us what a contemporary, and very astute, diplomat like Whitelaw thought would best please Richard, and also what assertions (with learned references and quotations) about the virtues of peace and the horrors and waste of war might be most effective. First there were the compliments. William Whitelaw listed Richard's general virtues: his humanity,[63] courtesy, liberality, loyalty, justice, his greatness of heart and his wisdom that made him kind to everybody, individually and collectively. Then he praised his military virtues: experience, courage, good fortune and authority,[64] and managed at the same time to link Richard to one of the great heroes of Greek mythology. Tydeus was the bravest warrior at the siege of Thebes and famous for his small stature, indomitable courage and his ancestral emblem of the boar.[65] Whitelaw promised permanence and glory to Richard's military and civil (*domesticus*) reputation, using a pleasant, pastoral quotation from Vergil, which had the boar peacefully roaming the mountains, and so came gracefully to the subject of peace and the purpose of the conference. He stressed dramatically how Christ had chosen a time of peace to come into the world and be made man. How the Romans had a temple built to Peace and Loyalty; how Christ had called those who make peace the sons of God. He described the horrors and folly of war:

The honour that is gained by force does not last. War gives the country a frightful aspect: houses burned, towns besieged, castles destroyed, dead bodies lying around everywhere in fields and villages; it makes the rivers flow with blood and everything resound with laments and sighs and the wailing of women.[66]

The blessings of peace:

In peace God is worshipped particularly because He is the provider of peace; strong and effective justice prevails; every virtue and good government flourish; farmers rejoice in peace; standing corn is safe; meadows are in flower, vines heavy with grapes and gardens adorned with fruit and flowers; there is great luxury in farms, houses and towns; princes, nobles, merchants and ordinary people are rich in gold, silver and jewels.[67]

Let every king be content with the limits, bounds and confines of his own kingdom and rather retreat than advance — reference to the return of Berwick and Dunbar! — lest he sins against God's commandments and brings himself to ruin. Finally, Whitelaw said, it was unnatural for English and Scots to be at war, for they were subject to the influence of the same sky and land, and they resembled each other in body, language and complexion.

Whitelaw's eloquence eased the formal opening of negotiations before the enthroned king — after that the genuine desire for peace of all negotiators brought the conference to a satisfactory conclusion, which, it was intended, should be refined by further negotiation in the coming years.

---

63. *humanitas* can also be translated as 'virtue'; Vanderjagt, *Qui sa vertu*, pp. 157–8.

64. These virtues were copied from Cicero, *De imperio Gn. Pompei*, ch. 28 (see e.g. *Cicéron, Discours*, vol. 7, ed. A. Boulanger, Paris 1929); *scientia* changed to *pericia*.

65. Whitelaw quotes many of the Latin texts on which Tydeus' reputation was based; he presumably did not know the Greek ones.

66. BL Cotton MSS Vesp. C xvi, f. 78r–v.

67. *Ibid.*, f. 78v.

All this is not to say that a soldier's work had no appeal for Richard, but, we would suggest, more so before he became king. 'Noble' men were expected to be inclined to war and Richard was fortunate that he could live up to contemporary expectations — whether he wanted to or not. He took an active part in the campaign which recovered the throne for Edward IV. One little known episode displays his daring and urgency in the matter. Jean de Wavrin, writing before 1475, recorded how Edward managed to secure entry to York by pretending he was merely seeking to recover his duchy, not the throne. At this point a local gentleman, Martin del See, supported by the city's recorder, insisted that Edward swear on the gospels to that effect. This, said Wavrin, prompted the duke of Gloucester and Earl Rivers to plot to kill the two men; Rivers, however, decided it was safer to organise the king's swift and secret departure from the city. For this and for the detail that while Edward entered York he left his army under Richard's command, Wavrin is the only source. There may be an element of truth in the story. Certainly it suggests that Richard took an active part in the enterprise and was prepared to threaten the lives of hostages to ensure the king's safety — it also may emphasise his extreme youth.[68] For Richard's subsequent exploits at the battle of Barnet he was likened to Hector, one of the Nine Worthies, in a rather standard but none the less flattering comparison.

In 1475 Richard took more men on the French campaign than any other English noble and was probably enthusiastic about the enterprise. Philippe de Comines reported that he was *comme mal content* at the treaty of Picquigny and absent from the interview on the bridge, but that he was in time 'bought' by the French king when he met him at Amiens and accepted gifts.[69] As so often with Comines, the truth is more innocent: Richard and Clarence visited Louis *together* on the morning of Thursday 31 August, less than forty-eight hours after the meeting of Edward and Louis, and they had a meal with the king while thousands of their troops were milling around in Amiens, which they all left on the same day.[70] Nor is Richard's absence from the necessarily limited party on the bridge itself evidence of his disapproval, for he had used the time of the conference to go and review the French army drawn up in the field, accompanied by the admiral of France.[71]

Another incident five years later illustrates one aspect of Richard's military interests. On 16 June 1480 he wrote to Louis XI to thank him for

the good favour you have always shown me and still show me, and among other things especially for the great bombard which you caused to be presented to me, for I have always taken and still take great pleasure in artillery and I assure you it will be a special treasure to me. I pray you . . . let me know if there is anything I could do for you . . .

68. Wavrin, ed. Hardy, v, pp. 643–7. For del See, see W.E. Hampton, *Memorials of the Wars of the Roses*, Upminster 1979, no. 421; Scofield, *Edward*, i, p. 569 n. 2. Del See was later knighted by Richard after the Scots campaign of 1481–2. W.C. Metcalfe, *A Book of Knights*, London 1885, pp. 5–7.

69. Comines' memoirs, bk. 4, ch. 10 (M. Jones, trans., *Philippe de Commynes. Memoirs*, Harmondsworth 1972, p. 259): 'plate and well equipped horses'. Richard's disapproval became widely known; Jean Molinet, *Les Chroniques*, ed. G. Doutrepont and O. Jodogne, 3 vols, Brussels 1935–7, i, p. 109, mentions no other objectors and does not suggest that Richard later accepted the peace. Dufournet, *Destruction*, pp. 493–4, on Comines general 'destruction' of Richard's character and reputation.

70. According to an anonymous, contemporary German report, printed in J. Chmel, *Briefe und Aktenstücke zur Geschichte des Hauses Habsburg. . .*, 3 vols, Vienna 1858, i, pp. 210–15, esp. 214.

71. For all references and further details, *Richard III's Books*, p. 94.

This conventional letter is in the same mode as Richard's letters to Louis when he was king.[72] The interesting facts are that Louis XI gave Richard a bombard rather than anything else, and that Richard confessed in an otherwise short and formal letter to a liking for guns, a liking of which Louis may have known and which there is no reason to doubt as genuine. Richard's fascination with artillery, may mean that he was interested in 'technology' and certainly indicates that he did not regard guns as 'unchivalric'. Richard's admitted 'pleasure' may have been bolstered by considerable knowledge, acquired in his youth from gunners and from the treatises available on sieges and guns,[73] augmented by solid, first hand experience in the Scots wars at the end of his brother's reign. Was it such glimpses of Richard's efficiency and interest in practical military matters when he was duke, visible to the French in 1475, cultivated by King Louis, and gleaned from the Scots at the French court, that frightened the minority-ruled French when he was king and made him a potential new invader in 1484–5?[74] A reputation which may justify us in describing Richard as truly 'chivalric', at least in the ambiguous terms of his own time?

Richard's motto as duke is not easy to identify. It is not known when and for how long he used the several early mottoes associated with him: *a vous me ly*, *tant le desieree* and *illa treztant desyree*.[75] All the occurrences of his *Loyaulte me lie*, 'loyalty binds me', are datable to 1483–5 — 'loyalty' and 'loyal' were commonly used 'good' words. This motto that Richard used as an adult needs to be considered — like that of Edward — to see if it can tell us anything about his view of himself as prince and king. In some of the books he owned, especially *De regimine principum* 'loyalty' was interpreted as 'justice', or rather 'doing what the law commands', treating everyone according to his status and merit, obeying God's law and man's. This 'loyalty' was directed not just to one person or cause — which is sometimes misguided — but to the community as a whole, in other words it was one of the main virtues of a king. It is to be identified as Aristotle's 'form of justice' which only exists in relation to others: 'Justice in this sense then, is not part of virtue but virtue entire'.[76] This concept was taken up by St Thomas Aquinas and later by Giles of Rome; Giles calls it *justitia legalis*, justice according to the law, and adds that it is 'as it were, every virtue in one'; this part of Giles' text is prominent in his work and may well have been familiar to Richard, who owned a copy. It is unlikely Richard was consciously aware of all the complexities of the meaning of the word, but he expressed an interest in the law, he did use the word 'loyalty' in his adult motto, and he is likely to have known several of the books in which the word was used in this specific sense.[77] Like his brother Edward, Richard chose a motto suitable to his kingly duties — a rather more 'active' and bookish one than Edward's and one that focused on government, but like Edward's, we suggest, it was preoccupied with peace and harmony.

---

72. For a full text and discussion, present authors, 'Richard of Gloucester and *la grosse bombarde*', *The Ricardian*, 10 (1994–6), pp. 461–5.

73. One such manual, 'The ordinance of laying a siege' was incorporated in Christine de Pisan's *Book of Fayttes* of 1408, printed 1490 in English, pp. 152–64, esp. pp. 154–6, 159 on guns.

74. For our assessment of Richard's role in the Scots campaigns and his policy towards France, *Richard III's Books*, pp. 96–7.

75. *Richard III's Books*, pp. 270–4.

76. Aristotle, *Ethica Nicomachea*, 5, 1, 1129b–1130a; quoted by P.M. Kean, 'Love, law and *lewte* in *Piers Plowman*', *Review of English Studies*, 15 (1964), p. 256.

77. See *Richard III's Books*, pp. 270–4.

The crusading 'ideal' may be perhaps called the greatest illusion of chivalry and it still played an important part in chivalric ideas in the Yorkist period. In Burgundy Duke Philip and his intimates — his son Charles to a lesser extent — were fascinated by anything to do with the East. Every aristocratic book collection contained a history of the crusades, descriptions of the marvels of the orient and romances in which the young hero won his way to glory by fighting the infidel. Defending Christendom was still the best justification for war and aggression. Gilbert de Lannoy in his *Instruction d'un jeune prince*,[78] written probably for the young Duke Charles, advised that, though no wars should be fought unless absolutely necessary, any youthful excess of energy should be vented on pagans.

Though western Europe was at a safe distance from the actual theatre of war, people were conscious of the Turkish threat; princes all had the defence of Christendom as the *next* item on their agenda, to be tackled just as soon as regional problems had been solved. One of the least known books that Edward owned was a text that stressed the necessity of a new crusade. In 1471 Cardinal Bessarion, the Greek humanist, theologian and papal legate composed a plea to the leaders of western Europe, including Edward IV, to settle their differences and join forces against the Turks. He explained the dangers and exhorted the princes directly, cleverly using the speech of Demosthenes which impressed the Athenians with the need of helping other city states of Greece against the Macedonian imperialist threat.[79]

In 1480 people in England and elsewhere had the danger brought home to them when the long expected attack of the Turkish fleet on the Hospitaller stronghold of Rhodes took place. The island was besieged from early June to the end of July; news was avidly sought, large sums of money were collected in England and Ireland, and Sir John Weston, the prior of the Order of St John, departed to assist the grand master. Despite Edward IV's objections to so much bullion, along with the prior, leaving the country he was later to own an English translation of the best known contemporary account of the siege and its successful conclusion for the knights.[80] In the dedication of his translation John Kay, the king's 'humble poete lawreate and moste lowly servant', wrote that Edward knew well how Christendom had suffered for forty years and how 'the grete Turke' had planned to invade Italy itself, but Christ himself had 'withdrawen hys rodde as a kynd father to his dere children contente with grete menasses and lytil punycion'. Reading the story of the defeat and death of the sultan would give 'joye and consolacyon' to Edward's people and they would know better the 'inestymable power and certentee of our crysten fayth'.[81] Though Kay tactfully attributed all possible virtues to Edward he nowhere suggested that the king might actually go and fight himself.

78. See C.G. van Leeuwen, ed., *Denkbeelden van een Vliesridder. De 'Instruction d'un jeune prince' van Guillebert de Lannoy*, Amsterdam 1975, and Ch. Potvin, *Oeuvres de Ghillebert de Lannoy*, Louvain 1878.

79. The First Olynthiac (349 BC), in which the orator urged the Athenians to take action while Philip of Macedon was still far away. Bessarion in his running commentary continuously emphasises the similarity of the situation in Demosthenes' time and in his readers'. See also *Richard III's Books*, p. 33, fig. 21.

80. A. Hanham, ed., *The Cely Letters*, EETS, os 273 (1975), pp. 103, 107, 108 (nos 114, 117, 118). C. Tyerman, *England and the Crusades 1095–1588*, Chicago and London 1988, p. 356. John Kay/ G. Caoursin, *The Siege of Rhodes (1482)*, ed. D. Gray, fac. New York 1975. *A Manual of Writings in Middle English, 1050–1500*, gen. eds J. Burke Severs / A.E. Hartung, 9 vols, New Haven, Conn., 1967–93, viii, [86].

81. *Siege of Rhodes*, f. 1r–v.

At about the same time William Caxton dedicated his translation of William of Tyre's *History of the Crusades* to Edward and his sons. The printer was more outspoken, and also more hopeful, or less realistic, or just more literary, than was John Kay.[82] In his long prologue he described all the Nine Worthies, the famous 'patron saints' of chivalry: Joshua, David and Judas Maccabeus, Hector, Alexander and Caesar, Arthur, Charlemagne and Geoffrey of Boulogne — the last three were said to have the first three 'stalls' among Christian men, like member knights at a chapter of their Order, or priests in the choir of their church. The life of Geoffrey of Boulogne, the subject of the book, said Caxton, was to be taken as an example, for he in his time had gathered together the 'prynces, lordes and comyn peple' to fight the heathen, 'to the resistence of whom, as yet' — Caxton added, referring to his own time — 'few Cristen prynces have put theym in devoyr'. Edward, the most successful soldier of his day should 'adresse, styre, or commaunde somme noble Captayn of his sugettes to empryse this warre agayn the sayd turke'. This 'captain' was not given a name, but in 1481 the only realistic candidate would have been Richard of Gloucester. Caxton ended his prologue by expressing the hope that Edward himself, or one of his sons, would eventually deserve the tenth place with the Nine Worthies and be another paragon of chivalry.

In 1463–4 it was rumoured that the king of England would send archers on Philip the Good's expedition to the East — which never happened.[83] Some of the prophetic texts which had reputedly predicted Edward's taking of the crown described him as the king who would clear the route to the Holy Land and win the Holy Cross,[84] but any direct, personal indication of Edward's interest in the reconquest of the holy places is lacking.

Richard, in contrast, does appear to have felt genuinely involved in the crusading movement. The evidence is not extensive but it is strongly personal. First there is the king's well-known, self-assured remark to Nicholas von Poppelau, telling him that given the opportunity he would defeat the Turks with only his own people to help him.[85] Secondly, there is the surviving fragment of what may have been a 'crusading litany' among the additions to Richard's book of hours. This text appears to be unique and may at least point to an awareness of the *languor* (inactivity) that affected western leaders as soon as they were actually asked to unite, organise themselves and rise above chivalric display. The litany beseeches God to destroy 'the peoples of the heathen' and preserve the earth from desolation. 'May your anger, Lord, now be lifted from your people'; its words are conventional but none the less forceful.[86] It has to be remembered that John Kay, in his introduction to the *Siege of Rhodes*, was convinced that it had been the repentance and the prayers of the pope, the princes and all Christians that had saved Christendom and slain the Great Turk 'in his moste pryde'.[87]

Equally important in this context is the evidence of Richard's veneration — there is no such evidence for Edward IV — for the oil given by the Virgin Mary to St Thomas Becket to anoint the English kings at their coronation. Divine assistance against all enemies, both

---

82. William of Tyre, *Godeffroy of Boloyne or The Siege and Conqueste of Jerusalem. Translated by William Caxton*, ed. M.N. Colvin, EETS, es 64 (1893), pp. 1–5.

83. Wavrin, ed. Hardy, v, p. 430.

84. *Richard III's Books*, pp. 197–200.

85. *Richard III's Books*, pp. 57, 101; present authors, *The Hours of Richard III*, Stroud 1990, p. 112, n. 305.

86. *Hours of Richard III*, pp. 62–6.

87. *Siege of Rhodes*, f. 1.

Christian and pagan, was expected from the holy oil: the first king to be anointed with it would recover Normandy and Aquitaine, 'build churches in the Holy Land and chase all the heathen from Babylon', and all kings who used it would be vigorous champions of the church. When 'carried in the breast' the oil would bestow victory over all enemies. Richard III was the king who decided that the holy relic of the oil should be kept with the other regalia in Westminster Abbey, making the particular reservation that it should be returned to him 'whensoever it shall please hym to ask it'![88] The overall message seems to be clear: Richard was both aware and moved by the contemporary demand for a crusade, more so than his brother had been, but neither of them took any real action.

By the time of the Yorkists, the Order of the Garter had been established for well over a hundred years.[89] It was celebrated in history and romance, and it was select, consisting of the sovereign and twenty-five companion knights. It had its headquarters at Windsor — its feast of St George was one of the most important dates in the king of England's calendar — and the Order was one of the most prestigious sources of patronage available to him. It was the means of creating his personal 'team'.

In 1461 the change of kings had repercussions for the Order. When was the new king himself admitted to the Order? Certainly sometime in 1461, but was it before or after his coronation on 29 June? This occasion might have been particularly splendid; Henry VII allowed himself a specially lavish gown of cloth of gold powdered with red roses for his admittance in 1485.[90] The first St George's feast of Edward's reign was held on 17 May by Viscount Bourchier, with Lord Berners, the duke of Norfolk (died 6 Nov. 1461) and Lord Fauconberg, in the absence of the new king and the rest of the knights. The achievements in the chapel were reorganised, Yorkist ones replacing those of Lancaster: Edward IV replaced Henry VI, the swords and helmets of Lord Welles and the earl of Wiltshire were removed; and those of the dukes of York and Buckingham, the earls of Salisbury and Shrewsbury, Viscount Beaumont and Lord Scales were offered at the altar with the usual ceremonies accorded to deceased knights of the Order.[91] Edward IV had thirteen vacancies to fill among the knights in his first year, a great opportunity for him to create a fellowship closely identified with his interests and to reward his friends and supporters. As Juliet Vale has persuasively written, Edward III's founding body of knights was composed of two finely matched fighting teams under the king and prince of Wales, carefully chosen

88. A.F. Sutton and P.W. Hammond, *The Coronation of Richard III*, Gloucester 1983, pp. 7–8.

89. There has been no study of the use of the Garter by the Yorkist kings. Compare H. Collins, 'The Order of the Garter, 1348–1461: Chivalry and politics in later medieval England', in *Courts, Counties and the Capital*, ed D.E.S. Dunn, Stroud 1996, pp. 155–80, and S. Gunn, 'Chivalry and the politics of the early Tudor court', in Anglo, *Chivalry in the Renaissance*, pp. 109–16; also D. Dunn in this volume.

90. The gown was the perquisite of Garter King of Arms who received all the gowns of new knights after they had been invested with the Order's robes, E. Ashmole, *The Institution, Laws and Ceremonies of the Most Noble Order of the Garter*, London 1672, p. 460.

91. London, Public Rcord Office, Great Wardrobe enrolled accounts, E361/6, m. 54, gives a few details. [J. Anstis], *The Register of the Most Noble Order of the Garter . . . usually called The Black Book . . .*, London 1724, i, pp. 172–4. G.F. Beltz, *Memorials of the Order of the Garter*, London 1841, p. lxvii. D. Schneider, *Der englische Hosenbandorden. Beiträge zur Entstehung und Entwicklung des 'The Most Noble Order of the Garter' (1348–1702) mit einem Ausblick bis 1983*, 2 vols in 4 pts, Bonn 1988, i, p. 360, n. 256, remarks on the fact that the same word used (in the French Register) to describe the expelling of a knight from the Order, *avaler*, was used for removing the helmet and sword of Henry VI.

with 'unswerving . . . loyalty' as 'the cornerstone'.[92] Later kings were never in a position to emulate this vision precisely, but, because of the circumstances of their accessions, Edward IV and later Richard III had unusually large numbers of vacancies to fill when they began their reigns. In 1472 Edward IV again had the large number of seven vacancies to fill. The evidence indicates that all kings first and foremost admitted those of the royal family whose position demanded admission, they then rewarded their friends and close associates, thirdly important magnates who might be offended by their omission, and fourthly a smattering of foreign princes, from among those they were least likely to fight, to cement alliances. Both Edward and Richard followed this pattern. The king's two younger brothers of Clarence and Gloucester were elected at some date before 4 February 1462, the date of the privy seal letter authorising delivery to Richard of his helmet, crest and sword which were to be installed at Windsor.[93] Clarence was old enough to be actually admitted on an unknown date sometime later. No issue of mantle, and the livery of gown, hood and garter powderings are known for Richard at any date,[94] but in 1465 he duly received a magnificent garter costing the king over £30, and apparently at some date between 27 April 1466 and 22 April 1467 he finally took possession of the stall assigned to him.[95] Apart from his brothers (who had automatically to be elected) and three foreign princes and lords, the rest chosen were Edward's supporters: John Neville, John Tiptoft, William Herbert, William Hastings, Lord Duras, Lord Scrope, Robert Harcourt, John Astley and William Chamberlain.[96] The surviving records do not tell us how Richard filled all the vacancies that occurred during his reign. His newly elected knights were: John Conyers, Thomas Howard, Francis Lovell, Richard Ratcliffe, Thomas Burgh, Thomas Stanley and Richard Tunstall.[97] Of these men five (Conyers, Howard, Lovell,

92. R. Barber, 'Malory's *Morte Darthur* and court culture under Edward IV', *Arthurian Literature*, 12 (1993), p. 138, gives 13; Anstis produces a possible 14 if Sir William died promptly after his election, pp. 172–5 and p. 175 note d. J. Vale, *Edward III and Chivalry*, Woodbridge 1982, ch. 5, esp. pp. 86–91.

93. Anstis, *Register*, p. 181, note q. Scofield, *Edward*, i, p. 216. Richard sat in stall 5 on the sovereign's side, which Jean de Foix, Vicomte de Castillon, Lord of Grilly, elected KG and created earl of Kendal in 1446, had surrendered, or been expelled from, in 1462. Schneider, *Hosenbandorden*, ii, p. 68, 157, 166 (n. 3a); *Complete Peerage*, ii, app. B, p. 541; vii, p. 110; Anstis, *Register*, p. 176, note e. Clarence was elected in the first year of Edward's reign, *ibid.*, p. 175, note d.

94. Scofield, *Edward*, i, p. 216. Clarence received the livery of 230 garters for powdering his gown (presumably for the gowns of 2 years, the correct number for his rank for two years, plus an extra 10, perhaps because he was heir apparent), and one large garter of 'ruddeur' with a shield in its centre showing the arms of St George, under an indenture dated 20 March 1465, and a great banner stamped with *armis domini Clarencie* was also made for St George's Chapel, PRO, Great Wardrobe Enrolled Accounts 1461–5, E361/6, mm. 53, 55d. No details are known of any issues of mantle, gown, hood and garter powderings to Richard. A.F. Sutton, ' "And to be delivered to the Lord Richard, the other brother . . ." ', *The Ricardian*, 8 (1988–90), p. 23 and n. 36. More is known of the supplies to the two brothers when they were made knights of the Bath at their brother's coronation, *ibid.*, p. 22.

95. Richard's garter, PRO, E404/73/1, no. 124A. Anstis, *Register*, pp. 182–3 and p. 183 note t.

96. The precise sequence and dating is not always clear. Ashmole, *Institution*, pp. 711–12; also Earl Douglas, the duke of Milan and the king of Naples. Barber, 'Malory's *Morte Darthur*', pp. 138–9.

97. Anstis, *Register*, pp. 219–21, esp. note e; certain 'vacant' stalls were apparently not filled by Richard (Ashmole, *Institution*, p. 712): marquess Dorset, the prince of Wales and Richard, duke of York; the princes' seats were not filled until 1491, by Prince Arthur, and 1496, by Edward Stafford, duke of Buckingham, according to Schneider's lists. Of the men elected in Richard's reign Thomas Stanley and Thomas Burgh had had many votes during Edward IV's reign, Tunstall and Lovell a couple, Conyers, Howard and Ratcliffe none; Schneider, *Hosenbandorden*, i, pp. 384–5.

Ratcliffe and Tunstall) were key supporters of his regime and his choice of them illustrates the rule that kings expected service and loyalty from their Garter knights — they were close to Richard, symbolically at the coronation when they supported the canopy over him during the anointing, the most sacred moment of the service,[98] and practically on the battlefield and in adversity. In none of these five men did Richard find disloyalty.

Edward IV certainly attended two feasts of the Order in the 1460s, 1463 and 1467; the records are by no means complete and he may have attended more.[99] In the 1470s and 1480s it appears he did better, and he was careful to celebrate the feast of St George at Windsor immediately after his return from exile, staying there from 19 April and leaving on the day after the feast.[100] The other times he attended in the 1470s and 1482 were also especially important occasions; he was present at a total of six feasts out of twenty-two. He attended more, probably all, of the chapters, which took place where the king was,[101] usually in his chamber; at these the statutes were amended, elections held and the Order administered. It has to be remembered that the records are not perfect for Edward's reign and are even worse for his brother's. While duke, Richard apparently only attended one feast at Windsor, that of 1472 — but he was probably there with Edward in 1471. He was habitually excused by the king because he was occupied elsewhere. He attended neither of the feasts of St George which fell in his reign, the deaths of his son and then his wife keeping him away.[102] The infrequent attendance of the Yorkist kings at Windsor to celebrate the feast day of St George should not be taken to indicate that they undervalued the Garter; Henry VI is known to have attended thirteen feasts in a reign of forty years,[103] and Henry VII ten in twenty-three.[104] The exigencies of busy royal itineraries and in Richard's case, profound personal reasons, prevented the kings from attending the great religious feast and annual ceremonies of the Order at the Order's home of Windsor regularly. It was mandatory that the feast day of St George be celebrated by the knights, but this could be done away from Windsor.[105]

98. As regards Richard's anointing itself there is uncertainty; of the four knights named, Sir Robert Greystock was dead, Sir William Parr was indeed a knight of the Garter and alive, Sir Richard Ratcliffe was not yet a Garter knight, and Sir Edmund Hastings never was one; Sutton and Hammond, *Coronation*, pp. 40, 221n, and biographies.

99. Neither occasion was remarkable, Anstis, *Register*, pp. 172–85. Beltz, *Memorials*, p. lxviii, giving no details. The Mercers' Company recorded how its members went to meet Edward after he returned from Windsor in 1463: 'Item to xvj persones of the Feloship to mete with the kyng on horsbak at his comeng to London from Seint Georges Fest with thambassatours of the Duc of Burgundy, x li. xiii s. iiij d.'. London, Mercers' Company, Wardens' Accounts 1348, 1390–1464, f. 205v; Scofield, *Edward*, i, p. 278.

100. Anstis, *Register*, pp. 186–215. Bruce, J., ed., *Historie of the Arrivall of Edward IV A.D. 1471*, Camden Society, os 1 (1838), pp. 24–5; Wavrin, ed. Hardy, v, p. 665.

101. See e.g. Statute 21 as printed in Schneider, *Hosenbandorden*, ii, pp. 461–6, for election meetings. L. Jefferson, 'MS Arundel 48 and the earliest statutes of the Order of the Garter', *English Historical Review*, 109 (1994), pp. 356–85, no. 19.

102. Anstis, *Register*, pp. 217–21.

103. Again the records are not complete. Barber, 'Malory's *Morte Darthur*', p. 138, citing Anstis, *Register*, and R.A. Griffiths, *The Reign of Henry VI*, London 1981. The calculations of Schneider, *Hosenbandorden*, produce 15, ii, pp. 130–41.

104. Schneider, *Hosenbandorden*, ii, pp. 183–91.

105. See e.g. Schneider, *Hosenbandorden*, Statutes no. 14, ii, pp. 436–41; Jefferson, 'Arundel 48', statutes, no. 12.

Edward IV's rebuilding and embellishment of St George's Chapel, his choice of it as his burial place, his generous endowment and incorporation of its college of dean and canons, is testimony enough to his commitment: as Ashmole wrote later 'his inclination to, and kindness for this place was extraordinary'. He also made some administrative changes to the Order: he is known, like other kings, to have had his own Garter seal and he modified the statutes regarding its seals; in 1475 he appointed as the Order's first chancellor, Richard Beauchamp, bishop of Salisbury, who was the devoted overseer of the rebuilding of the chapel; and on 10 February 1480 additions were made to the oath of all knights, new and old, that 'they will aid, support and defend with all their power the royal college of St George within the castle of Windsor, as well in its possessions as in all other things whatsoever'.[106] He also gave prestigious relics to the chapel, magnificent sets of vestments and a great statue of St George, as well as some Latin theological books to the library, though his plan to move all the books of Eton College there was not executed.[107] In 1471 Edward also instituted a new religious custom for the Order: remembering that it had been founded to the honour of the Virgin as well as St George, he had it laid down that all member knights on the five feasts of St Mary should wear their mantles 'during servyce tyme . . . bering . . . am ymage of our Lady with her son in her right arme of golde upon their mantells on their right shouldre'. They were to bear this same image in the same way every Saturday, and say five Pater Nosters and five Ave Marias in the Virgin's honour.[108] It is possible that these new instructions were inspired by Queen Elizabeth Woodville who is known to have had a special interest in the feasts of the Virgin Mary.[109] Perhaps most telling is the choice of the text of Psalm 20 (Vulgate 19) to decorate the fronts of the knights' stalls, presumably with the king's endorsement if not actually chosen by him. This prays for, and assumes as certain, the victory of God's anointed in war. In the surroundings of the Garter chapel the text appropriately blends faith with chivalry and is additional evidence of Edward's awareness of his duties as king. The choice of a carving of the meeting between himself and the king of France at Picquigny for the misericord of the sovereign's seat was undoubtedly personal, and reminds us again of the value Edward placed on that particular achievement of peace by a bloodless war.

While still duke of Gloucester Richard followed his brother's lead and endowed the college of Windsor with three manors,[110] but almost nothing is known of the chapters of his reign and the subject of their deliberations, although some voting schedules survive.

---

106. Ashmole, *Institution*, pp. 135–6, 149, 154–8, 169–71; Beltz, *Memorials*, p. lxxiii; Jefferson, 'Two fifteenth-century MSS of the statutes of the Order of the Garter', *English Manuscript Studies 1100–1700*, v (1995), pp. 18–35, esp. 27–31.

107. Anstis, *Register*, pp. 213–14 note n, citing Rous *Historia Regum Angliae*, for the head of St George. PRO, Issue Roll Mich. 1478, E403/848, m. 5: £50 is paid to the queen to make and *implement' pond' capit' imaginis sancti Georgii* in St George's Chapel. See also Issue Roll Easter 1478, E403/847, m. 5, for vestments embroidered with the life of St George, and Issue Roll Easter 1479, E403/852, m. 1, for vestments embroidered with golden angels for the chapel. M.R. James, 'The manuscripts of St. George's Chapel, Windsor, *The Library*, 4th ser. 13 (1932–3), pp. 55–76, esp. 65–6.

108. Schneider, *Hosenbandorden*, i, pp. 368–9.

109. See present authors, 'A "Most benevolent queen". Queen Elizabeth Woodville's reputation, her piety and her books', *The Ricardian*, 10 (1994–6), pp. 214–45, esp. 233–4. The image of the Virgin worn on the shoulder is also reminiscent of King Arthur's wearing her likeness on his shield into battle, Geoffrey of Monmouth, *The History of the Kings of Britain*, ed. L. Thorpe, Harmondsworth 1966, p. 217.

110. Ashmole, *Institution*, p. 149.

Perhaps most important for Windsor, if not the Garter, he had the pilgrim-attracting, money-making remains of Henry VI reinterred there.

There is one important text from the Yorkist period which gives an educated and sophisticated opinion of the value of such an institution as the Garter: the Latin speech made by John Russell, later bishop of Lincoln and chancellor of England, on 4 February 1470, to Charles of Burgundy when he was presented with the insignia of the Garter at Ghent.[111] It was important enough to be printed by Caxton in 1475, but we do not know whether this was done at the printer's instance, or at the author's, or even at that of Edward who wished to advertise the new alliance (or advertise it again in 1475). Russell began, of course, with compliments to Charles and praise of this third bond between Charles and Edward — already brothers of the Golden Fleece and brothers-in-law — forged, he believed, by the Holy Trinity and unbreakable. The substance of his text declared that orders of knighthood were not idle or superfluous but were one of those 'strong societies' or 'holy friendships' which support and unite nations. Man had emerged from his 'silvan huts and bestial life' because he realised the advantages of social ties, and from this 'fountain of social sense (*socialis nature fons*) welled up all order, all faith and all community of people'. Russell used the word *ordo* consciously in two senses, that of 'organised society' and that of 'order of knighthood', going on to say that thereby military men 'who are by nature very fierce' became restrained, obedient and devout in their way of life, 'excelling all others both in . . . courage in battle and devotion in church'. The greatest examples of such orders were the Round Table of King Arthur, the Garter of Edward III and the Golden Fleece of Charles's father. Russell finished by praying that from that time on Charles would be supported by his 'own' St Andrew, but also by St George. His text was in keeping with the chivalric message of Lull and other teachers: the idealism of the knight in the service of God as well as the underlying fear of the military man out of control.

The vast divide between the ideals of chivalry and real politics has been discussed in relation to the career of one man, a career given a brilliant chivalric gloss by certain contemporary chroniclers (Chastellain and Le Fèvre) and a writer of fatherly advice for princes and knights (Gilbert de Lannoy). Louis Robessart, knight of the Garter, decided to act out the role of chivalric hero, made his grand gesture, died for it, and was rewarded with the admiration of his contemporaries.[112] As chivalric tales are always those of individual heroes, the Louis Robessarts and the Sir Philip Sydneys — and it is they who, above all, bring the whole system to life and justify it — it is worthwhile considering if

---

111. Scofield, *Edward*, i, pp. 485, 507. The letter which informed Charles of his election, given at the chapter under Edward's signet and the common seal of the Order, was signed by all knights present and dated 13 May 1469. Lille, Archives departementales du Nord, série B, 862/16161/146. Charles thanked Edward for having received the garter, mantle and other ornaments, from Ghent, 4 Feb. 1469 [O.S.], T. Rymer, *Foedera* . . ., 20 vols, London 1704–35, xi, p. 654 (quoted in R. Putnam, *Charles the Bold*, New York and London 1908, p. 267). R. Vaughan, *Charles the Bold*, London 1973, p. 60, has 4 January for Russell's speech. See also Schneider, *Hosenbandorden*, ii, pp. 10, 168–9. Charles was later to have the seat vacated by Warwick, sovereign's side 3. Russell's speech is printed in *Propositio Johannis Russell, printed by William Caxton circa A.D. 1476*, introd. H. Guppy, Manchester and London 1909.
112. D.A.L. Morgan, 'From a death to a view: Louis Robbesart, Johan Huizinga and the political significance of chivalry', in Anglo, *Chivalry in the Renaissance*, pp. 93–106.

there were any such men in England in the Yorkist period.[113] First it must be admitted that civil war was not a good background for the potential hero — the French wars had been a better arena. A hero of the French wars, whose reputation was still revered in Richard's family, if not court, circle, was Richard Beauchamp, earl of Warwick, great-grandfather of Richard III's prince of Wales. The pageant of his life, composed probably at the order of his daughter, Anne, countess of Warwick and last of the Beauchamps, has been compared by modern historians to Malory's 'Tale of Sir Gareth' known as 'Beaumains' (of the White Hands), both Earl Richard and Sir Gareth being patterns of chivalry. The practical experience and the realities of the former's career in the Hundred Years War in France have been elevated by an unknown author to that of a story-book hero — probably for the delectation of Richard III's prince of Wales — and the Arthurian adventures of Sir Gareth are depicted in terms of fifteenth-century real life by Sir Thomas Malory, who had served with Beauchamp. When Beauchamp and Gareth both engage in a tournament wearing a variety of disguises, the earl in real life and Malory in his fiction were consciously acting out a chivalric tradition which went back to the twelfth-century romance of *Ipomedon* (of which Richard of Gloucester owned a fifteenth-century version).[114] Both the earl and his fifteenth-century biographer were well aware of the two sides of the coin and adopted which ever was most appropriate to each pageant or episode: the carefully staged display and rhetorical observance of the rules of honour and chivalry; or the down-to-earth necessity of coping with a military problem and the immediate need to win. Forty years after his death Beauchamp's career was given the necessary chivalric gloss.

One man who lived through the reigns of the Yorkist kings and who appears to have approached contemporary expectations regarding chivalrous behavior, even in the unpromising environment of intermittent civil war, was Sir John Astley. His main exploits were in the past by the time Edward IV took the throne, but he was one of Edward's first elected knights of the Garter, prominent as an adviser on protocol, and acceptable to all kings of England until his death in 1486. He was the son of Sir Thomas Astley of Nailstone, Leicestershire, and his wife, Elizabeth, the heiress of Richard Harcourt of Patshull, Staffordshire. He could claim kinship with the Harcourts, whose arms he quartered with Astley, and, through his grandmother, with the Beauchamps; his sister-in-law was nurse to Henry VI, whose tutor Beauchamp had been.[115]

113. For an interesting discussion of the hero in the early Tudor period, Gunn, 'Chivalry and the politics of the early Tudor court', in Anglo, *Chivalry in the Renaissance*, pp. 107–28, esp. 118–22.

114. See the study of the interplay of reality and ideals by J.R. Ruff, 'Malory's *Gareth* and fifteenth-century chivalry', in *Chivalric Literature. Essays on relations between literature and life in the later middle ages*, ed. L.D. Benson and J. Leyerle, Kalamazoo 1980, pp. 101–16, esp. 111–16. The tournament episode is one of the most engaging and regulary repeated motifs, see e.g. *Cleriadus and Meliadice*, ed. G. Zink, Geneva 1984, *passim*.

115. His arms of Astley and Harcourt quarterly with a label of three points ermine shows him to have been a younger second son, W. Dugdale, *The Antiquities of Warwickshire*, London 1730, p. 110; J. Nichols, *The History and Antiquities of the County of Leicester*, 4 vols in 8 pts, London 1795–1815, iv, pt 2, p. 811; brief biographies in F.P. Barnard, ed., *Edward IV's French Expedition of 1475*, repr. Gloucester 1975, pp. 42–7, and Barber, 'Malory's *Morte Darthur*', pp. 139–41. Margery, Sir John's widow, names his parents as Sir Thomas Astley and Dame Jane his wife in her will (PRO, PROB 11/8, f. 113v). Sir John's sister, Jane, married Sir John Clay of Cheshunt, Herts., and 'Shavesey', Cambs., (died 1464) who calls his wife 'Jane' in his will and has an influential collection of executors, including Hugh Fenne and Lord Wenlock (PROB 11/5, f. 41r–v). Jane Clay ended her days in the parish of St Benet Paul's Wharf, London, and died in 1477 making her brother one of her executors (PROB 11/6, f. 232r–v); the Clay's parish was remembered in the will of Margery Astley, ten years later. Pedigrees of the Astleys vary in details and do not include Jane Clay.

His fame rests on two single combats fought when he was a squire: the first in 1438 in Paris against Pierre de Masse whom he killed; the second at Smithfield in 1442 against Sir 'Philip Boyle', an Aragonese, over whom he was again victorious. Henry VI rewarded Astley with an annuity of 100 marks and a knighthood.[116] Thereafter he only advised at such combats, becoming a recognised authority. Little seems to be known of his subsequent career — he presumably took part in the French wars, as he was in Paris in 1438. That he supported York in the civil wars can be presumed from his election to the Garter on 21 March 1462 with a grant from the king of £40. Clearly he was very acceptable to Edward IV. He was on the king's 1462 expedition to the north, made captain of Alnwick in 1463, taken prisoner by the Lancastrians, sent to France and was finally ransomed in December 1466.[117] In his absence he was made *vexillarius regis*.[118]

He advised at the 1467 Smithfield tournament. In 1472 he was absent from the Garter ceremonials for an adequate reason, presumably the king's service at Calais, and had to be recalled suddenly so that there would be sufficient knights to elect.[119] In both 1474 and 1475 he was present at the Windsor Garter ceremonies in the absence of the king.[120] In 1475 he went on the French expedition. In 1478 he was on a commission to inquire into robberies and breaches of safeconducts and treaties by pirates and to punish the offenders according to the laws of the sea and the court of admiralty.[121] In 1479 he received a grant of £60 a year from Edward IV, later to be confirmed by Richard III.[122] He carried the canopy over Edward IV's body at his funeral and he attended the coronation of Richard III. It is not known whether he was at Bosworth, but it is likely he was not: he was in his seventies by 1485 and he managed to retrieve his £100 annuity from Henry VII in December 1485.[123]

He died in 1486 leaving no will; his widow, Dame Margery (*née* Kniveton, of Derbyshire), died two years later and was buried next to him in the London White Friars. Her will shows no great wealth, only the remains of a household which must have lived in some style, in the parish of St Sepulchre without Newgate, near the scene of one of Sir

116. *Chronicles of London*, ed. C.L. Kingsford, Oxford 1905, p. 150; J. Gairdner, *The Historical Collections of a Citizen of London*, Camden Society, ns 17 (1876), p. 220; Viscount Dillon, 'On a MS collection of ordinances of chivalry of the fifteenth century', *Archaeologia*, 57 (1900), pp. 35–6, Barnard, *French Expedition*, pp. 42–3.

117. Gairdner, *Collections*, p. 220; 'William Worcester', *Annales*, in J. Stevenson, ed., *Letters and Papers Illustrative of the Wars of the English in France . . .*, Rolls Series, 2 vols, London 1864, ii, pt 2, pp. 781–2; *Calendar of Patent Rolls 1461–7*, p. 262; J.A. Giles, ed., *The Chronicles of White Rose*, London 1845, p. lxxxviii. Anstis, *Register*, pp. 178–83, records him as absent from Garter ceremonies because of his imprisonment in 1464, 1465, 1466; he was present again 22 April 1467.

118. Anstis, *Register*, p. 179, note l.

119. Anstis, *Register*, pp. 186–7.

120. Anstis, *Register*, pp. 188–92.

121. With William Goodyere, doctor of law, and John Fortescue, esquire, *Calendar of Patent Rolls 1476–85*, p. 112.

122. *CPR 1476–85*, pp. 132, 377.

123. W. Campbell, ed., *Materials for a History of the Reign of Henry VII*, Rolls Series, 2 vols, London 1873–7, i, p. 203. He later recovered some of the Yorkist grants too, Barnard, *French Expedition*, p. 46.

John's victories, a parish in which she at least maintained many ties. Among her bequests were several fine clothes fit to have been worn at court in the presence of the great.[124]

It was perhaps inevitable that John's son, Thomas, was a disaster: in 1479 he was in prison and sick during 'the grete sekenesse that nowe reigneth' and his father was trying to get him released 'home to his hous' on his own recognizance to redeliver him to prison, if necessary, once he had recovered. Nothing more is known of him — one source says he was beheaded but gives no evidence; he certainly died before his mother.[125]

Sir John not only had great practical experience, he is also known to have owned the right books. A collection of his survives containing useful tracts on administrative, ceremonial and military matters, including a *forma et modus* of the coronation of the kings of England, a *De re militari*, treatises on jousting and how to arm a knight, a *Secreta secretorum*, details of the creation of a knight of the Bath, and the oath taken by a herald.[126] He also owned literary works, including a translation of the *Epistle of Othea* being decorated with his arms,[127] and illustrated narratives of his two famous *pas d'armes*. These last two items, at least, were undoubtedly commissioned by himself, although the other pieces may have been acquired piecemeal and then bound together.[128] His widow had a psalter to leave to one of her executors, Richard Jay, and a primer.[129]

In short Astley was a professional soldier and courtier learned in the protocol of his trade who lived on the money grants of his sovereign; his fame and reputation secured him patronage and an income from a series of kings independent of changes of dynasty. He was also apparently dependent on that 'earned' income, having no resources of his own, a fact illustrated by his provision for his widow before he went on the 1475 expedition and the need of him and his widow to resecure the annuities from Henry VII.[130] He conforms to a certain type of chivalric hero, a tournament hero, competent in war, respected for his courtesy and his knowledge of how to conduct the ceremonies of his chivalric world — and it is his 'need to earn a living' and the few known details of his personal life which link him to the real world.

The contrast between ideals and reality becomes almost painful in the story of a more famous paragon of chivalry, the Burgundian Jacques de Lalaing: 'a sweet, humble, amiable and courteous knight, who was generous and quick to feel pity. He had five gifts from

---

124. PRO, PROB 11/8, ff. 113v–14: she gives her parents as Thomas and Margaret Knyveton; her executors, Richard Jay serjeant at law, Christopher Hanyngton of the chancery (d. 1487, PROB 11/8, ff. 201v–02v), and especially the last, Nicholas Lathell baron of the exchequer, seem to have been chosen with an eye on the need to recover money owing. Barber gives her the name of Brice but this appears to be a confusion with her daughter, Margaret, who married a Brice alias Butterell.

125. Thomas had a surety of the peace obtained against him by the wife of William Meryot, PRO, C1/64/1155; his sickness and proposed release, C1/64/158 (21 May [1479]). Nichols, *Leicestershire*, iv, pt 2, p. 811.

126. Pierpont Morgan MS M 775. It also contained the assize of bread and a navigational directory with illustrations. See *Secular Spirit*, Exhibition at New York Metropolitan Museum of Art, 1975, no. 130. Described by Dillon, 'On a MS collection of ordinances of chivalry', pp. 29–70. See also Barber, 'Malory's *Morte Darthur*', pp. 147–8.

127. A commission dated to before his election to the Garter by C.F. Bühler, ed., *Epistle of Othea*, EETS, os 264 (1970), p. xvi.

128. A 17th-century 'descendant' appears to have had panel paintings made of his exploits, see Dugdale, *Warwickshire*, after p. 110. Compare Dillon, 'Collection', p. 33.

129. PROB 11/8, f. 113v.

130. PRO, C1/59/293 Fri. 23 Oct. [1475]. Campbell, *Materials*, ii, p. 99.

God: he was the flower of knighthood, as fair as Paris, as pious as Aeneas, as wise as Odysseus, in battle as stern as Hector, after battle kind and humble to the defeated'.[131] It is well known how de Lalaing spent the first half of his short adult life jousting across Europe, became a knight of the Golden Fleece, regarded war as a continuation of his jousting, and died during a 'real' siege, shot through the head by a cannon ball. The irony of the contrast between his life and his death has often been remarked upon.[132] For the modern reader it may epitomise, for example, the coming of a new, unchivalric age, or the clash between ideals and reality. To Lalaing's biographer, however, Jacques' death was just *moult grant dommage*, and he merely adds that the young man was planning to give his inheritance to his brother and go away and expose himself to danger in the service of God, fighting the infidel, never to return. Jacques had not lost sight of reality in all this: he planned to take enough money 'to maintain his estate'.[133]

It is likely that Edward IV and Richard III did not do badly in the eyes of their contemporaries, when compared to such heroes. Many people no doubt thought that there was much 'to be amended' in their actions and their rule, but most people would be blinded by the chivalric splendour in which the king and his court showed themselves to the world. There were also enough battles, adventures and quests in the lives of Edward and Richard to make people think they were comparable to the famous knights of the present and the past.

There is always a difference, however, between a king and his knights: King Arthur hardly stirred from his castle, Sir Lancelot was hardly ever at home. Arthur's life was full of adventure until he had established his position, after that he retreated into the background of the story, while his knights went about their chivalric business. Men like Sir John Astley and Jacques de Lalaing made being chivalric their profession; they had 'nothing else to do'. Once he was king the demands of government and diplomacy shaped Edward's attitude to 'adventures', that is to war; so, eventually, did they shape Richard's after a period of chivalric activity in his brother's service. As kings they naturally turned to peace, each in their own way: *confort* or *loyaulte*.

If we compare Edward to King Arthur, we may remember that in some versions of the Arthurian cycle he is known as the *roi fainéant*: the king who did nothing. We can perhaps relate Richard to Sir Gawain, whose reputation, in some traditions — but certainly not in all — is less than positive.

---

131. Georges Chastellain, *Oeuvres*, ed. C. Kervyn de Lettenhove, 8 vols, Brussels 1833–6, viii, pp. 252–3.

132. E.g. Huizinga, *Herfsttij*, p. 106; E. Gaucher, 'La confrontation de l'idéal chevaleresque et de l'idéologique politique en Bourgogne au XVe siècle: l'exemple de Jacques de Lalaing', in *Rencontres médiévales en Bourgogne (XIVe–XVe siècles)*, 2 (1992), pp. 3–24.

133. For Lalaing see R. de Smedt, *Les Chevaliers de l'Ordre de la Toison d'or au XVe siècle*, Frankfurt am Main 1994, no. 51, and references given there. For a realistic view of Jacques' career and death and similar deaths, Vale, *War and Chivalry*, pp. 98–9, 136–7.

The Lost St George Cycle of St George's Church, Stamford: An Examination of Iconography and Context

SAMANTHA J.E. RICHES

The lost St George cycle in the chancel glass of St George's church in Stamford (Lincolnshire) dates from the mid-fifteenth century. It formed part of the rebuilding campaign carried out by William Bruges, the first Garter King of Arms, but was destroyed more or less wholesale during the English Civil War. However, twenty-one of the images were fortuitously recorded shortly before this desecration in the herald William Dugdale's *Book of Monuments*, an illustrated manuscript now in the British Library.[1]

Bruges was probably born in 1375 or 1376. A native of Wiltshire, he followed his father Richard Bruges into royal service as a herald.[2] His first recorded appointment was as Chester Herald in June 1398;[3] he subsequently held the post of Guyenne (or Gujeune), and was raised to the newly-created post of Garter King of Arms in 1417. In 1420 he began the extravagant patronage of St George's church in Stamford which was to last until his death some thirty years later, and, through the terms of his will, beyond. He is known to have taken an interest in many other churches,[4] but St George's was certainly his main focus: the extent of his munificence, and the fact that he chose to buried in the choir there,[5] are ample testament. The reasons behind his decision to patronise this particular church are obscure; it has been suggested that he may have had links with the wool trade, and it could well have been this interest which led him to fix on Stamford. The dedication of the church would almost certainly have attracted Bruges' attention: St George is, of course, the dominant patron of the Order of the Garter,[6] but the condition of the fabric of the building may have been equally important. The church had been in existence, and dedicated to St George, since at least 1244, but it fell into disrepair, and possibly became completely derelict, following a fire in the early fourteenth century. The church was thus a prime location for redevelopment, and would have been of particular interest to someone

---

1. London, British Library Add. MS 71474, ff. 152–62.

2. H.S. London, *The Life of William Bruges the first Garter King of Arms,* Harleian Society Publications, 111 and 112 (1970), p. 1.

3. London, *William Bruges*, pp. 9–10.

4. *Ibid.,* p. 23.

5. *Ibid.,* p. 23. A monograph on the church by a former rector of St George's notes that Bruges' will makes reference to two chapels, of the Virgin Mary and St George, within the church: W.A. Rees-Jones, *Saint George, the Order of Saint George and the Church of Saint George in Stamford,* London 1937, p. 48. Bruges bequeaths to the Lady chapel two images, of the Virgin and St George, 'beyng in peynted stone & in my chapell at Kentishton'. Bruges makes provision for these images, and one of the Trinity, to be carefully boxed for the journey to Stamford.

6. The Order of the Garter was founded under the joint patronage of the Holy Trinity, the Virgin Mary and St Edward the Confessor as well as St George, but the other dedicatees were quickly relegated to a very minor role.

who would have wished to express his devotion to its patron saint through a display of piety mixed with largesse.

St George is now primarily identified, in Britain at least, as the patron saint of the English.[7] He is perceived as a mythic hero, a valiant Christian knight on a white charger, fighting under the emblem of a red cross on a white field, who rescued a princess from the predations of an evil dragon. Most people know little else about his legend or the development of his cult in England. Some English towns claim to be the place of his birth, or the site of his combat with the dragon, but any investigation into the development of his cult demonstrates that his links with this country are decidedly tenuous. The 'real' St George probably lived in modern-day Palestine or Turkey at the end of the third and beginning of the fourth century and was martyred under the Emperor Diocletian for refusing to sacrifice to Roman gods; there is some possibility that he may have been a Roman soldier, but no evidence at all to link him to the killing of a dragon. He was quickly identified as a Christian saint, with churches dedicated to him in the late fourth century. His devotion spread gradually throughout both the Byzantine and Roman church, and there is considerable evidence of the cult in western Europe well before the end of the first millennium. Narratives of his life were popular throughout the later medieval period, and included episodes such as the trial and torture of the saint, miraculous resurrections, and the casting down of a heathen idol in addition to the dragon legend, which became widely associated with St George from the mid-thirteenth century following its inclusion in the *Golden Legend* version of his life.[8]

St George was first identified as the patron saint of England during the reign of Edward III, the founder of the Order of the Garter, but he had begun to supplant the former English patron, St Edward the Confessor, some years earlier.[9] The reasons underlying this usurpation seem to relate to the identification of St George as a figure of chivalry and authority, and he was particularly linked with prowess in battle: in 1351 it was written that 'the English nation . . . call upon [St George], as being their special patron, particularly in war'.[10] Despite his role as the patron saint of this country, and the apparently wide circulation of literary narratives of his life (there are seven extant versions in various English and Scottish dialects),[11] vernacular visual imagery relating aspects of St George's legend other than the dragon story is surprisingly rare. There are only four (extant or recorded) medieval cycles likely to have been made by English designers and craftworkers which give any real sense of the complexity of the versions of his legend current during

---

7. Devotion to the saint was by no means confined to England. For example, it has been noted that St George was claimed as patron saint of Germany, Portugal, Barcelona, Genoa, Ferrara, Armenia, Antioch, Constantinople, various parts of France, and of the Coptic Christians, whilst 'St George for Holy Russia' was the battle-cry of the Czar: M.H. Bulley, *St George for Merrie England*, London 1908, pp. 21–2.

8. *The Golden Legend of Jacobus de Voragine*, trans. W.G. Ryan, 2 vols, Chichester 1993, i, pp. 238–42.

9. There seems to be no definitive evidence concerning the date when St George came to be recognised as the patron of the English people. A detailed analysis of the issues involved appears in my book, *St George: Hero, Martyr and Myth*, Stroud 2000, pp. 101–15.

10. T.H. Wilson, 'Saint George in Tudor and Stuart England' (unpublished M.Phil. dissertation, University of London, 1976), p. 21, citing E. Ashmole, *The Institution, Laws and Ceremonies of the Most Noble Order of the Garter,* London 1672.

11. See C. D'Evelyn and F.A. Foster, *A Manual of Writings in Middle English*, 2, pt v, Connecticut Academy of Arts and Sciences 1970, p. 589.

this period. Two of these cycles date to the period 1480–1500, and are both multi-panelled altarpieces in English alabaster, one at Borbjerg in Denmark and the other at La Selle in Normandy.[12] The third cycle, dated to the early sixteenth century, is a series of twelve images within a single window in St Neot's church, St Neot (Cornwall).[13] The Stamford cycle is not only the oldest of these four cycles, it is also by far the fullest, as it originally contained more than twice the number of images of the St Neot cycle, the next largest. However, the primary significance of the Stamford cycle lies in the ways in which it confirms and amplifies some of the rather troublesome imagery which appears in these other cycles, and consequently gives us strong evidence of a genuine localised English legend of St George. This narrative strand, first noted by M.R. James,[14] appears to be based on a legend associated with the Greek soldier-saint Mercurius, who was said to have been resurrected by the Virgin Mary in order to assassinate the apostate emperor Julian.[15] This story probably came to western Europe through a collection of miracles of the Virgin; in England St George seems to have been substituted for this little-known saint, although this incident does not occur in any written life of St George and is not alluded to in the *Acta Sanctorum*, even in the section specifically on England. Some early fourteenth-century English imagery seems to show St George resurrected to fight Julian: one example occurs in the sculptures of the Lady Chapel at Ely Cathedral, and further instances appear in the contemporaneous *Queen Mary Psalter* and *Smithfield Decretals*, as well as the rather later *Carew-Poyntz Hours* (*c*.1360) and a roof boss, *c*.1382, in the west walk of the cloister at Norwich Cathedral. Somewhat earlier, the *Lambeth Apocalypse*, *c*.1250–5, illustrates a legend of the Virgin resurrecting St Mercurius himself;[16] the device on his shield is very close to the cross of St George, and this may indicate the source of the English visual tradition which substitutes St George for St Mercurius. In later visual cycles of St George

12. On the Borbjerg and La Selle retables see S.J.E. Riches, 'The La Selle Retable: An English Alabaster Altarpiece in Normandy' (unpublished PhD thesis, University of Leicester, 1999); also S.J.E. Riches, 'The Alabaster Altarpiece of La Selle, Normandy: a Preliminary Report', in *Southwell and Nottinghamshire: Medieval Art, Architecture and Industry*, British Archaeological Association Conference Transactions, XXI, ed. J.S. Alexander, Leeds 1998, pp. 93–100.

13. On the window at St Neot see G. McNair Rushforth, 'The Windows of the Church of St Neot, Cornwall', *Transactions of the Exeter Diocesan Architectural and Archaeological Society*, 3rd ser. 4, pt iii (1937), pp. 150–90.

14. M.R. James, *The Sculptures in the Lady Chapel at Ely*, London 1895, pp. 5–9.

15. The *Golden Legend* gives an account of the assassination of Julian the Apostate by St Mercurius, stating that Julian had threatened to raze the city of Caesarea in Cappadocia following an argument with St Basil over a gift of barley loaves. St Basil had a vision of the Virgin summoning St Mercurius to despatch Julian, and the following day he visited the soldier's tomb to find that his lance was covered in blood; shortly afterwards he was informed that Julian had been murdered by a mystery assassin: *The Golden Legend*, i, pp. 128–30. Versions of the legend of St Mercurius circulated in England from the thirteenth century in collections of miracles of the Virgin, the *Speculum historiale* of Vincent of Beauvais and Gerald of Wales' *Gemma ecclesiastica*, amongst other texts: S. Lewis, *Reading Images. Narrative Discourse and Reception in the Thirteenth-Century Illuminated Apocalypse*, Cambridge 1995, pp. 275–6.

16. F.45, illustrated in Lewis, *Reading Images*, fig. 214.

Julian the Apostate seems to disappear from the narrative: at St Neot and La Selle, as well as at Stamford, St George seems to be resurrected in order that he should kill the dragon.[17]

The Stamford St George cycle formed the upper level of a two-tier arrangement of twenty-nine pairs of images in the chancel windows; the lower level was occupied by figures reputed to be the Founder Knights of the Order of the Garter. The lower level has received a considerable amount of attention because of Bruges' position as Garter King of Arms, notably in the form of debate over the identities of the figures, and in consequence it has entirely overshadowed the upper scheme in the literature concerned with the glass. For example, the historical background on William Bruges and the commissioning of the chancel windows was fully discussed by the herald Hugh Stanford London in a work of the 1950s. He devotes many pages to the figures in the lower cycle, yet he gives only two lines to the St George images: 'the upper row of panels depicted episodes in the martyrdom of St George ... These panels would doubtless repay study by someone versed in the hagiography of the saint'.[18] It seems that the time has now come to redress this imbalance.

One of the most significant problems about the Stamford St George cycle is that the sequence of images in the *Book of Monuments* provides only an incomplete record. Several of the drawings are clearly unfinished, but of greater significance is the fact that only twenty-one of the twenty-nine lights are recorded; the iconography of the missing scenes is unknown, and it is unclear where these images would have occurred in the cycle. However, comparison with the other English cycles of St George allows for several suggestions to be made; the Stamford imagery, in its turn, is able to offer an explanation of some of the more obscure imagery of the other known English cycles. Each subject, and its analogues, is now considered in turn.

(1)   An outdoor scene with St George standing on the left before a well, with a woman lying on the ground. She holds a jug which is spilling water near the saint's feet. St George brandishes a sword in his right hand whilst his left hand rests on the upper part of a golden scabbard which is attached to some kind of belt. It is unclear whether the saint has cast

---

17. It is interesting to note that the late fifteenth-century wall paintings of the miracles of the Virgin on the north side of Winchester Cathedral Lady Chapel include three subjects from the story of St George resurrected to kill Julian the Apostate; M.R. James has suggested that the subject probably also appeared in the wall paintings on the north side of Eton College Chapel, dated 1479–88. The re-emergence of this form of the narrative in English material at this late date tends to imply that the two forms coexisted. On the Winchester and Eton imagery see M.R. James, *The Frescoes in the Chapel at Eton College,* Eton 1907; M.R. James and E.W. Tristram, 'The wall-paintings in Eton College Chapel and in the Lady Chapel of Winchester Cathedral', *Walpole Society,* 17 (1928–9), pp. 1–45; A. Martindale, 'The Wall-paintings in the Chapel of Eton College', in *England and the Low Countries in the Later Middle Ages,* ed. C. Barron and N. Saul, Stroud 1995, pp.133–52. The links between the Virgin and St George are well attested: images of the two figures are commonly paired, such as in William Bruges' will (see note 5 above). Meanwhile, the *Scottish Legendary* contains one of several literary allusions to St George as the Virgin's champion: 'men callis hym oure lady knycht' (line 14 of 'George' in *Legends of the Saints in the Scottish Dialect of the Fourteenth Century,* ed. W.M. Metcalfe, Scottish Text Society 1891, pp. 176–203). However, whilst the legend of the resurrection of St George by the Virgin appears to be peculiarly English, there are signs of a connection between them elsewhere in Europe. For example, the Virgin is shown arming St George in the Valencia altarpiece, a work generally accepted to be German, dating from the period *c.*1410–20. It is treated at length in C.M. Kauffmann, 'The altar-piece of St George from Valencia', *Victoria and Albert Museum Yearbook,* 2, 1970, pp. 65–100, although there is no discussion of the links between the Virgin and St George.

18. London, *William Bruges,* pp. 60–1.

down the woman and her jug or is about to raise them up. The woman wears a long red robe, a white apron and a white headdress. The saint is dressed in a short blue robe with a high collar, long sleeves and white fringing at the edge of the skirt; he also wears red hose and black boots. The saint is nimbed, but is not identified by his red cross device: despite the presence of the sword he does not wear armour or have a shield. The well is depicted as a large yellow barrel filled with blue water sited beneath a pitched yellow roof supported on pillars. The winding mechanism, which holds a small yellow barrel, is depicted rather illogically, as it is attached to two pillars on the same side of the well rather than being centred over the well itself. The background of the scene is a forest and mountains; a single tree stands to the left of the well, immediately behind St George. This is an apparently unparalleled subject, and it seems likely that it is drawn from the obscure early part of the saint's career. It may reflect an otherwise lost English tradition associated with the narrative of the resurrection of the saint by the Virgin, which begins immediately afterwards.

(2)   An outdoor scene in a rocky landscape, with a single tree on the right of the scene. St George, still nimbed but now wearing armour with a red cross tabard and shield, is depicted on foot on the left of the subject. He uses a sword to fight a group of six armed men,[19] who are not identified by any device and wear a variety of styles of armour. One wears a red tabard, three others wear sleeved tabards in shades of blue with white cuffs. Two of the men in blue tabards are already falling, but the other four men threaten the saint with lances and swords. This subject is paralleled in the St Neot glass.

(3)   An indoor scene of a room with a floor tiled in a pattern of black and white triangles, a white rear wall with two round-headed windows and a ceiling covered with a blue brocaded cloth edged with gold fringing (Pl. VIA). St George, wearing armour and a red cross tabard, kneels in prayer on a gold brocaded carpet before an altar bearing a figure of the Virgin and Child. The sides of the altar have a number of arched recesses indicated, and it stands against a grey wall. St George is about to be beheaded by a bearded man in armour and a plain red tabard who wields a large axe. The quality of drawing in this image is rather variable, and the perspective of the carpet and the altar have given particular problems. This subject is also paralleled in the St Neot glass.

(4)   An outdoor scene of St George being resurrected by the Virgin and three angels from a stone tomb-chest (Fig. 23). The Virgin, who is crowned, wears a long-sleeved blue robe, lined with gold, over a second robe which is red and covers her feet. Her hair has not been coloured. The three angels all wear white robes and have golden hair and wings. St George is naked, but mainly covered by a white gravecloth. A wall and part of a substantial archway stands behind the tomb and to the left, whilst a tree occupies the right of the scene. The area around the tomb is rocky and grassy, whilst the background is mountainous. This subject is paralleled in the St Neot glass, and the alabaster retables at Borbjerg and La Selle.

(5)   St George, mounted on a white horse and armed as a knight, fights the dragon. In the main this is a very conventional treatment, with the dragon in the classic pose, under

19. St George holds the sword behind his head, a stance which is often used in images of the combat with the dragon as a variant on the standard pose of spearing the dragon in the mouth.

In quarto lumine dicto secunda Fenestra

Fig. 23. *St George is resurrected by the Virgin (London, BL Add. MS 71474, f. 153v)*

the horse's hooves, being speared through the upper jaw by the saint's lance. The princess kneels in the background on rising ground and her parents watch from a fortified city on top of a cliff. The only exceptional aspect is the lack of a lamb, which invariably accompanies the princess as a sacrifice in images of St George rescuing her from the dragon. St George wears a large red plume on his helmet and a red cross tabard. The background of the scene seems to be a thickly wooded mountainside, with a river or bay on the left of the image and the far coast in the distance. A small sailing boat is shown on the water. Versions of this subject are very common in the iconography of St George, and appear at St Neot and La Selle.

(6)   This subject shows St George baptising two long-haired women and a crowned, bearded man, who are shown naked, within a large yellow barrel-like tub filled with water. St George, who still wears his armour but now has a sleeved red cross tabard, holds a silver dish above the heads of the converts, who are likely to be the princess rescued from the dragon and her parents the king and queen. A group of five other converts are waiting their turn on the right of the scene; they are all naked, and the foremost, a short-haired figure with a rounded stomach who is almost certainly meant to be understood as a woman, covers herself rather ineffectually with a white sheet. The scene takes place in a setting which seems to be somewhere between a room and a stage set: two red masonry walls are indicated, and a black-and-white tiled floor, but the blue ceiling is edged with a white section, crenellated along one side with a spoked semi-circle protruding into the foreground and a short pillar, with rounded golden ends, marking the corner of the two

missing walls needed to complete the room. On the left side of the image the white edge section merges into a frame for the image, which continues down the left side and across the base. Three rounded windows appear in the back wall, and an arched doorway is indicated in the right wall. The background of the very top of the image, outside the 'room', is red. An image of the baptism of the king, queen and princess appears in the La Selle retable, and also occurs in non-English cycles such as the Valencia altarpiece.[20]

(7)   A scene of the trial of St George. He wears armour and a sleeved red-cross tabard and is nimbed; he is escorted by three guards who wear a variety of armour and carry weapons including an axe, swords and lances. The bearded heathen emperor, who is usually called Dacian in contemporary literary versions of the legend, wears a long red robe trimmed with ermine and a golden crown over a red crescent hat. Comparative versions of this subject are very common: examples include the cycles of St Neot, Borbjerg and La Selle. However, the Stamford treatment is unusual because Dacian does not seem to be enthroned, but is seated before a cloth of honour. Furthermore, Dacian has his hand on the head of a woman who appears to be denouncing the saint as she points towards him. She is dressed in a short blue robe with white cuffs, over a pink skirt, with a white wimple, and is seated on a white chest decorated with rounded shapes. Her identity is a mystery, as there is no known tradition which corresponds to this image.

(8)   This outdoor subject is in two parts. On the left side St George, still wearing armour and a red-cross tabard, is shown being pushed into a prison by a guard. This figure wears armour and a blue tabard; Dacian, wearing a red ermine-trimmed robe, a golden crown over a golden crescent-shaped hat and holding a golden sceptre, looks on from the far left. On the right St George is in prison, preaching through a window to a wimpled woman, wearing a long blue robe, who kneels in prayer outside. She is almost certainly to be identified as the Empress Alexandra, who was converted by St George in some literary versions of his legend. This is a relatively unusual subject; St George is shown in prison, visited by Christ, in the Valencia altarpiece, and in a mid-thirteenth century cycle in glass at Clermont-Ferrand Cathedral the empress is shown converted by St George.[21]

(9)   An outdoor scene of torture. St George, now stripped and wearing only a loincloth, lies on a rack. Two torturers pull on the ropes tied to his body, and Dacian looks on amid a group of six other men. The emperor is dressed identically to the previous panel, whilst his attendants wear a variety of robes and headdresses. This image departs from the overall format as it is presented in a fictive architectural frame, with a series of turreted towers, windows and crenellations. This subject seems to be very rare in extant visual cycles of the life of the saint, but it is commonly referred to in literary versions of the narrative, such as the *Golden Legend* and the *Scottish Legendary*.

(10)   An indoor scene, with a red rear wall and a floor tiled in a pattern of red and white, again framed by fictive architecture (Pl. VIB). St George, wearing a loincloth, his hair coloured yellow, is tied to the upright of a wooden cross and is scourged by two torturers

20. On the Valencia altarpiece see above, note 17.
21. On the Clermont-Ferrand cycle see Abbé R. Berger, *Les Vitraux de la Cathédrale Notre-Dame de Clermont*, Clermont-Ferrand 1968.

each wielding a morning-star, a spiked ball attached to a stick by a short length of chain. Dacian and another figure look on. The emperor wears a red robe trimmed with white rather than ermine, and has a blue crescent-shaped hat but no crown. His companion wears a long blue robe with lacing at the throat and a white hat. The torturer on the left wears a short blue robe with a white belt, pink hose and a red hat, whilst the torturer on the right has green hose, a grey hat and a pink robe with detailed lacing. Both men wear distinctive black boots with elongated points. The nearest parallel to this subject occurs in a cycle of the life of St George within the Salisbury Breviary (f.448v),[22] a French manuscript created for John, duke of Bedford, during the period 1424–35. In this version the saint is tied to a post rather than a cross; he is scourged by one torturer whilst a second apparently prepares to put salt in his wounds.

(11)   This is a rather indistinct, and evidently incomplete, subject in an outdoor setting of grass and bare earth. St George, wearing a loincloth but with no shading or colouration of his body or hair, is seated on a low table. He is assaulted by three torturers who are dressed in reds and blues and the pointed black boots, but whose faces and hats are uncoloured. They hold implements against his body; these objects are coloured yellow and look as if they are bunches of straw. This could be a scene of St George burnt by flaming torches, or the implements could be intended to be read as rakes. A similar subject occurs in the Borbjerg retable, although the saint is depicted standing rather than seated. The implements held by the torturers in this version are also indistinct, although they are somewhat smaller than those shown in the Stamford scene.

(12)   Another outdoor scene, with St George being boiled in a cauldron of water set over a fire in a grassy setting. Again, St George wears a loincloth but has no colouration or shading on his body or hair. Two torturers stir the liquid whilst a third, seated on the ground, looks on. All three are dressed in reds and blues, with hats which seem to be only partially coloured, and the elongated black boots. A gold radiance appears in the sky above the saint's head: this is the only scene where such a device is used. The subject of the boiling of St George is relatively common in visual cycles of the saint's life, occurring, for example, in the St Neot glass and the Valencia altarpiece.[23]

(13)   The torture of the millstones, in a rather unusual version. Rather than being suspended by his hands with a millstone tied to his feet to stretch him, as occurs in the St Neot glass, or crushed under a millstone, as described in the life of St George which appears in the early-to-mid-fifteenth century *Mirk's Festial*,[24] the saint has been seated on a mechanism with a large blade, a small millstone tied to each ankle. Two torturers are present, again dressed in reds and blues and the elongated black boots. The torturer on the right, who wears a yellow hat with a white brim, appears to be operating a mechanism to raise the blade and cut the saint in half. Drops of blood are indicated, running down the

22. Paris, Bibliothèque Nationale, MS. Lat. 17294.
23. An interesting comparative subject occurs in the St George imagery in the carved desk-ends of the south side of the choir of St George's Chapel, Windsor (lower row, third desk-end from the west end, facing west). Rather than being boiled entire, in this image St George is dismembered and his body parts are boiled in a small cauldron.
24. 'De festo Sancti Georgii, Martyris' in *Mirk's Festial: a collection of homilies by John Mirk*, ed. Theodore Erbe, EETS, es 96 (1905), p. 134.

saint's legs, but they have not been coloured. Dacian looks on from the left of the subject, wearing a blue robe under a red mantle trimmed with ermine. He carries a golden sceptre and wears a golden crown over a white crescent-shaped hat with a geometric pattern inscribed in gold. The subject is placed in an outdoor setting, with bare earth and grassy hillocks.

(14)   St George, wearing a loincloth, is bound to a post by ropes around his neck and ankles; his wrists are also bound. A torturer holds a golden chalice to his lips whilst three other men, all armed with large axes, look on. The four malefactors all wear the elongated black boots, three are dressed in reds and blues whilst the fourth wears a brown tabard. Several parts of the image have been left uncoloured, such as the torturers' faces and hands, one of their hats, a belt-purse and St George's entire body (although his hair is coloured yellow). The torture is again set in an outdoor scene with grass and bare earth. This subject is probably the poisoning of St George, although there is no sign of the conventional dragon in the chalice found in comparative images, such as in the Borbjerg retable.

(15)   This image depicts an indoor setting of a room with a floor tiled in a pattern of black and white and a rear wall coloured blue. Fan vaulting may be indicated in the ceiling. The image is framed with a simple white architrave; the top left corner of the image is cut off by the frame, and the area outside the frame is coloured yellow. St George, wearing armour and a sleeved red-cross tabard, baptises a figure of indeterminate gender who is shown in a small, yellow barrel-like tub. The saint holds a small golden bowl over the convert's head, which effectively forms a nimbus although the saint himself is unnimbed, just as he appears in most of the other subjects in this cycle. Two people, one a bearded man, look on; they are dressed in red and blue robes respectively, and the latter holds a purple robe with gold collar and cuffs. It seems likely that the convert is Athanasius, the magician who became a Christian when his poison failed to kill the saint, but the fact that St George wears armour is rather troublesome, as it would seem illogical to show the saint in armour as he is supposed to be imprisoned at this point in the story. The purple of the robe held by the bearded man is also problematic, as this colour is likely to be associated with a royal or imperial figure rather than a magician. If this is not the magician it is unclear who it is intended to be: the only royal person converted by St George, apart from the rescued princess and her family whom we have already seen in subject 6, was Dacian's consort the empress Alexandra. The short hair on the baptised figure, in stark contrast to the princess and queen's long hair in the previous baptism, makes it unlikely that this figure is female, although the short hairstyle on the near-naked woman in the first baptism scene could imply that this figure is a short-haired woman, or a woman with her hair tied up in some way. There is no known analogue for this image.

(16)   Another indoor scene, with a black-and-white tiled floor and a blue rear wall (Fig. 24). In this instance a plain white architrave cuts off both of the top corners of the image: they are each coloured yellow. The ends of the architrave are decorated with volutes, and the span between is filled with a simple trellis. St George, again wearing only a loincloth, is suspended by his hands, which are tied to the trellis. Two torturers are preparing to saw him in half vertically with a yellow two-handled saw. The torturers are dressed in reds and browns although their hats and elongated boots have not been coloured. It is interesting that the saw is not shown passing through the saint's chest, as is

In tertio lumine dicit Fenestra.

Fig. 24.   *St George is sawn in half*
(London, BL Add. MS 71474, f. 159v)

seen in parallel images such as the Valencia altarpiece; the torturers here are defying logic as they apparently float in mid-air to hold the saw at his head. There is clear evidence of redrawing of St George's lower legs and feet.

(17)   An outdoor subject which seems to be a second scene of resurrection. St George is shown in a similar chest tomb to that in subject 4, but wearing a loincloth rather than graveclothes. St Peter, dressed in red, stands on the extreme left holding his attribute of a golden key. Next to him stands a male figure, dressed in a blue mantle over a red robe. This is almost certainly Christ, who is holding the saint's right hand to raise him. Two angels also assist: one kneels in the right foreground, holding St George's left hand, whilst the second stands at the back of the tomb. All the figures have yellow hair, and the angels have yellow and green wings; Christ has a yellow beard but St Peter's is uncoloured. This subject is problematic as it seems to have no analogues. St Michael and a group of angels are variously credited with resurrecting St George in literary versions, and there is the English visual motif of resurrection by the Virgin, but there does not seem to be a tradition of Christ performing this function.

(18)   St George is depicted tortured on the wheel in an outdoor setting. This version of the wheel torture is unusual in that there are no knives or spikes, as found in the Valencia altarpiece, for example. This version shows the saint bound with ropes to two wheels which seem designed to move in opposite directions, working on a ratcheting system operated by two torturers. A third torturer, holding a large axe, looks on; all three are

dressed in blues and reds and have elongated black shoes; the hat of the third alone is uncoloured. Dacian observes from the right of the scene. He carries a golden sceptre and is dressed in his red robe trimmed with ermine and wears a golden crown over a pink crescent-shaped hat. St George wears a loincloth but his body and hair are otherwise unshaded and uncoloured.

(19)   An outdoor scene with hillocks of bare earth, grass and foliage before a castle with crenellated walls and two towers roofed in blue. St George, wearing a loincloth, his hair coloured yellow, kneels with his elbows and wrists bound with rope; his wrists are apparently tied to a short post. He is scourged by a torturer, dressed in a brown robe, blue hose and elongated black shoes, who holds a seven-headed whip. Dacian looks on from the right of the image. He wears a red mantle trimmed with ermine over a red robe belted in white, and a golden crown over a red crescent-shaped hat. In this image he holds a sword rather than a sceptre. On the extreme right of the image stands a man who appears to be dressed in clerical robes.[25] Two other men stand in the middle ground on the left. Their feet and legs are not visible; those of the man on the extreme left are plausibly hidden by a hillock, but the depiction of the man on the near left seems somewhat illogical. Both men are dressed in blues and reds; the man on the near left wears a hat with a green crown and a red brim. He seems to be pointing at the torturer, or possibly at the saint. Several elements of the composition are uncoloured, most notably Dacian's hair and beard, and the hair of the torturer. There are also two rather troublesome elements in the background: an elongated triangular shape appears in the sky immediately behind the torturer, and looks rather like the preliminary drawing of a spire. Furthermore, the blue roofs of the castle, one pointed, the other shaped like an onion dome, are each surmounted by what seems to be a circle topped by a cross. There are no direct parallels to this image, although, as noted above with reference to subject 10, the scourging of St George does appear in the Salisbury Breviary.

(20)   An outdoor scene with a similar foreground to the previous image, but an entirely different building. Dacian, wearing a red mantle trimmed with ermine over a pink belted robe and a golden crown over a pink crescent-shaped hat, and holding a golden sceptre, is shown in a loggia-type structure with a low wall and a stepped buttress supporting the left side. A poorly-drawn figure dressed in blue, with a green hat, is seated alongside Dacian on his left, and a green curtain lined with pink is draped in the extreme right-hand side of the window-like opening through which the figures are visible. St George, dressed in a loincloth, kneels in the foreground, awaiting his beheading by an executioner holding a large golden sword. This figure is dressed in a short pink belted robe and blue hose. His boots are of the usual elongated shape; one is uncoloured whilst the other has the colour of the surrounding grass. On the right of the scene is a curved ribbon-like uncoloured

25. Despite appearances, it seems likely that this figure is not intended to be read as a Christian religious. This kind of character regularly appears in scenes of martyrdom and seems to be a type of visual shorthand, as the term 'clerk', meaning a secretary, derives from 'cleric'. Examples of this figure occur in the La Selle retable, and also in wall paintings of the martyrdom of St Erasmus in Ampney Crucis church (Gloucestershire), *c.*1450, and the Commandery, Worcester, *c.*1480; both illustrated in E.M. Moore, 'Wall-paintings recently discovered in Worcestershire', *Archaeologia,* 88 (1940), pp. 218–88, plate lxxxvi, b and c. I am indebted to Miriam Gill for this reference.

area: its purpose is unclear. The execution of St George is a very common subject in cycles of his life, although it is more usual to show the moment after execution, with the severed head lying on the ground and his soul being carried off by angels. The La Selle retable utilises this form, although the St Neot glass, like the Stamford cycle, shows the saint awaiting decapitation.

(21)   The final scene shows a large golden reliquary, which presumably contains relics of St George. It has a pitched roof and pinnacled corners and is decorated with jewels and what is probably intended to be read as enamelling in red and blue. The reliquary is displayed on a large arcaded table-like structure, in a dark blue colour with an incised pattern on the top surface. Four male religious, representing two different orders, appear in the background, one pair on each side. The foremost of each pair is dressed in a brown habit, the hindmost in grey. The hair of each of them is uncoloured. The foremost on the left side rests his hand on the tabletop whilst his equivalent on the other side reaches out with his left hand as if about to touch the reliquary. In the foreground three lay people kneel on a floor tiled in a black and white pattern. The figure on the left wears a short red robe over blue hose; the hair and boots are uncoloured, and he gestures towards the reliquary with his left hand. The central figure, who is facing directly towards the reliquary, is a woman wearing a short red robe and a blue wrap over an uncoloured skirt. Her long hair is also uncoloured. The right-hand figure gestures towards the reliquary with his right hand. He has a golden sword on his belt and has red hose; his hair, robe and boots are uncoloured. This subject seems to be unparalleled in known narratives of the life of St George, but it does make a fitting conclusion to this cycle, as it clearly demonstrates veneration of the saint.

As noted above, the Stamford cycle forms an interesting counterpart to the English alabaster treatments of the life of St George at Borbjerg and La Selle and the version in glass at St Neot. Comparison of the four cycles shows a remarkable consistency of narrative form, with each version including imagery relating to the resurrection of St George by the Virgin Mary, the encounter with the dragon, the trial before the heathen ruler and the subsequent martyrdom. Imagery which appears at Stamford alone relates to the scene at the well, the baptism of 'Athanasius', the resurrection by Christ and the reliquary; subjects omitted at Stamford but appearing in the other cycles relate to St George being armed as a knight by the Virgin Mary and also to an episode where he casts down a heathen idol. Given that there are eight images missing at Stamford there is a clear possibility that these episodes were originally included but were lost before Dugdale's visit; in the case of the arming subject this is likely to be a probability. Both alabaster cycles begin with the resurrection of St George by the Virgin, but the glass at St Neot and the records of the Stamford cycle each present two episodes which precede this subject in an expansion of the 'English' narrative of St George noted above. In each of these latter cycles St George is shown (a) in combat with an enemy army and (b) being beheaded before an altar bearing an image of the Virgin and Child immediately before (c) the subject of the resurrection by the Virgin Mary. The implication is that St George was martyred by a heathen enemy whom he had opposed and then resurrected by the Virgin as a reward for his loyalty. At St Neot this narrative strand continues into (d) the Virgin arming St George as a knight and (e) the combat with the dragon. This format is exactly mirrored by the progression of the

La Selle retable, which includes subjects (c) (d) and (e) in that order.[26] The evidence provided by these English cycles indicates that the absence at Stamford of a scene of the arming of St George by the Virgin is quite extraordinary: as the subject following the resurrection is the combat with the dragon it is clear that the same narrative form is being used. Furthermore, given that Bruges, the patron of the Stamford cycle, was so deeply concerned with concepts of knighthood and chivalry it seems almost unthinkable that he would have omitted such a seminal subject as the conferring of the status of knight.

This assertion must be weighed against the evidence of the commentary which accompanies the drawings in the *Book of Monuments*. Brief captions on each picture state the location of the image, and the scheme set out in them indicates that the first four images are missing (on the north side of the chancel), also four images between subjects 10 and 11 (the final three lights of the five-light east window and the first light on the southern side). If correct, this would clearly rule out a scene of the arming of St George, which would occur in the north side between subjects 4 and 5. However, there seem to be good grounds for doubting the reliability of the captions, and, indeed, some aspects of the images themselves, as a consequence of what we know about the way that the *Book of Monuments* was produced. Dugdale travelled around the Midlands, East Anglia and Yorkshire during the summers of 1640 and 1641, in company with the limner and arms painter William Sedgwick, recording monuments, epitaphs and heraldry. It seems likely that they made notes and sketches on the spot, and that Sedgwick later worked up the sketches into the illustrations that we now have. The time delay involved, which seems to have been no less than three weeks in the case of St George's, Stamford,[27] must lead us to question the reliability of this source, for it would have been very easy for errors to creep in unless Sedgwick and Dugdale were scrupulously accurate in their preparatory work. Numerous examples of unfinished and poorly conceived images are observed in the record of the Stamford cycle, and whilst it is possible that shortcomings in perspective are attributable to the designers and artisans who made the actual windows, it is virtually impossible that obvious redrawing and omitted colour is due to anything other than deficiencies on the part of the manuscript. H.S. London has commented on errors in the heraldry represented in the images of the 'Founder Knights' and notes that three of the knights are misnamed.[28] As Dugdale was likely to have been considerably more interested in the Founder knights than in the St George cycle, these glaring errors considerably

26. The reasons for the omission of subjects (a) and (b) at La Selle are obscure, but may relate to the putative patronage of this altarpiece. The St Neot glass is embellished by short legends accompanying each subject, and the legends on subject (a) and (b) name the saint's heathen enemy as the 'Gallicani'. Rushforth glosses this as 'Gauls' (Rushforth, *St Neot*, p.174): the probability that the La Selle retable was made for a Norman patron (St George does not have a red cross device, for example) indicates that a reference to Gaulish heathens would not have been appropriate. The situation at Borbjerg is somewhat different, as there is a possibility that the narrative has been disrupted by losses, or perhaps altered in order to fit a rather limited number of subject panels and a specific design brief. St George is indeed shown in combat with a heathen enemy, then resurrected and armed by the Virgin, but the first episode is not obviously linked to the latter two by a scene of his death.

27. London, *William Bruges*, pp. 113–14. Interestingly, London observes that 'although not of outstanding merit . . . [the limnings] are carefully finished and it is manifest that they could not have been painted on the spot': the latter half of this statement seems incontrovertible, but close observation of the St George images demonstrates that 'careful finishing' is frequently notable only by its absence.

28. London, *William Bruges*, p. 59.

undermine the authenticity of the scheme of the St George images, and it seems quite possible that the captions on the images may well mis-site the lost subjects.

There is, however, some evidence to support Dugdale's contention that the first four images of the cycle are omitted from the *Book of Monuments*. Three otherwise unrecorded scenes occur in what purports to be a drawing of the first window on the north side of the chancel, made by Ralph Thoresby and collected in William Stukeley's Commonplace Book (f.100).[29] This image shows a draped scutcheon of the Bruges arms in the first light, followed by two scenes in a kitchen, or possibly a baker's shop, and an outdoor scene with two figures, one standing and one kneeling. All three scenes are unparalleled in the iconography of St George, both written and visual, a fact which leads to strong suspicions about the image. Furthermore, the very late date of the drawing casts considerable doubt on its veracity; it was made in September 1716, almost a century after the creation of the *Book of Monuments*, and it seems most unlikely that Dugdale and Sedgwick would have omitted this window from their scheme if it had still been in existence. The conclusion that Thoresby invented these images seems irresistible; to give him his due, his interest seems to have been in the 'Founder Knights' rather than the St George cycle. This impression is confirmed by reference to the next folio of the commonplace book (f.101), for here we see the knights in isolation, without the scenes of St George above; it can be argued that Thoresby is trying to give some impression of the original appearance of a destroyed window with no real claim to accuracy about parts of the iconography in which he was not personally interested. The presence of the Bruges arms may be correct, but in the absence of supporting evidence it seems that we may well be seeking four subjects from the life of St George, rather than three, for this window. It is very probable that, like the scene of St George and the woman by the well (subject 1), the missing subjects related to an otherwise lost tradition concerned with the early part of St George's career.

Dugdale's scheme implies that the second group of missing scenes, between subjects 10 and 11, formed part of the procession of grisly tortures inflicted on the saint. However, given that these lost subjects include the central image from the east window, it is possible that one may have had a different theme. A sketch of the lower scheme which was probably prepared by Wenceslaus Hollar for *Collections for the History of the Origin and Laws of the Most Noble Order of the Garter and the Lives of Its Illustrious Founder and Companions* (c.1664–72)[30] shows the central image as a standing figure of St George in armour, accompanied by a squire who holds his horse, standing before a canopied tent. If this sketch is accurate it suggests that the composition of this central light was quite different from the others; it seems likely that its counterpart in the upper scheme was a specifically complementary image, such as Christ blessing the scene, for example, rather than an image from the life of St George.

Whether or not this suggestion is correct, it is probable that some of the missing subjects were tortures, not least because of the relative completeness of the narrative of the life of St George within this cycle: there are a few notable omissions, such as the arming and the casting down of the idol, but it is difficult to suggest other subjects which are likely to have appeared. There is, however, no shortage of other possible tortures. Late medieval visual imagery and hagiography of St George is filled with a remarkable range of tortures;

29. Devizes, Wiltshire Archaeological Society, William Stukeley's Commonplace Book (1721).
30. Oxford, Bodleian Library MS Ashmole 1131, f. 162.

unlike most martyrs, he is not associated with any specific torture; rather, he seems to acquire tortures from other legends, such as St Catherine's wheel and St John the Evangelist's boiling. Comparison of the Stamford imagery with the St George roundels in the Bedford Hours (c.1422),[31] a second French manuscript commissioned by John, duke of Bedford, demonstrates that the sole torture they have in common is boiling. The Bedford Hours offers four other possibilities: St George is depicted being beaten whilst seated on a horse, tied to a saltire cross, sawn in half whilst seated, and being thrown into a well.

Another reason for asserting that several images of torture may have been lost from the cycle is that the subjects which do survive through the medium of the *Book of Monuments* demonstrate a strong emphasis on this theme, with approximately half of the recorded images concerned with torture in one form or another. This emphasis is very interesting, especially when we consider that the La Selle retable demonstrates that it was perfectly possible to construct a cycle of St George which omitted any reference to torture. The appeal of St George to Bruges is obvious: the great chivalric figure who was patron saint of both England and the Order of the Garter; indeed it was almost certainly this specific dedication which initially drew Bruges to the church of St George in Stamford. But the way that the cycle is constructed implies that there may have been a deeper agenda at work, and this may tell us something about Bruges' own convictions: whilst it is unlikely that the chancel windows were completed during Bruges' lifetime, it is very likely that he chose at least some of the subjects himself. Even if we add in a scene of the arming of St George we are still confronted with a cycle in which the chivalric code seems to be of only minor importance, where images of the suffering martyr far outweigh images of the heroic knight. There may well be an element of *Imitatio Christi* in this cycle, something which seems particularly apparent in subject 10 (Pl. VIB), where the figure of St George scourged whilst tied to a cross strongly evokes the scourging during the Passion of Christ. The emphasis on torture in the Stamford images can perhaps be read as a treatise on forbearance: St George suffers just as Christ suffered, he patiently accepts this suffering just as Christ had done. The viewer is shown that it is possible to emulate Christ under even the most severe duress, and if St George was able to forbear cannot every other true Christian forbear also?

Whilst it could be argued that the positioning of this cycle in the chancel, and hence beyond the rood screen, makes it unlikely that it was intended to be didactic, we should remember the fact that lay access to the chancel was limited to special occasions and this would have increased the impact of the glass.[32] The congregation knew that the St George cycle was there, and being allowed to see it would heighten the special atmosphere of the Easter vigil and Candlemas. There is also the possibility that Bruges himself anticipated

---

31. BL Add. MS 42131, f. 256v. Janet Backhouse has observed that, in the abscence of text, it is impossible to be sure that these roundels do actually depict St George (J. Backhouse, *The Bedford Hours*, London 1990, pp. 55–6). It has been suggested that the images represent the torture of the patron saints of the five leading members of the Order of the Garter, but, as all these tortures occur elsewhere in the iconography and hagiography of the saint, and the fact that he is clearly invoked in the dominant image on the folio, this explanation seems unlikely.

32. Eamon Duffy has argued quite persuasively that the rood screen functioned as a *permeable* rather than a solid barrier, and notes examples of occasions when laity were permitted to enter the chancel of their parish church: E. Duffy, *The Stripping of the Altars*, London 1992, p. 112.

being allowed more regular access to the chancel, and hence to his St George narrative; it is known that some patrons were granted such privileges, and a patron as munificent as Bruges would surely have had a strong claim to be given this special treatment had he lived to see the completion of the glass.

Ultimately it may not really matter whether or not the St George cycle was intended to be didactic. Bruges knew that he wanted to commemorate the first founders of the Order of the Garter, and to mark his exalted position in that Order; he also wanted to show his respect for the patron saint of the Order, and especially those aspects of the saint's life which were particularly pertinent to him. Regardless of whether it would be seen by anyone else, he knew that it would be seen by his God, the most important audience of all.

Memorials and Manuscripts of a Yorkist Elite

JANET BACKHOUSE

The close political, cultural and personal relationships which were fostered between the court of Edward IV and the Burgundian ducal court in Flanders are well documented and have been extensively discussed. The marriage of Margaret of York to Charles of Burgundy in 1468, resulting in the exchange of the Orders of the Garter and the Golden Fleece, Edward's period of exile in the Low Countries in 1470–1, and the diplomatic visit of Louis de Gruuthuse to Windsor in the autumn of 1472 are all historical landmarks in this process. Three of the men who in life participated in these events lie buried side by side to the north of the choir of St George's Chapel in Windsor. The first is King Edward himself, the second his close friend and supporter William, Lord Hastings, and the third Hastings's brother-in-law, Sir John Donne of Kidwelly. All three men have also been shown to have contributed at a personal level to the introduction of the Flemish taste into the court circle, for all three were significant purchasers of Flemish illuminated manuscripts.

St George's Chapel as a whole is perhaps Edward IV's most visible and lasting memorial and his unusual chantry chapel, spanning the first three eastern bays of the north aisle below the level of the vaulting and looking down directly onto the high altar, is one of its original features. Parallels can be drawn between this and the two-storey oratory inserted into the church of Onze-Lieve-Vrouwe in Bruges by Louis de Gruuthuse, but any direct influence must be at best only the result of hearsay. Edward fled into exile in Flanders early in October 1470 and was Gruuthuse's guest first at the Hague and subsequently in Bruges before he made his ultimately successful return to England in March 1471.[1] Arrangements for the construction of the present Gruuthuse chapel were not finalised until 7 January 1472.[2] The English king cannot therefore have seen it though he could well have heard it described, even by Gruuthuse himself, before he put his own plans for St George's into action in 1475. The two chapels do have in common the somewhat unusual facility of enjoying a direct and private view, from an upper level, of celebrations in the sanctuary of the church. In Bruges, however, the chapel incorporates a direct link between the church and the patron's existing residence which adjoins it. The Bruges church is moreover a public foundation belonging to the city. At Windsor the chapel is an integral part of a new building within the confines of a royal castle, adjacent to the supporting college rather than to the royal apartments. It furthermore provides the means of watching (or viewing) the north choir aisle as well as the sanctuary.

The direct influence of Louis de Gruuthuse has also been proposed as the inspiration behind Edward IV's activities as a collector of illuminated manuscripts. The lavishly

---

1. C.D. Ross, *Edward IV*, London 1974, pp. 152–60.

2. *Lodewijk van Gruuthuse, mecenas en Europees diplomaat ca. 1427–1492*, ed. M.P.J. Martens, Bruges 1992, pp. 39–42, 58. See also M. Vale, 'An Anglo-Burgundian Nobleman and Art Patron: Louis de Bruges, Lord of la Gruuthuse and Earl of Winchester', *England and the Low Countries in the Later Middle Ages*, ed. C. Barron and N. Saul, Stroud 1995, pp. 115–31, esp. 122–6.

decorated secular texts which he purchased survive as a foundation stone of the old Royal Library, given to the newly-established British Museum in 1757 by George II.[3] While he can hardly have been unaware of his host's enthusiasm for manuscripts and books, the collection which Edward may have seen in Gruuthuse's possession in 1471 was far from having achieved the richness for which it is admired today. Gruuthuse lived until November 1492 and many of his more spectacular acquisitions were made during his later years.[4] One at least of his manuscripts, its marks of ownership duly revised, did make its way into Edward's possession, possibly as a gift, though there is no way of recovering the circumstances.[5] However, the bulk of Edward's purchasing demonstrably took place around 1479 and 1480, long after his sojourn in Bruges. It was part of a more general campaign to acquire luxury accessories from the Low Countries, parallel to the major building campaigns at Eltham and, indeed, at St George's Chapel during the later part of the reign.

The Garter is consistently included among Edward's personal arms and badges in the margins of the manuscripts made for him in Flanders, though in a somewhat eccentric form. In place of the normal circular blue band with tag and buckle, the illuminators use a livery collar format. The blue and gold ribbon thus looks as if it should be hung around the neck with the buckle as a pendant, after the fashion of the insignia of the Golden Fleece. Edward was of course a member of the Order of the Golden Fleece and in 1478 was challenged by its new sovereign, Archduke Maximilian, husband of Duchess Mary of Burgundy, for his failure to wear its collar in accordance with its statutes.[6] Outside manuscripts and documents specifically associated with the Order, he is in fact depicted wearing it only once, in the frontispiece to the presentation copy of Wavrin's *Chroniques d'Angleterre*.[7] It does however surround his arms on the first page of the Luton Guild Book, opposite the miniature which includes figures of several members of the royal family. This was commissioned in 1475 and is the work of an outstandingly good Flemish hand, though whether it was painted in England or imported from the Low Countries is unrecorded.[8] The collar of the Fleece is commonly to be found surrounding the arms of its continental members in manuscripts which they commissioned for their own use, so

3. J. Backhouse, 'Founders of the Royal Library: Edward IV and Henry VII as Collectors of Illuminated Manuscripts', *England in the Fifteenth Century: Proceedings of the 1986 Harlaxton Symposium*, ed. D. Williams, Stamford 1987, pp. 23–41. See also Scot McKendrick, 'Lodewijk van Gruuthuse en de librije van Edward IV', in Martens, *op. cit.*, pp. 153–4.

4. C. Lemaire, 'De bibliotheek van Lodewijk van Gruuthuse', *Vlaamse Kunst op Perkament*, Bruges 1981, pp. 207–29 and nos. 99–118.

5. E.G. Millar, 'Les manuscrits à peintures des bibliothèques de Londres', *Bulletin de la Société française de manuscrits à peintures* (1914–20), pp. 9–14, for this Flavius Josephus, now MS 1 in Sir John Soane's Museum. See also Martens, *op. cit.*, no. 15.

6. See A. Payne and L. Jefferson, 'Edward IV: The Garter and the Golden Fleece', *L'Ordre de la Toison d'Or, de Philippe le Bon à Philippe le Beau (1430–1505)*, ed. C. Van den Bergen-Pantens, Brussels 1996, pp. 194–7.

7. London, British Library, Royal MS 15 E. iv, f. 14; reproduced in Payne and Jefferson, *loc. cit.*

8. R. Marks, 'Two Illuminated Guild Registers from Bedfordshire', *Illuminating the Book: Makers and Interpreters*, ed. M.P. Brown and S. McKendrick, London and Toronto 1998, pp. 121–41. See also Sotheby's sale catalogue, 13 June 1983, lot 19.

the decision to include it may have been made by the illuminator in the absence of specific instructions to the contrary.[9]

All the manuscripts associated with Edward IV are secular ones. No liturgical books for private or for public use have been identified. It is hard to believe that he had no personal prayerbooks, given the splendour of his library books.[10] He might also be expected to have commissioned service books of a standard commensurate with his building works at Windsor, though the general loss of this type of material is easier to understand. A very rare survivor of the period is a single leaf from the illuminated gradual which his sister, Duchess Margaret of Burgundy, presented to the Greyfriars at Greenwich.[11]

The chantry chapel of William, Lord Hastings stands between the pillars of the fourth bay of the north choir aisle. According to his will, drawn up in 1481, this resting place had been assigned to him by the king himself and the pledge was honoured after his summary execution at the order of Richard III in June 1483.[12] More traditional in form than the neighbouring chantry of his sovereign, Hastings's chapel has an open screen with a doorway on its aisle face and is enclosed on the south by the panelling at the back of the stalls in the choir. This southern wall is now adorned with paintings of scenes from the life of St Stephen.[13] The wooden enterclose was apparently completed in 1479–80 and it is likely that Hastings arranged for the chapel to be constructed in his lifetime but the paintings, which seem to convey a very pointed message, must be later. The saint, protomartyr of a new regime, is shown condemned not by the High Priest but by that pattern of all evil kings and slaughterer of the innocent, Herod himself. Stephen, like Hastings, was subject to summary execution without due process of (Roman) law. So very pointed a parallel cannot have been implied before Richard's overthrow at the hands of Henry Tudor in the summer of 1485. The paintings must therefore have been ordered by Hastings's widow or his heir. The costumes of the various characters, especially the headdress worn by a woman in the first of the scenes, suggest a date in the fifteenth rather than the sixteenth century. The heavy-handed style can in fact be compared with that of the less formalised of the two painters responsible for a sequence of pictures recording the ceremonies attendant upon admission to the Order of the Bath, now part of the composite volume known as Writhe's Garter Book.[14] The coarse-featured faces, the bold but crude

9. It appears routinely surrounding the arms of successive sovereigns of the Order. For a few other examples see B. Gagnebin, *L'enluminure de Charlemagne à Francois 1ᵉʳ*, Geneva 1976, p. 170 (Englebert of Nassau) and D. Thoss, *Flamische Buchmalerei: Handschriftenschätze aus dem Burgunderreich*, Vienna 1987, pls. 5 (Baudoin II de Lannoy) and 81 (Jean de Berghes).

10. It should however be remembered that Edward's brother and successor, Richard III, can be associated only with a fairly minor and certainly secondhand personal Hours, see A.F. Sutton and L. Visser-Fuchs, *The Hours of Richard III*, Stroud 1990.

11. BL Arundel MS 71, f. 9 (now bound separately), dated 1482.

12. The will is printed in full in N.H. Nicolas, *Testamenta Vetusta*, i, London 1826, pp. 368–75.

13. The scenes are described in W.H. St. John Hope, *Windsor Castle: An Architectural History*, London 1913, ii, p. 420. Reproductions are included in *idem.*, and P.H. Newman, 'The Ancient Paintings in the Hastings and Oxenbridge Chantry Chapels, in St George's Chapel, Windsor Castle', *Archaeologia*, 63 (1912), pp. 85–98. The second scene is given in colour in S. Bond, *St George's Chapel, Windsor Castle*, Pitkin Pictorials 1973, p. 17.

14. The entire sequence of Bath miniatures is reproduced in colour in *Medieval Pageant. Writhe's Garter Book: The Ceremony of the Bath and the Earldom of Salisbury Roll*, ed. A. Wagner, N. Barker and A. Payne, Roxburghe Club 1994. There is a single but relevant monochrome plate in K. Scott, *The Caxton Master and his Patrons*, Cambridge Bibliographical Society 1976, pl. xiv.

representations of rich fabrics and many incidental details, such as the ranks of little trees silhouetted along the skylines, are all common to both works. Costumes are also very similar. The Bath pictures can apparently be dated in the late 1480s, since they share a single run of paper leaves with Writhe's Garter armorial, the last entry in which is dated 1488, and with notes on the ancestry of Queen Elizabeth Woodville, mother of Henry VII's wife, Elizabeth of York, who was finally crowned in 1487. They were probably commissioned by Writhe, in his capacity as Garter King of Arms, from one of the professional painters in his employment, who could equally well have undertaken work for the widow of a Garter knight.[15]

The standard of the chantry paintings does not bear comparison with the best work of the day such as the exquisite series of grisaille paintings in the choir of Eton College chapel.[16] These, which are surely the work of a Flemish hand, would certainly have been much to Hastings's own taste. Painted works on a large scale cannot be directly associated with him but in recent years he has increasingly emerged as a bibliophile with a special liking for Flemish illuminated manuscripts. Like his king, he had substantial personal contact with the Low Countries. After a rapid rise to fame and fortune in the wake of Edward's successful bid for the crown in 1461, he frequently undertook the role of ambassador to the Burgundian ducal court and was particularly concerned with the negotiation of Margaret of York's marriage to Charles of Burgundy in 1468. He accompanied Edward into exile in Flanders in 1470–1 and was among those who welcomed Gruuthuse to Windsor on his behalf. During the latter part of the reign, as Lieutenant of Calais, he spent substantial periods of time in residence on the continent in close proximity to the chief centres of Flemish art.

The principal manuscripts associated with him are two exquisite Books of Hours, both probably made during the late 1470s, one of which is now in the Lazaro Galdiano Museum in Madrid, the other in the British Library. Both contain the arms of Hastings surrounded by the Garter. Although the Madrid Hours has long been recognised as an important example of the Flemish work of its day, it has often been associated with the name of William, Lord Hastings's descendant, Francis, earl of Huntingdon (d.1561) rather than with Hastings himself, the arms explained away as an addition.[17] Recent commentators on the history of the manuscript, including myself, failed to notice an article published by Joseph Hunter in 1855, when the Hours was in the possession of Lady Stourton, in which an entirely credible line of descent from Hastings in the late fifteenth century to Cardinal Howard's Dominican foundation at Bornheim in 1659, via the grandchild of Hastings's stepdaughter in the household of Princess Mary Tudor, was

15. The activities of a heraldic workshop of the next generation are examined by A. Payne, 'Sir Thomas Wriothesley and his Heraldic Artists', *Illuminating the Book: Makers and Interpreters, op. cit.*, pp. 143–61.

16. M.R. James and E.W. Tristram, 'The Wall Paintings in Eton College Chapel and in the Lady Chapel of Winchester Cathedral', Walpole Society, xvii (1928–9); A. Martindale, 'The Wall-paintings in the Chapel of Eton College', *England and the Low Countries in the Later Middle Ages, op. cit.*, pp. 133–52.

17. O. Pächt, *The Master of Mary of Burgundy*, London 1948, p. 68 no. 17 with previous bibliography. The miniatures are reproduced in G.I. Leiftinck, *Boekverluchters uit de omgeving van Maria van Bourgondie c.1475–c.1485*, Brussels 1969, pp. 109–25, pls. 165–201.

demonstrated.[18] The second Hastings Hours was bequeathed to the British Museum in 1968 by the widow of the well-known collector, C.W. Dyson Perrins. A particularly lovely example of the work of the anonymous book painter known as the Master of the Second Prayerbook of Maximilian, it was previously available only through a somewhat uncharacteristic reproduction in the Perrins catalogue.[19] Its transfer to a public collection quickly resulted in detailed study and publication, its miniatures and borders comprehensively reproduced in colour in two successive popular and widely circulated small books, bringing the Hastings name to the fore.[20]

The Hastings arms occur once in the Lazaro Galdiano Hours, in the form of a full page heraldic composition.[21] In the London manuscript they appear in the margins of folios 13 and 151, in both cases visibly inserted over existing decoration, which has again led scholars to query whether Hastings was the original owner.[22] In both cases the style in which the arms are painted seems perfectly consistent with a date in the fifteenth century. Furthermore, with the notable exception of a small group of suffrages which seem to have been added with special intent to the London manuscript, the two books are remarkably similar in content to a degree unusual in Books of Hours.[23] It seems too much of a coincidence to believe that they came by different routes into the hands of the next member of the Hastings family entitled to use the Garter as an accompaniment to his arms.[24] William Hastings's family certainly owned such prayerbooks. The will of his widow makes mention of two 'primers' and strenuous attempts have inevitably been made to associate these references with the two manuscripts which have come down to us, though without success.[25]

Hastings seems to have been given to asserting ownership by the use of arms and badges on his possessions. The heraldic manche of his coat-of-arms is picked out in the brickwork flanking the main entrance to his castle at Kirby Muxloe and Lady Hastings's will makes

18. J. Hunter, 'On the book of devotions by Cardinal Howard in the Library of the Dominican Convent at Bornheim in 1659', *Archaeological Journal*, 12 (1855), pp. 65–72. I had independently arrived at similar conclusions in *The Hastings Hours*, London 1996, pp. 57–9. However, David Rogers, 'An attempted reconstruction of the successive ownerships of the manuscript in the Museo Lazaro-Galdiano at Madrid', printed as an appendix to Leiftinck, *op. cit.*, produced a substantially different line of descent.

19. G.F. Warner, *Catalogue of Illuminated Manuscripts in the Library of C.W. Dyson Perrins*, Oxford 1920, no. 104, pl. lxxxviii.

20. D.H. Turner, *The Hastings Hours*, London 1983; J. Backhouse, *The Hastings Hours*, *op. cit.* See also *Renaissance Painting in Manuscripts: Treasures from the British Library*, ed. T. Kren, New York and London 1983, no. 3.

21. Folio 1 verso, Lieftinck pl. 193.

22. See, for instance, P. Tudor-Craig, 'The Hours of Edward V and William Lord Hastings: British Library Manuscript Additional 54782', *England in the Fifteenth Century: Proceedings of the 1986 Harlaxton Symposium*, ed. D. Williams, Stamford 1987, pp. 351–9.

23. Turner, *op. cit.*, pp. 116–17.

24. Francis Hastings, earl of Huntingdon, received the Garter in April 1549, his brother Edward, Baron Hastings of Loughborough, was elected in 1555, and his son and heir, Henry, in 1570.

25. Lady Hastings's will is printed in *Testamenta Vetusta*, pp. 450–6. See Tudor-Craig, *op. cit.*, pp. 358–61.

several references to soft furnishings bearing 'my Lordes Armes'.[26] Of more direct relevance to the examples in the manuscripts is the very grand armorial decoration in a niche high up on the wall of his grand tower house at Ashby-de-la-Zouche, directly above the only surviving door. This, though now very worn, clearly shows the arms surrounded by the Garter ribbon below the crest and between the supporters. One other Flemish manuscript was also originally intended to carry his arms, complete with Garter, though they are indicated only by an outline sketch and a painted blue ribbon. The book is a fine illuminated copy of volume II (1377–85) of Froissart's Chronicle and is now among the Royal manuscripts in the British Library under the number 18 E. i. The following number denotes a copy of volume IV of the same work bearing Edward IV's arms and devices and it has usually been assumed that Hastings relinquished his volume to the king to help him complete a set.[27] There is however no actual proof that this was the case and the Hastings Froissart is not the only manuscript of its date and type in the Royal collection to carry the arms of a contemporary owner other than the sovereign.[28] Its significance in the present context is its clear inclusion of the Garter as an accompaniment to the Hastings arms.

Given this fairly consistent use of the Garter in the various contexts in which the arms appear, it is only to be expected that the achievement of William, Lord Hastings on the outer face of his chantry chapel within the church devoted to the Order should include it. A sketch made by Nicholas Charles, Lancaster Herald 1608–13 (now BL Lansdowne MS 874, f.49v), would appear to show that the Garter was a prominent feature of the memorial, though it is not found there today.[29] As noted above, the chantry itself is likely to have been constructed within Hastings's lifetime. However, given the circumstances of his death and the difficulties which inevitably faced his widow and his heir, the final agreement between the family and the college for the saying of masses for his soul was not

26. Will, p. 453: 'two quishions of counterfeit arres with my Lord's armes . . . all such pieces of hangings as I have, of blew and better blew, with my lord's armes, with banquyrs and cupboard cloths of the same sort . . . four coverings for quishions with my lord's armys of counterfeit arres'. Lady Hastings's will mentions a number of service books in addition to the two primers. Two further books are specifically connected with Hastings himself — Caxton's *Mirror of the World*, printed in March 1481, was published at the request of Hugh Bryce, Alderman of London for presentation to him (the actual presentation copy is not known) and a *registrum brevium*, now MS 25 in the library of Harvard Law School, bears the Hastings arms, though apparently without the Garter. The latter cannot be earlier than 1476 (see J.H. Baker, *English Legal Manuscripts in the United States of America*, Selden Society 1985, no. 52).

27. No complete set of the four volumes of Froissart can be definitely attributed to Edward's library. Attempts have however been made to associate him with an odd copy of volume III which was a particular pride of the New York bookseller, H.P. Kraus, see his *In Retrospect*, New York 1978, no. 81. This was sold to the Ludwig collection and is now in the J. Paul Getty Museum in Malibu. Although it is certainly very closely connected to Edward's manuscripts in a stylistic sense, there is no evidence of ownership and plenty of other candidates.

28. See Backhouse, 'Founders of the Royal Library', *op. cit.*, pp. 30–1.

29. The boss in the vault of the north choir aisle opposite the chantry chapel which was originally painted in 1498–9 (St . John Hope, *Windsor Castle*, ii, pp. 420, 468) and renewed by Willement *c.* 1844 does not display the Hastings arms within the Garter. The centrepiece, however, is surrounded by a number of carved shields charged with the Hastings manche and encircled with the Garter.

concluded until 21 February 1503, only a few months before the death of Lady Hastings.[30] By this time Henry VII and his mother, Lady Margaret Beaufort, had scaled down direct Tudor royal interest in St George's in favour of their new chapel at the east end of Westminster Abbey, which was destined to become the mausoleum of their dynasty. The changed circumstances may have made it easier for the third of our prominent Yorkists, Sir John Donne, to obtain the right to burial alongside Hastings at Windsor when he died, also in 1503.

Donne, like Hastings, was a traditional supporter of the Yorkist cause and received substantial rewards from the victorious Edward IV, notably estates in Wales and in Northamptonshire. Shortly after Edward's accession, and certainly before March 1465, he married Hastings's sister Elizabeth. The two men were thereafter very closely associated, both in England and at Calais. Donne also held a series of appointments at court, in direct attendance upon the king. It is possible that he shared at least some part of Edward's exile in 1470–1 and he was certainly among the members of the court who welcomed Gruuthuse to Windsor in 1472. He was many times employed as an envoy, apparently accompanying Margaret of York on her marriage journey in 1468 and returning to the ducal court in 1477 during the intense diplomatic activity that preceded the marriage of Mary of Burgundy and Maximilian of Austria.[31] Although he was never to aspire to a political role as important as that of his magnificent brother-in-law nor to attract the type of recognition implicit in election to the Garter, Donne was nonetheless not insignificant in Edward's circle. It has recently become increasingly apparent that he was also a substantial patron of the arts.

No obvious trace remains of Donne's tomb, though he too was apparently buried in the north choir aisle of St George's Chapel, one bay west of Hastings.[32] It seems that no formal obit was set up at Windsor. The accounts of his son and heir, Sir Edward Donne, now in the Warwickshire County Record Office, include a number of direct payments to a succession of priests celebrating mass at Windsor for the souls of his parents at least between 1518 and 1536.[33] He would appear to have been largely forgotten little more than a century after his death, when Nicholas Charles made his sketches of the memorials in St George's.[34] In this collection he is represented by a shield surmounted by a helmet with a crest wreath but no crest. The shield, which has a lance notch, bears a rampant

---

30. The inscription once presumably over his tomb is recorded in Lincoln's Inn Library MS Hale 73, f. 210 (a reference I owe to Colin Richmond):

> Hastyns hic domini Willelmi corpus humatur
> Funde proces anima quod celi luce fruatur
> Centum namque dies venientur tociens et dantur
> A te quando pater et Ave prose recetantur.

31. Donne's career is best described and clarified by K.B. McFarlane, *Hans Memling*, Oxford 1971, pp. 1–15 and 52–5. He was the first to recognise that the patron of the Chatsworth Triptych had not been slain at Edgecot in 1469, as previously supposed, with unhappy consequences for the accepted chronology of Memling's work.

32. I am very grateful to Dr Eileen Scarff for informing me (in a letter dated 27 September 1996) that marks suggestive of iron railings and of an abutting stone structure are faintly visible in the appropriate part of the aisle.

33. Warwickshire County Record Office, CR 895/106, 107, studied and partially transcribed by the late Mrs Elizabeth Elvey. I am again grateful to Eileen Scarff for passing on this material.

34. Lansdowne MS 874, f. 50, in the British Library.

beast labelled 'ar' on a ground 'a', and the whole is identified merely as 'Sr Dune'.[35] There is no trace of any associated monument.

Today Donne's principal memorial is Hans Memling's celebrated triptych, *The Virgin and Child with Saints and Donors*, also known from its past home as the Chatsworth Triptych, which is now in the National Gallery in London.[36] Although it bears no written date, it is generally thought to have been executed in the late 1470s, suggesting a link with Donne's embassy to Flanders in 1477.[37] Donne's arms, azure a wolf salient argent, appear on it together with the Hastings arms of his wife, and both partners are shown wearing the Yorkist livery collar of suns and roses.

Until very recently the triptych seemed to be a unique instance of Donne's patronage. It then emerged that his arms, which are not of themselves particularly noticeable nor placed very prominently within the Memling where scholars are most likely to remark them, were also to be found in three Flemish illuminated manuscripts in the Royal collection, whose cataloguers had failed to identify them.[38] Studied originally as an appendage to the manuscripts of Edward IV, these three books were later looked at in more detail in their own right.[39] One in particular has proved to offer additional evidence for the part played by personal contact between individuals at the courts of England and Burgundy. Heraldic evidence and an ownership inscription, now almost completely eradicated, show that a handsome copy of Vasco de Lucena's translation of the *Res gestae Alexandri Magni*, now Royal MS 15 D. iv, belonged first to Guillaume de la Baume, one of Duchess Margaret's closest associates and advisers, who was particularly involved in her stepdaughter Mary's marriage negotiations. The addition of the arms of Donne, also obliterated but apparently executed in the same impressive style as those of de la Baume, suggests that the manuscript was a direct gift to the English envoy in 1477. Adjacent autograph inscriptions of greeting by both Duchess Margaret and Duchess Mary were probably added during the same period and seem clearly addressed to Donne. They postdate the erasure of de la Baume's ownership inscription. Furthermore Margaret, unusually for her, writes in English and signs herself 'Margarete of Yorke' rather than her more normal 'Marguerite d'Angleterre'.[40]

It is now becoming clear that Donne was also the original owner of an exceptionally fine Book of Hours, now in Louvain, which has attracted much discussion as the work on

35. The roof boss opposite the arch where Donne is apparently buried has an archangel holding a bouché shield which was found to be blank in 1844: T. Willement, *An Account of the Restorations of the Collegiate Chapel of St George, Windsor*, London 1844, p. 28.

36. Inventory number 6275, acquired from the Duke of Devonshire in 1957 under the terms of the Finance Act 1956.

37. McFarlane, *op. cit.*, followed by the relevant catalogues of the National Gallery.

38. Royal MSS 15 D. iv, 16 F. v and 20 B. ii. The two latter contain the *Livre de Sydrac* and Lives of saints respectively.

39. J. Backhouse, 'Sir John Donne's Flemish Manuscripts', *Medieval Codicology, Iconography, Literature, and Translation: Studies for Keith Val Sinclair*, ed. P.R. Monks and D.D.R. Owen, Leiden, New York and Cologne 1994, pp. 48–53.

40. *Ibid.*, pp. 50–1 for more explicit details.

which the identity of the putative Louthe Master has been based.[41] A part of the stylistic group associated with the name of Simon Marmion, the manuscript contains two representations of its patron, once in armour and once in the collar and gown of a layman, together with arms, in one place surmounted by a very curious crest of knotted snakes. The arms, of a leaping silver-coloured animal against an apparently black ground, were long ago attributed to one Thomas Louthe of Sawtry in Huntingdonshire, though he had no clear connections with the Low Countries and the arms lack a crescent which is proper to him.[42] In 1992 black and white reproductions of the pages carrying the arms were featured in the Proceedings of a symposium held two years earlier at the J. Paul Getty Museum in Malibu.[43] There they caught both my own eye, already attuned to the arms of Donne, and that of Lorne Campbell, currently working on a new description of the Chatsworth Triptych. Subsequent investigations suggest that the arms originally had a ground of blue and the crest has been associated with Donne's son and heir in the next century.[44] The new identification of patronage seems more appropriate than the old. Donne is now taking on the character of a major owner of Flemish works of art, giving to him a lasting memorial far beyond the survival of his earthly tomb and, at least for the present, placing him rather above his brother-in-law, Hastings, in the connoisseur stakes.

Much of the detailed work which has been done on the manuscripts of the three men discussed in this paper is of comparatively recent date. The questions involved can by no means be regarded as closed.[45] Nor are they in any way unique as English owners of Flemish liturgical and secular books, which were being produced in very large, not to say commercial, quantities during the latter years of the fifteenth century. Other known English owners such as Sir Thomas Thwaytes remain to be studied in detail.[46]. Two further personalities honoured with a resting place in St George's Chapel can be associated with relevant manuscripts. The arms of Charles Somerset, 1st Earl of Worcester, occur in a copy of the *Régime de Santé* in the Royal collection, surrounded by the Garter and thus

41. The Louthe Master owes his controversial separate existence to Antoine de Schryver, writing in 1969. The manuscript in question is now MS A.2 in the library of the Université Catholique de Louvain, Louvain-la-Neuve. The question is usefully summarised and brought up to date by Schryver himself in 'The Louthe Master and the Marmion Case', *Margaret of York, Simon Marmion and The Visions of Tondal'*, ed. T. Kren, Malibu 1992, pp. 171–80.

42. For fuller details and illustrations of the Louvain manuscript see J. Casier and P. Bergmans, *L'art ancien dans les Flandres: Mémorial de l'exposition organisée à Gand en 1913*, Brussels and Paris 1921, 2, pp. 67–75 and figs. 232–45.

43. *Margaret of York, Simon Marmion and 'The Visions of Tondal'*, figs. 124 and 125.

44. The discovery is now in print in L. Campbell, 'The Donne Triptych', *Memling Studies: Proceedings of the International Colloquium (Bruges, 10–12 November 1994)*, ed. H. Verougstraete, R. Van Schoute and M. Smeyers, Leuven 1997, pp. 71–80, esp. p. 76. I am very grateful to the author for keeping me abreast of the investigations which he initiated at Louvain. See also his National Gallery catalogue, *The Fifteenth Century Netherlandish Schools*, London 1998, p. 182. The manuscript also features in B. Brinkmann, *Die Flämische Buchmalerei am Ende des Burgunderruichs: Der Meister des Dresdener Gebetbuchs und die Miniaturisten seiner Zeit*, Turnhout 1997, pp. 153–9 and associated plates, though John Donne's ownership is not fully accepted.

45. Two individual books among Edward IV's collection have been the subjects of detailed studies by Scot McKendrick, placing them in the context of other contemporary copies of the same works, viz: 'La Grand Histoire Cesar and the Manuscripts of Edward IV', *English Manuscript Studies 1100–1700*, 2 (1990), pp. 109–38 and 'The Romuléon and the Manuscripts of Edward IV', *England in the Fifteenth Century: Proceedings of the 1992 Harlaxton Symposium*, ed. N. Rogers, Stamford 1994, pp, 149–69.

46. Backhouse, 'Founders of the Royal Library', p. 30.

after his installation in *c.* 1498.[47] And Katherine, wife of Sir Reginald Bray, has been identified as the owner of another Book of Hours of exceptional quality, closely related in workmanship to the London Hastings Hours, which is now in the library of Stonyhurst College.[48]

47. Royal MS 16 F. viii.
48. See J.J.G. Alexander, 'Katherine Bray's Flemish Book of Hours', *The Ricardian*, 8 (1989), pp. 309–17.

James Denton at Windsor

COLIN RICHMOND

All that now survives of the gift of a great benefactor to St George's is a fireplace; it is here in the Vicars' Hall.[1] Even less remains at Lichfield. Denton, a canon of St George's and dean of Lichfield, was, it seems to me, a good man, yet all that there is to remind us of his goodness, his pre-Reformation goodness, is a fireplace. Does the goodness of good men live on after them? Not, I think, if they lived and were good in the years immediately before the Reformation. Drastic change carries away the good as well as the bad. It is just as much the duty of historians to illuminate the former as it is to identify the latter.

INTRODUCTION

There are two matters by way of introduction. The first is personal. M.R. James writes that in addition to examining the documents in the Aerary while a schoolboy at Eton he climbed about the fabric of St George's.[2] Not only does that summarize our conference, an opportunity to re-emphasize the complementarity of those two forms of historical evidence, it also reminds me of myself. My parents in the second half of the 1940s invariably took their many visitors, chiefly distant relatives from Yorkshire and County Durham, to Windsor; there were two unchanging items on the itinerary: a river trip and St George's. What one does between the ages of seven and twelve cannot be forgotten. For Bruce McFarlane it was Norwich which made him a Medievalist.[3] What made me into a Fifteenth-Centuryist was St George's.

Secondly, there is the way in which a project, once one becomes committed to it, often changes direction. I embarked on a study of James Denton because he seemed an attractive character. He attracts me because he is one of those personalities whose interpretation is essential to an understanding of Past, Present, and Future: those whose work, and sometimes whose lives, are destroyed by what non-historians think of as History. Historians themselves tend to be worshippers of What Happened As A Good Thing. The English Civil War *and* the Restoration of the Monarchy are rationalized, justified, applauded. The Colonial victory in the American War of Independence is regarded as an Achievement for Mankind. The Renaissance is considered an Advance in Art, and until the collapse of Communism we were more often than not informed that Soviet Russia, for all its excesses, was a benevolent and progressive state. Now that Communism has fallen, commentators have fallen over themselves to inform us that it was Not Entirely a

---

1. In the lefthand spandrel is a scallop shell: the symbol of St James. In the righthand spandrel a barrel (tun) is pierced with an arrow or spear; to pierce was to dunt: hence Dunton or Denton.

2. See, for example, M. Cox, *M.R. James: An Informal Portrait*, Oxford 1983, p. 45.

3. 'I've got Norwich in the marrow; the place where I first became conscious enough of the architecture, yes and of the middle ages, to want to be a scholar, where my fondness for drawing turned to drawing churches in painstaking accurate pencil, wholly innocent of teaching, where I deserted Dickens for *Quentin Durward*, the *Magnet* for *The Cloister and the Hearth*': K.B. McFarlane, *Letters to Friends 1940–1966*, ed. G. Harriss, Magdalen College, Oxford 1997, p. 119. He was writing to Gerald Harriss in December 1954.

Good Thing. The English Reformation, it is true, is no longer presented as an inevitable step on the smooth path towards Enlightened Englishness; it might continue to be thought, for example by me, to be a necessary stage in the development of English bloody- and small-mindedness. These days, however, every historian of the sixteenth-century has the most mixed of feelings about the Reformation in England. Those who opposed it are no more seen as misguided than are those who reckoned British Rule in North America to be better than Colonial Independence.[4] As for those, like James Denton, whose life's work was overtaken by events and almost completely obliterated by them, or rather, because 'events' is in the passive tense, was wrecked by those intent on wrecking in the mistaken belief that what they were demolishing was something both historically unsuitable and unsafe, they are at long last getting their due. Far from being dinosaurs they are being re-assessed as dodos: not becoming extinct because they were redundant monsters but being extinguished because they were an anomaly in a Brave New World. In the course of learning about Denton he has not changed: he remains a dodo to whom I am devoted. The change relates to expectation. I had expected, as well as hoped, to come up with something new, to discover in the archive here some document which would alter, if only a fraction, your perception of him. That has not been the case. It goes without saying: all those who have written on James Denton, from Elias Ashmole to Neville Wridgway by way of the incomparable St John Hope, have been better scholars than I am.[5] There is nothing new to say, there are no unnoticed documents of significance to bring to your attention. All I can do, therefore, is repeat what is known but in a manner which does not send you to sleep. That is the direction the study has had to take: towards keeping you awake.

PART ONE: CONNECTIONS

Christopher Urswick was dean of St George's from 1496 to 1505. Denton was not appointed a canon until 1509, but I wonder whether Urswick's example as a benefactor and as a man of business did not have an influence on the younger man. Urswick was a Cumbrian; Denton might also have been one. They were both Cambridge men, although Urswick was not an Eton and King's man like Denton. They were both diplomats. The impact Urswick had on the chapter cannot now be gauged. It might have been negligible. On Denton it might have been considerable, especially where care for the choristers was concerned. Urswick repaired their house, and their prayers at his chantry in the chapel could have been the inspiration, if inspiration were needed, for those Denton also required them to offer for him there. Urswick, who resigned in 1505 to live at Hackney, did not die until 1522, the year Denton became dean of Lichfield.[6]

4. One of those rare books which make one think differently has been for me B. Bailyn, *The Ordeal of Thomas Hutchinson*, Cambridge, Mass. 1974. Another, in this context, has been J. McManners, *French Ecclesiastical Society under the Ancien Régime: A Study of Angers in the Eighteenth Century*, Manchester 1960.

5. N. Wridgway, *The Choristers of St George's Chapel, Windsor Castle*, Slough 1980, is a recent work I have drawn on heavily in this paper.

6. *Biographical Register of the University of Oxford to 1500*, comp. A.B. Emden, 3 vols, Oxford 1957–9, iii, pp. 1935–6; Wridgway, *op. cit.*, pp. 16–17 and appendix III. Wridgway calls Urswick 'a modest man' and I wondered whether his resignation might not have been out of religious conviction. Dr Babette Evans has disabused me; she writes in her authoritative notes on my paper: 'Concerning Urswick's resignation of the Windsor deanery: I think he just wanted a quiet life. Windsor was the only one of his many preferments which

Denton had been appointed a canon at Lichfield in 1509, the same year he had become a canon of St George's. If there could have been an inspiriting legacy of Dean Christopher Urswick at Windsor, at Lichfield there undoubtedly was the inspirational memory of Dean Thomas Heywood, who had held office for thirty-five years, from 1457 to 1492. To the cathedral Heywood was an unparalleled benefactor.[7] He had, for example, greatly improved the life of the fifteen or so chantry priests in the New College, built for them in 1414 on the south side of the close, adding a bakehouse and a brewhouse, and putting a stove in their common hall. Making these clerical proletarians more comfortable was, as we shall see, what Denton did at Windsor; at Lichfield he provided them with a water supply. It was, nevertheless, the Lichfield choristers who were Denton's principal concern, as those at Windsor had been. It was he who was responsible for the building of a house for them on the north side of the close, even if Bishop Geoffrey Blythe gave him some assistance. Blythe, it should be noted, was also at Eton and King's, having been there immediately before Denton, overlapping him briefly at Cambridge. He was another diplomat. He had been created bishop of Lichfield in 1503. Blythe died in 1531; Denton died in 1533. The gateway of the choristers' house survived until the eighteenth century; it bore the inscription: 'Domus pro Choristis Extructa 1531'. Denton appears to have increased the number of choristers by four; it was probably also he who gave them, as he had given the St George's choristers, a cook.[8]

By bringing in Urswick and Lichfield the aim is to do no more than indicate the way I believe benefactors and benefaction worked: by imitation, as well as by emulation. The later fifteenth- and early sixteenth-century canons of Lichfield like the canons of Windsor were highly educated men; they were, in consequence, wealthy men. They were, although this does not follow quite so automatically, generous, generous to the institutions and the members of those institutions (present and future) where they spent some, if not in some instances much, of their time. It is all very well to say what they did was 'the done thing' and leave it at that. The dedication of many of the later medieval and early modern canons of Lichfield cathedral to its 'improvement' has been remarked on by historians for decades past. Denton's generosity to both cathedral and town, where he 'improved' the market cross, is not remarkable considering the tradition of generosity which he encountered there.[9] Yet, he brought with him in 1522 a habit which while being personal,

required anything of him in the way of religious observance; all the rest, including Hackney, were sinecures. When he resigned the Windsor deanery, he kept all the other benefices (three archdeaconries, five prebends, the chancellorship of Exeter, a fellowship of Manchester collegiate church, and five rectories) until he died; he lived peacefully in Hackney (where his vicar did all the parochial work), retaining an interest in public affairs and attending the occasional royal function. It doesn't seem to me like a religious experience.'

7. For Heywood, see (all too briefly) 'The English Gentry and Religion, *c.* 1500', in *Religious Belief and Ecclesiastical Careers in Late Medieval England*, ed. C. Harper-Bill, Woodbridge 1991, p. 143, and the works cited in note 70.

8. For Blythe, *Biographical Register of the University of Cambridge to 1500*, comp. A.B. Emden, Cambridge 1963, pp. 67–8; for Lichfield, *Victoria History of the County of Staffordshire*, iii, ed. M.W. Greenslade, London 1970, pp. 164–5. Dr Evans's notes have also been of great assistance, and I am deeply grateful to her for them: just like her annotations on my undergraduate essays of the 1950s, they are meticulous, learned, and challenging.

9. 'There was of old tyme a fayre old crosse environid with stepps in the market place of Lichefeld. Denton Dene of Lichefelde invironyd this crose of late tyme with 8 fayre arches of stone, makynge a round voult over them for pore market folks to stond dry in. This *Octaplus* was made with the expence of a 160 l. [£160]': *Leland's Itinerary in England and Wales*, ed. L. Toulmin-Smith, London, reprint of 1964, ii, p. 100.

and while no doubt being shared by a slightly older contemporary, Geoffrey Blythe, was also a habit of the canons and deans of Windsor, at any rate of Dean Urswick. What had not been undertaken for the choir boys at Windsor and Lichfield Denton undertook: the house at Lichfield, the New Commons at Windsor.

PART TWO: BIOGRAPHICAL

James Denton's origins are as obscure as are Thomas Heywood's. Those were the days before one had to be the son of a gentleman to become a church dignitary: the gentrification of the English Church had to wait until its transformation into the Church of England. If James was a gentleman he might have been one of the Dentons of Hillesden, Bucks. The church at Hillesden was rebuilt around 1500 and is a St George's in miniature.[10] The Dentons, however, did not acquire Hillesden until 1547, although they were a family long settled in the area. Thomas Denton (d. 1533), father of the Thomas Denton (d. 1558) who purchased Hillesden and is buried there in a splendid tomb, was of Caversfield, Bucks. Yet, there is no evidence, heraldic or otherwise, to connect James with the family.[11] Although, therefore, probably not a local, he seems, nevertheless, to have come of gentle stock.[12]

After Eton, where he was a King's Scholar in 1483–6, which suggests, as I understand it, that he ought not to have been of the gentry, he went up to King's College, Cambridge, where he became a Fellow in 1489 and Bursar in 1496–7 and 1498–1500.[13] He also studied

10. 'Hillesden has one of the finest churches in England, all except the tower having been built at one time, about 1500. It would take pages to describe its beauties': K.B. McFarlane, *Letters to Friends 1940–1966*, p. 61, 5 August 1946 to Gerald Harriss. See also, Sir George Gilbert Scott, 'All Saints' Church, Hillesden, Bucks.', *Records of Bucks*, iv (1877), pp. 309–25.

11. *The History of Parliament. The House of Commons 1509–1558*, ed. S.T. Bindoff, ii, London 1982, pp. 29–31; *VCH Bucks*, iv, ed. W. Page, London 1927, pp. 173 and 175.

12. William Denton in a will of 1505 wished to be buried in the parish church of the Tower of London, although it was to the parish church of Babraham, Cambridgeshire, that he left a bequest for unremembered tithes. At the making of the will William's wife Mary was pregnant; if, however, no child was born or being born did not survive, William's heir was to be his nephew, George Denton; if George was to die without male heirs, William's lands were to descend to his cousin, William Denton of Henley on Thames, brother to William's cousin James Denton, Doctor of Laws. James was to have the guardianship of young George Denton, 'to see that he be instruct and informed in lernyng and vertue', and was both superviser of the will and a witness to its making: PRO, PCC, Prob. 11/5, f. 19v, dated 23 September 1505, proved 6 February 1506. William had been married before. In 1496 his wife Isabel, formerly the wife of Sir Humphrey Starky, chief baron of the Exchequer (d. 1486), made her will. She desired to be buried in the chancel of Babraham church. Isabel's will is PRO, PCC, Prob. 11/11, f. 50, dated 25 March 1496, proved 16 March 1497. King's carver to Henry VII (*CPR 1485–94*, p. 95), William Denton had been granted Babraham for life in 1488 (*CPR 1485–94*, p. 259; *VCH Cambridge and the Isle of Ely*, vi, ed. A.P.M. Wright, London 1978, pp. 22–3); he was a justice of the peace in Cambs from 1495 until his death (*CPR 1494–1509*, p. 632). Where did all these cousins come from? Perhaps James was a Thames valley man after all.

13. I have discovered nothing important to add to the standard entries in the *DNB* and Emden, *Biographical Register of the University of Cambridge*. There are two accounts in the St George's archives drawn up for Denton, the first when he was receiver-general and steward in 1517–18 (XV.49.13) and the second when he was precentor in 1522–3 (XV.56.36). They tell us nothing about him, anymore than does an interesting letter addressed to him, presumably when he was steward; it does, however, reveal a good deal about grasping farmers and evicted cottagers in Wiltshire, just as an earlier letter to Christopher Urswick from Richard Croft, steward of the chapel's estate at Monkland, tells us something about bad bailiffs in Herefordshire.

abroad after 1493, being awarded the degree of Doctor of Civil Law by the University of Valence in 1505. He was, one must suppose, in his late thirties when made a canon of St George's in 1509, the same year in which he became a canon of Lichfield. As a royal employee he was rewarded with other ecclesiastical preferments: the rectory of St Olave's, Southwark, in 1507, a canonry at Salisbury in 1510, a canonry at Lincoln in 1514, the archdeaconry of Cleveland in 1523, the mastership of the College of St John, Ludlow, at an unknown date. A king's chaplain, he was almoner to Henry VIII's sister, Mary, queen of France, in 1514, and after her return to England her chancellor. He led a successful diplomatic mission to Ireland in 1524, and the following year became chancellor of Henry VIII's daughter, Mary, in that capacity heading her council, which governed the Marches towards Wales from its headquarters at Ludlow. He died at Ludlow on 23 February 1533 and was buried in the parish church of St Lawrence. No trace of his tomb survives. Although no testament survives either, we can probably estimate his wealth from the contribution of £200 which he made to the Clerical Subsidy of 1522. The cartulary at Windsor known as Denton's Black Book, compiled on his initiative in 1517, indicates that Denton was conscientious; it may also indicate, practical compilation though it was, that he was scholarly.[14]

He was also, as we have seen, liberal in the distribution of his wealth. His greatest liberality was for St George's. In 1519 he built the New Commons in which the chantry priests and choristers were to eat their meals.[15]

PART THREE: THE NEW COMMONS

Denton's New Commons was demolished in 1859. All that was saved was the fireplace from the hall. There are a number of fine photographs taken while the building was being demolished enabling us to know what it looked like externally (Fig. 17, see p. 33 above). St John Hope has described it in detail. Denton put his new building directly in front of where the choristers had been taught since about 1475, and where they had lived and slept

---

14. The Black Book is catalogued as IV.B.2 and 3. What is called Denton's will (I.G.15) concerns only the endowment of the charities to be performed by his chantry priests of the New Commons, and precise instructions as to the nature of those charities.

15. He is also said to have constructed 'the flight of steps leading from the cloisters down to the dean's orchard . . . known as The Hundred Steps': R.R. Tighe and J.E. Davis, *Annals of Windsor*, 2 vols, London 1858, i, pp. 478–9, a reference I owe to Eileen Scarff. Along with John Clerk, the dean of St George's, Denton is also said to have received 'by indenture' from William, Lord Hastings, the sheets in which Henry VI was lying when he was murdered in the Tower of London (*ibid.*, p. 478), but that cannot be the case as Denton had not yet gone to Eton when Hastings was himself murdered in the Tower, without, so to speak, the benefit of sheets. For the famous sheets, see *The Inventories of St George's Chapel, Windsor Castle, 1384–1667*, ed. M.F. Bond, Windsor 1947, pp. 283, 285. They raise interesting questions. Who preserved the ex-king's bed-linen? Was he or she a distressed and devoted servant? Or did he or she have money in mind? How did the sheets come into the possession of William, Lord Hastings? Why did he want them? Did he buy them on behalf of Edward IV? Was St George's always their intended location? Did anyone preserve any of the bed-clothes, pillows for example, of Edward V?

since Denton had provided them with a partitioned chamber.[16] The New Commons was not a freestanding structure, being joined to the choristers' house (if it may be called that) by a block which had a storehouse on the ground floor and a chamber of undetermined purpose on the floor above. The New Commons itself was a two-storeyed block some 63 feet long and over 20 feet wide. There was a first-floor hall with a pantry and a kitchen below. A turreted staircase tower enabled communication between the two floors. There were also rooms for the cook and under-cook in an annexe to the north-west. On the east was a walled courtyard entered by a doorway on whose arch was carved an inscription: 'Edes pro Sacellanorum et Choristarum Conviviis Extructa 1519.'[17]

The overall cost came to £460. The building itself, including the paving of the yard, cost £310, fittings and furniture, all carefully itemized, cost £50, and Denton laid out a further £100 for the purchase of four properties to provide the revenue for the living expenses of the chantry priests and choristers, and for the maintenance and repair of the building, particularly, says the indenture of foundation, for the upkeep and mending of walls and windows, as if these might come in for the heaviest damage. The most valuable of the four properties were two houses in Peascod Street. There were eight chantry priests at the time the indenture of foundation was drawn up with them in April 1520. There were 13 choristers and their schoolmaster.[18]

What do the statutes of foundation of the New Commons tell us about Denton's ideas and attitudes? And by extension, because he was typical enough, what do they tell us of the minds of intelligent, successful, and well-intentioned churchmen in the years immediately before the Reformation? Possibly, Denton and his like should be reckoned civil servants as well as churchmen: it is hard to tell. This is a complicated matter on which DeLloyd Guth has recently been characteristically enlightening.[19] In whatever fashion we define James Denton, he was civilized, civilized by the standards of his time and ours. On that score one might want to hold his service to Henry VIII against him; to do so would be to condemn too many other men whose civility is not in doubt, Thomas More and Thomas Wolsey for example. I have no doubt that James Denton was complicated as well as civilized, and have no desire to reduce him, or his fellows to a stereotype. It is, nonetheless, how a man resolves his complications in action which counts, where civilization and, for that matter, everything else, is concerned. What Denton thought about the Divorce we do not know; what he might have thought about the Royal

---

16. Wridgway, pp. 13–14, marked A on his plan. Denton says in the Book of Statutes, when enjoining the choristers to remember him in their prayers, that one reason they should do so was 'For suche charges and costes and Emolumentes as they have had of me Nott onely in the howsynge necessary for ther newe commons Butt also in ther chamber with two partycyons where they Lye and use bothe day and nyghte Which two partycions with dyvers other thynges ther wer made at myn ownr propre charge and coste For the grete ease of the sayd Chorysters'.

17. St. John Hope, *Windsor Castle: An Architectural History*, London 1913, ii, pp. 513–14; Wridgway, p. 18.

18. The Statutes of the New Commons are in Cambridge University Library: MS MM Dd. 2. 26. They were copied by Ashmole and that copy is Ashmole MS 1123 in the Bodleian Library, Oxford. The costs are set out in the Statutes on ff. 4v–9, cf. Ashmole MS 1123 ff. 99–99v, 109–10. The two parts of the foundation indenture are in the archives of St George's: XI.D.9 and D.10. The indenture was copied both into the Statutes (at f. 1) and into Denton's Black Book (at f. 261).

19. DeLloyd J. Guth, 'Climbing the Civil-Service Pole during Civil War: Sir Reginald Bray (c.1440–1503)', in *Estrangement, Enterprise and Education*, ed. S.D. Michalove and A. Compton Reeves, Stroud 1998, pp. 47–61.

Supremacy we cannot tell. What we do have, what St George's once had, albeit not for very long, is Denton's New Commons: Denton in action so to speak.

One thing the statutes tell us is that Denton was pedantic, if signing the accounts included in the Book of Statutes amounts to pedantry rather than carefulness. It could simply have been a habit at St George's as well as of Henry VII. Denton also cared for cleanliness. A lead basin was provided in the courtyard for the choristers to wash in, while the under-cook had to sweep and make clean the courtyard and the 'Galarey' once a week and the hall, tables, cupboards, and stairs twice a day before and after dinner, to dust the 'cobwebs in the wyndows' as often as necessary, and once a month to sweep the storehouse and the chamber over the storehouse. He was to be fined if he failed to do so. Not only did Denton want everything to be clean, he also desired everything to be decent. The *raison d'être* of the New Commons, as the indenture of foundation has it, was that hitherto chantry priests and choristers 'daily were at no certain[ty] where to eat nor drink their meals and drinking but in sundry places in the town of Windsor to the great dishonour of the said college'.[20] He was insistent that the schoolmaster, who was to be continually resident in the New Commons to see to the good behaviour of the choristers, should eat with them, 'And nott the Chylderne to goo to Commons with hym as Tutor in any other place but onely in the sayd newe commons'.[21] The communalty of the New Commons was, therefore, a matter of decency and of discipline. It was also a late example of the medieval idea of community, an idea not without its critics in Denton's time, the early days of modernity.

What accompanied an insistence on cleanliness and good order was a concern for the health of those who were to be accommodated in the New Commons. It was not simply a healthy diet which occupied him; it was good health in general. The improved standard of living he desired for the choristers was necessary, he says at one point, 'consyderynge the tyms paste how they were deseasyd'. If he did not have in mind the plague year of 1479 when a number of choristers died, then it was 1517, another year of plague, which, as Neville Wridgway suggests, prompted him to action.[22] Probably, as Wridgway also suggests, he was thinking of smallpox and measles, more readily picked up in town than in the precincts of St George's. He was less likely to have been concerned about those adolescent pimples boys are prone to and paralysingly unhappy about: their healing was the province of St George's most lucrative saint, John Schorn. Here two diverging views coincide. On one hand an older, and shortly in England to be an old-fashioned, notion of healing, on the other new ideas about prevention. Denton was obviously an exponent of what some late Medieval historians call the New Morality. What one wonders did he

---

20. The whole passage reads, 'because they had no home habitation nor abiding to be at commons in nor to keep their commons within the said college but daily were at no certain[y] where to eat nor drink their meals and drinking but in sundry places in the town of Windsor to the great dishonour of the said college'. As the chantry priests did not lodge in the New Commons, even if four of them had small houses close by (St. John Hope, ii, p. 512), and the choristers lived next door, what is the meaning Denton attached to the words 'home' and 'habitation'? Apart from taking meals in the hall, were chantry priests and choristers expected to spend their free time (if they had any) there, as well as in the courtyard outside? If so, doing what?

21. Half-commoners, that is probationary choristers (Wridgway, p. 20), were obliged on pain of expulsion to serve at table in the hall.

22. Wridgway, pp. 11 and 18.

think of the fast-fading and traditional clerkly stance towards the laity of Live and Let Live? See under 'Football' below.

Education, it goes without saying, was important. If, however, the schoolmaster was to introduce New Learning to the choristers, it was old monastic ways which were to be followed at dinner and supper. The Bible or 'summe other devote and holy scripture for the gostly informacion of them that be present' was then to be read, the passage chosen by the two priests of Edward IV's chantry with the help of the schoolmaster. One of the choristers was to do the reading 'with a audible voys and that as long as hit shall please' the two chantry priests. Chained books were available in a cupboard in the 'vyse', that is, on the spiral staircase of the tower.

The healthier, tidier, happier, and better educated choristers (and chantry priests) were to be charitable. What remained from their income after they had been catered for was to be distributed to the impoverished males of Windsor: sixpence weekly to twenty-four poor men in farthing bread, three pennyworth on Mondays to twelve of them and three pennyworth on Wednesdays to another twelve. Anything still available after that gendered disbursement was to be given to the ungendered poor during Lent in the shape of herrings, shirts, smocks, shoes and stockings.

In return for his generosity Denton required prayers.[23] The choristers when they came into the chapel before Matins each morning were to kneel 'before the crucifix in the bodye of the Churche [and] sey pryvatly every chyld by himselfe Pater Noster [and] Ave Maria'. That done 'one knelynge in the myddys shall begynne with an audyble voyce' prayers for the souls of Denton and all Christian souls. 'And thus', Denton continues in the Book of Statutes:

the said Chorysters shall Refresshe all Cristyne sowls departyd unto God Bothe in the Morneynge and in the Evenynge For nyghtly after the Antem of the Crosse ys songe and all other suffragis sayde and fynesshed then in lyke manner the Choristers shall goo unto the seyd place and say as ys before Rehersyd.

And all this, he continues, 'I desyre them of their charyte and of no bondage butt for the Love that they bere to God to oue Blyssyd Lady and Saynt George', and in thanksgiving for what he had done for them. Prayers were a memorial. He also wanted his memory kept alive at other moments of the day. Once the after-dinner and after-supper prayers and graces had been said:

the Childe which begyn grace as long as I lyff [shall] sey this wordes foloyng God save the good state and prosperite of Master James Denton specyall benefactor and funder of this Commons Et post mortem God have mercy on Master James Denton soule sumtyme Chanon of this College specyall bebefactor and funder off this Commons And this to sey as long as ye kepe commons in this howse which shalbe ever with the myght of Jhesu.

Ever turned out to be thirty years. If one pauses to ponder how infrequently James Denton, busy between 1522 and 1533 at so many places, was likely to have been present to hear himself prayed for at St George's, one has to take a longer pause to wonder how he had what one might call, were it not an inappropriate phrase, all the time in the world in Purgatory to regret the Reformation putting an end to the prayers he had counted on to shorten his stay. Which brings me to the penultimate point about the New Commons.

23. The Book of Statutes, f. 8; cf. Wridgway, appendix IV. The folio was signed at the foot by Denton.

The fate of the New Commons was sealed in October 1550. In that month the Royal Commissioners ordered that the Reader of Divinity should have the New Commons as his house. It is a perfect comment on the times. A single family was to replace a commune. The choristers were given four little chambers elsewhere in the precinct, but nowhere to eat together. Twenty years later Sir Nicholas Bacon as College Visitor found that the chantry priests were misbehaving themselves in Windsor; he recommended that they should be brought back to live in community. How ironic one is bound to exclaim. The difference between 1519 and 1572, nonetheless, was that nothing was done in 1572. By that date what were then already called the Old Commons had become the residence of a canon.[24] Private interest won out over public welfare. What a reversal of values. It is a perfect example of the two sides of a single coin: the English Reformation and English Capitalism.

PART FOUR: FOOTBALL

English Capitalism features in this section also: in the unmistakable guise of its sanctification of Holy Property. The *first* clause of the Statutes for the New Commons prohibits ball games.[25] It does so comprehensively and not only in the courtyard of the new building. They are forbidden 'without the gatte of the north syde of the chirch and from the vicars well estward toward the Chapitre house'. The prohibition was made not only to prevent the breaking of windows in the New Commons, but also of the chapel itself, which 'by negligence and wantonnes of yowth hath in diverses places in tymes past before [been] hurt'. Denton felt that such breakages might now be laid to his charge. Any contravention of the prohibition was to result in a penny fine for men and 'beating and sharp correction' for boys. It is unlikely that the ban was effective; such bans never have been and never will be: boys will be boys and for that matter men will be men. If the breaking of glass and his liability for its replacement seems to have been what mainly worried Denton, there is surely more than that to his antagonism to football and tennis. It has long been evident that most English Protestants were spoilsports, John Stow being an unchallengeable witness to their effect on English games-playing. Denton was not a Protestant. He was one of a long series of those in authority, who condemned ball games for their unruliness and violence, and for the tendency of spectators to riot. Grown men were better employed turning themselves into more efficient killers at archery butts. He also had 'his' property, 'his' New Commons, much in mind. It is difficult, therefore, to know whether Denton was Medieval or Modern; no doubt, like Thomas More, he is most clearly to be observed on the margin between them. Hence, their attractiveness. The ball games played within the walls of Denton's New Commons or in the area between the chapel's north door and the chapter house are not known to us. We have to cross the river to Eton to discover what their nature might have been: there were walls enough there to make more than one Wall Game.[26] Whatever they were, they are likely to have ceased

24. For all this, see St. John Hope, ii, pp. 514–15.
25. The Book of Statutes, f. 9v; cf. Wridgway, appendix IV: another folio signed by Denton.
26. I have attempted an imaginative reconstruction of them in 'Thomas More at Windsor', *Common Knowledge*, 7 (1998), pp. 14–19.

abruptly when the New Commons became a private house, the absolute triumph of an unstoppable partnership: Property and Privacy.

CONCLUSION

Denton was not a Barchester clergyman. His studies abroad, his travelling as a diplomatic officer of the Crown, his involvement in the 'Grey Zone' of Tudor politics, would have made him much more than that. Yet, his care for the choristers does remind one of Septimus Harding, just as the tone of his regulations for the New Commons puts one in mind of Archdeacon Grantly. It does not need to be stressed that Windsor around 1500 was not Barchester in 1840: as Dr Bowers has demonstrated, the music the choristers sang was not only contemporary; it was also of a standard which was the envy of Western Europe. Precentor Harding's music did not match that. The architecture of St George's was contemporary too. Denton's New Commons was an exemplary Pre-Modernist building alongside it. The chantry priests and choristers were better and more regularly fed, were less often tipsy, were less smelly and dirty, and no doubt slept more soundly because of Canon Denton's generosity. Probably, the price they had to pay was in diminished leisure, more rigorous supervision, and greater restraint in the playing of ball-games. Much of this lasted less than a generation. Denton could not have foreseen the destructiveness of Reform, reformer in a pre-Royal Supremacy mode though he himself was. None but the spiritually foresighted are able to have any idea what the ever-ramifying consequences of self- rather than other-regarding actions will turn out to be. He did not have to witness the English Reformation of the years after 1533, of which his New Commons was a casualty, a minor casualty no doubt but a casualty all the same. Proust draws attention to human adaptablity in 1900 by taking the private telephone as his example: it testified to the speed and ease with which we adopt new-fangled notions and allow them to change our lives for the better. The mobile telephone in 2000 seems to support his idea, until one hears it put to public use and becomes at once the potential murderer of its user. In other words: with gains there are losses. Which is to admit that there were gains made by the English Reformation; I, for one, am willing to be convinced that there were. It is the losses, nonetheless, which historians should be mindful of, if only because others, who are not historians, forget what is no longer visible. Denton's New Commons, small loss though it might still be considered, comes into the category of Missing, presumed Dead.[27] In resurrecting the New Commons here, I hope it has been moved into the category of Missing, not Forgotten.

---

27. As Amy Clampitt has it: 'All history is an epitaph. . . what history there is is an erasure'. These are two lines from her magnificent poem, 'The Prairie', a History of the Western World pared down to its unattractive bones in some of the best poetry of the last fifty years. It is in her *Collected Poems* (1997), pp. 389–408.

The Music and Musical Establishment of St George's Chapel in the 15th Century

ROGER BOWERS

The principal purposes for which Edward III had founded the College of St George at Windsor in 1348, as may be discerned in the terms of the king's letters patent of foundation and of the statutes devolved upon it in 1352, were two-fold.[1] The first objective was the amplification, in obedience to Biblical exhortation, of the aggregated volume of universal worship rising to the Almighty from Earth below. The second was to seek, through prayer and enactment of the sacrifice of the mass, the good estate while living, and the salvation of the souls following death, of the king and his ancestors, of the knights of the Garter, and of the benefactors of the college. To these overriding duties all else was subservient and ancillary. Without its chapel and domestic buildings, of course, the college could not function; without sagacious management of its personnel, vigilant administration of its estates, diligent collection of its income and judicious acquisition of equipment and consumables, it could not endure. Nevertheless, these were but subsidiary and contributory functions, the discharge of which simply allowed the college to achieve what it had been created and existed to achieve — the observance of the divine liturgy, including the multiplication of celebrations of the mass, and some increment to the enduring lustre of the repute of the sovereign by whom it had been founded.

Music was one of a number of means by which the efficacy of the liturgical service could be maximised and enhanced, and in this respect the fifteenth century was to prove notably productive. Indeed, it witnessed the creation of the English tradition of ecclesiastical choral music as we now know it. The great secular churches, cathedral and collegiate alike, had long been staffed by teams of liturgical officiants, men and boys, by whom was observed the unceasing round of daily service in the choir. However, it was only between 1400 and 1500 that the inchoate body of singers in the medieval tradition, constituted primarily to render just the monodic plainsong chant of the liturgy, was transformed into a true choir. Now for the first time was there forged a balanced and structured musical force, managed by a designated and qualified director and constituted in such a way as to maximise its capacity to undertake the performance of a challenging repertoire of polyphonic music composed for choral execution (which it undertook in addition to, and not in place of, its long-standing and historic plainsong tradition). At few institutions in the land was this fifteenth-century transformation so marked as at St George's, whereby a well-favoured but relatively small-scale establishment was doubled

---

1. Letters patent: E. Ashmole, *The Institution, Laws and Ceremonies of the Most Noble Order of the Garter*, London 1672, Appendix, sig. k1v. The statutes have not been printed; the earliest manuscript copy which survives complete (*c*.1430) is St George's Chapel Archives (hereafter cited as SGC) IV.B.1, ff. 74–84. For a description of the original St George's Chapel of *c*.1240–1480, see W.H. St. John Hope, *Windsor Castle: An Architectural History*, London 1913, i, p. 55; ii, pp. 374–5.

in size and converted into an organisation blessed with the means and the potential to be among the finest choirs in the country.

I. THE CHORAL STAFF AND ITS ROLE IN c.1400

At the beginning of the fifteenth century the nature and scale of the resources with which the choral body found itself furnished were about typical of those of the more prominent of the second rank of collegiate institutions of the day. This was the immediate legacy of the manner in which the original foundation had been planned to meet the requirements of the liturgy. The statutes of 30 November 1352 had directed that so far as the appointments of the chapel and the provision of staff permitted, the liturgical use to be observed in the chapel be that of the cathedral church of Salisbury.[2] As well as being the appropriate diocesan liturgy for Windsor, this particular Use in any event was well on the way to achieving acceptance as the standard secular liturgy for all of lowland England from Dorset to the Wash. The daily services consisted of the eight Hours of the Office — Matins with Lauds,[3] Prime, Terce, Sext and None, and Vespers with Compline — and several celebrations of the mass. Principal among the latter was High Mass of the Day, with which the morning round of observance concluded. Also performed daily at Windsor, immediately before High Mass and by a team consisting of a proportion of the vicars choral alone (appointed probably by rote), were a celebration of the Mass for the Dead, and a celebration of the Mass of the Blessed Virgin (the Lady Mass).[4] One of the two altars in the ante-chapel was recorded in 1369–70 as dedicated to the Blessed Virgin;[5] nevertheless, the space available in this location probably would not have sufficed to accommodate a choral celebration of the Lady Mass, and in all likelihood these masses were sung at the high altar. All liturgy was to be sung to its proper chant 'as is accustomed to be done in cathedral churches'.[6]

Liturgical observance consisted of a fusion of three distinct elements: the verbal texts, the monophonic plainsong chant to which they were sung, and the elaborate ceremonial of vestment, artefact and movement by which all was accompanied. All liturgies for secular use in England predicated the provision of three specific ranks of clergy, to execution by one of which each distinct phase and component of the liturgy could be allotted. In the Ordinal and Consuetudinary these ranks were designated, respectively, the clerks of the upper, second and first forms. In choir the participants were appointed to stand and sit in two facing sets of stalls, each containing (in effect) three rows. To the clerks of the upper form the rubrics allotted those elements of the liturgy deemed to be of greatest weight and significance; to the clerks of the second form, those of lesser import; and to the clerks of

---

2. Statute 21: SGC IV.B.1, f. 76r.

3. From 29 September to 1 March each year, Matins — the night office — was to start at such a time as to be finished at day-break; in the summer season it was to commence at day-break. Statute 21: SGC IV.B.1, f. 76r.

4. Statutes 11, 26: SGC IV.B.1, ff. 77r, 76v. The statutory Mass for the Dead (the Mass *Requiem aeternam*) was to be omitted on any day on which High Mass was a mass for the dead, while on days on which High Mass was a Mass of the Blessed Virgin the Mass *Salus populi* replaced the Lady Mass.

5. *The Inventories of St George's Chapel, Windsor Castle, 1384–1667*, ed. M.F. Bond, Windsor 1947, p. 268; SGC XV.56.2; XV.56.5: (August 1380) in ligatura unius missalis capelle sancte marie ijs iiijd.

6. Statute 22: SGC IV.B.1, f. 76r.

the lowest form (in practice, a free-standing bench on the choir floor placed in front of the second row of stalls proper) those deemed suitable for execution by the young, by boys of the choir still possessing unbroken voices.

Meanwhile, the requirements of general administration necessitated the provision of both a principal manager and a group of — in effect — departmental heads and advisers, while the practicalities of the cleanliness and good order of the chapel building required the due provision of maintenance staff. To meet all these distinct requirements, the statutes supplied St George's with a warden (or dean) and twelve canons; a virger and his two assistants (non-statutory), the latter styled 'bell-ringers'; and for the choir, thirteen vicars choral — all in the orders of priest — to be the clerks of the upper form, four clerks in the order of deacon or subdeacon or in minor orders to be the clerks of the second form, and six boy choristers for the lowest form.[7] One of the canons was to be appointed to the office of precentor, to undertake and exercise ultimate responsibility for all aspects of the performance of the service.[8]

The three categories of person appointed to staff the choir of the college, that is, were determined by the requirements of the liturgy. The actual numbers of persons in each category, however, were entirely a matter for the founder to determine. The king's choice for St George's appears to have arisen from a number of stimuli. Contemporary values predicated the maximisation of the number of ordained priests on the foundation, so as to maximise the number of celebrations of mass observed each day within the chapel building.[9] To determine upon a directorate consisting of a dean and twelve canons was a common resort among the richer founders of the period, recalling and representing the elemental role of Jesus and the disciples in the establishment of the primitive Church. The same consideration informed the choice of thirteen to be the number of clerks of the upper form of the choir, the priest-vicars choral — a determination consolidated by the contemporary convention that each vicar served as the substitute-in-choir of one of the canons, predicating equal numbers in each category.[10] To appoint four to be the number of clerks of the second form appears wholly irrational by comparison; such a number was completely out of balance with their superiors of the upper form, and it does not seem possible that four can have sufficed to permit the accomplishment of the totality of the job appointed by the liturgy to be performed by the second-form clerks. In practice, it seems

7. Preamble to Statutes: SGC IV.B.1, f. 74v. At St George's the status in chapel of the knights of the Garter caused there to arise special seating arrangements unknown elsewhere. Only the knights and the canons were of status sufficient to occupy the upper stalls, and even a canon had to suffer displacement on any occasion on which his stall was required for a knight. Consequently, the Visitor ruled in 1432 that there be continued in perpetuity the then long-standing practice under which, despite their orders as priests, the vicars choral performed the liturgical duties of clerks of the top form from places on the second row of stalls: SGC IV.B.1, f. 87v (Injunction 32).

8. Statute 37: SGC IV.B.1, f. 79v.

9. The statutes amplified the requirements of canon law by stipulating that each priest-vicar choral celebrate his private mass daily. Statute 22: SGC IV.B.1, f. 76v.

10. The statutes provided for the presentation of aspirants for appointment to each vacant vicarage choral by individual canons (Statute 15: SGC IV.B.1, f. 77v), and the *Stalla vacantia* section of the Treasurer's accounts for the 1370s (SGC XV.34.10, 11, 14) show that at first individual vicarages were attituled to individual canons on the model of the prebendal cathedrals. However, this convention appears to have fallen into desuetude soon after 1378, and thereafter the right of presentation probably circulated among the canons by turn, falling in default to the chapter as a whole: see Injunction 9 of 1432, SGC IV.B.1, f. 85r.

that often the more junior of the vicars must have had to be deputed to help out the clerks of the second form.[11] Six was about the working minimum of choristers; it was adequate to meet most requirements, but not quite sufficient, for instance, to provide the seven boys properly required to sing the hymn *Gloria, laus et honor* at the procession preceding High Mass on Palm Sunday.[12]

Indeed, the principal criterion informing the precise choice of numbers of liturgical staff at St George's may have been one arising not from considerations of music or liturgy at all, but of royal prestige. St George's was one of a pair of essentially identical institutions, its twin being the College of St Stephen, Westminster, founded by Edward III on the same day, 6 August 1348. In terms of its architecture, the chapel of St Stephen's (already built) had been modelled directly on the Sainte-Chapelle, that dazzling reliquary in stone and glass erected in Paris between 1240 and 1248 by Louis IX within his royal palace on the Ile de France, housing his most precious relic, the Crown of Thorns. Now in constitutional terms also Edward III chose to model both St Stephen's and St George's directly on the example offered by the Sainte-Chapelle.

TABLE 1: THE CONSTITUTIONS OF THE SAINTE-CHAPELLE, ST STEPHEN'S WESTMINSTER, AND ST GEORGE'S WINDSOR

	CHAPTER		CHORAL STAFF			ANCILLARY CHAPEL STAFF
	Head	Prebendaries	Clerks of the upper form	Clerks of the second form	Clerks of the lower form	
Sainte-Chapelle (by the 1340s)	Trésorier	12 canons	13 priest-chaplains	4 clerks, deacon and subdeacon	6 choristers	3 clerks serving as 'marguilliers'
St. Stephen, Westminster 1348	Dean	12 canons	13 priests, vicars choral	4 clerks	6 choristers	3: one virger (two bell-ringers)
St. George, Windsor 1352	Custos	12 canons	13 priests, vicars choral	4 clerks, deacon, subdeacon & minor orders	6 choristers	3: one virger two bell-ringers

To serve this building St Louis had established in 1246 a college of priests, which by the 1340s had grown, very much piecemeal, to the following proportions: a dean (styled at that time *Trésorier*) and twelve canons; thirteen priest-chaplains; four (or just possibly five) clerks of the second form in the orders of deacon and subdeacon; six choristers; and three clerks serving as *marguilliers* — that is, minor officers fulfilling primarily non-liturgical

11. It was doubtless to accommodate this kind of infelicity that the statutes expressly permitted the stipulations of Salisbury Use to be modified with local adjustments when necessary, 'secundum loci congruenciam et exigenciam personarum'. Statute 21: SGC IV.B.1, f. 76r.

12. *Processionale ad Usum Sarum*, ed. W.G. Henderson, London 1882, p. 52. For their efforts in singing the *Gloria, laus et honor*, the Windsor choristers were rewarded with twopennyworth of ale: SGC XV.56.10, 11, 16, 17 (1388/9–1401/2).

duties such as virger, sacrist and bell-ringer.[13] In the case of St Stephen's, already by the day of its foundation in 1348 the king had determined its numbers of principal personnel, which were to be a dean, twelve canons and thirteen vicars choral.[14] The statutes of St Stephen's were promulgated on 8 December 1355, and long before this time the extent of all the *alii ministri congruentes* anticipated in the foundation charter must also have been determined; these numbered four clerks, six choristers, and the virger and his assistants, so completing its complement of staff.[15] In 1352 the College of St George at Windsor was by statute duly constituted in numbers of staff exactly the same. Allowing for the evident differences between French and English terminology, it can be seen that the common constitution devolved upon St Stephen's and St George's was as good as identical to that appointed for the Sainte-Chapelle. In the aftermath of Crécy and the capture of Calais, that collegiate expression of royal prestige and piety conspicuous upon the banks of the Seine was now to be replicated — twice, for good measure — by the banks of the Thames.[16]

II. THE DEFINING OF THE CRAFT OF CHURCH MUSIC: THE ROLE OF POLYPHONY AND THE RISE OF THE LAY CLERK, 1390–1430

So far as concerned its provision for liturgical observance, St George's entered the fifteenth century supplied with a choral staff that was very representative of its period; it was characterised by a considerable body of priests, all rather generously remunerated with

13. The constitution of the College of the Sainte-Chapelle as it stood in the 1340s (following enlargement in 1318–19) can, with some difficulty, be determined from the commentary and documents provided by S-J. Morand, *Histoire de la Sainte-Chapelle royale du Palais*, Paris 1790, pp. 65–70, 109–11 and 'Pièces justificatives' pp. 3–7, 8–13, 33–43; and M. Vidier, 'Notes et documents sur le personnel, les biens et l'administration de la Sainte-Chapelle, du treizième au quinzième siècle', *Memoires de la Société de l'Histoire de Paris et de l'Ile de France*, 28 (1901), pp. 213–383, at 221–42 *passim* but especially 221–2, 230–1, 237–9. Some of the material that is germane to the present subject was extracted from these volumes, and then supplemented with further matter, in M. Brenet, *Les Musiciens de la Sainte-Chapelle du Palais*, Paris 1910; reprinted Geneva 1973, pp. 1–24. It should be noted that the numbers of participants recorded on the accounts of the exequies of Pierre de Houdan in 1364 (Vidier, pp. 235, 237, 358) clearly represent the foundation staff of the Sainte-Chapelle greatly amplified by the presence of extra chaplains and clerks; and that everything about the language, style and content of the undated regulations for the training and upbringing of the Sainte-Chapelle choristers (Vidier, pp. 344–9; Brenet, pp. 15–20) bespeaks a date for their compilation of *c*.1450, not *c*.1350 as suggested by Vidier, so negating their relevance for the present purpose.

14. Letters patent of foundation: T. Rymer, *Foedera*, 3rd edn, 10 vols, London 1739–45; reprinted Farnborough 1967, iii, part 1, p. 37.

15. London, Westminster Abbey Muniments 18431. *Issue Roll of Thomas de Brantingham*, ed. F. Devon, London 1835, pp. 466–7.

16. The 'Croes Naid', the relic of the True Cross for which Edward I had begun to build St Stephen's (corresponding respectively to King Louis' Crown of Thorns and his Sainte-Chapelle) eventually was given to St George's by Edward III: A.K.B. Roberts, *St George's Chapel, Windsor Castle, 1348–1416: A study in early collegiate administration*, Windsor 1947, pp. 46, 94.

free lodging and a stipend of £8 os od per year,[17] an exiguous body of clerks of the second form, and about the bare working minimum of choristers. By 1400 the college had been a going concern for some fifty years, and this liturgical body was well established. Indeed, except for times of plague in the 1360s and 1370s, the chapter had proved reasonably diligent in keeping full the statutory numbers of vicars, clerks and choristers.[18] It could happen that there was a vacancy or two among the vicars and clerks — a not unreasonable consequence of illness, death or resignation; nevertheless, during 1398–9, for instance, at the ten obits held that year there was a complete choir in attendance at no fewer than six.[19] In addition, the choir was duly furnished with all the plainsong service books, vestments and liturgical equipment that were necessary to enable it undertake its observance of the liturgy of the Use of Salisbury.[20]

The resources devolved upon the choir answered to criteria unrelated to the needs of musical performance; rather, they were calculated to meet those twin cardinal objectives of maximising the number of celebrations of mass and of executing a reasonably faithful replica of the Divine Office as observed in its diocesan cathedral at Salisbury. Nevertheless, in this latter enterprise the plainsong chant was one of the three principal ingredients, and the statutes did require that all vicars, clerks and choristers possess serviceable voices for singing;[21] each chorister, moreover, had to surrender his place on his change of voice.[22] As a monodic music, though, matters such as considerations of balance between men's and boys' voices did not apply in execution of the plainsong. The boys were few in number but if, for instance, when singing in octaves with the men they were barely audible, that would scarcely have mattered.

There were resources enough, nevertheless, for the basic liturgical endeavour to be fulfilled. There were, moreover, a number of respects in which the character of the liturgical force at St George's can be seen to have been evolving at around the turn of the century, in a manner that enabled it to keep abreast of developments manifest at large among the most forward of the choirs of the period. These developments concern the projection of the performance of polyphonic music, and in particular the identity of the category of chapel staff principally concerned with its execution.

17. Statute 3: SGC IV.B.1, f. 75r. According to the deed of foundation made in 1402, the chaplain of the chantry of William Wykham, bishop of Winchester, was perpetually to complement his daily celebration of mass with observance of *secta chori*, attending all services in chapel under obligations the same as those undertaken by the vicars choral (SGC IV.B.1, f. 63r). However, no minimum qualifications in respect of musical or vocal skill were imposed on the recruitment of successive Wykham chaplains. Consequently, though this provision certainly amplified by one the number of those occupying the vicars' stalls at service, the chaplain was not necessarily able to contribute to the musical functions of the vicars choral, and has to be discounted as a member of the musical force of the chapel.

18. The numbers of staff in attendance at obits appear consistently on the Treasurer's accounts for this period; they yield absolute minima for those actually employed at the time, excluding all who were sick or absent on legitimate business.

19. SGC XV.34.19, *obitus*.

20. This included a complete set of vestments for the Boy Bishop. See the inventories of 1384–5 and 1409–10: *Inventories of St George's Chapel*, ed. Bond, pp. 32–4, 38–48, 62–72, 102–3, 105–8, 113–18. For a useful conspectus of 'The mediaeval services of St. George's Chapel', see *ibid.*, Appendix A, pp. 157–67.

21. No one was to be granted formal admission as either a clerk or vicar choral until he had given probationary satisfaction concerning his suitability, both of voice and of general demeanour. Statutes 13, 15: SGC IV.B.1, ff. 77r, 77v.

22. Statute 17: SGC IV.B.1, f. 77v.

There is a good deal of evidence to suggest that during the years 1380–1420 musical performance in the context of the liturgy was being advanced to a much enhanced level of priority in the values of those who were the patrons of the Church.[23] This provided an appetite for new composition, especially of polyphonic music, which the musicians were more than ready to satisfy. This volume of energy remained in full flow until around 1420; thereafter the actual impetus for innovation may have slackened a little for some years but was by no means extinguished, and a new plateau of heightened endeavour had been reached that was to serve as an essential springboard for the major innovations of the period between about 1455 and 1480.[24]

When the new choral force at the College of St George was assembled in the early 1350s it probably joined immediately a body of great churches, then numbering around forty, at which the observance of the liturgy was enhanced at suitable times by the singing of settings of texts individually composed in three- or four-part polyphony. These items, rendered by a group of adult solo singers who possessed the education and the training to read and sing from the mensural notation used for polyphony, were deployed as a means of conferring a special lustre upon services perceived as possessing particular distinction. The repertory created for this purpose during the second half of the fourteenth century extended primarily to settings of individual movements from the Ordinary of the Mass, principally for use at the daily Lady Mass; of texts in verse or prose in honour of the Virgin, principally for use in place of the sequence at Lady Mass; and to motets, which apparently were for use at High Mass of the Day on feast days, either to fill a liturgical hiatus commonly encountered at the time of the Offertory, or at the very conclusion of the service.

Nobody *needed* this polyphonic music; the corpus of plainsong was wholly self-sufficient, and the performance of polyphony — and also its composition — was undertaken at each church most probably as a hobby by a handful of enthusiasts, who prior to *c*.1380 very possibly did not number at any one time more than a couple of hundred individuals in the entire kingdom. From among the team of thirteen well-paid vicars choral at St George's there is every likelihood that there were always some three or four who were enthusiasts for this practice, and the frequent appointment by successive kings of chaplains of the Chapel Royal to canonries of St George's was certainly sufficient to establish in the chapel at Windsor a climate expectant of and receptive to the enhancement of the services, when appropriate, by the rendering of polyphonic settings.

Certainly there survives a good deal of evidence of an early impetus for the cultivation of polyphony at St George's. The early fifteenth-century binding of one of the seventy volumes donated to the Bodleian Library in Oxford by the dean and canons of Windsor in 1612 contains three fly-leaves drawn from a volume of English polyphony of about the

23. R. Bowers, 'Choral Institutions within the English Church: their Constitution and Development, *c*.1340–1500' (unpublished Ph.D. thesis, University of East Anglia, 1975), chapter 4.

24. The most comprehensive account of the history of polyphonic composition in England during this period is still F. Ll. Harrison, *Music in Medieval Britain*, 2nd edn, London 1963; see also J. Caldwell, *The Oxford History of English Music*, 2 vols, Oxford 1991, i. p., i: *From the beginnings to c.1715*, pp. 74–216.

third quarter of the fourteenth century.[25] These may well preserve some of the chapel's polyphonic repertory of the period *c.*1360–80. The leaves convey five settings of the Gloria of the mass, all fragmentary; all but one appear to include the Marian trope 'Spiritus et alme', confirming that their composition was for use at Lady Mass. The surviving music is poorly preserved, but it has proved possible to transcribe isolated passages from three of the settings.[26] All is composed in the standard texture of three men's voices, in an uncomplicated yet sonorous homophony; two pieces in particular employ an engagingly lively and extrovert triple rhythm.

It may be noted that, in addition, St. George's has been identified as a very plausible candidate for proposal as the provenance of a considerably more important fragmentary source of polyphony of this period; this is New York, Pierpont Morgan Library, MS 978, dating from *c.*1370.[27] Its contents are conspicuous for their diversity, since its fifteen items — some of considerable length — extend to six mass movements, a festal sequence for the proper of High Mass, one motet (its text Marian), one untexted item, five Marian pieces probably for use as the sequence at Lady Mass, and one similar votive piece in honour of St Edward. The texts to two pieces associate the manuscript closely with the courtly circle of Edward III. 'Singularis laudis digna' entreats the Virgin Mary to assure victory to the English in their conflict with the French, and to bring honour to Edward, 'worthy king of battle'. Its text was conceived among circles which could appreciate an obscurely allegorical reference to one of the contemporary Garter knights, Enguerrand de Coucy, and to his role in an episode within the family marriage diplomacy of Edward III which came to fruition in 1369. 'Regem regum collaudemus' extols the virtues of a canonised King Edward; of the two possibilities, the terms of the text appear to render Edward the Confessor somewhat the more likely. The invocation to the latter, one of the dedicatees of St George's Chapel, taken with the courtly and Garter connections of the former text, place St George's high on the list of possible provenances for this manuscript.[28] For the most part the music, in up to four parts but mostly for three, is characteristic of its time, though generally eschewing learned complexity in favour of direct projection of the text.[29]

The sense of musical endeavour at St George's may well have been much enhanced also by the existence among the canons, from 1362 until his death in 1373, of John Aleyn, one

25. Bodl. MS Bodley 384, ff. i–iii. Many of these seventy volumes contain inscriptions of origin showing that St George's had acquired them from previous owners; MS Bodley 384, however, exhibits no such mark to negate the possibility of a Windsor origin for its binding and fly-leaves. See *Inventories of St George's Chapel*, ed. Bond, pp. 289–92.

26. *English Music for Mass and Offices (I)*, ed. F. Harrison, E. Sanders and P. Lefferts, Polyphonic Music of the Fourteenth Century, 16, Monaco 1983, pp. 47–53, 269–70, 279.

27. The music is discussed in F. Harrison, 'Polyphonic music for a chapel of Edward III', *Music and Letters*, 59 (1978), pp. 420–8; E. Sanders, 'English polyphony in the Morgan Library manuscript', *Music and Letters*, 61 (1980), pp. 172–6.

28. For particular discussion of these texts and of the provenance of the manuscript, see R. Bowers, 'Fixed points in the chronology of English fourteenth-century polyphony', *Music and Letters*, 71 (1990), 313–35, p. 317; also *idem*, 'Postscript' to above article, *Music and Letters*, 80 (1999), 270–1, p. 270.

29. *English Music for Mass and Offices (I)*, ed. Harrison, Sanders and Lefferts, nos 44, 45, 58, 67, 73; *English Music for the Mass and Offices (II)*, ed. *eidem*, Polyphonic Music of the Fourteenth Century, 17, Monaco 1986, nos 1, 37, 47–51, 65, 67; *English Music of the Thirteenth and early Fourteenth Centuries*, ed. E. Sanders, Polyphonic Music of the Fourteenth Century, 14, Monaco 1979, no. 60.

of the chaplains of Edward III's Chapel Royal.[30] Aleyn can now with reasonable certainty be identified as author of both the texts and the music of *Sub Ar[c]turo plebs vallata / Fons citharizancium / In omnem terram*, one of the most complex and remarkable isorhythmic motets of the second half of the fourteenth century to have survived from anywhere in Europe.[31] This John Aleyn may very well also be the composer of a three-voice setting of Gloria in a simple cantilena style attributed to 'Aleyn' and preserved in an English source of *c*.1417–20, the 'Old Hall' Manuscript.[32] At his death Aleyn bequeathed to St George's a roll of polyphonic music (*unus rotulus de cantu musicali*), subsequently listed in the inventories of 1384–5 and 1409–10,[33] and it is tempting to wonder if the chapel book given by him which was sufficiently precious to have been supplied in 1394 with a lockable cover might also have been some finely prepared volume of polyphonic music.[34] Further, one Roger Gervays, formerly a minor canon of St Paul's Cathedral in London, served for a while in the 1390s as a vicar choral of St George's, and was employed for four and a half months of 1395–6 as Instructor of the Choristers.[35] He is very probably to be identified with the composer whose three-voice setting of Gloria is preserved in the 'Old Hall' Manuscript under the name 'Gervays' and, quite remarkably, also in a North Italian manuscript of *c*.1425, under the name 'Gervasius de Anglia'.[36]

Certainly, therefore, an early momentum for the cultivation of polyphony had been generated at St George's even before 1400. It is consequently no surprise to find that by 1415–16 the chapel possessed not one but some number of volumes of polyphonic music,

30. For Aleyn, see especially A. Wathey, 'The peace of 1360–1369 and Anglo-French musical relations', *Early Music History*, 9 (1990), 129–74, pp. 145–6, 151–4, 165–8. As canon of Windsor, Aleyn was no absentee passenger. During 1362–3 he and one of the vicars choral of St George's, Adam Pencrich, rode to Salisbury Cathedral and spent 86 days there correcting the chapel's collection of service books against authentic Salisbury exemplars: SGC XV.34.2, *expense necessarie*. Such correction of the service-books was a statutory obligation (Statute 51: SGC IV.B.1, f. 80v).

31. For the music, see *Two Fourteenth-century Motets in praise of Music*, ed. M. Bent, Newton Abbot 1977, pp. i, 1–7; *The Motets of the manuscripts Chantilly, Musée Condé, 564 (olim 1047) and Modena, Biblioteca Estense, alpha.M.5.24 (olim lat. 568)*, ed. U. Günther, Corpus Mensurabilis Musicae, 39, American Institute of Musicology 1965, pp. l–liii, 49–52. The literature is extensive; see especially B. Trowell, 'A fourteenth-century motet and its composer', *Acta Musicologica*, 29 (1957), pp. 65–75; Bowers, 'Fixed points in the chronology of fourteenth-century English polyphony', pp. 320–35; M. Bent, '*Subtiliter alternare*: the Yoxford motet *O amicus / Precursoris*', *Current Musicology*, 45–7 (1990), 32–65, pp. 60–5. It is now known that Aleyn forsook the court at about Michaelmas 1372 to take up residence at Exeter Cathedral, which is where he died. This was the most remote from London of his many canonries, and it seems very possible that this retirement from court supplies the scenario for the writing of the texts and composition of the music of his propitiatory motet: R. Bowers, 'Fixed points in the chronology of English fourteenth-century polyphony: a Postscript', *Music and Letters*, 80 (1999), pp. 269–70.

32. *The Old Hall Manuscript*, ed. M. Bent and A. Hughes, 2 vols in 3, Corpus Mensurabilis Musicae, 46, American Institute of Musicology 1969, i, p. 18.

33. *Inventories of St George's Chapel*, ed. Bond, pp. 34, 102; it seems fair to presume that had this been a scroll of monodic chant rather than of polyphony the inventory would have listed it simply as *rotulus de cantu*.

34. SGC XV.56.13: (July) item in j cera empta pro libro Johannis Aleyn iijd ob.

35. SGC XV.34.18, *stipendia officiariorum*. He was a minor canon of St Paul's from 1384 to 1393: G. Hennessy, *Novum Repertorium Ecclesiasticum Parochiale Londinense*, London 1898, p. 60.

36. *The Old Hall Manuscript*, ed. Bent and Hughes, i, p. 96; Bologna, Civico Museo Bibliografico, MS Q15, f. 22v. It may be noted that neither the 'Old Hall' Manuscript itself (London, British Library, Add. MS 57950) nor Bodl. MS Selden B26 are believed any longer to have had any connection or association with St George's (cf. *Inventories of St George's Chapel*, ed. Bond, pp. 263–4).

for the embellishment of which the precentor obtained in that year a quantity of vermilion.[37] Of the nature of the contents of these volumes there is no record.

It was at around this period that an abrupt change was wrought upon the identity of those members of the chapel staff by whom these collections of polyphony were actually performed. The polyphonic repertory of the period around the turn of the fifteenth century encompassed a particularly wide variety of styles. These ranged from those that were plain and unambitious and correspondingly quite easy to sing, all the way up to others that were of ferocious complexity, demanding virtuoso skills as much in simply reading the notation as in actually performing the notes.[38] Hitherto the necessary degree of specialist expertise required to sing polyphonic music had been found among some four or so of the ordained clergy appointed to be vicars choral, as actually the only members of the choir sufficiently senior to possess such accomplishments. As the fourteenth century closed, however, these skills were being sought at a time at which repeated onslaughts of plague had significantly reduced the overall national pool of manpower in which musical talent might appear, and at which the number of vocations to the priesthood was reaching a trough that was of a depth disproportionate even to the fall in population.[39] These seem to have been the circumstances generating the appearance at this time of a new category of expert church musician, through the progressive accomplishment of a complete transformation in the character of the clerkships of the second form. This resulted in the creation of a new class of career church musician, skilled men who were content to spend a lifetime in the service of the church but had no intention of entering major orders. Rather, they never advanced beyond the minor orders to which most had probably been admitted in boyhood, and remained at liberty to marry if they wished and raise families. It is in this development that there originated the modern lay clerk.

At Windsor the transformation was particularly marked. The statutes of 1352 had ordained that the clerkships of the second form fulfil their traditional role as a category of very junior liturgical officiant intermediate between the chorister-boys and the priest-vicars. Of the four, one clerk was to be in deacon's orders, one in subdeacon's, and the other two in minor orders, and it is clear that the clerks were originally envisaged as being youths and young men aged between about 15 and 24, progressing through the minor and major orders on their way to ordination to the priesthood. The stipend ordained for the clerks in minor orders, at £4 0s 0d per year, was only one mark more than that for a chorister; the deacon and subdeacon were more highly paid, at £5 6s 8d per year. Specific provision was made to ensure that as the two clerks in minor orders progressed to major orders on the title of the chapel they were to be admitted successively to the posts of subdeacon- and deacon-clerk. They were first to fill the vacancies that arose as the latter arrived at priest's orders, and thereafter were themselves eligible for promotion, if suitable, to vacant vicarages choral as opportunity arose.[40] In 1352, that is, it was not envisaged that anyone could make a lifetime career of being a second-form clerk in such a college — a

37. SGC XV.56.22: (April) . . . In vermylony empt' pro libris organ[icis] eliminandis [*sic: interlined* over 'limitandis' *lined out*, ?for 'illuminandis'] ijd.

38. It would not be unrealistic to suggest that the music notation of this period was among the most refined accomplishments of the late medieval intellect.

39. R.N. Swanson, *Church and Society in Late Medieval England*, Oxford 1989, pp. 30–6.

40. Statutes 3, 17: SGC IV.B.1, ff. 75r, 77v. The clerks were specifically identified as the *clerici secunde forme* on a document of 1378 (SGC XV.53.64) and as the *clerici secundarii* in 1376–7 (SGC XV.34.11, 13: *obitus*).

clerkship offered no opportunity for achieving anything at all, other than just the next stage upwards.

This is indeed the way in which at first the clerkships at St George's operated. With a high degree of consistency the obit payments entered onto the earliest treasurer's accounts, up to 1388,[41] note the presence of the deacon, subdeacon and other two clerks. By 1393, however, a new policy had been inaugurated; thereafter, none of the clerks was in other than minor orders, if in orders at all. One function of the subdeacon and deacon clerks had been to chant, respectively, the epistle and gospel at High Mass of the Day. From 1393 onwards there was no one to undertake these tasks. The obit payments for 1393–4 recorded the attendance throughout the year of just four *clerici*, and made no attempt to distinguish their orders. Each was paid £4 os od for the year, the rate of pay for clerks not in the major orders of subdeacon or above. The gospel at High Mass was read by the vicars, who received between them an extra payment of 40s od per year, and the epistle by the four clerks as a group, for which they were paid 26s 8d per year between them.[42] These became established practices, and in future years these payments were explained explicitly as being required by the absence of men in deacon's and subdeacon's orders.[43]

Around 1390, therefore, it was decided that rather than abide by the letter of the statutes it was in the college's interests that there be employed as clerks of the second form men bound neither by the constraints of major orders nor by desire to obtain them. The organised pattern of internal promotion from clerk to vicar and acolyte to priest predicated by the statutes was now abandoned, and the job of clerk became open to youths and men who were at liberty to serve in it for as long a time as they wanted. This development is seen not only at St George's but in a number of major choirs at this time, and soon became standard practice.[44] It appears to have originated merely as an opportunist response to a prevailing inability to recruit as clerks conventional youths and men who were proceeding through the orders and were seeking the priesthood; nevertheless, it turned very speedily into a positive and constructive departure, since it opened to the laity as well as to the ordained priesthood the door of opportunity to undertake a lifetime's professional career in the music of the church.

Indeed, it was not at all long before the greater collegiate churches and household chapels found themselves obtaining the highest levels of musical expertise not among the clergy but among the laymen now being admitted to the clerkships of the second form. The archives of other institutions corroborate the evidence yielded by those of St George's in making clear that from around the first years of the fifteenth century the clerks of the second form in the greater choirs took over from the priests the principal responsibility for

41. SGC XV.34.15★ (formerly CC 117558), *obitus*.

42. SGC XV.34.16: *obitus, dona et placita*. These payments added up to 66s 8d per year, and so absorbed the differential which the college saved through not having to pay two clerks at the higher rate in respect of their major orders.

43. E.g. SGC XV.34.24, *stipendia officiariorum cum rewardis*: item vicariis collegii pro lectura evangeliorum hoc eodem anno ex rewardo pro defectu unius diaconi ad hoc constituti xls. Item clericis eiusdem collegii pro lectura epistolarum hoc eodem anno pro defectu unius subdiaconi ad hoc constituti xxvjs viijd.

44. This development was not yet taken into account when the constitutions of the choirs of New College, Oxford, and Winchester College were being finalised late in 1391; its appearance can be detected later in the 1390s and early in the fifteenth century at such institutions as the Chapel Royal and Arundel College, and also in the statutes of colleges founded soon after c.1400, e.g. Fotheringhay (1415) and Stoke-by-Clare (1423): Bowers, 'Choral Institutions within the English Church', pp. 4040–50.

execution of the most demanding of the musical duties in the chapel, especially the
performance and composition of polyphony, the copying of the books in which it was
preserved, the playing of the organ and, presently, the instruction of the choristers.[45] The
efforts of the lay clerks might well be supplemented by any of the priests who happened to
be qualified and were minded to do so, but — for the first two-thirds of the century,
anyway — the latter were at liberty to concern themselves primarily with their sacerdotal
functions and with their contributions to the ceremony and plainsong of the liturgy, while
only the lay clerks undertook the rendering of the polyphony — in addition, of course, to
all their customary duties as clerks of the second form.

It may be noted that the much enhanced profile of musical enterprise manifest in the
years around the turn of the fifteenth century, and the emergence of a class of professional
lay church musician, are both well exemplified by a new level of prominence accorded at
this time to the use of the organ. At this period the church organ was no very imposing
piece of machinery.[46] It was a free-standing positive of perhaps a couple of octaves'
compass, still sufficiently compact in size to be movable if necessary, played by one man
and simultaneously blown by another. The organ was ubiquitous in the greater churches
by the middle of the fourteenth century, and there is every likelihood that St George's
possessed an instrument from very early in its foundation. In the surviving archives it is
first mentioned when materials were purchased for its maintenance and repair in 1395,[47]
and more substantial work was undertaken in 1397.[48] Its most likely location was on top
of the pulpitum, the screen dividing the chapel proper from the ante-chapel which
occupied its westernmost bay.

The contribution made by the church organ to the conduct of the liturgical service at
this period is wholly obscure. It possessed no written solo repertory and it was not an
instrument of musical accompaniment, either for plainsong or for improvised or composed
polyphony. One role, perhaps, was to play on the greater feast-days, sounding improvised
fanfares before the beginning and after the end of the major services in much the same
spirit as peals and clashes of bells. Actually within the services, its player might also
substitute for some of the less important items of plainsong, replacing the sung chant with
an improvisation upon it. At first, no member of the liturgical staff was either specifically
deputed or specifically remunerated for playing the organ; a vicar or — after about
1400 — a clerk merely discharged his duty of participation in the service by playing the
organ, as required, instead of singing.

Only special circumstances called forth a specific payment for playing, and instances of
this are recorded at St George's on three occasions in the first decade of the century. In
1403 an unnamed performer received 3s 4d for having played on two feasts of the Blessed
Virgin, namely the Assumption and Nativity, and had received 13s 4d for playing on an
earlier occasion — probably Easter.[49] At Christmas 1406 the dean himself ensured that a
distinguished visiting musician, Walter Whitby, receive the substantial sum of 13s 4d for

---

45. *Ibid.*, pp. 4049–50, 5056–76, 5085–93, 5096–8.

46. See e.g. S. Bicknell, *The History of the English Organ*, Cambridge 1996, pp. 16–43.

47. SGC XV.56.14: (January) Item in Wyr' empt' pro organ' jd.

48. SGC XV.56.15: (July) Dat' domino Nicholao clerico Regis pro emendacione organorum vjs viijd
precepto Custodis.

49. SGC XV.34.22[i], *dona et placita*: item organiste prima vice xiijs iiijd per Massyngham [canon] et altera
pro festis Assumpcionis et Nativitatis beate marie iijs iiijd — xvjs viijd.

having played at the festal services.[50] Whitby was already a prominent musical practitioner, and an early example of the careerist lay church musician. From 1384 to 1388 he had been the inaugural Master of the Lady Chapel choir at Westminster Abbey;[51] early in 1396 he was admitted a lay Gentleman of Richard II's Chapel Royal,[52] and doubtless it was in his capacity as a Chapel Royal member that he was present at Windsor and available to play the organ in St George's during the Christmas season of 1406. He was present again in the autumn of 1408, receiving on this occasion a gratuity of 3s 4d for his having performed on the organ.[53]

Some fresh impetus to the elevation of the ceremonial role of music in the promotion of liturgical observance at St George's arose during the reign of Henry V. This king's military endeavours and chivalric values ensured that the advancement of the fortunes of St George's was always likely to figure among his political and religious priorities. In 1415–16 Henry directed to St George's eleven fine service-books taken by forfeiture from the chapel of Henry, baron Scrope of Masham, lately convicted of treason, and it was from this king that the chapel obtained by gift its finest statue of the Blessed Virgin.[54] From Henry's brother John, duke of Bedford, the college received a substantial increase in its endowments in 1421–2,[55] and it is perhaps no coincidence that it was under a king who all but doubled the membership of his own Chapel Royal that there arose during 1415–17 a particular degree of intensity in the promotion of the music of St George's. This seems to have focused on one event of particular prominence, the magnificent ceremony held within the chapel on 7 May 1416 at which the Emperor Sigismund donated an important relic of St George and was personally invested by the king with a knighthood of the Order of the Garter.[56]

This particular period of vigour in the promotion of the music of the chapel had begun with an overall 'new deal' devised for the vicars choral, centred upon the expenditure during 1415–17 of no less than £88 16s 11¾d on the construction of a hall and a new range of lodgings specifically for their accommodation.[57] At the same time the chapter also

50. SGC XV.34.24, *stipendia officiariorum*: Item Waltero Whitby clerico existenti ibidem tempore Natalis domini ad instanciam custodis pro divinis in organis exequendis ex rewardo xiijs iiijd.

51. Westminster Abbey Muniments, 19371, *Minuta*; 19871–5, *Empcio liberature*; 18999, *Expense necessarie*; 23187–8, *Soluciones et stipendia*.

52. For Whitby as member of the Chapel Royal see London, Public Record Office (hereafter PRO), E101/403/10, f. 44v; E404/511/374; E101/404/21, f. 44v; E404/511/296; BL Harley MS 319, f. 46r; *Calendar of Close Rolls 1399–1402*, p. 198. He had left the Chapel Royal by 1413: PRO, E101/406/21, f. 19r. Richard Kingston was dean of both St. George's and the Chapel Royal, and it appears probable that it was through some enterprise of his that Whitby was present at Windsor on these occasions.

53. SGC XV.56.19: (September) Et Waltero Whyteby pro organisterio iijs iiijd.

54. SGC XV.56.22; PRO, E36/113, p. 107.

55. This took the form of a grant of spiritualities lately confiscated from the alien priory of Ogbourne (Wiltshire), dissolved: *Calendar of Patent Rolls 1416–22*, pp. 441–2; the grant was duly confirmed by the king (Ashmole, *Institution*, p. 159).

56. G.F. Beltz, *Memorials of the Order of the Garter*, London 1841, pp. lvi–lviii.

57. £67 14s 1¾d in 1415–16 and £21 2s 10d in 1416–17: SGC XV.34.28, *reparaciones*; SGC XV.48.5, *reparaciones*. St. John Hope, *Windsor Castle*, i, pp. 227–8; ii, p. 517. Described in 1432 as the *mansum vicariorum* (SGC IV.B.1, f. 87v). Some discrete suite of accommodation was also provided for the four clerks: SGC XV.34.41, *Custus caminorum clericorum* (1442–3); SGC XV.34.47, *Reparaciones* (1459–60). See further T. Tatton-Brown (*supra*, pp. 30–1).

undertook a substantial recruiting drive intended to replenish temporarily depleted numbers, which by Michaelmas 1415 had momentarily fallen to only ten. One of the existing clerks, Roger Everard, was sent to Oxford to seek men in priest's orders interested in taking up places as vicars choral at St George's. A reward was given to William Croydon, one of the vicars, for securing successfully the services of a new recruit, Richard Purdieu; another man invited to become a vicar choral, John Brynkman, was reimbursed the expenses he had incurred when he was inhibited by the bishop of Ely from acting upon his initial acceptance. William Kyrie, another of the existing vicars, was sent to the Midlands for ten days, 'to Lichfield and other places', to seek vicars for appointment to Windsor.[58] He had recently been recruited from the collegiate church of St Mary in Warwick, where he is known to have been a vicar choral in 1412,[59] so he was being sent back to trawl an area he knew. The number of vicars was complete again by 28 April 1416[60] — just in time for the investiture of Emperor Sigismund.

Moreover, the use of the organ seems to have been a matter of some priority to the chapter at this time. The term ending at Christmas 1415 had produced some special circumstances requiring particular resort to organ-playing,[61] and this time it was to one of the chapel's own clerks of the second form, Lawrence Dreweryn, that payment was made; he received five shillings 'by special grace of the Dean and College'.[62] In April 1416 the chapter ventured to decide that the instrument be substantially rebuilt. Two men were escorted to Windsor from London to undertake the job, for which the final inclusive settlement was 26s 8d.[63] It is actually possible that what St George's obtained at this time was a new organ altogether, since in March 1420 3d was spent on the mending of the 'old organs', indicating the recent acquisition of a new instrument.[64] There seems to be every likelihood that the work undertaken in April 1416 was put in hand in anticipation of the Emperor's installation the following month. Dreweryn was again paid a gratuity, on the

58. SGC XV.48.28, *Dona et placita* and *Expense Custodis Canonicorum et aliorum negocia Collegii prosequencium*.
59. PRO, E164/22, f. 186v.
60. SGC XV.34.28, *obitus*.
61. Some small repair had been effected upon the organ in January 1414: SGC XV.56.21.
62. SGC XV.34.28, 29: *Stipendia officiariorum cum rewardis*. On SGC XV.34.29, the fair copy account, the wording is 'et Laurentio Dreweryn uni clericorum collegii ex rewardo pro divinis in organis solempnizandis pro termino Natalis domini vs'. This wording is reminiscent of that employed in 1406 to describe the payment made to Walter Whitby (see note 50 above), and it must be acknowledged that such phraseology could conceivably refer to the singing of polyphony (*cantus organicus*) rather than the playing of the organ. Fortunately the wording used on the rough draft account for 1415–16 (SGC XV.34.28) makes clear that this payment (and by deduction that also for 1406) was indeed for playing the organ: 'et in rewardo facto Laurencio Dreweryn uni clericorum collegii de speciali gracia dictorum custodis et collegii pro quodam officio circa organa ludenda pro termino Natalis Domini tantum vs'.
63. SGC XV.56.22, April. The matter of payment was not settled without some dispute; the canon precentor, John Easton, had to travel to London to reduce the sum from 40s 0d plus expenses.
64. SGC XV.56.25: (March) Item in emendacione veterum organorum iijd.

instruction of the dean and again in the sum of five shillings, at the end of 1417–18 for having enhanced divine service with organ-playing.[65]

In respect of its cultivation of polyphony, the upgrading of the visual presentation of the existing accumulation of volumes undertaken during 1416 has already been mentioned.[66] To this collection a substantial addition was made in June the following year. For the making of a new book of polyphony the precentor paid out 6s 3d for fifteen skins of vellum, producing a volume of 60 folios.[67] Into a book of this size it would have been possible to copy a very substantial repertory of polyphonic settings; it is clear that the performance of this style of music enjoyed a high priority among the duties of the St George's singers, and it is most regrettable that none of the contents of this volume can now be identified.

III. THE MID-CENTURY CONSOLIDATION OF MUSICAL ENDEAVOUR, 1430–1475

After these flurries of excitement in Henry V's reign, the surviving archives up to the middle of the 1430s record no further unusual level of activity in any aspect of the chapel's music. The accounts surviving from the 1420s and early 1430s show that the college was then experiencing serious financial difficulties,[68] which may well have inhibited for a decade any appetite for undertaking major expansion of its musical endeavours. Rather, by about 1420 a new plateau of endeavour and stability had been achieved, which now was consolidated and maintained.

The terms of the Injunctions issued in 1432 by Archbishop Kemp, following his visitation as Lord Chancellor in 1430, do however indicate the manner in which the morale of the choir could be sapped somewhat and its efforts begin to be vitiated by the pressures arising both from financial under-provision and from the absence of the head of the college, John Arundel, about the business of the king elsewhere than in Windsor. Although the residentiaries chose to bear the brunt of the college's financial straits themselves, foregoing much of their own remuneration, they still were not able totally to avoid the singers' stipends falling into arrears. Hardly surprisingly, therefore, there was some slippage of standards. Nevertheless, despite its thoroughness the visitation's search for deficiencies in the college found little to record in respect of its manner of conducting

65. SGC XV.34.30, *Stipendia et vadia officiariorum*: et laurencio Dreweryn uni clericorum collegii ex rewardo pro divinis in organis solempnizandis mandato domini custodis (xs *lined out*) vs. The observation in E.H. Fellowes, *Organists and Masters of the Choristers of St George's Chapel in Windsor Castle*, London 1939, p. 6, that Dreweryn was named also as Instructor of the Choristers in 1417–18 is unfortunately erroneous; payment was made, but the recipient was not named (SGC XV.34.30, *Stipendia et vadia officiariorum*). That volume, and also Fellowes, *The Vicars or Minor Canons of His Majesty's Free Chapel of St George in Windsor Castle*, Windsor 1945, were both pioneering studies in their time; they offer mines of information, but do need to be used with circumspection in the light of subsequent increases in knowledge.

66. Above, note 37.

67. SGC XV.56.23: (June) Et in xv pellibus de velym emptis in Wyndesore pro uno libro vocato Organboke continente v quaternos, quolibet quaterno iiij pell' videlicet xij fol' vjs iiijd.

68. A.K.B. Evans, 'The Years of Arrears . . .' above, pp. 94–102. To make matters worse, in February 1418 the chapter had to go to law to recover choristers' salaries embezzled by a former Instructor, William Pounger: SGC XV.34.30, *dona et placita*, and "Dotted Crotchet" [*nom de plume*], 'St George's Chapel, Windsor', *The Musical Times*, 50 (1909), 701–11, p. 706.

the services in the chapel, and Kemp had reassuringly little to say about the work of the members of the choir, limiting himself to only two observations.

He had been advised of minor departures from certain of the finer intricacies of the Salisbury liturgy; on the principle that 'he who overlooks minor matters will lapse little by little into greater', he enjoined that practices incurring such departure from the authorised liturgy cease forthwith. In particular, he required that anyone claiming the debility of old age or sickness should obtain the leave of the chapter before departing from the liturgical rules for standing, genuflecting and kneeling. He also acted to terminate an infelicity of practice by which certain of the vicars and other ministers of the choir had become prone to seeking leave of absence from service for other than reasonable cause, an abuse which, through friendship or favour, the dean or vice-dean or precentor had been rather too readily prone to indulge.[69]

Kemp also sought to ensure that vacancies among the vicarages choral, which in the recent past had sometimes extended to six months or even a year through the negligence of the chapter, should henceforth subsist for no longer than a maximum of three months before a suitable man was found for appointment. In order to ease the achievement of this provision, Kemp also required that current opportunity for vicars and other minor officers of the college to leave their posts unserved through their 'sudden and unexpected departure' to employment elsewhere be terminated by requirement that henceforth a minimum of three months notice of intention to surrender office be given.[70] After what was plainly a very thorough visitation, this was all that Kemp had to say about the work of the choir. There had been, it seems, some slight attenuation of morale and of attention to duty, but clearly nothing had transpired which might have jeopardised the integrity of the service provided by the singers in chapel.

Indeed, viewed from around the mid-1430s the choral strength at St George's appears comfortably established among the second rank of professional choirs of its day, and in at least two important respects those responsible for the manner in which it undertook its duties were concerned to ensure that it kept abreast of developments being pioneered elsewhere. The early years of the fifteenth century had seen the appearance of rather a fashion for having the boys of any liturgical choir take a prominent role in the performance of the chant of the daily Lady Mass.[71] Evidently this practice had taken hold at St George's as elsewhere (superseding the injunction of the 1352 statutes that Lady Mass be performed by certain of the vicars choral alone),[72] and from Michaelmas 1435 onwards there occurs notice of the boys' attendance at daily Lady Mass with their Instructor.[73] Moreover, by this period the distinctive — if still unidentifiable — contribution to the conduct of the services made by the playing of the organ had grown into a feature sufficiently routine and regular for a particular member of the body of clerks to emerge for the first time as a

---

69. Injunctions 6–8: SGC IV.B.1, ff. 85r–v. In particular, no vicar or other minister of the choir was henceforth to be given leave for a whole day or more without the approval of the residentiary chapter.

70. Injunctions 9, 10: SGC IV.B.1, f. 85v.

71. Bowers, 'Choral Institutions within the English Church', pp. 4057–9, 4085–100.

72. Statute 26: SGC IV.B.1, f. 76v; and see note 4 above.

73. Treasurer's Account 1435–6: Winchester, Cathedral Library, MS L38/4/12 (Box 62), *Stipendia et vadia officiariorum*.

designated organist. It was from 1435 that his role was recognised by the appointment of a specified stipend in recompense for his work and recognition of his skills.[74]

It must be acknowledged that the locale of the work of the St George's choir may not have been particularly impressive; a building 70 feet long by 28 feet wide will be inspiring only if it also has great height, an attribute possessed by St Stephen's and the Sainte-Chapelle but not, it seems, by the old St George's.[75] The choir was indeed in no position to compete with the premier organisations of its time, namely the private chapels of the households of royalty and the greater aristocracy (spiritual and lay). Nevertheless, there were compensations. It was far more coherently organised than the choirs of the great cathedrals, and a membership of 23 rendered it compact and amenable to organisation and direction. Staff numbers on the whole were well maintained. It was unusual for fewer than eleven vicars choral to be present at obits, and at £8 0s 0d basic annual income, with free accommodation, a vicarage choral at Windsor could attract good men away from cathedral churches such as Wells and collegiate churches such as Warwick.[76] The vicars and clerks of St George's certainly worked hard for their money. The statutes of the greater cathedrals generally required full or almost full attendance of the clerks of the top and second forms at Matins and High Mass daily, but allowed attendance of about 50% at the remaining services.[77] Such latitude could not be extended at a much smaller organisation such as St George's, and the surviving attendance register for 1468–79 shows that out of eleven choral services a day (eight offices and three masses) every vicar and clerk was required to attend no fewer than eight. Nevertheless, basic conditions were good, and certainly the chapter was spared any necessity to suffer the prolonged employment of men who were unsatisfactory. Vacancies could readily be filled, and the 1468–79 register records not only the actual dismissal of around a dozen clerks and vicars in the wake of their failure to heed warnings concerning their conduct (mostly for contumacy, for quarrelsomeness, or for a propensity for fisticuffs) but also their rapid replacement.[78] In addition, there was patently no problem at all in keeping full all of the six choristerships.

In respect of the clerkships, however, matters were rather different. The principal reservoir of advanced musical skill and expertise now resided among the four lay clerks,

---

74. *Ibid.* The statutes of Eton College (1453) are the earliest to make specific provision for one of the clerks to serve as organist: *The ancient Laws of the fifteenth century for King's College, Cambridge, and for the public school of Eton College*, ed. J. Heywood and T. Wright, London 1850, p. 514.

75. For the dimensions and a description of the old St George's, see St. John Hope, *Windsor Castle*, i, p. 55; ii, pp. 374–5, 480. The overall height of St Stephen's was some 92 feet, that of its upper chapel being a remarkable 72 feet: M. Hastings, *St Stephen's Chapel and its place in the development of the Perpendicular Style in England*, Cambridge 1955, p. 63. A sketch of the north aspect of Windsor Castle as it appeared from Eton College in about 1450 shows the old St George's (built *c.*1240–50) as a relatively modest and unprepossessing building (Fig. 16, see p. 32 above).

76. For Warwick, see above, p. 184 and n. 59. Before coming to Windsor both John Rowley and Thomas Bible had been vicars choral at Wells, in 1460–1 and 1462–3 respectively: Wells, Chapter Archives, Muniments of the Vicars Choral, B41, B44; cf. Fellowes, *The Vicars or Minor Canons*, pp. 61, 63. The stipend at Windsor was paid as an assured lump sum, a system far superior to the receipt of an amorphous muddle of small sums, some of which could prove difficult to collect, which was the lot of many a cathedral vicar choral.

77. See e.g. R. Bowers, 'Music and Liturgy to 1642' in *A History of Lincoln Minster*, ed. D.M. Owen, Cambridge 1994, 47–76, pp. 49–50.

78. SGC V.B.2, *passim*.

from among whom, by now, were always chosen the music copyists, the organ-player and the Instructor of the Choristers. It was, however, not easy to retain the services of the ablest of the clerks. The statutes allowed them a stipend of only £4 0s 0d per year (now augmented by 6s 8d each for reading the epistle); such a sum had been appropriate for the youths and young men up to the age of 24 or so for whom the clerkships had originally been devised, but it was hardly sufficient for a mature man possessing highly marketable and very portable skills, and who was quite likely to be married and to have a family to keep. It was at Michaelmas 1435 that address began to be made to the issue of raising the remuneration of the lay clerks to a level appropriate to their degree of training and skill and to the responsibilities of their office.

The initiative came from the dean, John Arundel. Under his direction, the chapter determined that from Michaelmas 1435 the clerk serving as organ-player, currently Thomas Thomas, should begin to receive a supplementary stipend of 13s 4d per year. At the same juncture, the Instructor of the Choristers — an office also held at this time by Thomas Thomas — began to receive an annual stipend of 13s 4d for his being present at Lady Mass with the boys. Further, for each of the two longest-serving of the remaining clerks, John Mildenhall and Robert Walker, an augmentation of stipend of 53s 4d per year was now inaugurated, and to the fourth clerk, Walter Martyn, 20s 0d. The intention was salutary; at the time, however, the college was barely clawing its way out of its serious financial problems, and at audit the whole package was at first stricken out as unstatutory (or, more correctly, as contrary to the terms of Kemp's injunctions of three years earlier). Finally, however, the increments were restored, as a charge on that year's working surplus that clearly was perceived as possessing even greater urgency and importance than paying off some of the accumulated debt.[79] Thereafter, these increments to the clerks were paid in every year until the general re-foundation of the late 1470s; it appears that each was individually negotiable with the chapter, within a range of 26s 8d to 53s 4d per year per man.

The financial circumstances of the lay clerks were certainly ameliorated, but the resulting stipend still did not suffice to enable the College to retain the services of the very ablest men. Competition from rival choirs was simply too strong, and St George's was too impoverished to pay any more. Thomas Thomas, a clerk since at least 1435 and both Instructor of the Choristers and organ-player, left at March 1439 and occurs during 1450–1 as one of the four singing-men of the Lady Chapel choir of Westminster Abbey.[80] Richard Prideaux, a lay clerk throughout 1451–2 and a useful copyist of music manuscripts, had left by Michaelmas 1454 and at least by 1459 had made the same move to Westminster Abbey as Thomas Thomas before him.[81] John Mildenhall, a chorister-boy of Henry V's Chapel Royal in 1421, was a lay clerk of St. George's at least by June 1435 and received the most handsome of the increments of stipend available from Michaelmas that year.[82] Even so, he left at Michaelmas 1438, and he too was working in the London

79. Winchester Cathedral Library, MS L38/4/12, *Stipendia et vadia officiariorum* and final *Et debet* section.

80. Winchester Cathedral Library, MS L38/4/12; SGC XV.34.38★, XV.34.39, *Stipendia et vadia*; Westminster Abbey Muniments 19700, *Expense in ecclesia*.

81. SGC XV.34.44, *Stipendia et vadia* and *Custus necessarii*; absent from corresponding entries on SGC XV.59.4 (1454–5). Westminster Abbey Muniments 19066–70, *Firme domorum*; 23232, *Expense necessarie*.

82. PRO, E101/407/4, f. 46r. SGC XV.34.38, *obitus*; Winchester Cathedral Library, MS L38/4/12, *Stipendia et vadia officiariorum*.

area by 1448, when his name appears among those belonging to the Fraternity of St Nicholas, the London gild of parish clerks and professional church singing-men.[83] The total emoluments of John Wetherby were a generous £6 6s 8d during 1440–3 while he served at St George's as both clerk and organ-player; by 1451 he had moved on nevertheless.[84] In 1455–6 he likewise was admitted to the Fraternity of St Nicholas, and in 1466 he was recruited from London to become Master of the Lady Chapel choir at Ely Cathedral Priory.[85]

St George's was too prominent an institution to languish, however,[86] and its provision for the performance of the liturgy, especially with the extra distinction of polyphonic music when appropriate, underwent regular renewal. A climate of expectation in respect of the performance of polyphony may well have been sustained by the existence among the canons of the two most prominent composers of the Chapel Royal of Henry V and Henry VI, namely Thomas Damett, canon of the 5th stall, 1431–6, and Nicholas Sturgeon, canon of the 8th stall, 1442–54.[87] Accordingly, during 1438–9 parchment was bought for the compilation of a new volume to receive polyphonic settings, costing the considerable sum of 14s 0d for both the materials and the writing.[88] That this level of momentum was maintained thereafter is indicated by the payment to the clerk Richard Prideaux of 24s 0d during 1451–2 for the notation and text of yet a further large book of polyphony, this time of 72 folios. Payment of 2d per page suggests workmanship of a high order: this was a substantial and handsome volume.[89] The body of plainsong was finite and unchanging; it was in its polyphonic music for solo ensemble that the choir found opportunity for a renewal and updating of its repertory that was intensive and ongoing. It is especially regrettable that no immediate record survives of the contents of these two volumes.[90]

Nevertheless, on evidence that is suggestive but — it has to be acknowledged — less than conclusive, there has been attributed to St George's the provenance of one of the

83. SGC XV.34.38, *Obitus*; XV.34.38*, *Stipendia et vadia officiariorum*. Fraternity Register: London, Guildhall Library, MS 4889, f. 2r. His death was notified to the gild during 1464–5: *ibid.*, f. 11r.

84. SGC XV.34.40 verso; XV.34.41, *Clerici* and *Stipendia et vadia*; absent from corresponding entries on SGC XV.34.44 (1451–2).

85. London, Guildhall Library, MS 4889, f. 4v. Ely Cathedral: Treasurer's Account 1466–7: PRO, SC6/ 1257/9; Warden of Lady Chapel's Account 1466–7: Cambridge University Library, Ely Chapter Archives, MS Custos Capelle 11.

86. At Easter 1452 its festal witness was enhanced by a troupe of visiting actors, who mounted a play of the Four [*sic*] Maries with full scenery and properties: SGC XV.34.44, *Adhuc de custubus necessariis*.

87. S.L. Ollard, *Fasti Wyndesorienses*, Windsor 1950, pp. 91, 117. It should be noted that both were also canons of St Paul's, where Damett observed residence 1427–36 (with frequent absences) and Sturgeon from 1441 to 1447 and beyond: D. Lepine, *A Brotherhood of Canons serving God: English secular Cathedrals in the later Middle Ages*, Woodbridge 1995, pp. 109, 176. The *cotidiane* sections of the relevant Treasurer's accounts show that both Damett and Sturgeon commonly kept residence also at St George's.

88. SGC XV.34.39, *Expense necessarie*: in pergameno pro libro organizac[ionis] cum notacione eiusdem empto et soluta xiiijs.

89. SGC XV.34.44: *Custus necessarii* — et solut' Ricardo Prideaux pro scriptura et le notyng unius libri vocati le Organboke continente xij quaternos ad usum Collegii ad quemlibet quaternum pertinentia vj folia pro quolibet quaterno ijs — xxiiijs. See also below, pp. 190–2.

90. Attention has been drawn to some musical graffiti cut into one wall of the Tresaunt, the passage connecting the original St George's to its vestry: D. Jones-Baker, 'Graffito of medieval music in the Tresaunt, Windsor Castle', *Antiquaries' Journal*, 64 (1984), pp. 373–6. The staff-lines and note-shapes of mensural notation of which this consists appear consistent with a date of c.1420–70 for their execution; however, they add up to no more than incoherent and random doodlings, devoid of musical content or significance.

very few volumes of polyphonic music to have survived from this mid-century period. The manuscript Egerton 3307 in the British Library is generally dated to the decade 1440–50; it contains in its present slightly imperfect state 73 folios of music and is an ordered collection of miscellaneous occasional items. By this period polyphony for High Mass, Lady Mass and the Marian votive antiphon was commonly all copied into one volume available for daily use, while the pieces proper only to particular times of year were copied into another book altogether, to be fetched down from the shelf just when needed. Egerton 3307 is an example of the latter.[91] For liturgical use in church it contains an extensive and coherent set of items for performance during the principal services of Holy Week according to Salisbury Use; these add up to fifteen in all, running from Palm Sunday to Easter Day itself. There are also three items for later in the liturgical year, and a four-voice motet for the feast of St Dunstan, *Cantemus domino, socie*.[92] Egerton 3307 is also remarkable for being one of only four major sources which preserve a polyphonic repertory of fifteenth-century vernacular and Latin carols. A collection of 31, mostly in Latin and mostly appropriate to the season of the Twelve Days of Christmas, occupies a distinct section of 22 folios towards the end of the manuscript, with which is copied a three-voice isorhythmic motet setting a well-known text of secular conviviality, *O potores exquisiti*.[93] All the music is anonymous, of high quality, and set for two, three or four voices.

Clearly this manuscript was compiled for the use of some group of professional singing-men who were in secular ecclesiastical employment, and who performed conventional

91. For the principal discussions of this manuscript see B. Schofield, 'A newly discovered fifteenth-century manuscript of the English Chapel Royal', *The Musical Quarterly*, 32 (1946), pp. 509–36; M. Bukofzer, 'Holy-week music and carols at Meaux Abbey', in *Studies in Medieval and Renaissance Music*, New York 1950, pp. 113–75; G. McPeek, *The British Museum Manuscript Egerton 3307*, Oxford 1963, pp. 3–22. There are observations of varying degrees of appositeness in R. Strohm, *The Rise of European Music*, Cambridge 1993, pp. 383–5. For editions of the music excluding the carols, see McPeek, *The British Museum Manuscript Egerton 3307*, pp. 35–101 and *Fifteenth-century Liturgical Music I*, ed. A. Hughes, Early English Church Music, 8 (1968), pp. 44–132, 135–56. For the music of the carols (with texts in modernised spelling) see *Medieval Carols*, ed. J. Stevens, 2nd edn, Musica Britannica, 4, London 1958, pp. 33–62, 114; for the texts of the vernacular carols in original spelling, see R.L. Greene, *The Early English Carols*, 2nd edn, Oxford 1977, references on p. 299. The attribution to St George's Chapel, Windsor, was first suggested by Schofield, pp. 514–15; the choice of title for his article concealed this insight, for he failed to distinguish between St George's and the Chapel Royal of the king's household. Bukofzer accepted an attribution to Meaux Abbey (a Cistercian monastery located in the East Riding of Yorkshire) first suggested by R.L. Greene, 'Two medieval musical manuscripts: Egerton 3307 and some University of Chicago fragments', *Journal of the American Musicological Society*, 7 (1954), pp. 1–34. However, the case supporting this proposal is very weak, and it has been conclusively negated by Harrison, *Music in Medieval Britain*, p. 275; Greene, *Early English Carols*, pp. 299–301, disputes Harrison's conclusion, but has no response to the latter's apparently indefeasible point that liturgy and chant of the secular Salisbury Use could have had no place in the observance of a Cistercian monastery, least of all in Holy Week. The evidence, strong and less strong, favouring a St George's provenance is marshalled in McPeek, *The British Museum Manuscript Egerton 3307*, pp. 7–14.

92. For the vocal scoring of this motet as a very early instance of the use of boys' voices in composed polyphony, see R. Bowers, 'To chorus from quartet: the performing resource for English Church polyphony, *c*.1390–1559', in *English Choral Practice 1400–1625*, ed. J. Morehen, Cambridge 1996, 1–47, pp. 26–8. See also D. Hiley, 'What St Dunstan heard the angels sing: notes on a pre-Conquest historia', *Laborare fratres in unum: Festschrift László Dobszay zum 60. Geburtstag*, ed. J. Schendrei and D. Hiley, Hildesheim 1995, pp. 105–15.

93. For editions of this motet, see McPeek, *The British Museum Manuscript Egerton 3307*, pp. 92–5; *Fifteenth-Century Liturgical Music I*, ed. Hughes, pp. 141–7.

three- and four-part polyphony in their church but were just as adept at singing convivial carols and songs set to learned and elaborate music — either in the vicars' hall for their own pleasure, or round the fireside or at the table of the residentiary's mansion for his delectation.[94] The evidence suggesting St George's as the specific location for the provenance of Egerton 3307 is not explicit, but rather a matter of inference and circumstance. Most compelling is the set of verses provided for the processional hymn *Salve, festa dies*. This is furnished with the four standard texts supplied in Salisbury Use for feasts observed universally;[95] also it is supplied with a fifth set of words found almost nowhere else, which is proper for use on the feast of St George.[96] This occurrence indicates for certain that the manuscript was written for use in a church or chapel either actually dedicated to St George or in which he was particularly venerated.

Equally suggestively, a group of three carols copied together stands out from the rest as set to texts conveying sentiments specific to the location and social environment in which the manuscript was used.[97] Most conspicuously, the text of *Princeps serenissime* (62) is actually addressed directly and personally to the King, to accompany the offer of a gift at New-Year-tide. *Exultavit cor in domino* (61) invites the company present to thank God for the victories given to Henry V; *Enfors we us* (60) is a carol specifically in honour and praise of St George, 'Our Lady's knight', particularly for the potency of his support for the English cause at Agincourt. Moreover, others among the carol texts appear to have arisen within a milieu sufficiently adjacent to the wellsprings of political power for pious reflection urging an end to the prevalence and distress of war to appear not only apposite and timely, but also likely to fall directly on the ears of those influential in the political circles in which such decisions would be made. *Princeps pacis* (45) offers a prayer for the bestowal of the benefits of peace; *Anglia, tibi turbidas* (56) expresses anguish over the misery incumbent on the prosecution of war, and bids England to hope for light after present darkness; *Benedicite domino* (57) looks to a reconciliation of 'Anglia et Francia'.

Particularly intriguing is the coincidence between the physical aspects of MS Egerton 3307 and the details of a manuscript known to have been created at St George's during 1451–2. It is possible to show that the number of folios in Egerton 3307 executed by the

---

94. The role of the vernacular polyphonic carols of the fifteenth century has been much debated. Despite many suggestions to the contrary, it seems inconceivable that they could ever have been performed in the course of the liturgical service or during procession in church or chapel. In a kingdom which had lately proved itself an ardent persecutor of Lollard heterodoxy and heresy, there could have been no place in the ecclesiastical service for unwarranted and unauthorised interpolations expressed in populist vernacular text, no matter how devout. The liturgy likewise admitted no role to interpolated carols even in Latin. It may be noted in addition that whatever their role as simple poems, in polyphonic musical setting the carol is most appropriately perceived as 'popular' neither by origin nor by destination. Rather, it was music of elevation and refinement, created by learned composers for the entertainment and diversion of the educated, both performer and listener.

95. Namely, the Resurrection, the Ascension, Pentecost, and Trinity Sunday.

96. McPeek, *The British Museum Manuscript Egerton 3307*, p. 83. Bukofzer reports the occurrence of this text also in an early fifteenth-century processioner of Salisbury Use (Bodl. MS lat. lit. e 7): 'Holy-week music and carols', p. 114, n. 4.

97. *Medieval Carols*, ed. Stevens, nos. 60–2 (pp. 49–51). Throughout this paragraph, the numbers given are those of this edition.

original and principal hand added up to 72;[98] this is just the same number as that executed by Richard Prideaux for the manuscript of polyphony which he created at St George's for twopence per page during that year.[99] It may also be noted that the Holy Week music copied into Egerton 3307 includes the two earliest polyphonic settings of the liturgical Passions known to have survived from anywhere in Europe;[100] in this context it is certainly noteworthy that the sole surviving precentor's account from St George's for this period, that for 1457–8, includes a payment of 7d for food and wine given specifically as a reward to those singing the Passion.[101]

The overall character of the music, the address made directly to royalty, the prominence accorded to the veneration of St George, and the presence of music both liturgical and convivial within a single source, all combine to suggest that the manuscript was prepared for some major choir whose chapel was dedicated to St George or where St George was very specially honoured, and which was located within (or at least very close to) intimate royal circles and in a milieu which also cultivated an elevated secular conviviality. The case for an attribution to St George's Chapel, Windsor, is certainly strong but predominantly circumstantial and, regrettably, not conclusive. Indeed, the aggregated collection of evidence might be thought to point equally convincingly to the household chapel of any of the great magnates who was both a knight of the Garter and a Plantagenet loyalist.[102] The St George's attribution is best entertained, perhaps, as primarily an intriguing possibility.[103]

98. A detailed collation is given by Schofield, 'A newly discovered manuscript', p. 512; see also Bukofzer, 'Holy Week music and carols', pp. 115–16. The folios in the principal hand (identified as 'Copyist II' by McPeek, *The British Museum Manuscript Egerton 3307*, p. 4) are the following: the final folio of the first gathering; the six folios of the second gathering, and the six of the third (of which four are now lost); the next seven gatherings, each of eight folios (of gathering no. 8, which was of ten folios, two folios now represented by stubs were discarded or cancelled); and the first three of the penultimate gathering: total 72. The rest of the manuscript is in two or three minor hands, responsible for contributions at both beginning and end.

99. See above, p. 189 and note 89. According to the account Prideaux was paid for copying twelve quaternions each of six folios, and it must be acknowledged that this does not match the collation of Egerton 3307; this manuscript does indeed begin with gatherings each of six folios, but presently changes to larger gatherings of eight. This discrepancy, however, hardly seems significant. The accountant would simply have transferred to his account the wording supplied by Prideaux on his bill — and in all probability Prideaux would have composed his statement seeking payment for the writing of 72 folios in the plainest manner possible. In respect simply of obtaining full remuneration, neither to Prideaux nor to the treasurer's clerk did it matter in the slightest how the 72 folios were made up, and a claim for 12x6 folios had the same import as a claim for 1 + (2x6) + (7x8) + 3, and was far simpler to express.

100. This observation by Schofield, 'A newly discovered manuscript', pp. 519–20, and Bukofzer, 'Holy Week music and carols', p. 128, now requires only the slightest modification through the discovery of a third setting, contemporary and also English: Caldwell, *The Oxford History of English Music*, i, p. 167.

101. SGC XV.56.34: (March) et solut' pro pane et vino datis cantoribus passionis vijd.

102. The texts of some of the 'political' carols, especially *Anglia, tibi turbidas*, seem rather too blunt and direct for the provenance of this manuscript to have been Henry VI's Chapel Royal.

103. Into the decoration of the initial letter of one of the Passions (f. 20r, drawn apparently not by the principal text-scribe) is worked the platitude 'Mieulx en de cy' ("Better things from here on"). It was rather the habit of one of the contemporary St George's scriveners so to adorn his initial letters — see 'be true and serve god al wey' and 'pese causeth grace' on SGC XV.48.18 (*c.*1445), 'sey wel or noght' on XV.34.45 (1450–1), and 'parlez bien' on XV.48.22 (1449–50). Unfortunately, the drawing in Egerton 3307 is by too many degrees more elaborate than those on the St George's account-rolls for there to be entertained any realistic speculation that all may be by a single hand. No St George's connection has been discovered for the Egerton 3307 text; it does not occur as a motto on any of the surviving stall-plates.

This mid-century period was also conspicuous for the implementation of one particular development in the management of the music of the chapel that concerned the status and duties of the office of Instructor of the Choristers. The statutes of 1352 had directed that there be appointed to this office one of the vicars choral, at a stipend of 26s 8d per year.[104] The job then involved teaching the boys their Latin grammar and vocabulary, coaching them in the ceremonial of the services in which they participated, and training them in those chants of the liturgy that were deputed to be sung by *omnes* as well as in the relatively few and mostly (but not invariably) simple chants to be sung by one or a pair or all of the boys on their own. At that period the choristers were not expected to be able to sing from mensural notation; it was not among the skills taught to them, and boys' voices did not participate in the performance of composed polyphony. The instruction of the choristers, that is, was a task that had to be done by someone, but prior to about 1400 it was a chore rather than any source of satisfaction or pride. It offered little scope for the exhibition of real musical gifts or indeed of any expertise other than just the most routine. It was not an office which anyone retained for any length of time. Prior to 1410 or thereabouts the job at St George's frequently changed hands after a year, six months or even less, and no-one is known to have held it for more than two-and-a-half years.[105]

The scope, and with it the status, of the office grew in the early fifteenth century, particularly as the attendance of the boys at Lady Mass from about the 1420s onwards gave opportunity for them to deploy, on perhaps a daily basis, the skills of improvising descant to a given plainsong.[106] Under this technique a single boy followed the written plainsong performed by a colleague, singing a counterpoint to it *extempore* according to closely defined rules of consonance and cadence. Such a development required of their Instructor, for the first time, that he possess both real musical skills and the gift of teaching them. By the second quarter of the century the office of Instructor had become rather more respected and desirable than previously, which an individual might be pleased to retain for some number of years.

At Windsor, as elsewhere, the musical skills now required were to be found not among the vicars but among the clerks of the second form. Thomas Churchman, one of the lay clerks, was in office as Instructor of the Choristers by Michaelmas 1442 and occupied it at least until Michaelmas 1452;[107] this was quite a considerable tenure, and represented practice which, on the whole, was normal from then onward. The pattern is, nevertheless, somewhat confused by the career of Thomas Rolfe (clerk, 1455x9–1469, 1476–1484x5), who occupied the office for three separate brief periods in 1459–62, 1467–8 and 1477–8. It does appear, indeed, that his methods may have been somewhat too heavy-handed for any long-term success, judging by the number of times on which expense had to be made on recovering boys who had run away to London during his periods of tenure as

---

104. Statute 16: SGC IV.B.1, f. 77v; also Statutes 11, 15: *ibid.*, ff. 77r, 77v.

105. See the list of Instructors of the Choristers below, p. 214.

106. See above, p. 186. In Salisbury Use the daily Lady Mass was considered to be always a festal mass, rendering it amenable to enhancement with polyphonic performances on a daily basis, if desired.

107. Clerk from June 1439 until 15 August 1478: SGC XV.34.38*, *Stipendia et vadia officiariorum*; V.B.2, p. 122. He occurs as Instructor during 1442/3 and 1451/2: SGC XV.34.41 and XV.34.44, *Stipendia et vadia officiariorum*.

Instructor: one boy in 1461–2,[108] one in 1467–8,[109] and two at the beginning of 1468–9.[110] The Instructors of this period are mostly figures now little known; however, they do include the widely experienced Adam Roke, whose career can be traced at Eton College and at King's College, Cambridge, as well as at St George's, where he served as Instructor from June 1462 probably until Michaelmas 1467.[111]

The specific contribution made by the boys to observance in the chapel was increased again between 1463 and 1468, when there was introduced the singing in plainsong of *Nunc Christe, te petimus*, an antiphon in honour of Jesus.[112] The performance of this sort of paraliturgical commemoration took place in the evening, following Vespers; usually it originated in a specific endowment made by some particular individual, in which the singing of the antiphon prefaced the recitation of prayers for the good of the benefactor, or of his soul.[113] The circumstances of its introduction at St George's are unknown. In the new St George's in the sixteenth century this observance was made before the Great Rood and was known as 'the Antem of the Crosse'.[114] Most commonly the Jesus antiphon was sung once weekly, on Fridays; at Windsor, however, it was sung daily, and each boy was paid 2s 0d per year for his effort, and their Instructor 6s 8d.[115] In addition, at some point in the 1450s the organ-player began to join the Instructor, boys and men at the daily Lady Mass. Probably his role there was to enhance the mass with an additional timbre of sound,

108. SGC XV.34.49, *Stipendia, vadia et regarda officiariorum*: et solut' eidem [Thome Rolfe] in regardo dato ex concensu capituli quando chorista recesserat ab ipso vjs viijd; *ibid.*, *reparaciones*: et solut' Thome Rolfe pro expensis suis pro equitacione usque london' pro Willelmo Tilley chorusta ut patet per billam super hunc compotum ostensam etc iijs iiijd.

109. SGC XV.48.37 verso, [*Expense necessarie*]: Et solut' Thome Rolf pro suo labore et costagio usque london' per preceptum decani et Capituli ad referendum quendam puerum nomine Marchaunt Choristam iijs iiijd. This was not the cost of recruitment of a new chorister; William Marchant was already a chorister at 1 June 1468: SGC V.B.2, p. 48.

110. SGC XV.34.56, *Soluciones*: Et solut' Thome Rolf pro expensis suis equitanti london' ad revocandum Johannem Cowper et Johannem Mayster chorustas extunc per iij dies iijs iiijd.

111. 1449–50: junior lay clerk, Eton College chapel; 1450–2: lay clerk, King's College chapel; 1452–61: lay clerk, Eton College chapel; Michaelmas 1461–Michaelmas 1463 (probably to Michaelmas 1467): lay clerk, St George's Chapel, and Instructor from June 1462; Michaelmas 1467–Michaelmas 1468: Instructor of the Choristers, Eton College chapel. See Bowers, 'Choral Institutions within the English Church', pp. A041–3.

112. SGC XV.34.56, *Stipendia, vadia et regarda officiariorum*. This text originated as the last of the three verses of *Libera me, domine*, the ninth responsory at Matins of the Dead. Detached from their source, these words constituted a very suitable Jesus antiphon; either with or without the larger text of which they form a part, *Sancte deus, sancte fortis*, they exist in a number of polyphonic settings of English origin.

113. See e.g. Harrison, *Music in Medieval Britain*, pp. 83–4; also 168, 174, 182, 338, 341.

114. SGC IV.B.1, f. 156v; Cambridge University Library, MS Dd.2.26, f. 14r; St. John Hope, *Windsor Castle*, ii, p. 467. Windsor's manner of observance was emulated elsewhere. In regulations made in 1523 for the establishment of a choir in the parish church of St Mary, Newark (Lincolnshire), the founder, Thomas Magnus (canon of Windsor, 1520–47), stipulated that every evening the Master of the Choristers and his six boys 'shall nyghtly kepe our Ladyes Antyme in the saide Churche in the Place accustumed; and forthwith after that Antempne doon, another Antempne of Jhesus to be by theym solempnely and devoutly song afore the Roode in the Bodye of the Churche of Newarke aforsaide; the same Scoolmaister and Chylder knelyng in manner and forme as at the Antempne of Jhesus hath [been] and ys usyd to be song before the Roode of the North Dore in the Cathedrall Churche of Seynt Paule in London, and in the College of Wyndesore, with lyke Prostrations and devout Maner': N. G. Jackson, *Newark Magnus*, Nottingham 1964, p. 280.

115. SGC XV.34.56, *Stipendia, vadia et regarda officiariorum*.

improvising on the plainsong in alternation with the voices; for this service he was receiving a modest payment of 3s 4d per year by 1459–60.[116]

For some thirty years between 1454 and 1484 the choir of St George's benefited from supplementation by the presence as a supernumerary member of John Plummer, one of the principal mid-century English composers. Plummer first occurs in 1438 as a lay Gentleman of the Chapel Royal of Henry VI,[117] where he also served as Master of the Choristers from at least May 1444 until succeeded by Henry Abyngdon at Michaelmas 1455.[118] Plummer continued to serve as a Gentleman of the Chapel Royal until at least the summer of 1467.[119] However, by Michaelmas 1454 he had also been appointed to the staff of St George's, though not ostensibly as a member of the choir; he appears in occupation of the office of virger. It is possible to suggest an explanation for this peculiarity, for St George's was by no means the only institution of its kind to find employment for a senior musician at this time by appropriating to him nominal occupation of the office of virger. It was part of a pattern.

As the profile and prominence of polyphonic performance advanced throughout the fifteenth century, many of the longer-established collegiate churches found that they were inadequately endowed with places for the singers who were now its principal executants, namely the lay singing-men of the second form. Consequently, they took steps to contrive to increase the number of their second-form clerkships. At institutions such as New College, Oxford, at Winchester College, at St Mary Newarke, Leicester, and St Mary's, Warwick, resort was made during the 1440s and 1450s to a variety of devices intended to achieve this end; in each of these particular instances the necessary objective was achieved by the creation of one new place for a specialist musician who would also serve as Instructor of the Choristers.[120]

St George's twin institution of St Stephen's, Westminster, appears to have experienced a like need at this same time, and found an ingenious way in which to meet it without resort to the creation of a new office. Its constitution exhibited one particular peculiarity — the astonishingly high rate of 6d per day, adding up to £9 2s 6d per year, paid to the chapel virger.[121] At St Stephen's by the 1450s this office and its generous stipend were being pressed into a novel though no less useful and even more productive service. In 1454 the composer John Bedyngham had been serving as one of the singing-men of the

---

116. SGC XV.34.47, *Stipendia, vadia et regarda officiariorum.*

117. PRO, E101/408/25, f. 2r; on a list ordered by seniority, Plummer appears fourth from the end, and was quite a recent appointee.

118. A. Wathey, *Music in the royal and noble Households in late medieval England*, London and New York 1989, pp. 78, 154–5, 159, 166–7, 291–6; *Calendar of Patent Rolls 1452–61*, p. 279.

119. PRO, E101/412/2, f. 36v.

120. Bowers, 'Choral Institutions within the English Church', pp. 5088–93.

121. That the stipend of the virger at St Stephen's was sixpence per day is known from the contract of employment of Nicholas Ludford, 1526: PRO, E40/13426 (a transcription is given in D. Skinner, ' "At the mynde of Nycholas Ludford": new light on Ludford from the churchwardens' accounts of St Margaret's, Westminster', *Early Music*, 22 (1994), 393–413, pp. 408–9 (though for 'mea parte edicorum' read 'in ea parte editorum')). Twopence per day was a more usual level of pay for this kind of office.

Lady Chapel choir of Westminster Abbey,[122] but by 1456 he had stepped through the boundary wall to accept employment on the staff of St Stephen's. However, it was in the office of virger that he was employed there,[123] and it is clear that at some point in probably the recent past this well-rewarded post had been abruptly and arbitrarily converted to become a vehicle for the employment of a principal musician for the chapel, supplementary to its statutory staff.[124] At St Stephen's, indeed, this expedient proved permanent and was still in effect at the time of its dissolution 100 years later.[125]

Other examples may be found in a very similar vein. In c.1454 Ralph Cromwell, Baron Cromwell, instructed those to whom he had given authority to compile a code of statutes for his newly founded collegiate church of Tattershall (Lincolnshire) to collect ideas from the existing statutes of three similar colleges, namely Fotheringhay, Manchester and St Stephen's, Westminster; probably it was from the latter that they drew the idea (eventually abandoned) of creating an office of virger-cum-organist, to be paid 4d per day.[126] Only a little later, at some point probably in the 1470s, the post of virger (worth £5 0s 0d p.a.) at the collegiate church of Stoke-by-Clare (Suffolk) was likewise appropriated to the use of a resident supernumerary musician. This arrangement was made at the instance of Cecily, duchess of York, in favour of her servant William Lessy, a lay Gentleman of the choir of her household chapel who was sufficiently distinguished in both the practical and theoretical aspects of his profession to have been admitted to the degree of Mus.B. by Cambridge University in 1471.[127]

What was planned for St George's appears to have been similar in principle to each of these instances, though somewhat different in detail. The constitution of St George's exhibited a peculiarity the same as that of St Stephen's, namely the very high stipend of £9 2s 6d per year paid to the Chapel virger.[128] It appears that it was shortly prior to his relinquishing office as Master of the Chapel Royal choristers in 1455 that John Plummer was appointed to this post and stipend at St George's.[129] Like Bedyngham at St Stephen's,

---

122. On the 'Wages and Stipends' section of the Sacrist's account for 1453–4 (Westminster Abbey Muniments 19704, *Vadia et stipendia*) the notice of the payment of the contribution due annually from this office towards the wages of the four (unnamed) singing-men of the Lady Chapel choir is followed immediately by the entry 'Et solut' Johanni Bedyngham pro Roba sua hoc anno xiijs iiijd'. This indicates that Bedyngham was employed by the Abbey during that year, in close association with — and almost certainly as one of — the singing-men of the Lady Chapel choir, and had earned himself an extra gratuity in that year.

123. PRO, C54/308, m. 21v (*Calendar of Close Rolls 1451–61*, p. 283).

124. In such circumstances a sub-virger, sacrist or vestry clerk could always be employed (at a rather less elevated rate of pay) to fulfil the actual work of the virger, except for those duties of the office which were primarily ceremonial and which probably its official holder was happy to execute as a symbol of his status.

125. In 1548 the composer Nicholas Ludford was in employment there as the chapel's principal musician; ostensibly, however, he was engaged not as a member of the choir in any capacity, but was rather — and no doubt purely nominally — in occupation of both the office and the generous stipend of the chapel virger, just as Bedyngham had been before him. Skinner, ' "At the mynde of Nycholas Ludford" ', pp. 395–7.

126. Maidstone, Kent Archives Office, Manuscripts of Lord De Lisle and Dudley, U1475/Q20.

127. Original letter, with signature of Duchess Cecily: Cambridge, Corpus Christi College, MS 108, p. 91; *Grace Book A*, ed. S.M. Leathes, Cambridge Antiquarian Society, Cambridge 1897, p. 86. See also *Visitations in the Diocese of Norwich A.D. 1492–1532*, ed. A. Jessopp, Camden Society, ns 43 (1888), p. 238.

128. Statute 54: SGC IV.B.1, f. 80v.

129. Plummer was in office by Michaelmas 1454: SGC XV.59.4, *virgebaiulus*. His predecessor, Richard Brun, had still been in post at Michaelmas 1450: XV.48.22, *Feoda et robe*. For confirmation that John Plummer of the Chapel Royal and John Plummer of St George's are identifiable as the same individual, see SGC XV.45.194.

however, he was no ordinary virger. It is very noticeable that when a schedule of the annual income and outgoings of the college was made in 1476 (Plummer being still in office at that time) the list of stipends paid included the office of virger among the members of the choir, between the clerks and the boys, rather than further down the list with the bell-ringers and similar custodial staff.[130] Moreover, for the duration of Plummer's occupation of this office St George's created an *ad hoc* post of 'clericus vestibuli' (clerk of the vestry), presumably to create an officer by whom the routine custodial duties of the virger would actually be performed.[131] It seems certain, therefore, that like Bedyngham at St Stephen's Plummer was expected to serve not actually as virger but as a non-statutory principal musician and perhaps 'composer in residence' for the chapel.

For so long as Plummer retained his office of Gentleman of the Chapel Royal he could give only a proportion of his time to Windsor. Nevertheless, during the last confused and dangerous years of the reign of Henry VI St George's must have seemed to offer a reasonably comfortable refuge, and during 1454–5 he was paid at Windsor for 258 days' attendance, and during 1459–60 for 298.[132] Under Edward IV he was recalled to the Chapel Royal, spending but 23 days at Windsor in 1461–2 and 95 in 1462–3.[133] However, following his final retirement from the Chapel Royal in 1467 or 1468 he moved home to Windsor and thenceforth occupied his office at St George's full time until a successor replaced him during 1483–4, a little before his death on, apparently, 5 November 1486.[134] By then Edward IV's re-foundation of the choral strength of the chapel was complete, and upon Plummer's death the office of virger at St George's (unlike that at St Stephen's) was restored to its original nature and intention.

Plummer appears to have been greatly respected in the College, for he carried enough prestige for two of the canons, Thomas Passhe (d. 1489) and William Hermer (d. 1473), to associate with him in founding a joint chantry, eventually established by their executors in 1494 in the new chapel.[135] He was sufficiently wealthy also to found an obit in Eton College Chapel.[136] So far as is known, he never served in offices such as Master of the Choristers or organ-player at Windsor; nevertheless, during the years 1454–61, and again from his retirement in 1467–8 until his death, St George's did enjoy the company, the services and the expertise of one of the mid-century's more individual composers, as a supernumerary member of its musical strength. Some half-dozen of his works, all for three or four men's voices, still survive; they include one complete setting of the Ordinary of

130. SGC XV.3.11. See also XV.43.33, a lease dated 25 March 1472 of property held jointly as a group by Plummer and the four lay clerks.

131. For the departure of Richard Foster from this office on 29 January 1473, and the appointment of a chain of successors, see SGC V.B.2, ff. 28r, 35v, 39v, 67r.

132. SGC XV.59.4; XV.34.47, *virgebaiulus*.

133. SGC XV.34.49; XV.34.50, *virgebaiulus*.

134. SGC XV.34.56; XV.34.51–5; XV.34.57; XV.34.59–60, *virgebaiulus*. V.B.2, ff. 1r–67v. XV.48.25–48 passim, *Robe generosorum*. For his date of death, see note 136 below.

135. SGC IV.B.3, f. 241r. For the location of its altar see T. Tatton-Brown, *supra*, p. 20.

136. Both Windsor (Treasurer's accounts, *obitus*) and Eton (Audit Rolls and Books, *Custus forinseci*) observed Plummer's obit on 5 November annually. Eton College received the endowments of his obit in October 1486, and observed it for the first time on 6 November that year, indicating that it was on the day previous that his death had occurred: Eton College, Audit Roll 22 (1486–7), *Custus forincici*.

the Mass and two movements from another, and four votive antiphons.[137] It has to be acknowledged, however, that none displays any overtly evident association with St George's.

IV: THE CHALLENGE OF CHORAL POLYPHONY: THE NEW CHAPEL AND ITS EXPANDED CHORUS, 1475–1500

It is from 19 February 1473 that notice first appears of Edward IV's intention to build a new chapel for the College of St George, when the king appointed Richard Beauchamp, bishop of Salisbury, to be master and surveyor of the king's new works there. A start was made on the preliminary clearing of the site in June 1475, and actual building began in March 1477. It appears that by 1482 the raising of the walls of the choir and its enclosure by a roof and temporary western partition were essentially complete, and that work on the erection of the choir stalls was well advanced. Possibly the conduct of services had been transferred from the old chapel to the new choir by the time Edward IV died in April 1483, and almost certainly by the time further construction work was suspended at the end of 1483.[138] And even as a start was made on the clearing of the site in 1475, thought was already being given to ensure that the manner of the worship of God to take place in the new chapel should be worthy of the sumptuousness of its setting. Indeed, scope existed for a total review and revision of the chapel's provision for music, since during the twenty or so years prior to the king's initiative the composition and performance of polyphony for the church services had undergone a revolution.

The key to this development was a progressive simplification in the notation used for polyphonic music, whereby it was transformed from a mystery the command of which could be tackled by only a gifted few, to a relatively simple means of communication that could be learnt and mastered by any literate individual minded to do so, including the young. In particular, therefore, from the 1450s onwards, but especially during the 1460s, 1470s and 1480s, institutions began to seek to appoint as Instructor of the Choristers a specialist musician able to teach to the boys of the choir the novel skills of reading from the mensural notation used for polyphonic music. These skills, once learnt, progressively filtered through to the adult departments of the choir, for within a short space of time the first cohorts of trained boys began to grow up to become the lay clerks and vicars choral of the next generation. Thereupon it became possible for those selecting new members for the choirs of the greater secular churches to seek among all their newly appointed adults the capacity to sing not only plainsong but also polyphony. They were enabled, that is, to demand from the ordained priests desiring appointment to vicarages choral the range of skills they had long required of the lay clerks of the second form. By 1500 or so, therefore, the priests of the major choirs were largely just as capable of participating in the performance of polyphony as were the clerks and boys, and the rendering of a truly choral sound had become possible.[139]

---

137. *John Plummer: Four Motets*, ed. B. Trowell, Banbury 1968; *idem*, 'Plummer, John', *New Grove Dictionary*, ed. Sadie, xv, p. 15.

138. St. John Hope, *Windsor Castle*, ii, pp. 375–83; T. Tatton-Brown (*supra*, p. 15) and *idem*, 'Vaulting St George's Chapel, Windsor', *Report of the Society of the Friends of St George's* (1994–5), 238–43, p. 242. See also M. Bond, 'Acoustic Pots in St George's Chapel', *ibid.* (1953), pp. 8–10.

139. Bowers, 'To chorus from quartet', pp. 26–34.

This transformation was accompanied by a revolution in the palette of sound available for use, since the composers found themselves able to take the long-established three-part scoring for solo adult voices, consisting of one alto and two tenors, and to add beneath this historic core a part for genuine bass voices and above it a line for the voices of the boys. The result was a rich five-part texture of boy's treble, adult alto, two tenor and bass voices rendered not by soloists but by the choir as a corporate unit. Between 1455 and 1480, indeed, these initiatives created what is now thought of as the quintessential sound of English cathedral music, rendered by a balanced chorus of the voices of men and boys.[140]

Church musicianship had now reached its maturity as a recognised and respected craft. Conventionally, modern ecclesiastical historians — and especially Reformation historians — have regarded the singing-men of the pre-Reformation cathedral and collegiate churches as troupes of little better than unskilled clerical parasites, who fed off the endowments of their institutions and gave back little or nothing of value in return. In the face of the evidence, however, such an evaluation cannot be sustained. In reality, by 1500 church musicianship was a well-defined craft, which enjoyed both a regular training programme and a recognised career structure, and occupied a perceptible proportion of all the educated males in England over the age of eight. Indeed, following the introduction of degrees in music by the two universities in the 1460s and 1470s, it was even on the verge of developing into a learned profession.

The choral force established by the mid-fourteenth-century statutes of St George's had not been constituted to sing choral polyphony, and like many another English choir in the second half of the fifteenth century it now required expansion and re-formulation.[141] As it stood, the composition of the chapel staff remained designed to meet the needs of a hundred years earlier — a priest-vicar for every canon, and just about enough clerks and choristers to make possible a tolerably efficient performance of the plainsong and ceremonial of the daily liturgy according to Salisbury Use. Edward IV now proposed to make substantial additions to the endowment of the college, and much of the income so arising was to be consumed on the expansion of the choral force from 23 to no fewer than 45 singers, so yielding the large and fulsome sound now newly fashionable.

The king's initial attempt at defining the choir's needs for new personnel dates from 1475. The income from the newly-appropriated St Anthony's Hospital was earmarked for application to the expansion of the choir, and was intended at first to establish ten new places for priest-vicars, six for lay clerks and four for choristers,[142] so yielding a choir of 23 vicars, ten clerks and ten boys. However, the new choral polyphony required not only virtuoso skills of its individual executants, but also a sense of balance in the resulting sound arising from one boys' and four men's parts. It did not take long for there to arise the realisation that in so large a choir a corps of ten boys would not suffice to sustain a good choral balance, and within a year it was being proposed to add to the ten priest-vicars and six 'gentilmen Clerkes' already agreed not four but seven new choristers, establishing a boys' choir of thirteen.[143] An inaugural expansion was implemented as early as the

---

140. For a fuller discussion of this revolution in composition and performance, see *ibid.*, pp. 20–39.
141. Bowers, 'Choral Institutions within the English Church', chapter 6.
142. S. Bentley, *Excerpta historica*, London 1831, p. 375.
143. SGC XV.3.11, dated 1476.

beginning of 1476, when on 28 January two extra choristers were admitted, and during March three new lay clerks.[144]

At this point numbers were pegged until September 1477 when, probably in anticipation of the imminent arrival of the necessary income from St Anthony's Hospital, new recruitment resumed and advanced apace. By now, also, altogether more practical considerations had supervened. What the new music required was not more priests of the choir, but more professional singing-men to be lay clerks of the second form. Consequently, when during 1478–9 the first income began to arrive from St Anthony's, its receipt was described specifically as intended to pay the salaries of seven lay clerks and seven choristers 'of the new foundation', and not of any new vicars at all.[145] By now, that is, a chorus eventually to be of thirteen vicars, eleven clerks and thirteen choristers was envisaged.

Attainment of that target was still not fully achieved when in the summer of 1479 there came a setback. In July the district was stricken by plague;[146] the college decamped, and by 21 July the services in chapel were being maintained by a skeleton staff of just two canons, two vicars and two poor knights. The contagion was short-lived; nevertheless, when the staff returned to celebrate the feast of the Assumption on 15 August four vicars choral, one clerk and four choristers were gone. Throughout September obits were being attended by a much depleted choir of only eight vicars, nine clerks and five boys.[147]

Recruitment was promptly resumed, and now that anything up to £260 per year was arriving from St Anthony's a final constitution for the expanded choir could be determined. Moreover, in order to attract the services of high-quality singers in a very competitive field, it became necessary to settle also on a level of increase in stipend to be paid to each category of membership. Ultimately it was found that there were resources enough to restore to the dignity of the celebration of High Mass the presence of a deacon to read the gospel,[148] and of two clerks to share the reading of the epistle;[149] it was possible also to increase the number of lay clerks not just to eleven but to thirteen, and to raise the number of vicars to sixteen.[150] By Christmas 1482 the new choral strength for St George's was settled and had been achieved, and stood as follows: sixteen vicars choral paid £10 0s 0d p.a. each; one deacon, gospeller, at £6 13s 4d p.a.; thirteen lay clerks at £10 0s 0d p.a.; two clerks, epistoler, at £6 13s 4d p.a.; and thirteen choristers at £4 0s 0d

144. SGC V.B.2, ff. 46r, 47r, 47v; XV.34.56, *clericis* and *choristis*.
145. SGC XI.B.26; XV.34.55, 57: *recepta*.
146. In the Treasurer's account for 1478–9 (SGC XV.34.55) there appears to be no overt mention of this occurrence of plague; however, there are references to it in the accounts of the Bursars of Eton College for the following year (Eton College, MS Audit Roll 18 (1479–80), *Custus forincici*: payment to two of the chaplains of the chapel 'pro laboribus eorum quos sustinuerunt tempore pestis ultimo anno'), while in the St George's Attendance Register the words 'propter pestilenciam' appear in the margin against the name of one vicar choral whose attendance ceased on 5 July: SGC V.B.2, f. 67r.
147. SGC V.B.2, f. 67r; XV.34.55, *obitus*.
148. SGC XV.3.11 (1476). The stipend of the deacon was recorded as paid specifically 'pro lectura evangelii' in 1477–8: SGC XV.34.54, *diacono*.
149. At least until Michaelmas 1504 the two epistolers were listed consistently among the clerks on the records of stipend payments. Their stipend was identified specifically as paid 'pro lectura epistole' in 1496–7: SGC XV.34.70, *clericis*.
150. For certain periods between December 1482 and October 1492 not sixteen but seventeen vicars were attending obits (SGC XV.34.59–66, *obitus*); after the latter date the number settled finally at sixteen.

p.a. For the accommodation of the vicars choral and even for some of the clerks the handsome set of twenty-one lodgings known as the Horseshoe Cloister was built during 1478–81.[151] It seems likely that the influence of Richard Beauchamp, the king's appointee as master and surveyor of his new works at Windsor, had been much to the fore in many of these procedures of recruitment. If coincidences of names can be trusted, then among the vicars choral newly appointed between 1475 and 1480 Hugh Latham, Michael Dulard, John Rogers, Thomas Phillips and John Kynred had all been drafted in from the choir of Beauchamp's cathedral at Salisbury.[152]

When Edward IV died in 1483, he had lived long enough to see his grand design for the choral personnel of St George's completed, even if not yet that for its building. He had furnished it with a sufficient and satisfactorily balanced team of well-paid singers, men and boys, totalling 45 in all, adequate to satisfy any king's need for a conspicuous display of the wealth, resources and creative talent at his disposal in the ordering of the daily services of his principal religious foundation, within which his body was eventually to rest.

Up to the end of the reign of Henry VIII only two modifications were made to this constitution. At some point early in the sixteenth century the two epistolers were, perfectly rationally, reduced to one. Rather more significantly, in 1489 there first appears record of the payment to certain of the vicars choral of the increment of stipend of £3 6s 8d per year which eventually became the mark of the holding of a minor canonry. Six vicars were so rewarded from 1489 to 1492, seven in 1492–3, and eight from 1493 onward,[153] and certainly by 1511 the term 'minor canon' (alternatively, 'petty canon') had been adopted to designate this senior element among the vicars.[154] By 1522 at the latest it had been enacted formally that of the sixteen vicars choral, eight each year should hold the rank of minor canon and receive the designated increment of salary accordingly.[155] There appears to be no rationale in either liturgical or musical terms that can explain the creation of this category of senior vicar. It seems, rather, to have constituted a means of offering to the more experienced and senior of the ordained priests a differential that recognised the special status of their orders above that of the lay singing-men, who otherwise, in terms of pay and esteem, had now caught up with the ordained clergy of the choir. The minor canonry was a device whereby the pre-eminence of priesthood could be demonstrated and preserved.

151. St. John Hope, *Windsor Castle*, ii, pp. 517–20. For other clerks such as Robert Rede — probably those who were married with a family — the college provided accommodation in the town close by the castle: SGC XV.48.46, *Expense senescalli* (1480–1).

152. Salisbury, Cathedral Archives, Register Machon, pp. 143, 144, 154, 157, 158; cf. Fellowes, *The Vicars or Minor Canons*, pp. 64–8.

153. SGC XV.34.62–66, *Stipendia, vadia et regarda officiariorum et aliorum*.

154. SGC XI.B.27, XI.B.28. The term 'minor canon' appears to have been adopted from the usage of St Paul's Cathedral in London, where it denoted the body of personnel which elsewhere was designated as priest vicars choral.

155. Ashmole, *Institution*, Appendix, p. [27]. For confirmation that Ashmole's 'viii Peticanons and xiii Vicars' is an error of transcription for 'viii Peticanons and viii Vicars', see *Valor Ecclesiasticus*, ed. J. Caley and J. Hunter, 6 vols, Record Commission 1810–34, ii, p. 153.

V. THE SEED-CORN OF THE ENGLISH CHORAL TRADITION: THE CHORISTERS AND THEIR INSTRUCTOR, 1475–1500

The engagement of a much enlarged corps of choristers in the performance of polyphony constituted the greatest single innovation of this period in the resources available for the observance of the liturgy. Indeed, although the most conspicuous element in the transformation in the choral strength at St George's was clearly the increase in the number of lay clerks from four to fifteen (including the two epistolers), that which had greatest impact on the actual production of music-making was the rise in the number of choristers from six to thirteen. The polyphony for church use being composed in the last third of the fifteenth century made immense demands on their training and skills, and extended to a number of diverse categories. These included expansive settings of the Ordinary for High Mass on feast-days, and Magnificats for use at first Vespers on the previous evening; somewhat slighter settings of the Ordinary for use daily at Lady Mass, with settings also of its Kyrie, Alleluia and Sequence; and imposing settings of Marian votive antiphons, for use daily at an evening devotion, extra-liturgical, widely observed in the greater secular churches towards the end of the working day. The music now being composed cultivated great floridity of melody and complexity of rhythm, and required true professional virtuosity of its performers, of the boys no less than of the adults.

Singing-boys trained and skilful in this capacity became a valuable commodity, and the successful location and appointment of a musician specially skilled and experienced in imparting such instruction to them came to be perceived as the cardinal ingredient in the creation of any satisfactory choir.[156] Perhaps an initial attempt to achieve this at St George's may be discerned in the arrival of John Kegwyn as a vicar choral in May 1475, since he is known to have been an early exponent of the skill of teaching to boys the skills of singing composed polyphony. Indeed, it is likely that the influence of Richard Beauchamp lay behind this appointment also, since Salisbury Cathedral was one of the institutions at which Kegwyn had served as Instructor of the Choristers in polyphony, between 1463 and 1467.[157] For some reason, however, this appointment turned out to be unsuccessful; the attendance register shows that prior to July 1475 Kegwyn put in few appearances at service in St George's, and that he soon gave notice and left in October of the same year.[158]

As the expansion of the choir progressed, attention was paid to the whole issue of the tuition of the singing-boys, and from 1 January 1479 the chapter instituted numerous improvements in the arrangements for their education, keep and training, so ensuring for them a culture of esteem and reward. Their stipends of £3 6s 8d per year each were raised at that point to £4 0s 0d, so providing extra resources for their clothing, food and keep.[159]

---

156. For some idea of the negotiation sometimes necessary to obtain the services of the right man, and the sense of satisfaction at having done so, see (in respect of Cardinal College, Oxford and Cardinal College, Ipswich) R. Bowers, 'The cultivation and promotion of music in the household and orbit of Thomas Wolsey', in *Cardinal Wolsey: Church, State and Art*, ed. S. Gunn and P. Lindley, Cambridge 1991, 178–218, pp. 196–200.
157. Salisbury, Cathedral Archives: Register Newton, p. 57 (Kegwyn's contract of employment); accounts of Choristers' Collector, 1463–4, 1467–8. Immediately prior to his arrival at Windsor, Kegwyn had been Master of the choir of the parish church of St Michael, Cornhill, in the City of London (London, Guildhall Library, MS 4071/1, f. 26r).
158. SGC V.B.2, ff. 42v–45r.
159. SGC XI.B.26; XV.34.55, *Chorustis*.

The salary devolved upon the Instructor of the Choristers, for addition to his stipend as lay clerk, was raised at the same point from 26s 8d to 66s 8d per year, in recognition of its newly enhanced role.[160] The chapter also returned to the appointment of a specialist Instructor, and in Walter Lambe, who joined the team of lay clerks on 13 February 1479 from Holy Trinity College, Arundel,[161] St George's obtained the services of a musician and composer of the highest quality. In about November of that year he undertook in addition the duties of Instructor of the Choristers,[162] and there can be no doubt but that his appointment set the seal on the training of the boys to participate in the singing of composed polyphony for Mass, Magnificat, and votive antiphon. Among his successors, Richard Hampshire (1493–c.1512) is also known as a composer. He had been a chorister of St George's from November 1474 to March 1479, and was a scholar of Eton College and lay clerk, scholar and Fellow of King's College, Cambridge, before returning to Windsor in 1487x9 to spend the rest of his career at St George's as a remarkably highly-educated lay clerk and (from 1493) Instructor of the Choristers.[163]

The nature of this office was also streamlined. Prior to the re-foundation by Edward IV, the Instructor had been charged with full responsibility for the whole range of supervision and general stewardship of the boys' affairs, as well as for their liturgical and musical training and their other education.[164] Now, apparently with effect from Michaelmas 1477, the chapter created a separate office, that of Supervisor of the Choristers, to take over all aspects of the direction of the financial, domestic and other routine management of the boys' maintenance. Usually this office was conferred on one of the vicars choral or chantry chaplains; its first occupant was William Paynell, sometime vicar choral and now chantry priest and chapter clerk.[165] Its creation ensured that thereafter the specialist musician appointed to be Instructor of the Choristers could devote the totality of his time and energy to their musical training and general education, without the distractions of having to serve as housemaster, caterer and probably makeshift matron as well.[166]

The domestic buildings adjacent to the chapel preserve to this day an intriguing memorial of the first generations of St George's choristers to be taught the skills of reading the mensural notation used for polyphonic music. A first-floor room now part of 25, The Cloisters, was identified by Sir William St John Hope as that appropriated at some time

---

160. SGC XV.34.55, *Stipendia, vadia et regarda officiariorum*.

161. SGC V.B.2, f. 64v; he was paid as from 5 January 1479: XV.34.55, *Clericis*. For Lambe's previous career at Arundel, see R. Bowers, 'Arundel, The Castle, Archives of the Duchy of Norfolk, MS A340', in *idem* and A. Wathey, 'New sources of English fifteenth- and sixteenth-century polyphony', *Early Music History*, 4 (1984), 297–346, p. 303.

162. SGC XV.34.57, *Stipendia, vadia et regarda officiariorum*.

163. SGC V.B.2, f. 39r; XV.34.52, 55: *chorustis*; XV.34.64, *Stipendia, vadia et regarda*. A.B. Emden, *A Biographical Register of the University of Cambridge to 1500*, Cambridge 1963, p. 284. Hampshire's death as 'Instructor Choristarum apud Wyndesoram' was recorded, apparently between 1509 and 1515, on a list of members of King's College, Cambridge (Cambridge, King's College, MS Inventory of 1445, f. 74r: the same composite entry included record of the appointment of Nicholas West to the office of dean of Windsor in 1509, but not his elevation to the bishopric of Ely in 1515).

164. Statutes 4, 11, 15, 16, 30, 37: SGC IV.B.1, ff. 75v, 77r, 77v, 77v, 79r, 79v.

165. SGC XV.34.54, *Chorustis* and *Stipendia, vadia et regarda officiariorum*.

166. In the larger choirs the creation of the office of *Supervisor Choristarum* or equivalent soon became standard practice: Bowers, 'Choral institutions within the English Church', pp. 6089–91.

for the lodging and schoolroom of the boys; it must have been so used between the demolition of their former residence in the vicars' lodgings in 1475 and the building and equipping of Denton's Commons in 1519–20.[167] One wall preserves traces of an extensive mural painting covering an area of many square feet. On large five-line staves, with an associated verbal text, appears a single line of melody in music notation of the period around 1480 (Fig. 25). In their very fragmentary state of preservation neither the music nor the text can be identified; however, it is noticeable that, among other features, the music contains all the shapes that could be taken by one of the more awkward ingredients in this notation, the ligature *cum opposita proprietate* of two adjacent semibreves. Overall, it appears certain that this was an extended musical exercise painted onto the wall of the boys' schoolroom, for use as a visual aid in teaching them to recognise and sing from this style of notation.[168]

The recruitment of the choristers was a never-ending task. A certain number shared a surname with some current lay clerk, and doubtless were their sons or other close kin. In addition the chapter possessed a licence or commission, almost certainly first issued by Edward IV and renewed by subsequent sovereigns, to requisition for membership of the choir the services of chorister-boys raised and trained in other institutions. On 15 April 1493 Robert Rede, then Instructor of the Choristers, was reimbursed in the sum of 10s 0d for the expenses he had incurred in travelling to take up choristers by virtue of the commission.[169] In 1527 the then Instructor of the Choristers, John (or Robert) Wenham, appropriated one boy from Winchester and another from London.[170] The archives of Salisbury Cathedral for 1536–7 record the visit of John Sharp from Windsor to take one of the cathedral choristers 'by virtue of the commission of the lord king', and in the same year Lincoln Cathedral paid Windsor's Master of the Choristers 7s 6d as an incentive to buy off his unwelcome attentions 'habens Commissionem ad pueros capiendum'.[171] The records of Canterbury Cathedral note a similarly predatory descent made by John Hake,

---

167. St. John Hope, *Windsor Castle*, ii, p. 516. In 1424–5 and 1459–60 the boys had been using as their accommodation a single dormitory provided within the then vicars' lodgings: SGC XV.48.8, *Custus domorum ac murorum infra Collegium et Wyndesore*; XV.34.47, *reparaciones*. They had taken meals with the vicars in the vicars' hall: XV.34.46, *cotidiane* (1428–9); XV.34.56, *chorustis* (1468–9); XV.34.59, *expense necessarie* (1482–3).

168. It appears that at some stage an initial exercise was limewashed over and replaced by a new one. P.E. Curnow, 'Royal lodgings of the thirteenth century in the lower ward of Windsor Castle: some recent archaeological discoveries', *Friends Report* (1965), pp. 218–27; E.C. Rouse, 'The recently discovered wallpaintings in the lower ward, Windsor Castle', *ibid.* (1965–6), 275–81, p. 277; A. Hughes, 'The painted music in no.25, The Cloisters', *ibid.* (1965–6), p. 282.

169. SGC XV.48.55, *Expensa necessaria*: Et in denariis liberatis Roberto Rede pro expensis equitandi virtute Comissionis in capiendo chorustarum xs [the date is given on an inadvertent duplicate of this entry, subsequently lined out]. The king's commission also authorised the requisition of singing-men, a licence used during 1499–1500 to take two, both priests, from Arundel College to be vicars choral of Windsor. SGC XV.48.68, *Soluciones Forinsecorum Necessariorum*: Et in denariis solutis Simoni Wallyngford le messenger equitanti usque arundell cum Commissione domini Regis ad capiendum duos presbyteros Cantatores per mandatum Magistri decani xiijs iiijd.

170. S. Bond, *The Chapter Acts of the Dean and Canons of Windsor, 1430, 1523–1672*, Windsor 1966, p. 8; Fellowes, *Organists and Masters of the Choristers*, p. 11.

171. Salisbury, Archives of the Dean and Chapter, Fabric A/c 1536–7, f. 5r. Lincolnshire Archives, Archives of the Dean and Chapter, MS Bj.3.5, unfoliated (account 1536–7, *curialitates*).

Fig. 25a and b. *Exercise for reading musical notation, painted onto the wall of the choristers' schoolroom, c.1480 (Conservation of Wall Painting Department, Courtauld Institute)*

then Instructor of the Choristers at St George's, so late as 1553–4,[172] and it seems unlikely that such a privilege did not date back all the way to the time of the re-foundation by Edward IV. Moreover, at least from 1484 onwards commissions to other royally-favoured choirs to requisition singing-boys commonly expressly inhibited the beneficiaries from robbing St George's,[173] while grants of immunity from such predation frequently excluded immunity from impressment by all the royal choirs, commonly including St George's.[174]

The extraordinary survival of the attendance and admissions register for 1468–79 and of eighteen annual lists of names from the treasurer's accounts for the years 1468 to 1499 permits unusually detailed analysis of the careers of the choristers to be made. They yield precise dates of both admission and departure for 41 of the 91 boys who are known to have been choristers during those 31 years,[175] while among the remainder the duration of service entered by another ten is known to within a year or less. In addition, a further eleven boys certainly served for four years or more, and four certainly for under three years. Thus the duration of 51 careers is known exactly or to within one year, and 15 more are known certainly to have been relatively brief or relatively long. The body of data relating to these 66 boys constitutes a source of information for the analysis of choristers' careers unequalled for any other pre-Reformation choir in England. Admittedly, such analysis can only be rather rough and ready, but some intriguing conclusions do emerge. It is known from the statutes of other collegiate churches that boys were admitted as choristers at the age of eight or nine.[176] The most durable chorister at St George's, John Kyngford, served for just four days less than eight years,[177] but he was wholly exceptional; only one other boy exceeded seven years' service (and that by only a few days),[178] and only five more are known to have exceeded six. A good clutch of boys served five years (17) and four years (17). Only three are known to have served for three years but less than four, but no fewer than 22 enjoyed a career certainly of under three years. This latter statistic — one-third of the sample — suggests that St George's depended to a substantial extent on the requisition of boys from other choirs, who arrived fully trained and gave to Windsor their best couple of years or so before their change of voice.

172. Canterbury, Cathedral Library and Archives: MS Misc. A/cs 39, ff. 17v, 18r; A/c Treasurer 2, f. 10v. R. Bowers, 'The liturgy of the cathedral and its music, c.1070–1642', in *A History of Canterbury Cathedral,* ed. P. Collinson, N. Ramsay and M. Sparks, Oxford 1995, p. 432.

173. See e.g. *British Library Harleian Manuscript 433,* ed. R. Horrox and P.W. Hammond, 4 vols, Richard III Society, Gloucester 1979–83, ii, p. 163 (Chapel Royal, 1484); PRO, C82/609, no. 189 (King's College, Cambridge, 1528); PRO, C82/676, no. 2 (household chapel of earl of Huntingdon, 1533).

174. See e.g. the grant of qualified immunity to the master and fellows of Pleshey College (Essex), 1527: PRO, DL12/44/2, no. 2. Such immunity notwithstanding, any of its six choristers might still be taken for service by the Chapel Royal, St George's Windsor, St Stephen's Westminster, or the household chapel of Cardinal Wolsey.

175. SGC V.B.2; XV.34.56–71, *chorustis*; Bodl. MS Berkshire Roll 4 (Treasurer's Account, 1495–6), *chorustis*. In addition, there are lists for 1459–60, 1461–2 and 1462–3, and one for 1503–4.

176. E.g. Fotheringhay College, where boys already coached in elementary plainsong but knowing no more could be admitted up to the age of nine. Statute 3: 'The statutes of the College of St Mary and All Saints, Fotheringhay', ed. A. Hamilton Thompson, *Archaeological Journal,* 75 (1918), 241–303, p. 272.

177. 10 August 1471–5 August 1479: SGC V.B.2, f. 20r; XV.34.55, *chorustis*. By the time of his approaching retirement Kyngford was sufficiently grown-up to be pressed into service as temporary vestry clerk during a vacancy of seven weeks in June–July 1479: SGC XV.34.55, *clerico vestibuli*.

178. William Chard, 26 March 1486–6 April 1493: SGC XV.34.61, 66: *chorustis*.

Most remarkably, perhaps, the length of a singing-boy's career seems then to have been only a little longer than that experienced now. Among those raised at St George's from the age of eight or nine very few lasted beyond six completed years, four-and-a-half to six being about the norm. Voices were breaking, it seems, at about the age of fourteen. It was indeed a statutory provision that boys leave upon their change of voice, and fourteen was the age reached by John Goldyng (1468–73), William Tylle (1462–8) and Thomas Greneway (?1468–72) when each left the choir to become a scholar of Eton College.[179]

These observations appear to render possible the presentation of a tentative hypothesis concerning an aspect of the style of singing taught to these boys. It has been noted that some 200 years later, during the years 1660–1733, the choristers of St George's continued singing to an age much greater than had their predecessors. The average age of admission for the ninety-seven boys who served as choristers during that period was just over nine years and six months, and their average age of retirement was sixteen years and five months. Of the seventy-nine boys for whom full data are available, almost two-thirds (50) served for six years or more; five tenures even exceeded nine years.[180] So startling a divergence between practices separated by these 200 years probably is best explicable in terms of the nature and demands of musical repertory, and of singing style.

The body of eight to ten choristers of 1660–1733 sang a repertory commonly reaching in terms of pitch no higher than e'' or f'', and were balancing with a men's ensemble of only thirteen to fourteen voices.[181] It appears likely that the longevity of these boys' voices is explained by their having been taught to sing in the light head tone that was all that was necessary for their particular repertory and circumstances; such a training commonly leaves the treble register still usable for some considerable time after the voice has in fact broken. However, the thirteen boys of the late fifteenth-century choir sang a repertory which frequently and ordinarily took their voices as high as g'', and on those occasions on which all the choir was present (for example, the daily votive antiphon) they were required to balance with a chorus of no fewer than thirty-two adult voices. The production of a vocal technique capable of sustaining the top part under such circumstances seems likely to have involved dedicated and calculated use of the more powerful chest register. This technique is believed commonly to be associated with the loss of the treble voice at the time of puberty, and it may be surmised that its cultivation was the reason for the comparatively early age of retirement of the choristers of the late fifteenth century.

179. Statute 17: SGC IV.B.1, f. 77v. Emden, *Biographical Register of the University of Cambridge*, pp. 264, 588; W. Sterry, *The Eton College Register 1441–1698*, Eton 1943, p. 148. For further grounds for concluding that the voices of singing-boys changed at about 14 or 15 years at this period (c.1465–1548), see R. Bowers, 'The vocal scoring, choral balance and performing pitch of Latin church polyphony in England, c.1500–1558', *Journal of the Royal Musical Association*, 112 (1987), 38–76, p. 48 and n. 23. Claims that the change of voice was occurring at an age much later, derived largely from evidence that is circumstantial or arises in relation to other periods or places (e.g. R. Rastall, *The Heaven singing: Music in Early English Religious Drama*, Woodbridge 1996, pp. 308–20), seem less securely based than the present conclusions drawn from contemporary documentary evidence.

180. K.J. Dexter, 'The provision of choral music at St George's Chapel, Windsor Castle, and Eton College, c.1640–1733' (unpublished Ph.D. thesis, Royal Holloway University of London, 2000), pp. 73–8. I am most grateful to Dr Dexter for his kindness in communicating these findings to me, and for his permission to quote them here.

181. *Ibid.*, p. 75; I. Spink, *Restoration cathedral music 1660–1714*, Oxford 1995, pp. 370–2.

For many boys a St George's education proved to be the springboard to a noteworthy career, for theirs was a well-rounded schooling. Despite the musical bias of their training they still required thorough tuition in Latin vocabulary, syntax and grammar, and what Dr Emden considered may have been the manuscript *Grammar* actually owned and used by Richard Hampshire, Instructor 1493–*c*.1512, still survives as Cambridge, Corpus Christi College, MS 233.[182] Hampshire himself (chorister 1474–9), Edward Martyn (1478–1484/5), Richard Frevell (1486x9–1494x5), and particularly Thomas Ashwell (1491–3) and William Rasor (1499–1504–>), took up distinguished careers in the music of the church and became composers. Hampshire became Instructor of the Choristers at Windsor itself,[183] and Frevell at St Giles' Hospital, Norwich, while Ashwell became Instructor at Lincoln Cathedral (1506–11) and later Master of the Lady Chapel choir at Durham Cathedral (1513–*c*.1524x5).[184] John Watkins (1499x1503–1504–>) became an early recipient of the Cambridge degree of Bachelor of Music (1516), for the award of which he was required to compose a mass and a votive antiphon; he served from 1521 to 1542 as a vicar choral of Lincoln Cathedral. Robert Wetwood (1486x9–1492) became a Gentleman of Henry VIII's Chapel Royal.[185] A fair number of boys went from choristerships at Windsor to scholarships across the river at Eton, whence some progressed in due course to scholarships and fellowships of King's College, Cambridge.[186] From there the careers of some can be traced yet further: Robert Hobbs (1485–91), for instance, concluded his career as Registrary of the University of Cambridge.[187] With only a handful of exceptions, however, what the boys did *not* do was to return to, or stay on at, St George's as singing-men. Their education was no mind-narrowing and imagination-stunting experience serving as little other than a card of life-membership to a well-heeled but inward-looking gentleman's club; rather, it was a passport to the wider world.

VI. THE FULFILMENT OF ROYAL AMBITION: THE MUSIC OF THE OLD AND NEW CHAPELS, 1475–1500

In respect of the musical content of the work of the choir of St George's, no less significant than the construction of the new chapel by Edward IV was the conversion by Henry VII,

182. Emden, *Biographical Register of the University of Cambridge*, p. 284. This volume also contains (f. 95v) texts of songs.

183. See above, p. 203 and n. 163.

184. For some further account of each of these, except Richard Frevell, see *New Grove Dictionary*, ed. Sadie, *sub nomine*. For Frevell, see A. Wathey, 'Newly discovered English fifteenth-century polyphony at Oxford', *Music and Letters*, 64 (1983), 58–65, pp. 58–9; I am most grateful to Dr Carole Rawcliffe for the information concerning Frevell at St Giles' Hospital.

185. Watkins: R. Bowers, 'Music and worship to 1642', in *A History of Lincoln Minster*, ed. Owen, p. 61. Wetwood: PRO, LC 2/1, f. 170r; *Letters and Papers, foreign and domestic, of the reign of Henry VIII*, ed. J.S. Brewer and R.H. Brodie, 22 vols, London 1864–1932, i, no. 381(8).

186. A trawl through Sterry, *The Eton College Register 1441–1698*, and Emden, *Biographical Register of the University of Cambridge*, reveals that despite the very imperfect recording at this period of the names of any Eton boys other than those who progressed to King's College, Cambridge, out of the *c*.60 Windsor choristers of the period 1465–90 ten are known to have become King's Scholars at Eton (to Thomas Ayloffe, Richard Blackburn, John Goldyng, Thomas Greneway, Richard Hampshire, Robert Hobbs, Thomas Massey, Thomas Scalon and William Tylle, add Edward Dylcocke (SGC V.B.2, f. 59r)). Of these, six went on to achieve admission as scholars to King's College, Cambridge, and four became Fellows.

187. Emden, *Biographical Register of the University of Cambridge*, p. 307.

complete by 1500, of the former St George's into a Lady Chapel for the new building.[188] In the principal chapel were sung the plainsong observances both of the numerous obits,[189] and of all the daily office, of the Jesus antiphon, and of High Mass. On major festivals and principal Garter celebrations the ordinary of the latter was conventionally rendered in polyphony, as was the Magnificat at Vespers on their eves. In the Lady Chapel were sung the Lady Mass and evening Marian antiphon, both rendered in polyphony almost certainly on a daily basis.

Concerning the actual music-making undertaken by the newly enlarged choral body during the last quarter of the century the records are reticent, but fortunately not entirely silent. The loss of the chapter acts is a major obstacle to research for the entirety of the century; also lacking are the texts of any contracts made between the chapter and each successive Instructor of the Choristers, who in the new régime of choral polyphony was universally regarded as the principal musician in his institution and, under the precentor, head of the singing staff. Nevertheless, although the performance of the plainsong liturgy remained the staple fare of the singers of every choir in this pre-Reformation period, it was probably by its rendering of the newly-devised choral polyphony that the patrons and sponsors of choirs judged how good a service their beneficiaries were doing them, and the clearest available indications of the content and nature of this, the most high-profile work of the choir at St George's, arise from consideration of the music created by those of its members who were composers.

Of these, Walter Lambe was the most distinguished. He served as a lay clerk from January or February 1479 until some point during 1484–5, and again from 1 July 1492 until Michaelmas 1504 and beyond.[190] All of his surviving works are found in the Eton College Choirbook of c.1502–5.[191] Its index reveals that originally this source contained twelve pieces by him, rendering him the best represented composer therein after John Browne. These compositions consisted of one setting of Magnificat and eleven Marian antiphons; however, four of the latter are now lost altogether, and one survives in only a fragmentary state. It is most regrettable that no volume comparable to the Eton Choirbook preserving a repertory of masses survives from this period; during 1503–4 Lambe was paid 6s 8d at St George's for the copying of four settings of the mass, very probably of his own composition.[192]

The amplitude of the resources available to Lambe at St George's allowed him to compose in up to six parts and on the very grandest scale; indeed, the most imposing of his votive antiphons take little less than a quarter of an hour to sing. His standard ensemble was that usual for this period, namely the five-voice pattern of treble, alto, two tenors and bass; it was the abundance of men's voices at St George's that he exploited when writing

188. St. John Hope, *Windsor Castle*, ii, pp. 478–82.

189. By 1503–4 no fewer than 57 obits were being celebrated annually: Bodl. MS Berkshire Roll 5, *obitus*.

190. SGC V.B.2, f. 64v; XV.34.55, 60, 65: *clericis*; Bodl. MS Berkshire Roll 5, *clericis*. During the interval between 1484/5 and 1491 he was back at Arundel College whence he had come: see above, note 161. Soon after he arrived at Windsor in 1479, 9d was spent on the purchase of ink and two quaternions of paper specifically for him to use in the writing out of music: SGC XV.34.57, *reparaciones*.

191. Eton College, MS 178: *The Eton Choirbook*, ed. F. Ll. Harrison, 3 vols, Musica Britannica 10–12, 2nd edn (1967–73).

192. Bodl. MS Berkshire Roll 5, *In regardis vicariis et aliis*: Et solut' Waltero Lambe pro le prykking iiij[or] missarum et pro papiro et forell' vjs viijd.

in six parts, adding a baritone between the two tenors and bass.[193] These latter four also yielded him a rich palette of tone colour when writing for lower men's voices alone.[194] Given a choir of thirteen boys and some thirty men, he never divided the treble part in chorus work; however, there is a magical passage in his *Salve regina* in which a solo trio of one treble and two altos gives way almost imperceptibly to the even more ethereal texture of two trebles and one alto. His setting of *Stella celi* looks earlier than his other surviving works, particularly in respect of its scoring, which engages two altos and two tenors for its ensemble of four men's voices. Its text is a plea to the Blessed Virgin for relief from plague, and it may have been written in the summer of 1479 when the choir of St George's was so severely stricken by a visitation of the disease.[195] In works such as *Nesciens mater* Lambe was content to adopt a relatively direct idiom, little enhanced with vocal decoration. Elsewhere, and especially in *Gaude flore virginali* for four men's voices, he could write music of ferocious rhythmic complexity, indicating the presence among the St George's choirmen of singers possessing truly formidable technique, in reading the intricacies of the notation no less than in producing the notes.[196] Lambe's work was widely copied, and it appears to have been this degree of versatility of approach combined with his technical assurance in contrapuntal finesse that led to his contemporary recognition as among the foremost composers of his day.

The Eton Choirbook also contained a Magnificat for a full choir of five voices by a composer named Mychelson; probably this was one or other of the brothers John and Robert Mychelson, respectively vicar (2 August 1492 — 21 March 1499) and lay clerk (21 December 1492 — beyond 30 September 1504) of St George's.[197] Unfortunately, the music is lost.

The organ in chapel continued to make its contribution to the execution of the services. It did not accompany polyphony, and — in England, anyway — may even yet have possessed no written solo repertory. However, many inventories of this period record the provision of plainsong service-books 'pro organis', and it is evident that one of its player's principal functions now was to alternate with the singers, probably at the minor services on days of little liturgical significance, improvising upon the plainsong while the singers took a brief rest. Probably it was for such a practice that one of the clerks, John Scalon, supplied the chapel in 1482–3 with a plainsong hymnal 'for the organ'.[198]

Normally, as in the manner observed since 1435, one of the clerks was designated as organist. In 1477–8 Thomas Rolfe received 13s 4d for playing the principal organ; he was also paid 3s 4d for playing the small organ used at the Lady altar for the daily Lady Mass, where again the function of the organ probably was to relieve the singers at certain points

---

193. See *O Maria plena gratia* (*The Eton Choirbook*, ed. Harrison, i, p. 31); probably also the fragmentary six-voice *O regina celestis glorie* (*ibid.*, iii, p. 161).

194. See *Ascendit Christus* and *Gaude flore virginali* (*ibid.*, iii, pp. 37, 42).

195. See above, p. 200, and note 146.

196. *Ibid.*, i, p. 131 (see p. 137); iii, pp. 32, 10, 42.

197. John: SGC XV.34.65, 71, *Stipendia, vadia et regarda officiariorum*. Robert: SGC XV.34.66, *clericis*; Bodl. MS Berkshire Roll 5, *clericis*. For record that they were brothers: SGC XV.34.66, *Stipendia, vadia et regarda officiariorum*.

198. SGC XV.34.59, *Expense necessarie*: et solut' Johanni Scalon pro j ympnario pro organis 2° folio uni in trinitate et aliis necessariis pro choro vjs viijd.

in the service by improvising upon the plainsong as a *cantus firmus* while they rested. In 1478–9 these payments were consolidated into a single remuneration of 16s 8d.[199]

There is every likelihood that it was between 1480 and 1482 that a new organ was commissioned for installation in the new chapel — about which, unfortunately, very little is known. Certainly by Michaelmas 1482 the player's annual remuneration had been raised to 20s 0d, and in 1496 was raised again, to 33s 4d.[200] Very probably these increments reflected increasing levels of frequency of performance on the new instrument, and also of rising expectations of musical skill and content in its playing. It is known that within the new St George's there was a small organ in addition to the principal instrument. In 1496–7 the well-known builder John Howe came from London to repair an organ at a cost of 56s 8d, and this job involved two workmen temporarily shifting the small organ out of the choir of the new chapel and subsequently returning it.[201] It is likely, therefore, that this repair was to the organ of the old chapel, by then designated and used as the Lady Chapel.[202]

The secular environment of the royal castle yielded to the St George's musicians the opportunity to compose secular song in addition to their church music. The surviving output of Richard Hampshire (Instructor of the Choristers from 1 November 1493 until *c.*1512)[203] and of Thomas Phillips (vicar choral, April 1477 — March 1490)[204] adds up to only one song each, but they are preserved together in a collection compiled in the autumn of 1501.[205] Indeed, their compositions appear to have arisen as responses to the same event. The texts of both exploit the imagery of the rose to evoke the royal couple Henry VII and Elizabeth of York, and both offer in allegorical terms a celebration of the birth in 1486 of Prince Arthur, their son and heir.[206] The music of Hampshire's song 'Lett serch your myndis, ye of hie consideracion' is unfortunately incomplete; only one of its two voices has survived. Phillips's song 'I love, I love, and whom love ye?' is for three

199. SGC XV.34.54, 55: *Stipendia, vadia et regarda officiariorum.* Repairs to the instrument were paid for in 1478–9 (26s 8d): XV.34.55, *reparaciones.*

200. SGC XV.34.57, 59, 70: *Stipendia, vadia et regarda officiariorum.* During 1489–94 the playing was committed to a team of four, consisting of the Instructor of the Choristers and three of the other lay clerks; the rationale for this expedient is not clear. SGC XV.34.62–6: *Stipendia, vadia et regarda officiariorum.*

201. SGC XV.34.70, *reparaciones.* The chapter had originally sent to London for a man called Wheyllar: XV.34.70, *Stipendia, et vadia ac regarda officiariorum.* Either Wheyllar or Howe may have been the builder of the first organ for the new chapel.

202. St. John Hope, *Windsor Castle*, ii, pp. 478–82; also see above, pp. 208–9.

203. See above, note 163.

204. SGC V.B.2, f. 54r; xv.34.62, *Stipendia, vadia et regarda.* The signature of Thomas Phillips, as succentor and keeper of the Attendance and Admission Register, occurs on each of its leaves from October 1477 until its end in July 1479: SGC V.B.2, ff. 57r–67v. He was sometime chorister (and Boy Bishop in 1465) and vicar choral (admitted 1473) of Salisbury Cathedral (Salisbury, Cathedral Archives: Register Machon, p. 157; Register Newton, p. 81), and in 1508 chaplain of the household chapel of Edward Stafford, duke of Buckingham (Staffordshire Record Office, MS D(W)1721/1/5, pp. 84, 88).

205. R. Bowers, 'Early Tudor courtly song: an evaluation of the Fayrfax Book (British Library, MS Add. 5465)', in *The Reign of Henry VII: Proceedings of the 1993 Harlaxton Symposium*, ed. B. Thompson, Stamford 1995, 188–212, p. 194.

206. *Ibid.*, pp. 193–4. Although the texts seem most likely to be celebrating the birth of the Prince, it is not impossible that texts and music were written for a somewhat later event in Arthur's life that took place at St George's itself, namely his installation as a knight of the Garter on 8 May 1491 (Beltz, *Memorials*, p. clxviii).

voices, and for sheer disingenuous charm has few equals among the secular repertory of its day.[207]

It was the role of St George's as spiritual home of the Order of the Garter that yielded the principal opportunity for the chapel singers to take on a secular role as performers of polyphonic vernacular song. The manner in which a body of professional singers such as the choir of St George's tackled the performance of secular song at around this period is indicated by an early sixteenth-century drawing (Pl. VII), one of a pair purporting to illustrate the celebrations conducted overseas on the occasion of the investiture, in a secular environment by English ambassadors, of a foreign ruler as a knight of the Garter.[208] The pictures are evidently of English origin and decorative rather than 'authentic' in intent; they were produced by an artist drawing not on foreign but familiar local practice and experience for his subject-matter. The drawing purporting to illustrate the investiture of Ferdinand, archduke of Austria, in 1523 depicts the entertainment of the party by singers. The performance is undertaken by a group of six, all in secular dress; the singers include boys, and men both clerical (tonsured) and lay. They are performing *a cappella* without instrumental participation. The three in front appear to constitute an ensemble of soloists; they are two laymen (untonsured) and a boy, each singing from his own individual copy.[209] Behind stand three more singers, being two adults (both tonsured) and either a third man or another boy; these are evidently ready to join in when required, reading from the same copies and thus establishing the sound of a small three-part chorus. These resources match exactly those required to render the structure of alternating burden and verse, respectively for chorus and soloists, that was characteristic of the polyphonic carol and of the song-forms derived from it that are encountered in English song of the late fifteenth century. There is every likelihood that this drawing — the sole example of its kind yet known of English origin — depicts the manner standard at the turn of the sixteenth century for the performance of polyphonic song by members of a group of trained singers such as the St George's choir.

VII. CONCLUSION

By 1500 the choir of St George's had had devolved upon it resources sufficient to render it a cynosure among its counterparts elsewhere in the land. Indeed, as the sixteenth century progressed, its artistically and politically balanced constitution turned out to be uncommonly influential, for it soon was chosen as a model to be emulated by other choirs seeking a similar plan of modernisation. For instance, the rank and office of minor canon was introduced at Hereford Cathedral before 1535,[210] and also at the royal chapel and collegiate church of St Michael in Stirling Castle in Scotland; indeed, this latter collegiate and choral foundation, created by James IV in 1501–3, was clearly modelled on St

207. *Early Tudor Songs and Carols*, ed. J. Stevens, Musica Britannica, 36 (1975), pp. 36, 70.
208. College of Arms, MS Vincent 152, f. 178.
209. On the creation of single parts as performance media for early Tudor song, see the observations on certain of the items considered in D. Fallows, 'The Drexel fragments of early Tudor song', *Royal Musical Association Research Chronicle*, 26 (1993), pp. 5–18.
210. *Valor Ecclesiasticus*, iii, p. 12.

George's Chapel to a considerable extent throughout.[211] Finally, in c.1532 St George's provided the pattern on which the constitution of King Henry VIII's College in Oxford was devised,[212] which in turn provided the template for the constitutions of all the New Foundation cathedrals created in the 1540s.[213]

By the end of the fifteenth century there can be little doubt but that the choir of St George's was considered to be among the finest out of over 200 professional church choirs in England.[214] Quite possibly, indeed, it was reputed as the very finest among those which enjoyed a fixed site rather than the uncomfortably peripatetic existence of the chapels of the king and of the upper ecclesiastical and secular aristocracy.[215] Its enjoyment of royal favour, its association with the nation's highest order of chivalry,[216] its location in an imposing royal residence of character both military and domestic, the splendour and grandeur that would pertain to its building when complete, and its generous staffing level of no fewer than 45 well-paid professional singers constituting a balanced chorus, sufficed to confer upon it a prominence and a cachet few others could match.

211. Following its establishment in 1501, the king added to the foundation in 1503 a team of ten minor canons (*pauciores canonici*), so that the total constitution was for a dean and six dignitaries, ten other canons, ten minor canons and six boy choristers: C. Rogers, *History of the Chapel Royal of Scotland*, Edinburgh 1882, pp. 3, 7, 26–7, 55–6, cxxxi–cxxxiii; I.B. Cowan and D. Easson, *Medieval religious houses: Scotland*, London 1976, pp. 226–7; R. Bowers, 'Robert Carver (1487/8–c.1568) at Scone and Stirling', *Early Music Review*, 48 (March 1999), 8–10, p. 10.

212. For the statutes of King Henry VIII's College, which, in respect of the choir, even incorporate almost *verbatim* considerable passages from those of St George's, see *Statutes of the Colleges of Oxford*, ed. Her Majesty's Commissioners, 3 vols, Oxford 1853, iii, part xi, pp. 185–210.

213. As noted by A. Hamilton Thompson, *The Statutes of the Cathedral Church of Durham*, Surtees Society, 143 (1929), p. xxxix, though Thompson may have overlooked the intermediate role of King Henry VIII's College.

214. On 8 March 1560 Elizabeth I issued her licence to St George's authorising the chapter to impress men and boys for its choir, 'willing it should not be of less reputation in our day, but rather augmented and increased': N. Wridgway, *The Choristers of St George's Chapel, Windsor Castle*, Slough 1980, p. 32.

215. Only choirs such as these latter could now tempt singing-men to leave St George's: for instance, Thomas Phillips to the household chapel of the duke of Buckingham (see note 201 above) and the lay clerk William Edmunds (1478–83) to the Chapel Royal (SGC V.B.2, f. 59v; xv.34.59, *clericis*; *Calendar of Patent Rolls 1485–94*, p. 309).

216. In c.1500 it was recorded that on his arrival at Windsor for the annual Garter meeting and feast on St George's Day, each knight was required to hasten straight to the chapel to make his offering to the high altar without even changing from his riding clothes. Some of the choristers were to be in attendance on each knight as he made his way from the chapel door to the choir door, ready to bear up his Garter mantle lest it catch on his spurs (Bodl. MS Eng. misc. b.208, f. 94r). No doubt the boys' expectations of a small cash tip for their services were not disappointed, so originating the practice of 'Spur Money', recorded well into the nineteenth century.

APPENDIX 1: ST GEORGE'S CHAPEL, WINDSOR CASTLE: THE MASTERS OF THE CHORISTERS, ORGAN-PLAYERS AND SUPERVISORS OF THE CHORISTERS, *c.* 1360–1500

Masters of the Choristers		Organ-player		Supervisor of the Choristers
Adam [?Hull]	M1361–M1362			
Adam Penkridge	M1366–Mar 1367			
John Dyer	Apr 1367–Mar 1368			
Thomas Horn	Apr 1368–M1368			
Roger Brancote	M1370–M1372			
Thomas Wybourne	9 months within M1375–M1376			
Nicholas Chandel	Jan 1377–Mar 1377			
Nicholas Mason	Apr 1377–M1377			
Richard Geddynge	3 months within M1377–Jan 1378			
Thomas Grys	3 months within Jan 1378–M1378			
John Gloucester	some time within M1385–M1386			
John Perye	some time within M1385–M1386			
Walter Cumberton	M1393–Mar 1396			
Roger Gerveys	4½ months within Apr 1396–M1396			
John Kelly	some time within M1407–M1408			
William Pounger	some time within M1407–M1408			
Thomas ——	some time within M1407–M1408			
		Laurence Dreweryn	1415, 1418	
Thomas Thomas	M1435–Mar 1439	Thomas Thomas	M1435–Mar 1439	
Thomas Churchman	M1442–M1452	John Wetherby	M1440–M1443	
		John Wem	M1451–M1452	
Thomas Rolfe	M1459–June 1462	Thomas Rolfe	M1459–July 1469	
Adam Roke	July 1462–M1463			
Thomas Rolfe	M1467–M1468			
Richard Prudde	M1468–June 1469	Robert Cotyngham	Aug 1469–M1472	
John Chard	July 1469–M1476	John Brown	M1474–M1476	William Paynell
Thomas Rolfe	M1477–M1478	Thomas Rolfe	M1477–M1484	M1477–M1479
Thomas Gossyp	M1478–M1479			
William Edmunds	a few weeks at start of Mich term 1479			Thomas Raynes M1479–M1484
Walter Lambe	*c.* Nov 1479–M1484	John Tuke, Richard Bowyer, Matthew		William Paynell
John Tuke	M1489–Dec 1492	Bednall, William Bell, M1489–Dec 1492		M1485–M1486
Robert Rede	Jan 1493–M1493	Robert Rede, Richard Bowyer, Matthew		John Friendshyp
		Bednall, William Bell, Jan 1493–M1493		M1489–M1504→
		Richard Bowyer, Matthew Bednall,		
Richard Hampshire	Nov 1493–1509 x 15	William Bell,	M1493–M1494	
		Richard Wood	M1495–M1504→	

NOTES

M = Michaelmas

Surnames of clerks of the second form indicated by SMALL CAPITALS; all others were vicars choral (except John Friendshyp: chantry priest).